This book was donated to us.
Please treat it as the gift it is.

*"There is more treasure in books than in all the
pirate's loot on Treasure Island." ~ Walt Disney*

To Tell the Truth Freely

TO TELL THE TRUTH FREELY

THE
LIFE
OF
IDA B.
WELLS

MIA BAY

HILL AND WANG
A division of Farrar, Straus and Giroux
New York

Hill and Wang
A division of Farrar, Straus and Giroux
18 West 18th Street, New York 10011

Grateful acknowledgment is made for permission to reprint the images that appear throughout the book. Image on page 8 courtesy of the North Carolina Collection, University of North Carolina Library at Chapel Hill. Image on page 18 courtesy of HarpWeek., LLC. Image on page 37 courtesy of the Library of Congress, Rare Books Division. Image on page 46 courtesy of Princeton University, Firestone Library. Images on pages 75, 80, and 128 were originally printed in the *Indianapolis Freeman*, reprinted courtesy of the University of Pennsylvania, Van Pelt Library. Images on pages 86, 88, 107, 117, 225, 277, 303, 319, and 322 courtesy of the Special Collections Research Center, University of Chicago Library. Images on pages 123, 143, and 174 courtesy of the Manuscripts, Archives, and Rare Books Division; Schomburg Center for Research in Black Culture; The New York Public Library; Astor, Lenox and Tilden Foundations. Image on page 135 courtesy of Vron Ware, Personal Collection. Images on pages 160, 195, 210, 215, and 229 courtesy of the Library of Congress, Prints and Photographs Division. Image on page 171 courtesy of the Rare Book Collection, University of North Carolina at Chapel Hill. Images on pages 251 and 291 courtesy of Rutgers University Library, Alexander Library. Images on pages 254, 261, and 299 courtesy of the Department of Special Collections and University Archives, W.E.B. Du Bois Library, University of Massachusetts Amherst. Image on page 306 is from the *Chicago Daily News* negatives collection (DN-0071303), courtesy of the Chicago Historical Museum.

Library of Congress Cataloging-in-Publication Data

Bay, Mia.
    To tell the truth freely : the life of Ida B. Wells / Mia Bay.— 1st ed.
        p.   cm.
    Includes bibliographical references and index.
    ISBN-13: 978-0-8090-9529-2 (hardcover : alk. paper)
    ISBN-10: 0-8090-9529-7 (hardcover : alk. paper)
    1. Wells-Barnett, Ida B., 1862–1931.   2. African American women civil rights workers—
Biography.   3. Civil rights workers—United States—Biography.   4. African American women
educators—Biography.   5. African American women journalists—Biography.   6. United
States—Race relations.   7. African Americans—Civil rights—History.   8. African Americans—
Social conditions—To 1964.   9. Lynching—United States—History.   I. Title.

E185.97.W55B39 2009
323.092—dc22
[B]

                                                                                                    2008047116

Designed by Patrice Sheridan

www.fsgbooks.com

1   3   5   7   9   10   8   6   4   2

Contents

	List of Illustrations	*vii*
	Introduction: "If Iola Were a Man"	3
1:	Coming of Age in Mississippi	15
2:	Walking in Memphis	40
3:	The Lynching at the Curve	82
4:	Exile	109
5:	Capturing the Attention of the "Civilized World"	151
6:	"Although a Busy Woman, She Has Found the Time to Marry"	191
7:	Challenging Washington, D.C.—and Booker T.	232
8:	Reforming Chicago	274
9:	Eternal Vigilance Is the Price of Liberty	314
	Notes	329
	Acknowledgments	359
	Index	361

Illustrations

Collage from Henry Davenport Northrop et al., *The College of Life*
    (1895)   8
Holly Springs, Mississippi, 1863   18
Wells as a young woman   37
Diagram of a ladies' car   46
Wells in *The Indianapolis Freeman*   75
Cartoon from *The Indianapolis Freeman*   80
McDowell and Moss in *The Memphis Commercial*   86, 88
Wells, c. 1893   107
Ida, Betty Moss, and the Moss children   117
Cover of Wells's *Southern Horrors* pamphlet   123
Frederick Douglass, c. 1890   128
Catherine Impey with her sister Nellie   135
Postcard of Clanton, Alabama, lynching   143
"Darkies' Day at the Fair" cartoon from *Puck*   160
Ferdinand Lee Barnett, c. 1890   171
Lynching of C. J. Miller   174
Booker T. Washington, c. 1890   195
Frances Willard, c. 1880–98   210

Susan B. Anthony, c. 1890   215
Wells-Barnett and Charles Aked Barnett   225
Mary Church Terrell, c. 1900   229
W.E.B. Du Bois, 1903   251
William Monroe Trotter, 1905   254
The Niagara Movement meeting, 1905   261
Wells-Barnett with her children, 1909   277
Wells-Barnett at the suffragists' parade, 1913   291
East St. Louis riot, 1917   299
Wells-Barnett, 1917   303
Chicago riot, 1919   306
Barnett family portrait, 1917   319
Wells-Barnett in her sixties   322

To Tell the Truth Freely

Introduction:

"If Iola Were a Man"

AS THE NINETEENTH CENTURY CAME TO A CLOSE, A YOUNG African American woman named Ida B. Wells was acclaimed "the most widely known woman of her race in the world."[1] Born a slave in Civil War–ravaged Mississippi, Wells achieved freedom with emancipation, and international renown in the 1890s, when she rose to fame as a journalist, speaker, and civil rights activist who led an international crusade against lynching. She was just thirty years old when she first began her campaign to end the brutal white-on-black mob violence that took the lives of at least 3,220 African American men, women, and children between 1882 and 1930—a period that marks the high tide of this violence. Wells would remain an antilynching crusader all her life, with good reason. During much of it, lynching was so popular in the South that it was commemorated in postcards featuring the dead black bodies hanging from trees, bridges, and streetlights. And even outside of the South, the mob violence went almost wholly unchallenged until Wells began her antilynching crusade. The lynch mobs' victims, usually both black and male, were sometimes accused of rape, and invariably condemned as criminals after the fact—although they were put to death without judge or jury. As the postcards advertising these lynchings testify, the practice was not covert. Instead, it was the work of white mobs who displayed dead African American bodies to underscore their continuing racial dominion over a people only recently freed from slavery.

A member of that new generation of ex-slaves, Ida B. Wells came of age at a time when her people needed aggressive leaders who could combat the erosion of black civil and political rights that accompanied the end of the Reconstruction era. By the late nineteenth century, the voting rights, political power, and social freedoms that African Americans had won when the South was first reconstructed after the Civil War were under assault. Anxious to restore the white supremacy that slavery had once guaranteed, white Southerners used mob violence, political terrorism, and election fraud to drive the freed people and their Republican allies out of politics. What came next was a Jim Crow South, where few African Americans voted, and all were subject to segregation and many other forms of legal and economic discrimination. While white Southerners called the end of Reconstruction a blessed "Redemption," among African Americans it represented a devastating setback in the struggle for freedom that dated back to slavery. Moreover, it came at a time when many of the black leaders who had led that struggle were too old to head the new battle now needed to protect emancipation's freedoms. A new generation of black leaders was needed, and Wells would become one of them.

Born to slave parents in 1862, she had defied remarkable odds before she ever embarked on her antilynching campaign. Orphaned at age sixteen when her parents died in the yellow fever epidemic that swept the Mississippi Valley in 1878, she raised her five younger siblings by herself, taking a teaching job in a rural school that same year. Her own education remained incomplete as a result, but Wells pursued a tireless course of self-education, reading and writing her way into a career in journalism under the pen name "Iola." By her late twenties, Wells had become one of the preeminent female journalists of her day, and the editor and co-owner of the Memphis, Tennessee, newspaper *Free Speech and Headlight*. Now widely acclaimed as "Iola, the Princess of the Press," Wells saw her career almost derailed in the spring of 1892, when a white mob lynched three black businessmen in Memphis.

Shocked by the violence and mourning the death of three men she had known for years, one as a close friend, Wells protested the murders.

She also began an investigation of lynching that would last a lifetime and see her exiled from the South. The three men who died in Memphis had committed no crime other than to open a store that challenged a nearby white-owned business. Accordingly, their deaths inspired Wells to research the causes of lynching. White Southerners justified lynching as a necessary "check on the horrible and beastly propensities of the black race." Black men were prone to the crime of rape, they insisted. Only "the most prompt, speedy and extreme punishment" could prevent them from preying on "weak and defenseless [white] women."[2] But as Wells soon discovered, more than two-thirds of the African American men murdered by lynch mobs were never even accused of rape. Indeed, like her dead friend, many of the victims of white mob violence were never accused of any serious crime. Outraged by her findings, Wells wrote an editorial indicting Southern whites for lynching black men "on the old threadbare lie that black men rape white women," which soon brought death threats that forced Wells to leave the South.[3] She left just ahead of the white mob that attacked the offices of *Free Speech*, smashing her presses and shutting down her paper. But the attacks made her all the more determined to expose lynching's true cause by telling "the truth freely."[4]

After she left Memphis Wells launched an antilynching campaign that took her from Tennessee to New York, Great Britain, and Chicago, and garnered her new acclaim as one of the most forceful African American leaders of the day. Her antilynching campaign, as one contemporary commentator noted, addressed the most urgent issue facing black America at a time when "none of our representative and most prominent black men would take up the lead." Another deemed her "the only successor to Frederick Douglass"—the former fugitive slave who became black America's great antislavery leader. As such observers were well aware, the two black leaders had much in common. "Both were editors, both were orators, and both began their careers passionately committed to righting the worst forms of injustice that, in their respective times, were inflicted on their people," writes

Douglass biographer William McFeely.[5] Moreover, after the two met in 1892, they became fast friends; Douglass wrote a number of letters of support for Wells, including testimonials for the antilynching pamphlets Wells published before Douglass's death in 1895—providing a public record of his support for her.[6] In his seventies by the time they met, Douglass served as both a mentor and a role model to Wells, whose antilynching campaign mobilized some of the same international reform networks Douglass had once rallied to the antislavery cause.

The British, in particular, had lent powerful moral authority and financial support to the abolitionist movement. They proved a crucial audience for Wells, who, at the beginning of her campaign, had trouble even gaining a hearing among whites at home. American whites in both the North and the South chose to regard lynching as a Negro problem largely brought on by the criminal character of the race, but the British proved more receptive to Wells's well-researched analysis of its true causes. Moreover, they were also supportive when Wells asked them to once again champion the unrealized liberties of the freed people—just as they had supported their emancipation. The result was the formation of a much publicized British Anti-Lynching Committee, which shamed a number of American states into drafting, and in some cases even passing, antilynching legislation, and fostered an Anglo-American discussion of lynching that made headlines in both countries.

Lynching did not end in the 1890s, or for many years to come. But Wells's campaign transformed lynching from a practice that went largely uncontested even among Northern whites into an ugly symbol of the racial injustices of Jim Crow. Not the first African American to speak out against lynching, Wells was the first to gain a broad audience. Her work is notable for crafting an analysis of lynching that remains pathbreaking even to this day. In challenging the practice, Wells cut through the myths about black rapists that white Southerners used to defend lynching. Lynching had nothing to do with rape and everything to do with power, Wells argued, presenting the facts and figures to prove it. White men policed the color line even to the point of murdering black men who engaged in consensual relationships with white women, and most lynchings did not involve allegations of rape. Instead, lynchings sustained the all-encompassing system of racial domination that marked the New South by terrorizing blacks and "keeping the nigger down."

Subsequent civil rights activists would agree, organizing much of the early twentieth-century civil rights struggle around antilynching strategies pioneered by Wells. But Wells would not lead them, nor go on to be Frederick Douglass's successor. Although she appears among the major leaders of the race in an 1895 photo collage that includes Frederick Douglass and Tuskegee Institute principal Booker T. Washington, she would have trouble sustaining prominence as a national leader even through the remainder of the 1890s. Eclipsed at least in part by Washington's meteoric rise to fame on a platform of black accommodation to Jim Crow, she also during those years became a wife and mother, marrying the Chicago-based African American lawyer Ferdinand Barnett. Thereafter, she juggled her public life with domestic responsibilities that included two stepsons and soon came to include four children of her own. But neither motherhood nor the growing power of Booker T. Washington fully explain why Wells's sojourn in the national spotlight was so brief. An activist all her life, Wells would continue to battle lynching and other forms of racial injustice for the remainder of her days. But she ended her life as a leader more prominent in Chicago than the nation as a whole.

Undoubtedly, sexism circumscribed her career, as did her assertive personality, which many contemporaries found to be at odds with her gender. Even her admirers could never compliment her leadership without noting that it was ill-suited to her sex. "If Iola were a man," black journalist T. Thomas Fortune said of Wells after first meeting her, calling her by her pen name, "she would be a humming independent in politics. She has plenty of nerve, and is sharp as a steel trap." And over time, such admirers would often turn on Wells for possessing traits admirable only in men. Fortune himself was a case in point. By 1899, Fortune, who had once employed

This photo collage of some of the day's most prominent African Americans appears at the beginning of The College of Life, or Practical Self Educator: A Manual of Self Improvement for the Colored Race *(1895), by Henry Davenport Northrop, Joseph R. Gay, and I. Garland* Penn. *The only woman among the five figures pictured, Ida B. Wells is one of the four younger leaders whose portraits circle an image of Frederick Douglass—black America's elder statesman. Above Douglass are newspaperman T. Thomas Fortune and Tuskegee Institute principal Booker T. Washington; beneath Douglass, on the left, is writer I. Garland Penn—*The College of Life's *only black author.*

Wells at his newspaper *The New York Age*, had allied with Booker T. Washington, and began to dismiss his former protégée as "a bull in a China shop."[7]

Whether Wells's career would have indeed taken a different path if she had been a man remains impossible to say, although her contemporaries' persistent unease with her gender suggests as much. An activist by nature, Wells had limitations above and beyond her sex when it came to sustaining a following. She often resisted the "restraints of organization," as a later critic would note. Hardheaded to a fault, and possessed of a temper that she acknowledged to be a "besetting sin," Wells helped build a stunning variety of black organizations, including the National Association for the Advancement of Colored People (NAACP), only to find herself comfortable in none of them. More radical than most of her contemporaries, she also had no gift for compromise and often departed in a huff from the organizations that she helped create, her famous temper flaring when negotiations did not go her way. As a result, her contemporaries considered her difficult, although even that assessment cannot be decoupled from her gender. With the possible exception of Booker T. Washington, most of the leading African Americans of her era *were* difficult, in one way or another.

Early twentieth-century black leaders had to contend with a racist white majority that questioned their qualifications for leadership, while defending their community against a relentless assault on black civil rights. Not surprisingly, strong personalities prevailed among their ranks. Such personalities included the NAACP leader W.E.B. Du Bois, who deposed Booker T. Washington to become the early twentieth century's most preeminent leader. A man who frequently butted heads with Wells, Du Bois was often described as "arrogant." He spent much of his career battling with both black and white contemporaries—without ever being written off as "a bull in a China shop." A strong mind was more of a liability in a woman.

Moreover, Wells-Barnett—as she renamed herself after her marriage—had other leadership liabilities as well. Born at the end of the slavery era, she became a leader without the help of the kind of educational or social credentials that would help younger black leaders such as Du Bois earn the respect of the increasingly educated black middle class—and their white allies as well. Although Wells was active in the Progressive-era reform community, her credentials as wife, mother, and self-educated journalist paled next to the academic credentials that supplied many black and white progressives with their leadership qualifications. She was also less educated and socially elite than many of the black club women she helped organize during her antilynching campaign. Founded in 1896, the National Association of Colored Women (NACW) first took shape around her work, but she was never considered for any leadership post in that organization.

Disappointed but never despairing about the many obstacles her leadership faced, Wells remained committed to the "preservation of our [African American] liberties" all her life. Tireless foes of mob violence in Illinois, she and her husband, Ferdinand, fought a successful battle for effective antilynching legislation there, and then moved on to fight injustices within the state's legal system, offering representation to blacks who had been unfairly imprisoned, and support and guidance to black prisoners as a group. Moreover, even though Wells would not remain active in the NAACP or the NACW or any other national organization, she continued to fight lynching and other forms of racial injustice in Illinois and elsewhere, protesting the race riots of the twentieth century's first decades as well as the federal government's mistreatment of black soldiers during World War I. Also active on behalf of early childhood education, women's suffrage, temperance, and the social welfare of Chicago blacks, Wells was involved in Republican politics, and even made an unsuccessful bid for a state senate seat in Illinois in 1930—at age sixty-eight. Her campaign capped a life committed to a range of causes so extensive that they defy easy summary. Raised by ex-slaves and informed by an education that included reading the Bible cover to cover and imbibing all the most activist elements of the Judeo-Christian tradition, Ida always felt compelled to "do something" in the face of "injustice or discrimination." Her life bears eloquent testimony to the power of that commitment. An African American leader barely a generation removed from slavery, Wells drew on forms of antebellum politics that survived the Civil War but have not always been appreciated by historians since. In particular, the keen political insights that Wells brought out of her ex-slave upbringing lend strong support to the work of scholars such as Steven Hahn, who maintains that black Southerners greeted emancipation with enduring political and moral commitments forged during slavery and fostered thereafter in the kinship networks that guided the freed people through emancipation.[8] Moreover, Wells embraced the tradition of noisy public protest nourished among antebellum-era blacks who escaped the slave South, combating lynching with protest strategies once used by black abolitionists and allying herself with the ex-slave leader Frederick Douglass.

Although the African American protest strategies and political traditions that Wells did so much to help sustain would shape the twentieth-century civil rights movement, Wells herself was underappreciated during her own lifetime. As she got older, she found herself increasingly overshadowed by a new generation of black leaders—many of whom were active in organizations she had helped found. She had spent most of her life far "too busy trying to do what seemed to me to be my share of work for the race . . . to write about myself," so in her sixties Wells decided to "set it all down." Intent on leaving "some record of the beginnings of agitation against lynching," she interrupted her busy career as a reformer to write a long autobiography that she never managed to finish.[9] Despite this effort, after her death in 1931 her reputation languished for many years, neglected by a historical profession long uninterested in the history of African Americans or women.

But as the twenty-first century opens, Ida B. Wells is well on the road to achieving all the honors and recognition never accorded her in her lifetime. Even as Wells's star dimmed after her death, her youngest daughter, Alfreda Duster, preserved her mother's papers, edited her autobiography, and worked tirelessly to secure its publication. She finally succeeded in publishing *Crusade for Justice: The Autobiography of Ida B. Wells* in 1970, at a time when black history and women's history were finally beginning to receive widespread attention. Since then, Wells has been studied by an ever increasing number of scholars and biographers, whose work appreciates the importance of her antilynching campaign and pioneering history as a female leader. Far from forgotten, Wells now receives a full measure of the public recognition that eluded her during the second half of her life. Studied and taught in school and college curriculums, she was even featured on a U.S. postage stamp issued in 1990. And in 2005, her work was lauded on the floor of Congress. The Senate adopted a "nonbinding" resolution "apologizing to the victims of lynching and the descendants of those victims for the failure of the Senate to enact antilynching legislation" (which did not receive a unanimous vote). Too little, too late, Wells might have thought with reference to the Senate resolution. But she might also take comfort in the fact that today her life and work are not just honored but also studied and taught, ensuring that her "crusade for justice" will have a continuing impact on future generations.

Wells is now appreciated as an important historical figure not in the least because her life and work illuminate dilemmas that still vex us today. Racism and sexism still shape American politics in myriad ways, coloring popular perceptions of both black and female leaders and perpetuating the challenges to black female leadership that Wells faced. Moreover, Wells's life provides invaluable historical testimony on the often contradictory impact of being black and female at the turn of the nineteenth century—a time when the lives of most black women went unrecorded. Among the relatively few African American women of her era to leave a life chronicled well enough to be studied or remembered in any detail, Ida documented experiences that would otherwise be lost to history. A journalist and an activist, she left behind many news articles, editorials, petitions, and protest pamphlets. She was also a prolific correspondent and compulsive writer who recorded the details of her life in diaries, letters, and a long autobiography. Many of her diaries and much of her personal correspondence are long gone—burned in a house fire that destroyed many of her papers. But, carefully preserved by Alfreda Duster, Wells's autobiography and her surviving diaries and papers combine to provide a rich documentary record of the life of a woman whose observations about her world remain insightful even today.

Not the least bit representative of mainstream modes of thinking common to her day—among whites or within her own community—Wells was an extraordinary individual. Her biography offers far more than a useful chronicle of her times or a life characteristic of her era. An unrelenting and insightful social critic, Wells spent her life testifying to the social, political, and economic evils of her era and thereby recording the toll they took on a generation of African Americans who, by and large, lacked the education, opportunity, and political freedom to speak for themselves. An indignant witness to the violence, segregation, and other forms of racial discrimination white Southerners used to restore white supremacy, her life preserves a history of black activism and female leadership that historians are just now beginning to recover. Moreover, her commitment to "'do something' about every item of injustice and discrimination . . . whatever the matter happened to be" makes her a hero whose life still stands as both a lesson and a challenge to modern-day Americans—black or white, male or female. Always impatient with anyone unwilling to speak out against injustice, Wells reflected on the ongoing challenge faced by those who shared her commitment to equality and civil rights. "Eternal vigilance is the price of liberty" was the motto she used to begin the final chapter of an autobiography too often interrupted by her protest activities to be completed.[10]

· 1 ·

Coming of Age in Mississippi

WE ARE ALL SHAPED BY OUR CHILDHOODS, BUT IDA B. WELLS'S childhood was more formative than most. The time, place, and circum-stances of her birth structured her life in decisive ways, as did the early death of both her parents when she was just sixteen years old. To be black and born a slave in the American South in 1862, as Wells was, was to enter the world in the middle of a revolution brought on by a cataclysmic civil war and its aftermath. A member of the first post-emancipation generation of African American Southerners, Wells grew up during a unique moment in American history. Contrary to our often romantic notions of African American emancipation, slavery did not just go out in a blaze of glory with the Union Army's hard-fought victory. Instead, the Civil War was followed by an almost equally bitter struggle between the South and the North over the fate of the freed people, in which the ex-slaves allied with their North-ern emancipators in a desperate struggle to secure their rights as American citizens. Known as Radical Reconstruction, this period spanned the years 1866 to 1877, and saw Northern Republican leaders impose black voting rights on a defiant white South, while the ex-slaves educated themselves, participated in politics, and tried to create a free and equal world for them-selves and their children.

Reconstruction did not last long or fulfill the freed people's hopes. Instead, it ended in 1877, after a series of state-by-state defeats that marked the power and persistence of white Southern resistance to black empowerment as well as the fleeting nature of Northern concern for the freed people's well-being. But for all its brevity, Reconstruction loomed large in Wells's life. The revolutionary hopes, dreams, and dangers of Reconstruction shaped her childhood, which ended in 1878 with the death of her parents. Raised by ex-slaves who were fiercely committed to the brave new world that newly freed blacks sought to create during Reconstruction, Wells lost both her parents and the prospect of that brave new world at the same time.

Its memory shaped her life, perhaps because these combined losses were so devastating. Indeed, a half century later, when Wells sat down to write her autobiography, Reconstruction loomed largest in her mind. In her preface she explained that she was committing to paper her life story for young people "who have so little of our race's history." And then, quite strikingly for someone who lived most of her life after Reconstruction, Wells went on to stress that she felt especially "constrained" to write "because there is such a lack of authentic race history of the Reconstruction times written by the Negro himself." Seemingly writing an introduction to her parents' biography rather than her own, Wells continued, "We have Frederick Douglass's history of slavery as he knew and experienced it. But of the time of storm and stress immediately after the Civil War, of the Ku Klux Klan, of ballot box stuffing, of wholesale murders of Negroes who tried to exercise their new-found rights about which the white South has published so much that is false, the Negroes' political life of the era—our race had little that is definite or authentic."[1]

In Wells's own lifetime, the memory of what W.E.B. Du Bois would call "Black Reconstruction" was distorted by white Americans from both regions. The myth of Reconstruction that emerged after the North and South reconciled in the late nineteenth century cast Reconstruction as a scandalously corrupt period of "Negro rule," in which unscrupulous "carpetbaggers" from the North collaborated with self-serving Southern "scalawags" to turn the government of the South over to ludicrously inept freedmen. This national fable allowed white Northerners to turn a blind eye to the disenfranchisement of blacks in the post-Reconstruction South and assume no responsibility for abandoning the protection of freed people's rights during Reconstruction. Embraced by American popular culture as well as American political leaders, it helped whites in both regions justify the entrenched racial inequities and pervasive racist violence that persisted into twentieth-century America. As commemorated in popular works such as D. W. Griffith's film *The Birth of a Nation* (1915), Reconstruction was a disaster remedied only by the forcible restoration of the "white man's government" that came afterward. An ode to the Ku Klux Klan, the film featured white actors in blackface who depicted African American men as lust-crazed savages.

Lost in all the convenient mythologizing was the black experience, or as Wells writes, "the gallant fight and marvelous bravery of the black men of the South fighting and dying to exercise and maintain their newborn rights as free men and citizens, with little protection from the government that gave them those rights and with no previous training in citizenship or politics." Personally galling for Wells was the absence of any record of the courage and convictions of her parents and the political and cultural dramas of her own childhood, all of which had combined to give Wells an enduring faith in the power of black people to educate themselves and govern their own destiny. These beliefs shaped her life and also helped form her conviction that the story of Reconstruction would fire the "race pride" of America's black youth, if only "it had been written down."[2]

A Child of Freedom

The sweeping social and political changes that structured her life started early. Ida Bell Wells came into the world in the town of Holly Springs, Mississippi, just as Union troops began to sweep through northern Mississippi in preparation for General Ulysses S. Grant's Vicksburg campaign. Her birth on July 16, 1862, must have been a source of both joy and anxiety to her parents. James and Elisabeth Wells greeted their firstborn in a prosperous Mississippi town where the outcome of the war was far from certain. The site of both a Rebel armory and a Union supply depot, Holly Springs was continually under siege by either Union or Confederate forces. Contested territory, it changed hands more than fifty times over the course of the war. The wartime violence and uncertainty was devastating to all concerned, and weighed especially heavily on slave families such as the Wellses. Terrorized by Confederate raids that sent "Negroes and abolitionists begging for mercy," Holly Springs's African American residents saw their hopes for freedom dashed so often before the Confederate forces finally surrendered the town on May 4, 1864, that even then many must have wondered whether freedom had come to stay.[3] By Ida's third birthday, however, the war was over and the slaves were free.

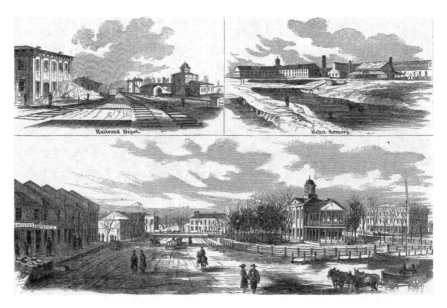

Holly Springs in January 1863—less than a year after Ida B. Wells was born. This wartime sketch shows the town in the wake of a Confederate raid that destroyed its railroad station and several blocks of buildings.

Emancipation was the long-awaited day of jubilee across the slave South, which the ex-slaves greeted with celebrations, thankful prayers, and countless efforts to take immediate advantage of their liberty. Wells's parents were not among those many ex-slaves who took their freedom on the road in search of lost relatives or greater liberties—although they did, in a solemn ceremony, exercise these liberties by legalizing their slave marriage. A proud and independent man even as a slave, Wells's father, known as Jim, was an apprentice to a contractor and builder, Mr. Bolling. Jim's wife, Elisabeth ("Lizzie"), served as Bolling's cook. After the war, the Wellses initially chose to stay on with Mr. Bolling. But they did not remain in Bolling's household long. Unlike many ex-slaves, Lizzie and Jim Wells prospered during Reconstruction, rapidly achieving a political and economic independence that was all too rare among African Americans in the post-emancipation South. In doing so, they sought independence for their children as well, preparing them for freedom in a household that abhorred slavery, honored education, and achieved self-sufficiency.

As skilled urban laborers, the Wellses escaped the poverty that was among the most acute problems faced by black Southerners after the war. The vast majority of the freed people were agricultural laborers who came out of slavery with "nothing but freedom."[4] Landless, unskilled, and uneducated, most black Southerners had to depend on bitter and vanquished white Southerners for their livelihood during the hard economic times that followed the war. All across the Southern countryside, Reconstruction was shaped by the often futile struggles of freed people to receive fair wages for agricultural work from impoverished Southern planters who were both unwilling and unable to pay them a living wage. With the collapse of the Confederacy, white Southerners lost their capital in both Confederate currency and slaves. With defeat their currency lost all value, and emancipation wiped out their investment in slaves—who prior to the Civil War had been the most valuable form of private property other than land in the United States. Stripped of their most valuable investments, former slaveholders still remained among their region's largest landowners. But they owned virtually nothing other than their land, and therefore rarely had enough cash to pay for wage labor. Sharecropping was the compromise ultimately reached between the land-rich and the landless. Blacks ended up tending plots of land in return for a share of the crop produced. Sharecropping, while offering black families a little more independence than slavery, was almost equally exploitative. Dependent on the planters to advance them food, clothing, and other necessities from the plantation store, and subject to interest rates often exceeding 50 percent, many sharecroppers ended up in debt even after they had received their share of the crop. Sharecropping was a "state of servitude but little better than slavery," one freedman complained. Freed "without any chance to live to ourselves . . . we still had to depend on the southern white man for work, food and clothing."[5]

By contrast, Reconstruction dawned much brighter for the Wells family. Ida's parents, as she remembered, were never poor because they were "able," a word that reflected her pride in her parents' skill and independence. Ironically, Jim Wells owed his independence, at least in part, to his slave owner father. The only son of a slaveholder who had no children with his wife, Jim Wells received some recognition and privileges from his powerful parent. He grew up on his father's plantation in Tippah County, Mississippi, where his workload was relatively light. According to Ida, he served primarily as "the companion and comfort" of his slaveholding parent's old age.[6] Moreover, his father provided him with what would prove to be a valuable education, sending him to Holly Springs to learn the carpenter's trade when he reached eighteen, which is how he began his apprenticeship with Bolling. According to Ida, her grandfather expected his enslaved son to use his skills on the plantation once his training was complete. But once apprenticed, Jim Wells never returned. Following the war's conclusion, he remained with Bolling only until election time, when Bolling instructed him to vote for the Democrats. Wells refused, choosing instead to vote for the party that had brought Radical Reconstruction and black voting to the South, the Republicans. When he returned from the polls, he found himself locked out of Bolling's shop. Wells promptly set out on his own, purchasing his own tools and renting a house for himself and his family.

Thereafter, Jim Wells was able to support himself and his family as a carpenter. Although he owed his preparation for independence at least partially to the education provided by his slave owner father, there is little evidence that Jim felt any filial ties to the man who fathered him. Indeed, both of Ida's parents expressed only negative memories of their slave days. Ida's strongest impression of her father's childhood revolved around the bitter household relations that existed on the plantation where he grew up, evidence of which she recorded in her autobiography.

Like her son, Jim's mother, Peggy, and her husband, a man whom she married after emancipation, achieved economic independence once free. Buying a farm in rural Mississippi, the couple raised corn, cotton, and hogs, which they sold at harvest in Holly Springs, where they also visited with the Wells family. During one of these fall visits, Ida's grandmother brought pork from her farm and news from the old plantation. Their former mistress, "Miss Polly," wanted Jim Wells to "come and bring the children. She wants to see them." The irony of a former slave mistress's request to meet her husband's slave grandchildren may have been lost on the young Ida, but not the bitterness of her father's reply: "I never want to see that old woman as long as I live." Still haunted by his father's wife's cruelty toward his mother, Jim told Peggy, "I'll never forget how she had you stripped and whipped the day after the old man died . . . I guess it is all right for you to take care of her and forgive her for what she did to you, but she could have starved to death if I'd had my say-so." The exchange made a lasting impression on Ida, who later reflected that while she did not understand what her father said at the time, she never forgot his words: "Since I have grown old enough to understand I cannot but help feel what an insight into slavery they give."[7]

If the tangled family relations in which Jim Wells grew up were scarcely benign, Ida's mother's slave experience was still more painful. Born Elisabeth Warrenton, Ida's mother met her husband in Mr. Bolling's household, where she served as cook. Eighteen years old when Ida was born, Lizzie Wells was one of ten children born to a Virginia slave couple. What we do know about her early life speaks to the power of the domestic slave trade to wreak havoc on the lives of individual African Americans. Lizzie Wells suffered the double misfortune of not only being born a slave but also serving in antebellum Virginia, an upper South state with a surplus of slaves. Virginia planters participated in a lively domestic slave trade, selling off unneeded slaves to the rapidly expanding cotton states of the Southwest. Sold to a slave trader at the age of seven, together with two of her sisters, Lizzie was among the hundreds of thousands of surplus slaves carried from the upper South to the Southwest during the antebellum era. Young Elisabeth changed hands several times before she ended up at Mr. Bolling's. Her early hardships were literally written on her back, which bore scars from the beatings of "overseers and mean masters."[8]

Equally enduring was Lizzie Wells's anguish over her separation from her family. Proud of her family's Native American ancestry, Lizzie, who would go on to have seven more children after Ida, often reminded her children that her father was half Indian and her grandfather a full-blood. But as much as she valued her heritage, she was only ever able to introduce her children to the two sisters who were sold with her and moved to Mississippi as well. Even after emancipation, Lizzie was never able to locate any of her other siblings or her parents. As a child, Wells used to see her mother writing letter after letter to Virginia "trying to get track of her people." She never succeeded. In her autobiography, Ida reflected that the details of her mother's family history died with her, as her children "were too young to realize the importance of her efforts, and I have never remembered the name of the country or people to whom they 'belonged.' "[9]

Her parents' experiences made a sufficiently vivid impression on the young Ida that she would later regale her own children with "many stories of slavery time."[10] Wells's enduring preoccupation with slavery is not surprising, given that she grew up in the midst of Reconstruction and was raised by adults who were themselves making the transition from slavery to freedom. Indeed, this remarkable experience was one of the sources of Ida's lifelong belief in activism and social change. Her childhood coincided with her parents' first years of freedom, and she grew up alongside parents who were intent on remaking themselves and their children as free people.

The Wellses seized Reconstruction's opportunities eagerly. Chief among them was education, which had been forbidden to blacks by law under slavery. One of the most dramatic changes of the Reconstruction era was the sudden appearance of hundreds of schools for blacks. Such schools marked the beginning of a broad system of public education in the South, which prior to the Civil War was not always available even to whites. The first black schools were established by Northern churches in collaboration with the Freedmen's Bureau—a short-lived federal agency established by President Lincoln in 1865 to oversee the welfare of the former slaves. Holly Springs was the site of one of these early schools. Initially known as Mac-Donald Hall, it was established by the Freedmen's Aid Society of the Methodist Church in 1866. An elementary school at first, it was chartered in 1870 as Shaw University in recognition of the freed people's desire for an education that extended from grade school to college. Informally known as Rust College until 1915, when the name became official, it soon expanded to offer both elementary and higher education and is now Mississippi's oldest historically black college.[11] Despite the fact that in most black families all members had to work to make ends meet, ex-slaves sent their children to school wherever possible, and often attended night school themselves. In the Wellses' home state, black children's school enrollment reached 50 percent by 1875, a figure that reflects the sacrifices many hard-pressed black Southern families made to educate their children. Better off than most blacks in their region, the Wellses' commitment to education represented less of a sacrifice, but Ida was still raised to regard her education as serious work. Of herself and her siblings, she wrote, "Our job was to go to school and learn all we could."[12]

The importance of this job was clearly impressed upon the Wells children by both parents. In addition to sending all their children to school, the Wellses were also active in the daily affairs of the school. Jim Wells was a trustee at Rust, and when Ida began school, her mother attended courses alongside her daughter. In addition to an education, Rust College provided the "deeply religious" Lizzie Wells with a thoroughly Christian environment in which to educate herself and her children.[13] Students attended chapel daily and were also expected to attend weekly prayer meetings as well as

Sunday church services. Pursuing religious knowledge as well as literacy, Lizzie studied with her children until she learned how to read the Bible. After that, she confined her own schooling to Sunday school, winning a prize for regular attendance, but she continued to visit Rust regularly to observe her children's progress. She also tended to the children's education at home, teaching them morals, manners, and housework—lessons that left an enduring impression on Ida.

"She was not forty when she died," Ida wrote of her mother in her autobiography, "but she had borne eight children and brought us up with strict discipline that many mothers with educational advantages could not have exceeded."[14] Among Lizzie Wells's legacies to her daughter were her religious convictions and devotion to Bible study. Ida learned to read at a very young age, probably alongside her mother as she mastered the Scriptures at Rust College. By the time she was a teenager, Ida had "read the Bible through," as her parents did not permit her "to read anything else on Sunday afternoons at home." Moreover, she also imbibed its lessons: Ida would draw on the Scriptures for guidance, strength, and comfort for the rest of her life, frequently turning to Bible passages for direction in times of duress or indecision.

Reading also gave Ida an early acquaintance with another defining feature of black life during Reconstruction: African American political participation. One of her earliest memories was of reading the newspaper to her "father and an admiring group of his friends." Whether or not Jim Wells needed Ida as a reader is not clear. Certainly many former slaves were not literate, and Jim Wells may have been among them. Or his training as a carpenter may have given him a chance to acquire reading skills—and to encourage his daughter's precocious reading ability. Either way, when Ida read to her father and his friends she participated in a drama that was unfolding in black communities across the South. With freedom, African Americans sought not only literacy, but also news and political information. African American readers and nonreaders alike devoured newspapers, with those who could not read gathering in homes, stores, and saloons to hear the news from anyone who could.

Educated or otherwise, Jim Wells took an intense interest in politics. During Mississippi's Republican Reconstruction period, from 1867 to 1875, black political participation was perilous, as Jim Wells found when he defied Mr. Bolling. Despite the fact that African Americans comprised the overwhelming majority in the Wellses' electoral district of Marshall County, the Democrats were able to use intimidation and election fraud to hold on to power for much of Reconstruction. In addition to discouraging African Americans from voting, they stuffed ballot boxes and forged ballots. Democratic ruffians threw sticks and brickbats at Republican speakers, who were also whipped, beaten, and in one case even murdered.[15] Neither the threat of violence nor the loss of his job with Bolling, however, deterred the independent-minded Jim Wells from participating. He attended political meetings, even though his wife feared for his safety. Ida learned to associate politics with danger at an early age. She "heard the words Ku Klux Klan long before I knew what they meant," and "knew dimly that it meant something fearful, by the anxious way my mother walked the floor at night when my father was out to a political meeting."[16]

Lizzie Wells had good cause to be anxious. Founded immediately after the Civil War, the Ku Klux Klan was a paramilitary terrorist organization dedicated "to serving the interests of the Democratic party, the planter class, and those who desired white supremacy."[17] As black Republicans, the Wellses and their friends were acutely conscious of Klan activities. The Klan staged at least one attack on the Holly Springs branch of the Loyal League, a Republican political group composed primarily of black members. The Klan detested the league, since it brought white and black Republicans together in a coalition government. During the late 1860s and early 1870s, Klan members plotted to destroy the group in Holly Springs by killing Nelson Gill of the Freedmen's Bureau, a "negro lover" from Illinois who had helped organize the league. An attempt on Gill's life took place during a Loyal League meeting held at Gill's house, when armed Klansmen hid under the house and fired into the meeting.[18] But the gunmen's shots went off course, and the league thereafter stationed armed guards outside its meetings.

Still, if Ida B. Wells grew up aware of the dangers, she also grew up far more aware of the promise of politics than would later generations of African Americans. Despite local Klan activity, electoral politics were in fact less violent in Holly Springs than in many parts of the South, where Klan violence decimated many Republican organizations, and Republicans were sometimes attacked and even murdered at the polls. More important, black politics were, at least briefly, a success story both in Mississippi and Holly Springs. Mississippi sent two African American men to the U.S. Senate—Blanche K. Bruce and Hiram Rhodes Revels. And as a Holly Springs resident she must have been particularly aware of the accomplishments of Revels, who was the first African American senator in U.S. history; Revels moved to Holly Springs in the mid-1870s, shortly after his Senate term. Moreover, Holly Springs had its own political triumphs. Starting in 1873, the dogged persistence of black Republicans such as Jim Wells paid off. That year, the Republicans swept the Marshall County offices, sending three African Americans to the Mississippi state legislature. Still more impressive, one of them, James Hill, a Holly Springs resident, rose from the legislature to serve as Mississippi's secretary of state between 1874 and 1878. Even before Hill's term ended, the Democrats would return to power, reclaiming the state in 1875. But the brief years of Republican rule were a source of pride to black families, such as the Wellses, whose attempts to gain a voice in politics had succeeded against the odds. Moreover, they exposed young Ida to a level of black political participation and leadership that would not be seen again in the South until the civil rights movement of the 1960s.

Ida would spend much of her adult life trying to regain the black political rights and power that as a child she had seen Mississippi freedmen hold so briefly. By 1877, Reconstruction was over, not only in Mississippi but throughout the South. The contested national election of 1876 resulted in the infamous "Compromise of 1877." An unwritten agreement between Northern Republicans and Southern Democrats, the compromise allowed the Republicans to retain the presidency despite the fact that Democratic presidential candidate Samuel Tilden had won a plurality of the uncontested electoral votes and a majority of the popular vote. In return, Democrats claimed home rule—and an end to Reconstruction. When the Republican candidate, Rutherford B. Hayes, assumed the presidency, he withdrew the troops stationed in the South to protect the freedmen, and the Republican Party abandoned any protection for black civil rights. The Democratic Party returned to power in the South, and the party's "redemption" marked the beginning of the end of black political participation for many years to come. "The Negro," The Nation accurately prophesized at the time, "will disappear from the field of national politics. Henceforth the nation as a nation will have nothing to do with him."[19] Free to use violence, poll taxes, and ultimately disenfranchisement to eliminate black voters, the Southern Democratic self-styled redeemers took over the region. But the end of Reconstruction in the late 1870s must have passed in a blur for the teenage Ida, for it coincided with her stormy adolescence and ended with tragic family losses that utterly transformed her life.

Tragedy, of course, came unanticipated. The mid-1870s saw Wells advancing to college courses at Rust College. They were years that she would later describe as joyful, characterizing herself as "a happy light-hearted school girl." She experienced the joys and sorrows of "first love," falling hard for James B. Combs, a "mulatto" student from Georgia who boarded with a local family.[20] Five years older than Wells, he evidently ended the relationship, leaving her disappointed and enduringly apprehensive about giving her heart to any one man. Other passions were less disappointing. At Rust, Ida developed a lifelong admiration for the Northern Methodist Episcopal teachers who ran the school. Considered "carpetbaggers" by white Southerners, these white teachers shared Ida's parents' vision of black independence and worked to prepare the freed people to be self-sufficient citizens. A. C. MacDonald, the Methodist minister who founded Rust, stressed that the school's educational goal was not to "hurry the students through a college curriculum . . . but to take the far more difficult and tedious plan of trying to lay a foundation for a broad, thorough and practical education."[21] Ida would honor such ideals and appreciate the work of the devout men and women who taught at Rust. Mostly Northerners, they were despised by local whites, who did not share their commitment to educating the freed people. As a result, the Rust faculty were subject to insults, slander, and physical threats—up to and including a sexual assault on one white female teacher's favorite student. Not surprisingly, Ida would long remember them as "consecrated teachers" and looked back on Rust as a "splendid example of Christian courage."[22] Rust also exposed Ida to another great love, books. She read all the fiction in the college library, shaping her ideals on "the best of Dickens's stories, Louisa May Alcott's, Mrs. A.D.T. Whitney's, and Charlotte Brontë's books, and Oliver Optic's books for boys."[23]

Not even Dickens, however, could prepare Ida for the tragedy that struck next. In 1878, shortly after her sixteenth birthday, she was visiting her grandparents' farm when a yellow fever epidemic broke out in the Mississippi Valley region. Initially hardest hit was Memphis, Tennessee, fifty miles from Holly Springs. On hearing the news from Memphis, residents of Holly Springs were not concerned. Memphis had been the site of previous epidemics, and yellow fever was widely believed to be caused by the "swamp vapor." On relatively high ground, Holly Springs was considered safe, so much so that the town mayor refused to impose a quarantine on travelers from Memphis. As Wells put it: "Our little burg opened its doors to any one who wanted to come in."[24] When news of the epidemic finally reached her grandparents' farm in rural Mississippi, Ida and her grandparents also remained calm. Mail arrived only intermittently at the farm, so they could expect no direct news of the Wells family, but they knew that yellow fever was nothing new in Memphis, and had never spread to Holly Springs. Moreover, should Holly Springs become dangerous, they assumed that Jim Wells would move his wife and children to the country.

And dangerous it became. The mayor's hospitality had disastrous consequences. People began to die shortly after the first "refugees" from Memphis arrived. A virus more common to lowlands, yellow fever is not confined to them. At the time linked to "swamp vapors," yellow fever is transmitted by mosquitoes, and passes easily from human to human. An unseasonably mild winter followed almost immediately by a very hot summer had made conditions especially ripe for the transmission of the virus in the Mississippi Valley in 1878. The hot weather had allowed mosquitoes to breed in unprecedented numbers, expanding their territory and spreading yellow fever as their population grew. The effect was devastating, as yellow fever is more easily tolerated by people with a long history of exposure to it, and most lethal to people without any. Worse, the yellow fever of 1878 was a particularly virulent strain. It left few survivors.[25]

By early September, fifty cases of fever had been reported in Holly Springs, and a mass exodus was under way. Streets "were jammed with every conceivable type of vehicle loaded with baggage and human beings," as some two thousand people fled the city. Only fifteen hundred remained behind in a city soon utterly overcome by fever. A resident reported in an anguished telegraph: "The stores are all closed . . . Physicians are broken down . . . Many cases will die today . . . Gloom, despair, and death rule the hour, and the situation is simply appalling."[26]

Among those who stayed were Jim Wells and his family. Ida's mother was nursing a nine-month-old baby, Stanley, and one of her older children also required a lot of care. Ida's sister Eugenia, the family's second child, had become paralyzed below the waist two years earlier after a severe case of scoliosis had deformed her spine. Stanley and Eugenia may have made it particularly difficult for the family to travel. In any case, Elisabeth Wells herself was soon too sick to travel. Although Jim Wells quarantined his family at home once the fever struck, Elisabeth was the first to get sick. Next was Jim. A hero of the epidemic, Jim Wells had spent its early days ministering to both the town and his family. During the final weeks of his life he nursed the sick, prayed for the dying, and built coffins for the dead, all between visits to the gate of his house, where he delivered food and monitored the health of his family. When his wife fell sick, Wells returned home to care for her and promptly fell ill himself, dying September 26, one day before his wife passed.

Too far out in the country to receive newspapers or regular mail, Ida and her grandparents did not hear the news until October. She and her relatives were outdoors picking the first fall cotton when three men from Holly Springs arrived on horseback. Still confident that her family had left Holly Springs, Ida thought they were paying a social call. Only once the men had been greeted and seated did she ask for news of Holly Springs. One of them then handed her a letter he had received from the Wellses' next-door neighbors, which she scanned with little expectation of reading anything of direct "personal interest." Midway through the first page she was brought up short: "Jim and Lizzie Wells have both died of fever. They died within twenty-four hours of each other. The children are all home and the Howard Association has put a woman there to take care of them."[27]

Three days later, Ida rode home aboard a freight train. "No passenger trains were running or needed," and the caboose that Wells rode in was draped in black to honor the recent deaths of the train's two previous conductors. How Ida's relatives made the difficult decision to let the sixteen-year-old brave the deadly epidemic in Holly Springs is not clear. Perhaps they, like Ida, were moved by a letter from a doctor in Holly Springs telling her that her siblings needed her care. Others, however, clearly thought that Ida's mission was foolhardy. She traveled against the advice of everyone at the railroad station where she boarded. They told her she should stay put. No "home doctor" would have ever asked her to come, they suggested, voicing their suspicions of the visiting doctors from outside their region who had been called in to help during the epidemic.[28] Their fears were clearly shared by the train's conductor; he told Ida in no uncertain terms that traveling to Holly Springs was a mistake.

Ida's response to the conductor was marked by the defiant and fearless sense of duty that she had learned from her parents and would display for her entire life. She turned the question around, asking him why he continued to run the train when he was equally likely to contract the fever himself. And when he replied that he did it because "somebody had to do it," Wells said, "That's exactly why I am going home. I am the oldest of seven living children. There's nobody to look after them now. Don't you think I should do my duty, too?"[29]

Wells's decision marked the end of her childhood. She arrived home to find her baby brother, Stanley, dead, and all her other siblings, save her crippled sister Eugenia, who had never contracted the disease, recovering from mild cases of yellow fever. Both in the Wellses' household and elsewhere in Holly Springs, the epidemic was over. But Ida's "Hard Beginnings," as she would later term them, had only just begun.[30]

Hard Beginnings

Although sixteen when her parents died, Wells would always remember herself as only fourteen when she became the head of her family. Her slip may reflect simply how very young she felt in the face of the enormous adult responsibilities she assumed after the death of parents. Indeed, none of the adults who gathered to consider what was to be done expected Ida to take care of her family. Jim Wells had been a Mason, and after his death, his brother Masons rallied around his family. Members of a fraternal organization that provided many African Americans with a social safety net, black Masons often took responsibility for the welfare of its members during times of distress. Accordingly, a meeting at the Wellses' house was called to decide who would take the children. Though Ida attended, she was not consulted; she could only listen with growing dismay as Jim Wells's Masonic brothers discussed a plan to divide up the six children. Ida's two younger sisters would go with two Masons whose wives wanted little girls, and her brothers would be apprenticed out to learn their father's trade. Eugenia could not be placed and would have to go to the poorhouse, while Ida was deemed old enough to fend for herself.

The meeting was abruptly interrupted by young Ida, who announced that "they were not going to put any of the children anywhere." Invoking the memory of her parents, she insisted "it would make my parents turn in their graves to know their children had been scattered like that." The Wellses owned their house and "if the Masons would help me find work, I would take care of them." Initially dubious, the Masons questioned whether Ida, who had never even had to care for herself, was old enough to look after her family. But they eventually let the "butterfly fourteen-year-old school girl," as Wells remembered herself, have her way. Confronted with

Ida's adamant resistance to their plans, Jim Wells's friends ultimately "seemed relieved that they no longer had to worry about the problem."[31]

"I suddenly found myself head of a family," Ida wrote without exaggeration. The Masons appointed two of their members to stand as legal guardians for the Wells children, but Ida took over the family finances, and went from being a schoolgirl to being a schoolteacher. On the Masons' advice, she applied to teach at a country school, and once she passed the corresponding teacher's exam, she had her "dresses lengthened . . . and got a school six miles out in the country."[32] Adult pressures on Ida only grew as she waited for the school term to begin. Financial issues were not the problem. Jim Wells had owned his house free and clear and the family had no debts. Moreover, Jim Wells had left at least three hundred dollars in cash, a sum that Ida's sister Eugenia had given to the family's doctor, Dr. Gray, to put in the town safe. The money would be more than enough to tide the family over until school began. When Ida set out to recover it, however, she found herself catapulted into the treacheries of adult life.

At sixteen, Ida "had never had a beau" or "been out in company except at children's parties," but when she went into town inquiring after Dr. Gray, who was white, rumors began to swirl around her. Townspeople who overheard them jumped to the wrong conclusion when Dr. Gray said he would bring Ida the money that night. "As young as I was," Ida recollected, "it was easy for a certain type of mind" to conclude that "I had been heard asking white men for money and that was the reason I wanted to live there by myself with the children." Looking back as she wrote her autobiography, Wells remembered "this misconstruction" as one of the greatest shocks of her life, and its emotional impact is in fact hard to fully imagine.[33] Young, naive, and traumatized by the recent deaths of her parents and baby brother, Wells had her first encounter with what would be an enduring problem and preoccupation: the sexual slander that she and other black women could so easily become subject to in the racially and sexually polarized world in which they lived.

Victorian mores made Ida appear suspicious to gossiping minds in Holly Springs simply by virtue of the fact that she lived alone, with no other adult in the household. Moreover, as a black woman, Wells was especially vulnerable to allegations of sexual impropriety. In a racist America black women and black men were traditionally seen as especially lascivious and morally "loose." These notions of black sexuality developed hand in hand with racial slavery. Enslaved African Americans were not allowed to have legitimate sexual liaisons or granted the power to control their own sexuality—deprivations that white Americans justified by choosing to view blacks as naturally wanton beings who had no desire to confine their sexual relations within the restrictions of marriage or monogamy. Moreover, in the years that followed emancipation, racial contests over political power and social status only heightened such distortions of black sexuality. The Southern Democrats who retook the South in the 1880s and 1890s were led by men such as the South Carolina politician Benjamin "Pitchfork" Tillman, who, as part of a white supremacist campaign to eliminate black voters from Southern politics, branded black men as rapists who lusted after white women. "We of the South have never recognized the right of the negro to govern white men, and we never will," Tillman told the U.S. Senate in a 1900 speech explaining why black voting rights had all but disappeared in the South. "We have never believed him to be equal to the white man, and we will not submit to his gratifying his lust on our wives and daughters without lynching him."[34] Meanwhile, black women never figured in such expressions of white Southern chivalry, which protected the virtue of white women but assumed that black women did not require similar protection.

This double standard could not be further from the truth, as Ida would later learn and emphasize in her writings: black Southern women were often exploited and victimized by white men. What she learned at sixteen was that African American women were often suspected of sexual improprieties—so much so that black as well as white mores dictated that respectable black women be hypervigilant in protecting their reputations. Chastened, Ida sought out a chaperone, writing to her grandmother in the country asking her to come and stay with them. In her seventies, Peggy joined Ida, taking care of the children and helping with the household chores, but soon further tragedy struck. After one long day's work, Peggy had a paralyzing stroke from which she never fully recovered. An invalid for the remaining years of her life, she returned to the country to live with her daughter. Left alone again, Ida still needed an adult in the household, especially as she had begun teaching at the country school. She was able to find an old friend of her mother's, who came and looked after the children during the week, when she was away at the school.

Ida's late teens found her teaching at Marshall and Tate County schools in rural Mississippi, as well as taking a six-month assignment across the border in Cleveland County, Arkansas. Throughout, she traveled back to Holly Springs on weekends, coming home every Friday "on the back of a big mule." Her short weekend was spent "washing and ironing and cooking for the children" before getting back on the mule on Sunday afternoon to return for Monday's classes. Ida says relatively little about her three and a half years of teaching in rural schools, making no comment on the grueling schedule or what must have been a hard and lonely life for a young girl. But it is clear that those years made an enduring impression on her.[35]

For one thing, these years gave Wells a broad and intimate familiarity with uneducated rural black Southerners, a familiarity many middle-class black leaders of her generation never acquired. Other black leaders, such as Massachusetts-born W.E.B. Du Bois, also taught in the rural South in the 1880s, but usually far more briefly than Wells. During his college days at Fisk University, Du Bois taught for two summers in Alexandria, Tennessee, where he was regarded as a "biggety nigger."[36] Moreover, he clearly never interacted with the country people on the same terms that Wells did. Far from appearing "biggety," Wells traveled to her country schools by mule. A teenager with a high school education and the descendant of rural Southerners herself, Wells was only a few steps removed from the people she taught. Indeed, her daughter Alfreda Duster, recalling her mother's life during those years, suggested that the country people took as much care of their young teacher as she took of them. In particular, Duster described the country people rallying around their young teacher after "the news of Miss Ida's family spread around the countryside." "Friday afternoon was a hilarious time at school. Each student vied with the other to bring something [for Miss Ida] to take home. Fresh butter, sorghum, home grown things she could carry would be piled up ready for her trip."[37]

The bounty that Ida brought home each week no doubt provided a much-needed supplement to the twenty-five-dollar monthly salary she earned. It also may have pressed her to think about how she could best help the rural black folks she taught. In her autobiography she reflected that "as a green girl in my teens I was of no help to people outside the classroom, and at first, I fear, I was very little aid in it, since I had no normal training. The only work I did outside my schoolroom, besides hard study to keep up with the work, was to teach Sunday school." Writing a half century later, Wells still sounded a little overwhelmed as she recalled the challenge of meeting the needs of rural black Mississippians as a teenager. She "found out in the country that the people needed the guidance of everyday life and that the leaders, the preachers were not giving them this help. They would come to me with their problems because I, as their teacher, should have been their leader. But I knew nothing of life but what I had read."[38]

But if Wells could not meet this challenge right away, it was one that she continued to wrestle with. In "A Story of 1900," one of Wells's early journalistic pieces, which appeared in the Fisk Herald in 1886, Wells looks back as if writing in 1900 to tell the story of a Southern-born black woman who taught "among her people" twenty years earlier. Teaching in the country in 1880, as Wells had in fact done, this young woman "perform[s] her duty conscientiously with a desire to carry the light of education to those who dwelt in the darkness, by faithfully instructing her charge[s] in their text-books and grounding them firmly in its rudiments." But she neglects their religious education. "She never thought of the opportunities she possessed to mould high moral character by—as the Episcopalians do in their religion—instilling elevated thoughts, race pride, and ambition, in their daily lessons."[39]

These were lessons that Ida had learned from her parents and also from the teachers at Rust College, and the woman in the story learns them when a visitor to the school critically observes that the boys are getting "enough education to send them to the penitentiary and the girls do worse."

Thereafter, the young teacher understands that blacks lacked "proper home and moral training, combined with mental," and that the duty of black teachers is to supply this lack. Fired with this new mission, the young teacher begins to teach lessons that go beyond schoolwork, exhorting her students "to cultivate honest, noble habits, and lay the foundation for a noble character that would convince the world that worth and not color made the man." She also teaches their parents, visiting homes and "talking earnestly" with them about "laboring to be self-respecting so they might be respected; of a practical Christianity; of setting a pure example of cleanliness and morals before their children."[40]

On the one hand, Ida's message in "A Story of 1900" might seem merely conventional. During the late nineteenth century, middle-class black and white leaders alike often bemoaned the lack of cleanliness and moral education among black Southerners and called upon teachers to teach this recently emancipated population morals and middle-class habits. On the other hand, Ida was no stranger to black life in the rural South even before she started teaching, and seems to have spent her years in the country reflecting on what she could actually do for people. Teaching would not ultimately be Ida's contribution to the betterment of rural black Southerners. As we shall see, she never enjoyed teaching and abandoned it as soon as she could. But when in her early twenties Ida first began to write, she did so with the country people who were her first pupils and their parents in mind. "I had observed much and thought much of the conditions as I had seen them in the country schools and churches," she wrote. "I had an instinctive feeling that people who had little or no schooling should have something coming in their homes weekly, which dealt with their problems in a simple, helpful way."[41]

But before Ida could realize this goal she first had to leave rural Mississippi and, remarkably, she managed to do so. Here, too, Wells drew on lessons learned early in life, most notably the legacy of her parents' Reconstruction dreams. Like the mother she admired so much, Ida did not let her family obligations stand in the way of her education. Indeed, throughout her teens Ida pursued the higher education that both parents had envisioned for their eldest daughter. While teaching in the country school, Ida educated herself by reading at night. With "no oil for lamps" and "no candles to spare," during winter nights she would "sit before the blazing wood fire" with a book in her lap.[42] Moreover, during the summers she continued to attend Rust College until she was expelled in 1881 or 1882. The reasons are elusive, but Wells recalled the incident in a diary written some years later as one of the most "painful memories of my life." The headstrong young woman evidently lost her temper with some of the teachers at Rust, giving voice to "hateful words" that she later regretted. Remembering the incident three years later, Ida was still moved to self-recriminatory prayer: "O

Ida B. Wells as a young woman

My Father forgive me," she wrote in her diary, "forgive me & take away the remembrance of those hateful words, uttered for the satisfaction of self. Humble the pride exhibited and make me Thy child."[43]

Wells would struggle to control her temper later in life as well, but rarely at such a high cost: she long regretted not finishing her degree, which would have made it easier for her to advance as a teacher. According to Wells's daughter Alfreda Duster, Wells tried to complete her studies after she moved to Memphis, attending Fisk University during at least one summer session. But little other evidence exists to show that she even studied there. She attended Fisk commencement exercises one spring, and confessed her "craving" to study there to a reporter for the *Fisk Herald*, which may in fact be the sum of her contact with Fisk's Nashville campus.[44] Still, it remains clear that Ida B. Wells continued her intellectual education long after she left Rust. Rather than being defeated by the educational limitations imposed on her by her precipitate path to early adulthood, Wells seems to have been determined to honor her parents' legacy by retaining all her ambitions. Her first opportunity came in 1881, when her father's sister Fannie Wells invited Ida and her younger siblings to come and live with her in Memphis. Ida's aunt was a widow with three small children of her own, so she could not relieve Ida of all her caregiving responsibilities. But her invitation did offer Ida a way to escape her poorly paid and unsatisfying work in the country schools. In Memphis, she would be able to take the city schoolteachers' exam, which would qualify her to earn a higher salary teaching in better schools.

Urban Tennessee also offered Wells a world beyond rural Mississippi. Memphis was home to a dynamic black middle class with a lively intellectual milieu that would foster her talents, helping her transform herself from a teacher to a journalist, editor, and activist. And during her years there, the schoolgirl-turned-schoolteacher would also become a woman. Leaving Holly Springs three years after her parents died, Wells moved to Memphis less encumbered by family obligations than at any time since her parents' deaths. Her two brothers, James and George, had both left home to become carpenters' apprentices, while Ida's disabled sister Eugenia went to live with another aunt in the country. Now nineteen, Wells moved to Memphis, with only her two youngest sisters, Lily and Annie, in tow. Moreover, with her aunt Fannie on hand to help her raise the girls, Ida finally became free to do some growing up herself. In Memphis she would socialize and date for the first time, discovering a both frustrating and liberating world of love and romance in which her ambitions were often in conflict with social norms. In the end, however, Wells's career in Memphis would be more notable for its successes than its frustrations. She would spend a little over a decade there, rising from her humble origins to become a well-known journalist and activist, and acquiring a much more minor reputation as a "heartless flirt."[45]

· 2 ·

Walking in Memphis

MEMPHIS PROVED TO BE THE MAKING OF IDA B. WELLS. OR, AT the very least, Memphis was where Wells remade herself from a country schoolmistress to an elegant and accomplished young member of the New South's urban black elite. The transformation was not easy, and it did not happen overnight. Instead, Wells's transition to city life was gradual. She moved to Memphis in 1881, but a couple of years passed before she was able to complete the city's schoolteachers' exam and find a job there. In the meantime, she continued teaching rural schoolchildren, taking a job ten miles outside of the city in Woodstock, Tennessee. Still boarding in the country during the week, Wells first got to know Memphis on the weekends, easing into a new life in a city that was very different from her rural hometown.

A bustling city of 35,000, Memphis was approximately ten times the size of Holly Springs and growing by the day. At the crossroads of several major Southern railroads, it was a commercial hub for the South's cotton belt and lumber trade. A prosperous and rapidly modernizing city, during the 1880s Memphis was among the first Southern cities to introduce such newfangled conveniences as electric streetcars. More important to Ida was the fact that the Tennessee city housed a much more vibrant and diverse black community than her small Mississippi hometown. Memphis's population was over 40 percent African American during Ida's years there. Free to migrate for the first time, during the decades following the Civil War rural black Southerners flocked to urban areas in search of education, autonomy, and work that paid better than sharecropping, and Memphis, in particular, was "a mecca for African-Americans in the region." Among its attractions was the still-famous Beale Street. Now known as the birthplace of the blues, in Ida's day the street had a seedier reputation. It was known as the "black magic district."[1] A mile-long strip jammed with gamblers, prostitutes, voodoo doctors, and saloons, Beale Street housed a new black urban underclass that had emerged with emancipation. But farther down Beale Street was another class of black people—the respectable middle-class kind. The office buildings on the first three blocks of Beale Street were occupied by black professionals and businessmen, such as Robert R. Church, a wealthy real estate mogul who, like Ida, had started out in Holly Springs. Also on one of Beale Street's respectable blocks stood the Beale Street Baptist Church, one of the dominant cultural institutions of black Memphis.

Although by no means well-to-do herself, especially when she first arrived, Ida identified from the start with Memphis's black elite, and spent her years there carving out a place for herself among the leading black citizens of Memphis. As a rural Southerner and a child of former slaves, Ida's claim to middle-class status when she first arrived in Memphis was fragile at best. She had only a modest education, her parents were dead, and she was perennially strapped for cash. By and large, her financial troubles were the inevitable and unavoidable result of her familial obligations. In addition to taking care of her youngest siblings, Lily and Annie, during her early years in Memphis, Ida also sent money to her two brothers and supported her disabled sister Eugenia. Moreover, Ida's finances remained precarious even after her aunt Fannie moved to Visalia, California, in April 1886, taking Lily and Annie with her. Relieved of caring for the two girls, Ida still had to contribute to their support and struggled to find the ten dollars a month she sent to Fannie on their behalf. Once her aunt left she also had to find her own accommodations, which meant paying from ten to fifteen dollars a month to board with a variety of landladies, who changed over time in part because Wells had trouble keeping up with her monthly obligations.

A diary kept by Wells during her years in Memphis, containing entries running from 1885 to 1887, dramatizes both her precarious finances and her middle-class aspirations. One of her few surviving personal documents, it shows her moving from boardinghouse to boardinghouse in a vain attempt to find suitable long-term housing. One of Ida's landladies moved away; another mistreated her children; one woman had to give up her home when she could not make ends meet; and Ida's attempt to live with her friends the Settles, a wealthy Memphis couple, foundered when she believed that they had overcharged her. "Sick & tired [of] begging people to take me to board," Ida dreamed of going "into housekeeping by my own hook." But her hopes of getting a loan to purchase her aunt Fannie's Memphis house never came to fruition. Far from being in a position to buy a home, during most of her time in Memphis Wells was constantly in debt. "Mr. F[roman] was up last evening & loaned me the $3 I asked," she wrote on December 3, 1885, in a typical diary entry. "M[enken] sent a bill of $78 and I have no money to pay it. Looking back at my debts I am thankful I could not accomplish my purpose and borrow money to get away—I would have been more deeply in debt."[2]

In the diary, Wells kept an ongoing record of her expenditures and debts, which reveals how tenuous her claim to an elegant middle-class life was. She had grown up to be a very pretty young woman who enjoyed dressing well. But she rued the money she spent on clothes and expressed reservations about almost every purchase. "I am very sorry I did not resist the impulse to buy that cloak" she concluded one discussion of her finances. "I would have been $15 richer." Elsewhere she worried about the expense of a new outfit: "Wore my new dress & hat as they were finished up and like the dress very much. Paid the woman $7.60 for making it and altogether it cost a good deal." Wells clearly regarded her clothing expenditures as a self-indulgence that she could neither afford nor avoid. "I have bought enough silk to finish my dress with, and buttons, thread, linings etc. Amounting to $15.80 & yet have no parasol, or other things I would like to have," she fretted in another diary entry. "My expenses are transcending my income; I must stop."[3] Yet her unfulfilled longing for a parasol and her reference to sewing her own dress in an age when many middle-class women left such work to dressmakers suggest that no amount of self-discipline could have curbed her aspirations.

Instead, what we see during Wells's early years in Memphis is a determined young woman cobbling together a middle-class life on a teacher's salary that was perennially stretched to support too many people, resulting in repeated emergency recourse to credit and loans. Despite her modest means, Wells had access to Memphis's black elite by virtue of her late father's many friendships and good reputation in Holly Springs. Among the many friends and possibly Masonic brothers of Jim Wells were men who later left Holly Springs to become prominent Memphis businessmen and professionals. They included the black millionaire Robert R. Church and the businessman Alfred Froman, as well as attorney Benjamin F. Booth and teacher Green P. Hamilton. Although Ida initially knew Church only by reputation, she knew at least some of the other men well. She regarded Froman, especially, as a mentor and second father, referring to him as "Dad" and "Pap" in her diary.[4] Solicitous of her interests, he likely played a crucial role in helping Wells get settled in Memphis. Appointed to the Memphis School Board in 1883, Froman may have used his influence to help Wells secure her teaching position the following year. At the very least, she relied on Froman for counsel and much-needed loans, and would later develop a similar relationship with Church.

Still, Wells's success at gaining access, no matter how tenuous, to nineteenth-century America's black elite should not be attributed to family connections. Family ties, no doubt, helped Wells survive her early years in Memphis, but they cannot explain her remarkable social and professional achievements there. When Wells arrived in Memphis she was a small-town nineteen-year-old whose unfinished education qualified her only to teach in rural schools; in less than five years she transformed herself into city schoolteacher and published writer. Within ten, she became the best-known black woman journalist in America, earning the nickname "Iola, Princess of the

Press." And all the while, Wells helped support her siblings and enjoyed an active social life. Attractive, outgoing, and interested in men, Wells embraced the opportunities Memphis offered young women of her era, entertaining suitors and looking for love even as she developed a career that would make marriage less of a necessity for her than it was for many young women of her generation.

Wells's remarkable accomplishments in Memphis attest to her extraordinary energy and sense of purpose. The personal and financial obligations that raising her siblings imposed on her, along with the limitations of her education, should have kept her teaching in rural schools for the rest of her life. And, if the educational aspirations Ida inherited from her parents helped her avoid that fate, neither her parents nor anyone she knew steered her toward her career as a successful writer. In the 1880s, when Wells first rose to fame, there were only forty-five black female journalists in America, many of whom lived and worked outside the South. In joining the nation's first generation of black female journalists, Wells forged a path largely unfamiliar to her ex-slave parents and their contemporaries. But her career certainly honored the occupational ambitions of her parents, which were high for both themselves and their children. And by all evidence she also took her political sensibility from Jim and Lizzie Wells, whose fierce commitment to Radical Reconstruction had been evident to Ida even as a child.

By the 1880s, however, Ida lived in a different world from the one her parents had known. Black men still voted in Memphis, but largely due to a stalemate in municipal politics that left the black vote uncontested. In the wake of Reconstruction, the political possibilities available to blacks were under attack in both Tennessee and the rest of the South. Southern Democrats had reclaimed state governments with a vengeance, and moved quickly to bar blacks from regaining political power. Starting in the 1880s, Democratic state governments began to exclude black voters from the political process altogether through the passage of prohibitive poll taxes, literacy tests, and other legal exclusions such as the grandfather clause, which barred most African Americans from voting by limiting the franchise to men whose grandfathers had voted. But, despite the political climate, Wells was not ready to abandon the Reconstruction-era ideals of racial equality and black political participation. Indeed, more than anything, it was her political commitments that combined with her energy and determination to launch her extraordinary career.

"Like a Lady": Wells's Railroad Lawsuits

As a writer and activist, Wells's primary preoccupations would be political, so it is only fitting that her career first took shape around a one-woman political battle she launched in 1883 at age twenty. That year, she became embroiled in two civil rights suits against the Chesapeake, Ohio, and Southwestern Railroad, which repeatedly refused to seat her in its first-class car. Wells's first published article chronicled her legal battle with the railroad, and her subsequent writings were as political as her editors—who usually expected women journalists to write about domestic subjects—allowed them to be. In the long run her passion for politics and journalism would also end up helping her make ends meet. She began her writing career penning free articles for black newspapers and church publications. In 1889, when she finally bought her first property, it was not a house but a one-third interest in a newspaper, *The Memphis Free Speech and Headlight*. A local black newspaper, *Free Speech* was the property of two African American men, who signed Wells on as both part owner and full-time editor of their fledgling publication. Ida B. Wells's position at *Free Speech* marks the utter singularity of her career. When she bought an interest in and assumed editorship of the paper, she became the first woman owner and editor of a black newspaper in American history.

Wells's road to journalism began with nothing more complicated than a trip to work. In 1883, two years after her move to Memphis, Ida was still teaching in Woodstock and traveling home on the weekends. In some respects, her life must have seemed largely unchanged from what it had been in Mississippi, where she also had a grueling commute. But gone at least was the indignity of the contrary old mule she had ridden to work during her years teaching outside Holly Springs. Years later, Wells still remembered her battles with Ginger—an "antiquated [and] slow-moving" creature who always refused to go "even a mite faster no matter how many 'Giddaps' were yelled."[5] No mule was needed in Memphis, which had a rail line that took her directly to Woodstock. Indeed, Wells traveled in style, riding first class on the Chesapeake, Ohio, and Southwestern Railroad. But traveling by rail ultimately posed more serious problems than Ginger ever had.

Railroad travel did not become commonplace in the South until the 1870s and 1880s, when the railroad companies began to expand and consolidate their lines to offer regular passenger service across much of the region. A far more public mode of travel than horse-drawn carriages, railroad cars posed a serious challenge to "respectable" women of the Victorian era, whose delicate sensibilities were thought to flourish only in the home. Indeed, the moral dangers of train trips were routinely addressed in etiquette manuals. Women traveling unattended ran the risk of being compromised by overly familiar male passengers, and were advised to avoid speaking to male strangers and make sure to "find a seat next to another lady, or near an elderly gentleman."[6] Railroad companies addressed such concerns by providing a special "ladies' car" for first-class passengers, which offered shelter to unaccompanied traveling women such as Ida B. Wells, who seated herself in the ladies' car as she rode back and forth from school.

Wells no doubt chose to travel first class on her journeys for several

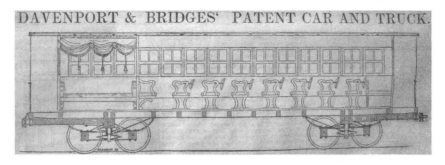

Diagram of a ladies' car

reasons. Not only did her choice of the ladies' car mark the young teacher as a respectable member of Memphis's black middle class, but a first-class ticket offered her a quieter and far more comfortable journey. Usually known as "smokers," the second-class cars provided nothing beyond hard wooden seats and accommodated any number of male tobacco smokers drawn from all classes. Moreover, on nineteenth-century passenger trains, which typically consisted of a locomotive and two passenger cars, the smoker was typically the forward car. In addition to tobacco smoke, its passengers were exposed to the heat, soot, and noise from the engine. By contrast, the ladies' car rode at the end of the train. Typically more plush and comfortable than the smokers, ladies' cars featured upholstered seats and sometimes even sofas, along with ice water dispensers and two water closets. Designed to shield women from having to share a bathroom or other facilities with unfamiliar male travelers, the ladies' cars were reserved for women and their male traveling companions, a distinction which at least theoretically made them open to any black woman able to pay the price of a first-class ticket.

By the 1880s, however, the color line had become the preeminent social divide in the South, and gender distinctions on the railroad were giving way to distinctions of race. Black women were increasingly unwelcome in the ladies' car, as Wells found out one Saturday in 1883. Wells was returning to Memphis after a week in Holly Springs when her journey came to an abrupt end. Having bought a first-class ticket, she boarded the train and seated herself in "the ladies coach as usual." For two years she had ridden the rails between Woodstock and Memphis without incident. But when the conductor came by that day, he told her he could not take her ticket in the ladies' car. Initially, their exchange was polite, Wells would later testify: "He said that he would treat me like a lady . . . but that I must go to the other car." Wells recalled replying, "If he wished to treat me like a lady, he would leave me alone," while remaining in her seat. The conductor finished taking tickets from the other passengers and then returned, moving Wells's bags and umbrella to the forward car in an effort to get her to move there. Wells did not follow, telling him that "the forward car was a smoker, and as I was in the ladies' car, I intended to stay."[7] Losing patience, the conductor then grabbed her arm and tried to drag her out of her seat. Utterly determined to stay, Wells managed to retain her seat by hanging on to her chair and sinking her teeth into the conductor's hand.

At twenty-one years old, Wells had grown up to become a petite woman. She was a little under five feet tall and had a trim figure, but despite her diminutive size she put up an impressive fight. In the aftermath of her first round with the conductor, she "braced her feet against the seat in front and was holding on to the back, and as he had already been badly bitten he didn't try it again himself." Still determined to pry her loose from her chair, the conductor sought assistance from the baggage clerk and another man, and only with their help was he finally able to dislodge Wells and drag her out of the first-class car. As the three men carried her out, they were congratulated by "the white ladies and gentlemen in the car." Indeed, some of the other passengers, Wells recalled in her autobiography, even "stood in the seats so that they could get a good view and continued applauding the conductor for his brave stand."[8]

Wells's altercation dramatized the day-to-day indignities that African American women could expect to meet when they ventured into public spaces, and especially when traveling by rail. It also underscored the dilemmas they faced in responding to such indignities. Writing in 1892, another black Southerner, Anna Julia Cooper, reflected that black women travelers who sought to defend their dignity were caught in a double bind. Extended few courtesies by white train officials, even when allowed to travel, black women often received no assistance in getting on or off the train or moving their luggage. At stations with no raised platform, "Gentlemanly and efficient" railroad conductors would help the white female passengers off the train and then "deliberately fold their arms and turn away when the black woman's turn came to alight—bearing her satchel and bearing besides another unnameable burden inside her heaving bosom and compressed lips." Yet any protest would only make black women look even less ladylike to scornful white audiences, who never saw middle-class white women fight to be treated courteously. "The feeling of slighted womanhood is unlike any other emotion of the soul," Cooper reflected mournfully. "Its first impulse of wrathful protest and self-vindication is checked and shamed by the consciousness that self-assertion would outrage further that same delicate instinct."[9]

Such emotions may have torn at Wells, but they did not curb her determination—throughout her life she would rarely back down in a fight. On that fateful day in 1883, Wells ended up on the next station's platform, "the sleeves of my linen duster torn out," but otherwise unharmed and still fighting. She got off rather than accept a seat in the smoker, returned to Memphis, and promptly filed suit in Tennessee state court. Charging the Chesapeake, Ohio, Southwestern Railroad with both assault and discrimination, she complained that the conductor had "laid violent hands on her," and that the railroad had refused to provide her with the first-class seat for which she had paid.[10] And, as her lawsuit was pending, she continued to lay claim to the ladies' car. Indeed, even before her first suit was settled, Wells found herself compelled to launch another one after being refused entry to the ladies' car yet again in May 1884 during an excursion to Woodstock.

By that time Wells was no longer riding the train regularly, having finally obtained a teaching job in Memphis. But the one time she did return to Woodstock to visit the friends she had made there, the conductor would not even let her set foot in the ladies' car on her return trip. With her first suit still pending, Ida must have been furious. Even before leaving Memphis, she had taken the precaution of sending her lawyer, Thomas J. Cassells, to talk to the railroad about whether she would be seated in the ladies' car if she took the train again. Through Cassells, she had received assurances from the railroad that she "would not be disturbed anymore." But despite her precautions and their assurances, Wells was once again manhandled by the conductor, who "put his hands upon her to push her back" as she attempted to enter the car. Left standing outside the ladies' car, Wells refused to give the conductor her ticket, at which point he stopped the train and ordered her to get off. This time, Wells got off without a fight— "politely assisted" by the conductor.[11] Left stranded outside the station, Wells then had to walk back to Woodstock, where she remained until the following day, when she was able to get a ride to Memphis in a wagon. She arrived home too late to teach her classes and was docked a day's wages.

In filing her suits, Wells joined a long line of African American men and women who fought for their right to equal treatment on public means of transportation in nineteenth-century America. African Americans frequently encountered segregation or outright exclusion on steamboats, railroads, and streetcars, especially after emancipation, when all of a sudden four million African Americans were free to travel by themselves for the first time. In hearing African American challenges to segregation and exclusion, antebellum state courts typically held that common carriers such as railroads and steamboat companies were required to serve blacks, but were under no legal obligation to offer them the same accommodations as whites. As privately owned entities that served the public, they could adopt any "reasonable regulation" they chose with regard to passenger accommodations. Accordingly, an African American couple who sued after being denied a cabin on a steamboat in 1855 lost their case because the steamship company did offer them passage on deck. The court ruled that the law "gave passengers a right to passage, not a right to choose their seat."[12] However, among the arrangements commonly adopted by railroad carriers was one that complicated the practice of segregation: the ladies' car.

For much of the nineteenth century, separate ladies' cars and cabins were the most common of the "reasonable regulations" that transportation companies imposed on passengers. Indeed, the necessity of dividing passengers by sex was so widely accepted that as segregation cases began to multiply during Reconstruction it became the "socially irrefutable analogy for separating passengers by race." In 1877, a lawyer defending segregation aboard the steamboat *Governor Allen* argued:

> A male passenger, basing his right on the law of the United States, might have complained that he was not allowed a stateroom in the ladies' cabin, with as much force and propriety as a colored passenger could have complained that he was furnished compartments and accommodations not inferior to, but different in locality, than other passengers.[13]

Middle-class black women such as Wells, however, posed a challenge to this analogy between race and gender. Both black and female, they defied any attempt to equate race with gender. Unlike most blacks, whose poverty confined them to the second-class smoker cars, middle-class black women could and did seek accommodations set aside for ladies. Not only were ladies' cars smoke-free and more comfortable, they were also far safer, providing black women in particular with shelter from predatory white men, too many of whom considered sexual access to black women, willing or otherwise, an entitlement. Moreover, the letter of the law was actually on the side of African American women: by virtue of their gender they had every right to ride in the ladies' car under common law.

As a result, case law on suits such as the two filed by Wells was complicated and contested. Black women could claim access to the ladies' car by virtue of a "common law tradition privileging separate superior facilities for women." And black women such as Wells took full advantage of this legal tradition, filing the majority of challenges to racial discrimination on common carriers. Indeed, African American women often won such cases, although their suits were much less successful on appeal.[14] In the 1880s, however, black women's legal options would begin to narrow as Southern states blocked off such suits by passing Jim Crow laws that explicitly separated railroad passengers by race. As Ida's luck would have it, Tennessee introduced the first such law in 1881: a "colored car" law requiring the railroads to provide separate accommodations for black railroad passengers. No boon to African Americans, this measure was intended to block black challenges to racial discrimination on the railroads by providing legal sanction for racial discrimination.[15]

Yet, as can be seen in Wells's suits, the new law had little immediate effect on actual practices. The custom of the ladies' car continued, and no separate first-class seats were provided for black women. Accordingly, when the Wells cases went to trial in 1884, the Chesapeake had no easy defense against her charges. Holmes Cummins, the railroad's lawyer, argued in both cases that the railroad's smoking cars were equal in every way to the ladies' cars that Wells had not been permitted to ride in. But his argument made little headway with the judge. He found for the plaintiff in both cases, awarding her damages in the amount of $500 for the first case and $200 for the second.

Wells had the good fortune of having her cases appear before Judge James O. Pierce, an ex–Union soldier from Minnesota, who explicitly affirmed her right to ride in the ladies' car. Pierce dismissed her assault charges against the conductor, accepting the railroad's argument that the conductor had acted on his own. But he recognized her right to ride in the ladies' car, judging it to be a matter of class and gender rather than race. Wells, Pierce found, was "a person of lady-like appearance and deportment, a school teacher, and one who might be expected to object to traveling in the company of rough or boisterous men, smokers and drunkards."[16] But Pierce's favorable assessment of Wells's character and of her right to ride in the ladies' car would not stand on appeal, and Wells would never receive her damages. Her early victory was fragile and transient, for, as can be seen in the wording of Pierce's ruling, access to the ladies' car turned on class as well as gender, and the class status of black women in the South was under constant assault.

While Wells celebrated her initial verdict, Memphis whites were appalled. DARKY DAMSEL GETS DAMAGES, *The Memphis Daily Appeal* huffed when the verdict was announced. "What It Cost to Put a Colored School Teacher in a Smoking Car—Verdict for $500."[17] Amused by this clunky sobriquet, Wells would forever remember being labeled a "darky damsel" and laugh about it with her children.[18] But in all other respects, her confrontation with segregation was no laughing matter. The Chesapeake, Ohio, and Southwestern Railroad appealed both cases, embroiling Wells in litigation that would last until 1887. Moreover, as the cases proceeded, Wells lost confidence in Thomas Cassells. A prominent black lawyer and politician who provided Wells with able representation in her first suits, Cassells displayed little enthusiasm for litigating the appeals which followed her cases or helping Wells obtain the damages she had been awarded. After enduring a series of delays, Wells found out that "he had been bought off by the road" and promptly replaced him with James M. Greer, a white lawyer who had done some work on the original cases.[19] Irate over being fired, Cassells became one of Wells's lifelong enemies.

Still more serious was the opposition Wells faced from the railroad. Wells's lower court victories had set a precedent that the railroad was not prepared to maintain. So in addition to appealing both cases, Holmes Cummins, the railroad's lawyer, "tried every means in his power" to get Wells to "compromise the case." He offered her an out-of-court settlement, which she "indignantly refused."[20] When that failed, the railroad began a "smear campaign" to discredit Wells. Exactly what kind of misinformation the Chesapeake, Ohio, and Southwestern's lawyer spread to undermine Wells's case is not clear. But in April 1886, Wells wrote in her diary that her case was slated to "come up before the Supreme Court some time this month and a true friend of mine has unfolded a conspiracy to me that is on foot to quash the case." Still more obliquely, she added, "It is a painful fact that white men choose men of the race to accomplish the ruin of any young girl but that one would deliberately ask a man of reputation to encompass the ruin of one's reputation for the sake of gain is a startling commentary on the estimation in which our race is held."[21]

A diary entry a month later indicates that Wells received more information on the conspiracy from her old friend and mentor Alfred Froman. "Saw Mr. F[roman] today," Wells wrote in May, "who told me the dirty method Mr. Cummins is using to quash my case." Froman also attempted to intervene, ordering Cummins "to stop it." Froman's intervention was not successful, but he and Wells were not alone in seeing a conspiracy. The black-owned *Cleveland Gazette* also spoke of foul play in the Wells case, reporting that "the most ridiculous and despicable part known in the proceedings is the attempt on the part of the defendant to put up a blackmailing job and attempt to tarnish the character of the fair prosecutrix."[22]

Although the details of Cummins's attacks on Wells's character outside the courtroom have been lost, the trial transcripts from her Tennessee State Supreme Court cases reveal that the railroad lawyer also employed character assassination in his courtroom challenges to her circuit court victories. In contesting Wells's right to ride in the ladies' car, the railroad lawyer questioned whether Wells was a lady, branding her instead as an overly aggressive black woman who was determined to sit where she was not wanted. In doing so, he also maintained that all seats on the railroad's trains were equal.

Both lines of argument involved much sophistry. In one trial, Cummins called the conductor to the stand to testify that he did not allow smoking in the forward car—known as the smoker—and frequently asked people to stop; a move which Wells's lawyer countered by introducing witnesses who had smoked in the forward car. Mocking the conductor's blatant falsehood, her lawyer also asked why, given that smoking was not allowed in either of the train's two passenger cars, so many people had to be discouraged from smoking in the forward car.

Ultimately, however, the case turned not on the question of smoking, but on the issue left open by Judge Pierce's ruling—which had accorded Wells a seat in the ladies' car because of her ladylike appearance and deportment. The railroad lawyer successfully challenged Wells's status as a lady, using her very insistence on sitting in the ladies' car as evidence against her. His major witness was Victoria Kimbrough, a white woman who claimed that Wells had attempted to sit beside her in the ladies' car "sometime in November or December 1883." Kimbrough did not even claim to have been present during either of the train rides that precipitated Wells's suits: her testimony simply served to portray Wells as a black woman who felt entitled to seat herself next to a white woman. Although legally dubious and not accepted by the circuit court, Kimbrough's evidence was accepted by the Tennessee State Supreme Court, which ruled against Wells in both cases. In an 1887 decision that was a blatant triumph of prejudice over logic, the judges declared that the ladies' car and smoking car were "alike in every respect as to comfort, convenience and safety" and also accused Wells of filing suit only to "harass" the railroad company. Her "persistence" in the case, the court concluded, "was not in good faith to obtain a comfortable seat for a short ride."[23] Also reversed were her awards for damages. Instead of receiving money, Wells ended up liable for more than two hundred dollars in court costs.

These expenses alone were no doubt devastating to the financially overextended young schoolteacher, whose monthly salary was seventy-five dollars. But a still more bitter pill to swallow was, in Wells's eyes, the terrible insult done to African American rights. "I felt so disappointed," Wells writes in an anguished passage in her Memphis diary, "because I had hoped such great things from the suit for my people generally."

> I have firmly believed all along that the law and the world was on our side and would, when we appealed to it, give us justice. I feel short of that belief and utterly discouraged, and just now if it were possible would gather my race in my arms and fly far away with them. O God is there no redress, no peace, no justice in this land for us.[24]

Ida's anguish was entirely warranted. In her 1887 diary entry she recorded the writing on the wall. We now know that the Tennessee State Supreme Court's decision in her case was one of the many state-level stops on the road to *Plessy v. Ferguson* (1896). In *Plessy v. Ferguson*, another railroad case, the United States Supreme Court resolved the legal uncertainties around segregation on state railroads by affirming the constitutionality of Louisiana's separate car act. The sweeping decision all but eviscerated the first section of the Fourteenth Amendment—which promises all Americans "equal protection before the law." Qualifying that Reconstruction-era promise, the Court ruled: "The object of the [Fourteenth] Amendment was undoubtedly to enforce the absolute equality of the two races before the law, but in the nature of things it could not have been intended to abolish distinctions based upon color, or to enforce social, as distinguished from political equality, or a commingling of the two races upon terms unsatisfactory to either."[25]

Least among *Plessy's* effects was the demise of the ladies' cars, which had given way to cars separated by race well before 1896. As historian Barbara Welke notes, the passing of the ladies' car reflected the white South's attempt to curb the self-assertion of black women such as Wells, who sought access to ladies' accommodations as "the gender equivalent of the political and economic power that men of color had gained with freedom."[26] *Plessy* brought still more radical infringements on black freedom. Indeed, until it was overturned in *Brown v. Board of Education* (1954), *Plessy* ruled over an era of cast-iron segregation under which blacks were required to use not only separate train seats, but separate schools, hospitals, orphanages, insane asylums, poorhouses, and public bathrooms. Segregation was still informal when Ida lived in Memphis, but by the early twentieth century signs marking everything from building entrances to water fountains as WHITES ONLY or COLORED would be ubiquitous throughout the South.

For all her forebodings about the future, however, Ida understood the grave import of her failed legal defense through the lens of the past. Even when she looked back on the case in her autobiography, she did not link *Plessy v. Ferguson* and the final triumph of Jim Crow with her own struggles. Instead, she mourned it as a tragic consequence of the repeal of the Civil Rights Bill of 1875, which had been declared unconstitutional in 1883. Crafted by a coalition of Radical Republicans under the leadership of the fiery abolitionist hero Charles Sumner, the bill had provided federal protection for citizens' rights under the Constitution—protection that had allowed cases similar to Ida's to be moved to federal court. In the results of its repeal, Ida saw nothing short of the final bitter death of Reconstruction. "The Supreme Court of the land has told us to go to the state courts for the redress of our grievances," she reported, "but when I did I was given the brand of justice Charles Sumner knew the Negro would get when he fathered the Civil Rights Bill during Reconstruction." The New South that emerged after Reconstruction, she noted caustically, "wanted the Civil Rights Bill repealed but did not want or intend to give justice to the Negro after robbing him of all sources from which to secure it."[27]

In her autobiography, Wells was almost equally bitter about the black community's response to her suits. She recalled that she was left with only her "salary to fall back on to help pay the costs" of the court cases. She complained that "none of my people had ever seemed to feel it was a race matter and that they should help me in the fight. So I trod the wine press alone."[28] While her long legal struggle must have placed a great and somewhat solitary strain on Wells, her memory of it may have been colored with bitterness over later experiences—in the many subsequent political battles that left her feeling that she did not have the support of her community.

At the very least, her Memphis diary, written at the time the trials were unfolding, suggests that she did not in fact battle the railroads alone. Her first response to her defeat was protective rather than dismissive of other blacks—as we have seen, she wanted to "gather my race in my arms."[29] Moreover, she both heard about and contested the smear tactics used by the railroad only through other members of her community. A "true friend" alerted her to the conspiracy, and both Alfred Froman and the editor of *The Cleveland Gazette* spoke out in her defense.

Admittedly, Ida had some cause to resent the lack of activism among other middle-class black contemporaries, who sometimes used money to bypass the indignities of discrimination rather than defending their race. Through the 1890s, black travelers were still permitted to purchase tickets for the deluxe Pullman accommodations offered on many trains—which were sold without restrictions as to race by Chicago's Pullman Palace Car Company, which owned and operated the cars. Such services allowed many affluent blacks, as Wells complained in an early article, to dodge discrimination rather than contest it. "Railroad officials don't bother me, in traveling," they would maintain, content to buy their way out of Jim Crow travel.[30]

But whatever her quibbles with the black elite, Wells's struggles were not as isolated as she remembers. The years of country teaching that frame Wells's account of her legal struggles in her autobiography ended less than six months after she began her first suit, when she secured a teaching job in Memphis. As the case stretched from the fall of 1883 through the spring of 1887, Wells was no longer a lonely country teacher, reading by the firelight, but instead led a very active social life in Memphis.

Indeed, during the period covered by Wells's Memphis diary, 1885 through 1887, she mentioned her lawsuits far less frequently than her clothing purchases, romantic life, and professional activities. Displaying an emotional equanimity in the face of hardship that seems to have been one of her particular gifts, Ida simply went on with her life as her case was appealed. When the case headed to the Tennessee State Supreme Court, she had to stretch her small budget to pay Judge Greer's traveling expenses, and pledge that she would pay court costs. But despite the financial burden the case imposed on her, and the smear tactics the railroad used against her, Ida expressed little anxiety about the case in her diary. When the trial date was set, she reported it, also referring briefly to the railroad's campaign against her. But she concluded on a calm note: "I shall watch and wait and fear not." And true to her promise, Ida did not mention the case again until after it was decided.[31]

"Every Young Woman's Ambition": Work and Womanhood

Rather than portraying her as a lonely political martyr, her Memphis diary reveals a lively, flirtatious young woman struggling to find her place and purpose in the world. In her midtwenties as she wrote, Wells was at the age when young women of her day were expected to be married, or energetically pursuing the goal of marriage. Black women were far more likely to work for wages than white women, and it was not uncommon for even married middle-class black women to work. But, employed or otherwise, like all nineteenth-century women, African American women were expected to build their lives around marriage. "Every young woman's ambition is to have a home of her own someday," wrote the editor of *The Indianapolis Freeman*, a black newspaper, in 1893. Marriage was a woman's God-given purpose in life. A woman must be able to achieve a home that is "just right," the editor advised. Otherwise, it would make "no difference how much wealth, how much beauty you may possess, your brilliant talents, if you are void of purity of purpose, [and] nobleness of soul, you are not what God intended."[32] Clearly aware of such ideas, Ida chafed under the expectation of marriage. She enjoyed male company, but was not anxious to marry. Aware that she was unusual in that regard, Ida wrote in her diary, "I am an anomaly to my self as well as to others. I do not wish to be married but I do wish for the society of gentlemen."[33] Still responsible for her siblings, Ida may have feared that marriage would mean a lifetime of uninterrupted mother-hood and domestic drudgery. Certainly she did not romanticize marriage. "Went . . . to call on Mrs. Neal," she wrote in her diary of a young married acquaintance, "who is very bright complexioned, with fair skin & dark hair, and rather pretty—was more so before she married. The inevitable baby is there with the habits peculiar to all babyhood."[34]

The oldest of eight children, Ida knew babies, but men were another matter. Memphis introduced Ida to a whole new world of male companion-ship, which she was anxious to explore to its fullest. During the years her family responsibilities had kept her teaching in the country, she had little opportunity to meet eligible men. But that changed when she moved to the city. There, Wells had a continual stream of suitors. Described in an 1885 newspaper account as "about four and a half feet high, tolerably well-proportioned . . . of ready address," and elsewhere as "young and comely," Wells was admired for her striking dark eyes and ready wit.[35] "Just now there are three [men] in the city," she wrote in her diary at one point, "who with the least encouragement, would make love to me; I have two corre-spondents in the same predicament." Expressing no ambivalence about jug-gling her plethora of suitors, Ida continued: "I am enjoying my existence very much just now; I won't wonder longer, but willingly enjoy life as it comes."[36]

Dating for the first time after years of isolation and hard work, Ida rev-eled in the experience. Beyond male companionship, Ida's abundance of suitors and men friends opened up a world of new social and cultural op-portunities. She was taken to the theater, lectures, and parties—all new ex-periences for the young country girl. As a single woman with no parents, Wells was more dependent than most young women on male escorts to ac-company her to such events, since women of her era did not socialize by themselves. Her reliance on her beaux as companions can be seen in a February 1887 diary entry where she bemoaned a falling-out with an unnamed male friend. "Expected to attend a party given last week," she wrote, "but my escort did not come."[37]

Ida's escorts, however, often resented her ability to see them as little more than friends and escorts. "I must try & curb myself more, and not be so indifferent to the young men," she chided herself in her diary, "they feel & resent it." She lamented in another entry, "It seems that I can establish no middle ground between me and my visitors—it is either love or nothing." Ida wrote the latter comment while reflecting on two of her most persistent suitors, I. J. Graham and Louis Brown, whom she never managed to choose between. "I feel that I have degraded myself in that I had not the courage to repulse one or the other," she noted in her diary. "I know not which of the two I prefer. I don't think I want either for a husband but I would miss them sadly as friends—and that of course would be the intermission of friendship if I said nay."[38]

A fellow teacher in Memphis, Graham courted Wells for over a year without ever being sure of her. Theirs was a tempestuous relationship in which her feelings for Graham seem to have never been entirely clear, even to Ida. As the relationship progressed, she grew impatient with Graham for not proposing marriage. Meanwhile, Graham was evidently reluctant to take this step without some kind of invitation from Ida, because he knew both from town gossip and from Ida herself that she was seeing other men. However, his diffidence only made her more impatient. On February 14, 1886, she wrote in her diary: "Mr. G[raham] and I had a bout last week . . . He renewed his question from a former occasion as if I would tell him I cared for him without a like assertion on his part. He seems to think I ought to encourage him by speaking first—but that I'll never do. It's conceding *too* much and I don't think I need to buy any man's love."[39]

Yet it is unclear that Ida ever truly wanted to marry Graham. Her desire for a proposal from him seems to have been spurred by an indiscretion on her part. Reflecting that their physical relationship had gone past the very narrow bounds of Victorian middle-class propriety, Ida wrote that she was willing to bid good-bye to Graham as a suitor, but "blush[ed] to think

I allowed him to caress me, that he would take such liberties and yet not make a declaration."[40]

Moreover, when the hapless Graham finally declared his love to her, Ida's response was lukewarm. She wrote in her diary, "I told him I was not conscious of an absorbing feeling for him but I thought it would grow. I feel so lonely and isolated and the temptation of a lover is irresistible." Even after that admission, however, her feelings for him did not blossom. She remained reluctant to commit herself to him, and questioned his feelings for her, complaining, "I wish to be loved with more warmth than that." In the end, the problem seems to have been more hers than his. In a diary entry written August 2, 1886, Ida recorded: "received a letter from Mr. G[raham] who . . . wishes to know if I love him & will live with him. I fear I don't but then I also fear I shall never love anybody."[41]

Ida might well have feared that she did not love Graham, since his attentions never inspired her to drop any of her other suitors. Indeed, even after telling Graham that she thought her feelings for him would grow, she did not regard herself as "pledged to anyone." Most prominent among her other suitors was Louis Brown, a journalist whom she met as she began writing for *The Living Way*, a local black Baptist newspaper. Still more tempestuous and stormy than her relationship with Graham, Ida's relationship with Brown seems to have been marked by a strong sexual attraction, combined with doubts about Brown's strength of character and professional prospects. Brown's kisses "blistered" Ida's lips but also made her "humiliated in my own estimation," since her feelings for him were entirely uncertain and she "believed him to be incapable of love in its strongest best sense." A man who "bounce[d]" from city to city and job to job, Brown struck Ida as a young man "still hunting for his place." Even at her most optimistic, she saw him as a man who would have to change himself to earn her love. Her most favorable assessment of him in her diary came after receiving a "manly" letter from him, after which she wrote: "He is developing symptoms more to my ideas of what becomes an earnest man and I told him so, as well as that if he succeeded in this new venture & in winning my love in the meantime, I would help him prove to the world what love in its purity can accomplish." However, Ida's fantasy of redeeming Brown through her love was undercut by an additional note in the same entry. "Dreamed of Mr. P[oole] last night," she wrote, referring to yet another suitor.[42]

The strength of Ida's feelings for her various suitors is also called into question by her trip to California in the summer of 1886. She was in fact many miles away from Brown, Graham, and other beaux, even as she wrote them the letters in which she questioned their affections. That July she left them all behind, leaving for Visalia, California. Uncertain when or whether she would return to Memphis, Wells traveled to the West Coast for an extended visit with her aunt Fannie, Fannie's children, and her two younger sisters, Lily and Annie. Fannie had moved to Visalia several months earlier, taking Ida's sisters with her. But they all missed Ida and had been urging her to move to California to join them ever since they left. Anxious to see her niece rejoin the family permanently, Fannie assured Ida that she could find work in California, instructing her to arrive by mid-June so she could take the state exam for new teachers on June 15. Ambivalent about any permanent move, Wells ignored these instructions. Instead, she took her time traveling west, stopping first in Kansas City, attending a National Teachers Association meeting in Topeka, Kansas, visiting Manitou Springs and Denver, Colorado, and stopping in San Francisco, before finally proceeding to Visalia. En route, Wells expanded her journalistic repertoire, writing letters back to *The Living Way* describing the cities she passed through. Far from pining for Graham or Brown, Wells seems to have enjoyed her trip immensely and attracted new suitors as she traveled, including one who "was ready to propose on the spot almost," and another whom she liked "better than any one I've known so short a time."[43]

Wells proved no more ready to settle down in California than she had been in Memphis. Indeed, despite Aunt Fannie's hopes, Ida traveled to California still uncertain as to whether she planned to visit or to stay. On arriving, she was very glad to see her sisters, who she noted were "near my height and look very much like women." In her diary, Wells usually speaks of her siblings primarily in terms of her obligation to them, but their reunion in California moved her to express a sense of kinship with them evidently brought on by the growing maturity that she saw in her "little sisters." Amazed by the changes in them after months apart, she described them as "shooting into my own world, and ripening for experiences similar to my own."[44]

But as much as she enjoyed her sisters' company, Wells was dismayed to find Fannie pressuring her to "stay the year" in Visalia—regardless of whether or not she secured a teaching job. Wells did not like Visalia, which she found "hot & dusty" and "dull and lonely." "Not a dozen colored families lived there," and Ida sorely missed the active social life she had enjoyed in Memphis, perhaps all the more keenly because several of her suitors there continued to write. Left to her own devices, she confided in her diary, she would have left immediately, taking her sisters with her if at all possible. But finding Fannie "careworn . . . with hard work and solicitude for the children," Wells sold her return ticket, resolving to "help her share the responsibility" for at least a year.[45]

Wells regretted her decision almost immediately. Her aunt had been drawn there by "good work and good wages," and a climate more suited to her health than that of Memphis, but Ida felt isolated and depressed. Even her journalism suffered, as she found it "a trial to get the opinions of others." Securing work was not difficult, even without California teachers' credentials, but Wells found a job that only made matters worse. The beginning of September found Ida registering Visalia's eighteen colored students in a dilapidated one-room school devoted exclusively to their use. Given her Southern background, Wells could not have been surprised to find herself teaching in a segregated school. But she was disgusted to learn that this separate school was not mandated under California law. Rather, it had been requested by "the colored people themselves," who chose to be educated in isolation while Visalia's white, Indian, "half-breed," and Mexican children all attended school together in a "commodious building on a hill." Doubly unhappy to be "helping to perpetuate this odious state of things," Wells became ever more determined to leave Visalia as soon as possible.[46]

Fortunately, she already had an exit strategy in the works. Even before school started, Wells had confided her doubts about Visalia to a number of people, including her mentor Froman, to whom she wrote for advice. And once school started, she also informed her aunt of her change of heart. Wells simply could not reconcile herself to life in the sleepy little town, she told her aunt. Even Fannie herself granted that Visalia was dull. "It is worse for me," Wells told her: as "a young woman, to have nothing to look forward to, as I was just beginning to live and had all my life before me."[47] Sorely disappointed, Fannie Wells told Ida that if she left she must take her sisters with her—an ultimatum meant to keep Ida in Visalia, since, as Fannie well knew, Ida lacked the funds to cover three tickets east.

But Fannie underestimated Ida's resourcefulness. Encouraged by Froman, who reminded Ida of her railroad lawsuits and advised her that she should not seriously consider staying in California until they were resolved, Ida sought out teaching positions in both Memphis and Kansas City, and then went to work figuring out how to get herself and her sisters out of California. If the Kansas City job came through, she was confident that she could borrow the train fare she needed from friends there. But the long trip to Memphis was an expensive proposition that would cost Ida far more than she could hope to borrow from any of her friends. Undeterred, she wrote Robert Church, the wealthy Memphis businessman. Church had hailed from Holly Springs, and was likely a onetime acquaintance of Ida's late father. But Ida knew him only by reputation, which did not keep her from asking for a loan of $150 to finance her return home. Wells told him that she sought his help "because he was the only man of my race that I knew who could lend me that much money and wait for me to repay it."[48] By way of security, she referred him to the Board of Education; if it reappointed her that fall, Wells would be able to repay the money.

Ida's audacious plans worked, but not easily. Her hopes for working anywhere but California rested on the fact that the school term started later in Kansas City and Memphis than it did in Visalia, allowing her to take a job in California without giving up on her other prospects. Indeed, Wells had already spent several "dreary days" teaching in Visalia before she heard back from either city, receiving a job offer from Kansas City. Now even more anxious to go, she faced serious opposition to her departure. Her aunt

Fannie did her best to persuade her not to go and then "cried all night & half the morning at the thought of her leaving," while Annie refused to leave California with her sisters. Shaken to the point of second thoughts but very unhappy at the prospect of staying, Ida wrote with reference to Fannie in her diary: "I know I owe her a debt of gratitude but she makes it all so burdensome for me as to be very distasteful. Forced acts of gratitude are not very sincere I should say."[49] In the end, Ida decided against the dictates of gratitude. On receiving a letter from Robert Church not only informing her that she had been reappointed by the Memphis School Board but containing a bank draft in the amount of the loan she requested, Ida left the next day. She took only Lily with her, as Annie remained steadfast in her desire to remain in California.

Though now in the company of one sister, Wells left California as she had come, not quite certain where she was going. She was willing to work in either Kansas City or Memphis, depending on where she could arrive in time to secure a position. Missing the first day of school in Kansas City, she arrived to find a young woman teaching in her place, which made Wells's appearance the subject of some controversy among the teachers there. So she moved on to Memphis, where school had not yet started. By then Wells had taught, as she proudly recalled in her autobiography, "in one month in the states of California, Missouri and Tennessee."[50]

Among other things, Ida's sojourn across these three states illustrates her continuing doubts about her future. California seems to have appealed to her primarily as a refuge from some of her suitors. Writing from Visalia, she told one longtime correspondent that she felt torn "between marrying and staying here to raise the children."[51] Yet, in the end, Wells seems to have realized that she could remain in Memphis and unmarried. For although she returned, she did not end up marrying any of her Memphis suitors. Less than a month after Ida returned from California, Graham surprised everyone who had witnessed his courtship of her by abruptly marrying someone else. And Louis Brown never lived up to her expectations.

Still, Ida's diary records few regrets about losing either Graham's or Brown's attentions. Instead, both before and after her California trip, Ida struggled with not just the idea of marriage, but the challenges of remaining single. Aware that she had failed to observe Victorian mores with regard to marriage, Wells was also troubled by the physical allure her suitors held for her. She faced one of the quintessential dilemmas of Victorian womanhood. Women were not supposed to have strong sexual feelings, especially for men that they did not intend to marry. So what Ida did end up regretting were passionate kisses she exchanged with suitors such as Graham and Brown, which she feared reflected poorly on her moral character. Yet, by all evidence, her transgressions did not extend beyond a few kisses, for Ida went into her marriage nearly a decade later still unfamiliar with the mechanics of birth control.

Like many other middle-class female contemporaries, black and white, Ida evidently adhered to a Victorian sexual ideology that prohibited sex before marriage.[52] However, Ida gained little credit for her self-restraint. As an attractive, unmarried woman in her midtwenties with an active social life, she often generated suspicion and talk. The story of her rumored involvement with Dr. Gray followed her to Memphis, where it was alleged she had been involved with a "white man" in Holly Springs for money. And after that, her social life in Memphis created rumors of its own. Her dating habits clearly attracted some male censure, which seems to have been one source of the talk that swirled around her. Her ever ambivalent suitor Mr. Graham, for example, heard whispers that Ida believed that "any young man I went out with ought to feel honored because of the privilege & that whenever any one was with me all the young men in the town knew it and said of him he was highly honored"—a story clearly designed to convince him that Ida got around. Mad at Graham for even repeating this bit of gossip, Ida understood the male hostility that lay behind it and reflected, "He did not add (altho' I knew it must be so) that they hastened to tell such an one of the rumor & thus maliciously have been setting all the young men against me & by their cock & bull stories, have kept them away, for a silly speech of mine—if, indeed—I really said it (of which I have not the slightest remembrance)."[53]

Ida faced a new set of ugly rumors about herself on her return from

California in 1886. Her decision to decline a job in Kansas City in favor of returning to Memphis came back to haunt her. In refusing that teaching job, Wells had unwittingly angered several of the teachers who had helped her secure it. After she left, they retaliated with a rumormongering campaign in which they wrote letters to Memphis school officials alleging that Wells was having an affair with Graham, and that her youngest sister, Lily, was in fact her daughter. Faced with such mean-spirited misrepresentations of her own behavior, Ida was once again hard-pressed to defend herself.

Suing the railroads for discrimination was one thing, finding a way to protect her personal reputation was another. As a sixteen-year-old in Holly Springs, Ida had been able to correct the stories about her and Dr. Gray only by calling in her grandmother as a chaperone. And early in her Memphis years, Ida had been literally struck dumb by the stories she heard about herself. Told by a male acquaintance that he had heard "bad things" about her, Wells reported, "I was so angry I foamed at the mouth, bit my lips & and then realized my impotence—ended in a fit of crying."[54] On hearing the rumors coming out of Kansas City, Wells felt similarly silenced and powerless. Enraged by the gossip about Graham and herself, she viewed the rumors as "premeditated and deliberate insults" and wrote, "My blood boils at the tame submission to them." But Wells took no action, simply telling Graham, who mentioned the allegations, that she had "been misrepresented." And although she yearned for revenge, she settled for "praying for enlightenment." Dismissing the idea of retaliation, she wrote, "I have never stooped to underhanded measures to accomplish an end and I will not begin at this late day by doing that which my soul abhors; sugaring men, weak deceitful creatures, with flattery to retain them as escorts or gratify a revenge, and I earnestly pray my Father to show me right."[55]

Besieged by rumors about her personal life, Ida also wondered "what's the matter with me." In 1887, after three years in Memphis, she was the "only lady teacher left" in her school still unmarried. Worse, being single did not always make her happy. When her last unmarried colleague wed she felt "singularly lonely & despondent."[56] But Wells always stopped short of embracing marriage as a remedy for her loneliness, though she was often tempted to do so. In the fit of despondency mentioned above, for example, she wrote her former suitor Mr. P[oole], telling him that "if he desired my happiness to come home & help make me happy." But Ida had already dropped the idea two weeks later when the surprised Poole wrote back asking "if his coming will really contribute to my happiness." By then, Ida did not even consider a serious reply. "Shall write and ask to forget & send me back those letters," she noted in her diary.[57]

An "emotional loner," Ida was often unhappy while in Memphis.[58] As the oldest member of her immediate family, she received limited emotional support from her siblings, whom she rarely mentions in her diary other than to chronicle her brothers' money problems and the domestic conflicts she had with her sisters. Moreover, she had little sustained contact with other relatives, especially after her aunt Fannie moved to California. She had a cousin in Memphis, Stella Butler, for whom she served as maid of honor in 1886, but the two were not close—Stella is rarely mentioned in Wells's diary. And she seems to have lost all contact with her grandmother Peggy and her Holly Springs relatives after Peggy's stroke. When her aunt Margaret wrote in 1887 to tell her that Peggy had died that March, Wells was surprised to "know that she had been alive all that time & I never knew it or where she lived."[59]

Emotionally isolated and overburdened, Wells suffered from a sadness that may have had more to do with depression than her remaining single. As biographer Linda O. McMurray points out, Wells clearly endured intense bouts of depression during her Memphis years. There were times when her chronic money troubles, grueling work schedule, and unending familial obligations, coupled quite possibly with the stresses of the lawsuits, got to be too much for her. She referred, for example, to the winter of 1886 as "the winter of my discontent," and her diary entries bear her out. Frequently physically ill, she complained of neuralgia and thought that her "system was not in good order." Still more problematic was her mood, which she reported as "sluggish" and "blue." There were days when the busy young teacher accomplished nothing. On March 30 she wrote, "No lessons of any-kind were covered Saturday or sewing done, the biggest job undertaken and finished was—a bath."[60] In her low moods, her social life and her suitors were a diversion, but could not always lift her spirits. A visit from Graham on a bad day, for example, did little to change matters. "Have been very blue all day," she wrote, "& G[raham] was in trying to comfort me but he makes a mess of it as always."[61] But having no company could be worse. "I had no visitors today," wrote Ida at a low point in her diary. "I am in as correspondingly low spirits tonight as I was cheerful this morning. I don't know what is the matter with me. I feel so dissatisfied with my life, so isolated from all my kind. I cannot or do not make friends & these fits of loneliness will come & I tire of everything. My life seems awry, the machinery out of gear & I feel as if there's something wrong."[62]

Wells's low mood that winter may also have been influenced by her "wavering steps" along a still uncertain career path. Established in the Memphis school system, where she "had made a reputation . . . for thoroughness and discipline in the primary grades," Wells was increasingly conscious that in her teaching assignments, she would never be "promoted above fourth grade." By 1886 she had begun to find the "monotony and confinement of primary work . . . distasteful," but saw little way out of it. She had no normal-school training—as the college-level preparation courses for schoolteachers were then called—which meant that she had little hope of being assigned to teach any of the higher grades. Although she contemplated further education, she lacked the time and money to attend summer courses at Fisk University in Nashville, where many black teachers received their training. Moreover, a lack of money was not the only issue holding her back. Responding to a friend who asked her whether she thought she would be able "to stand examination in algebra, natural philosophy, etc"—as she would need to do to advance as a teacher—Wells could only "confess my inability." At issue seems to have been a lack of dedication as much as anything else. Contemplating the limits of her teaching career in her diary, Wells regretted "those golden moments wasted, the precious hours I should have treasured and used to store up knowledge for future use." But, try as she might, she could not make training for teaching her first priority. "It seems so hard to get at it [study]," she fretted in her diary. "I've made so many resolutions I am ashamed to make more."[63]

Wells's Memphis diary reveals that her energies were in fact directed elsewhere, toward a writing career that would ultimately provide her an "outlet through which to express the real 'me.' "[64] But in 1886, the success of her career as a journalist was by no means assured. So Wells's doldrums may also have reflected doubts about her future as a writer. Increasingly widely published, Wells saw her articles for *The Living Way* reprinted in T. Thomas Fortune's New York–based paper *The Freeman*, and was also invited to write for Kansas City's *Gate City Press*. But she was rarely paid for her work, so she had scant hope of writing full time. Run by Baptist ministers, *The Living Way* had little or no resources with which to pay Wells, and they allowed other papers to reprint her work as part of a free exchange of copy common among nineteenth-century publications. Other papers behaved similarly, offering her no remuneration even when they solicited original articles. In lieu of pay, T. Thomas Fortune sent her ten copies of *The Freeman* for an original article titled "Woman's Mission," while the *Gate City Press* initially had her writing regularly for free. Frustrated in her hopes of becoming a "full-fledged professional journalist," in 1885 Wells published a piece in *The Living Way* criticizing the editors of black newspapers for not compensating their authors.[65] It brought her a stinging rebuke from Calvin Chase, the editor of *The Bee* (Washington, D.C.), who contended that magazines, not newspapers, were the appropriate venue for authors who sought pay for their writing. He also questioned whether Wells's journalism was worth paying for, with the nasty suggestion that "if 'Iola' should write anything worthy of public interest *The A.M.E. Review* will no doubt publish it, and allow her something by way of compensation."[66]

Chase's comments did not crush Wells, who noted in her diary, "I would not write for him for great pay & I will write something someday that makes him wince." But their exchange does underscore the difficulties that Wells faced making a living as a writer. Increasingly bored by teaching, she not only pursued journalism but also dreamed of writing a novel with one of her suitors, Charles S. Morris, a journalist from Louisville and for a time one of her favorite correspondents. But even as Wells sketched out a plot for a novel in her diary entries, fiction must have seemed even more unlikely than journalism to offer her a career path. Black novelists were even rarer than black journalists, as Wells knew all too well, having "never read a Negro book or anything about Negroes," prior to arriving in Memphis. Indeed, only Morris's steady encouragement allowed her even to contemplate "the stupendous idea of writing a work of fiction," which she could hardly do without a "smile in derision" at herself for thinking of such a thing.[67]

Perhaps for this reason, Wells never began her novel. Even early in her career, journalism was clearly her métier, despite her love of fiction. "A Story of 1900," which appeared in the *Fisk Herald* in 1886, was among the few fictional pieces Wells would ever publish if the story's obviously autobiographical reflections on how black teachers in the rural South could best serve their students can be called fiction.[68] Likewise, Ida's Memphis diary suggests that the novel she contemplated writing would have been all but true to life. Among her entries are plotlines of court cases involving black women, which she jotted down to "remember . . . when I write my 'novel.' " One was the case of a young black woman who got into a fight with a white woman after being abused by both the white woman and her brother, and ended up remanded to the workhouse for defending herself.[69] Far from fictional, the cases Ida recorded dramatized her concerns about the difficult and dangerous course that black women navigated in Southern society—as well as the legal injustices they faced.

In journalism, Wells found the perfect place to express such messages and share the dogged commitment to black progress inculcated in her by her parents, as well as her growing unease about social relations of all kinds in the late nineteenth-century South. Writing as "Iola," she was a persistent critic of the black leadership class, whom she faulted for not "exerting their talents and wealth for the benefit or amelioration of the condition of the masses."[70] Not even the Masons were sacrosanct, despite their effort to help Wells and her family following the deaths of her parents. She worried that the Masons and other black secret societies achieved little beyond fellowship, at a time when African Americans needed leadership and support. In 1885, when several Memphis ministers denounced the power and mysterious practices of these fraternal orders—which often drained resources away from black churches—Iola agreed with them. The Masons and other fraternal orders had a "history of an enormous amount paid into their treasuries with nothing to show for it in the way of real estate, parks, or even [the care of] a multitude of widows and orphans."[71]

Wells's discussions of black leadership and organizations established her credentials with the largely male fraternity of black journalists, who praised her for plunging "into politics and other matters of national importance with the vivacity of a full-fledged journalist of the masculine gender."[72] But she also spoke, as one contemporary noted, to "women . . . around the fireside," in articles clearly written for the "Woman's Corner" departments then featured in many black newspapers.[73] In pieces such as "Woman's Mission" and "The Model Girl: A True Picture of the Typical Southern Girl," Wells offered flowery assessments of the womanly ideals to which black women should aspire. In keeping with the nineteenth-century cult of true womanhood, Wells celebrated the importance of "women's influence" in the "making of great men," and urged black women to eschew "fashion, idleness, and usefulness" in favor of a standard of "earnest, thoughtful, pure noble womanhood." The "model girl" must have a "character in spotless purity," and esteems "it among her best accomplishments that she can cook, wash, iron, sew, and 'keep house' thoroughly and well."[74]

At first glance, such columns speak more to the conventions that prevailed in Woman's Corner columns of the nineteenth-century press than they do to Wells's experience. A woman who took more pride in her intellect than her domestic accomplishments, Ida did not care for cooking and found most housework tedious. But she was partially sincere in her admiration for "ladylike refinement" in other women, and often rued her own "tempestuous, rebellious hard-headed willfulness." Like many black women of her era, Wells was attracted to the feminine ideals enshrined in the cult of true womanhood, even though such ideals located women in a sheltered domestic feminine sphere largely alien to her experience. Her Memphis diary contains lavish praise for a white teacher, whom she met on a return visit to Rust in 1885 and who struck Wells as the embodiment of all feminine ideals. "Was introduced to Miss Atkinson, the music teacher, who seemed fair and pure, so divinely good, whose notions were grace and poetry personified—she seemed to me, one of the few women I have met who came near justifying the ravings of the poets and proving their metaphors not inspired alone by imagination."[75]

At the same time, however, Wells's appreciation for middle-class ideals of white womanhood was complicated by her awareness that many white Southerners considered black women incapable of attaining them. "Unmindful of the fact that our enslavement with all the evils attendant thereon was involuntary," she noted in one of her columns on women's issues, "there are writers who have nothing to give the world in their disquisitions on Negroes, save a rehearsal of their worthlessness, immortality, etc." Black women were especially subject to "wholesale contemptuous defamation," she contended. "Among the many things which had transpired to dishearten the Negroes in their effort to attain the level in status of civilized races . . . none sting so deeply and keenly as the taunt of immorality; the jest and sneer with which our women are spoken of, and the utter incapacity or refusal to believe there are among us mothers, wives and maidens who have attained a true, noble and refining womanhood."[76] Such assumptions must have been all the more galling to Wells since she knew full well that female morality was not the exclusive preserve of the well-bred. According to her autobiography, her own determination to keep herself "spotless and morally clean" derived from the teaching of her "slave mother."[77] But in her early newspaper writings, Wells seemed less than certain about the morality of slave women, and instead highlighted the progress made by blacks since emancipation.

Seen in hindsight, Wells's early columns on women show her beginning to make sense of the gendered character of white supremacy. As we have seen, with the end of Reconstruction, white Southerners campaigned for segregation and disenfranchisement by questioning not only the racial character of black people but also their gender characteristics—often construing black sexuality as a racial threat to the white race. Black women were deemed too base and immoral to deserve a place in the ladies' car, while black men were stereotyped as sexual predators who lacked the disciplined and autonomous manhood required for voting. Wells's years in Memphis saw an ever increasing sexualization of racism across the South that ultimately strained all social relations between the races. Whites became increasingly hostile to even largely apolitical middle-class blacks, whose hopes for advancing the race had rested on the achievement of a bourgeois respectability that whites were no longer willing to accord to any black people. In time, Wells would develop a hard-hitting analysis of the middle-class sexual mores with which Southern whites masked their attacks on the political and social rights of all black men and women. But, both in her early writings and in her personal life in Memphis, she struggled to reconcile class-bound white ideals such as "true womanhood" with the African American experience.

In addition to providing a forum for her concerns, Wells's columns on women's issues helped her to advance in the newspaper business, where she was increasingly in demand both as one of the country's few black women journalists and as a political reporter whose gender made her work a "novelty." Although she continued to make her living as a teacher, in 1886 Wells was elected editor of *The Evening Star* (Memphis), and also became a regular correspondent for *The American Baptist Magazine*, a national publication which offered her "the lavish sum of one dollar weekly."[78] Thereafter, the network of publications that solicited and featured Wells's work increased steadily and soon included the *A.M.E. Church Review*, *The Indianapolis World*, the *Kansas City Dispatch*, and *The American Baptist*.

By the late 1880s, Wells was one of the most prolific and well-known black female journalists of her day. Her nickname "Iola, Princess of the

This unflattering drawing of Wells appeared in The Indianapolis Freeman.

Press" marked Wells's increasing visibility in the profession, which stemmed not only from her publications but also from her involvement with the National Colored Press Association, which she attended as a representative of the *Little Rock Sun* in 1887, the first year that organization welcomed women. She came back from the meeting "tickled pink over the attention I received from those veterans of the press."[79] Evidently Wells made a good impression on the pressmen as well; the following year saw her elected first assistant secretary. Not surprisingly, the attractive young woman was evaluated on her appearance as well, with one commentator deeming her "pleasant-faced," while another wrote of an unflattering drawing of Wells published in a Louisville paper, "Iola will never get a husband so long as she lets these editors make her so hideous."[80] Never indifferent to comments on her appearance, Wells complained about the sketch, only to face further mockery from a columnist in *The Indianapolis Freeman*, who told her that she need not "be pretty as well as smart," since "beauty and genius were not always companions."[81]

But evaluations of her feminine charms were the least of Ida's concerns when it came to her journalism career. On attending her first Colored Press Association meeting, she gave a paper titled "Woman in Journalism, How I would edit," which expressed her ambition to edit her own paper.[82] Still poorly paid as a writer, Ida had decided that there would be more money in journalism if she published her own work, and in 1889 she purchased a one-third interest in a new paper, *The Memphis Free Speech and Headlight*. In doing so, she joined forces with the paper's founders and co-owners: the Reverend Taylor Nightingale, who also presided over the Beale Street Baptist Church, where the paper was published and sold, and J. L. Fleming. Fleming was the former editor of a black paper published in Marion, Arkansas—*The Marion Headlight*, where Wells had published several articles in the past. Fleming's collaboration with Nightingale had begun in 1888 when he was forced out of Marion by armed white men intent on eliminating African Americans from local politics. Despite Fleming's background in journalism, Wells soon become editor of *Free Speech*, while Fleming served as its business manager and Nightingale managed sales. With the well-known Iola at the helm and the support of Nightingale's large congregation, whose members bought at least five hundred copies every Sunday, the paper thrived.

Free Speech was soon in the black and not a moment too soon, since Ida's days as a teacher were numbered. In the end, it was not Wells's mixed feelings about teaching but her opinionated journalism that ended her career as a teacher. Already disliked by some black leaders in Memphis for her critiques of black secret societies, in the winter of 1891 Wells waded into another, still more perilous controversy when she protested the conditions in Memphis's black schools. Intimately acquainted with school affairs after many years of teaching, Wells not only complained about the "few and utterly inadequate buildings" that housed black students, but she also challenged the school board's hiring practices. In particular, she noted that some of the teachers working in colored schools "had little to recommend them

save an illicit relationship with the school board." Though Wells had long
been troubled by conditions in Memphis's black schools and disappointed
by the school board, which had not had a black member since 1886, it is not
clear why she chose to comment on improprieties involving a member of
the school board. Clearly, she anticipated that in doing so she might put her
job in jeopardy, for in her autobiography she noted that she initially asked
the Reverend Nightingale to sign the critical article, and published it under
her own name only after "he refused to father it."[83] She also explained that
she considered the not-so-clandestine affair between a black schoolteacher
and a young white lawyer who worked for the school board and had been
instrumental in securing the teacher's job to be a "glaring evil."[84] When
Wells lost her job as a consequence of the article, she told the disappointed
parents of her students that she had acted on behalf of their children. But,
one suspects, the tangle of sex and power in the illicit relationship she exposed galled her as much as any particular teacher's lack of qualifications.
Further, she may have reasoned that the liaison jeopardized the status of
other teachers such as herself, who thereafter might be expected to trade
sexual favors in exchange for employment.

Certainly Wells was sensitive to how easily the reputations of black
women could be compromised. Her own had been attacked time and again,
to the point where she was ready to embrace patrolling the morality of others as her best defense. But the volatility of the color line made African
American attempts to address white immorality—of any kind—a dangerous proposition. Indeed, Wells and fellow teachers were the only ones to
suffer for her actions. The lawyer for the school received no censure, and he
even continued to call on the teacher he had hired, "growing bolder as time
went on."[85] The affair came to a tragic end only for his lover, who committed suicide when the liaison led to disapprobation from her family. Meanwhile, the other black teachers were tainted by the scandal when another
Memphis paper alleged that several of them had entertained white callers.
And last but not least, the article and its aftermath compromised Wells's
livelihood and reputation. She returned to school that fall only to find that
the school board had revoked her teaching position. And shortly afterward

she became the subject of ugly rumors about the circumstances under which she had lost her post.

Free Speech

Jobless and subject to scandal yet again, Wells rebounded, with a resourcefulness that demonstrated the confidence and credentials she had built up over her decade in Memphis. No longer defenseless in the face of false accusations, she reacted promptly when a black minister whom she encountered while traveling on *Free Speech* business drew all the wrong conclusions about the end of her teaching career, telling several young men that Wells's dismissal was "suspicious." Outraged, she confronted and corrected him, making him issue a public statement renouncing his insinuations. After a decade in Memphis, the orphan from Holly Springs had matured into a formidable woman, more than capable of protecting herself from gossip. Wells had established a secure place in her region's middle-class black community, and built a network of influential friends in both the press and the pulpit—which included the unfortunate minister's denominational superior, Bishop Henry MacNeal Turner. After years of remaining quiet in the face of attacks on her reputation, she was no longer willing to suffer in silence. Dressing down the minister, Wells told him that her "good name was all I had in the world, that I was bound to protect it from attack by those who felt that they could do so with impunity because I had no brother or father to protect it for me."[86]

Likewise, even after losing her job as a teacher, Wells was far from down and out. She had a well-established career as a journalist to fall back on, as well as her shares in *Free Speech*. Prior to the fall of 1891, the newspaper had not been earning enough to allow Ida to support herself without her teaching job. But after being propelled into full-time journalism by her outspokenness, Wells built up the paper's business by using her railroad press pass to traverse the Delta selling subscriptions. Soon *Free Speech*'s circulation all but tripled, providing Wells with "an income nearly as large" as the salary she had earned while teaching. The paper's growing revenues also allowed Wells and Fleming to buy out the Reverend Nightingale, after he attempted to use the paper to "flay" enemies in a dispute with his congregation that ultimately ended in assault charges and Nightingale's flight to Oklahoma.[87] By the time Nightingale left town Wells and Fleming had moved *Free Speech* out of the Beale Street Baptist Church into its own office.

Tirelessly promoted by its charismatic female editor, the paper acquired a distinctive reputation "up and down the Delta spur of the Illinois Central Railroad." Like its sales, its news coverage extended far beyond Memphis, offering Ida an expansive forum for her increasingly militant political journalism. The paper chronicled, for example, the Mississippi Constitutional Convention of 1890, which saw the state adopt a new constitution designed to effectively disenfranchise its black population. The key legislation was an "Understanding Clause" that limited voting rights by way of a verbal test on the constitution administered by white men convinced "that very few Negroes understood the clauses of the Constitution."[88] Bitterly disappointed by this retreat from the black voting rights enshrined in the Fourteenth and Fifteenth Amendments, Wells wrote an editorial excoriating Isaiah Montgomery, the convention's only black representative, who had voted in favor of the new constitution. Although aware of the difficulties that black leaders faced in opposing powerful white interests, and later a personal friend of Montgomery, Wells had little patience with black accommodations to the politics of white supremacy. "It would have been far better to have gone down in defeat," her editorial told Montgomery. And elsewhere she railed far more frankly against "Negroes who persecute and betray their race of their own accord to curry favor with white people and win the title of 'good nigger.'"[89]

Ida's forthright style created controversy, but it also attracted a large and diverse readership. Among other things, *Free Speech* fulfilled her early ambition of explaining the world to rural black Southerners. For, as Ida noted in her autobiography, even blacks who could not read sought out copies of *Free Speech*—presumably for public reading by a literate member of their community. Indeed, this phenomenon was common enough that

As the editor of Free Speech, *Wells was subject to still more unflattering portraits. An 1890 cartoon dramatized the lively editorial differences among black newspaper editors by portraying Wells and T. Thomas Fortune of* The New York Age *as small, noisy dogs barking at* The Indianapolis Freeman. *Inset on the upper left-hand corner of the cartoon is yet another unappealing portrait of Wells. Almost unrecognizable, except for the bun in her hair, she is dressed in men's clothing and wistfully maintains, "I would I were a man."*

Wells and Fleming were ultimately compelled to begin to print *Free Speech* on distinctive pink paper, after realizing that unscrupulous vendors were substituting copies of *The Police Gazette* for *Free Speech* when selling it to people "who could not read for themselves." The format change guaranteed that even illiterates could identify *Free Speech*, by "asking for the pink paper."[90]

With the success of her pink paper, Ida escaped the professional uncertainties that had plagued her for most of her adult life. She "thoroughly enjoyed" producing and promoting the paper, and felt that she had "at last found my real vocation."[91] But the increasingly militant *Free Speech* would not see another year before its office went up in flames at the hands of a white mob intent on driving its editor out of town. The conflagration marked the end of Ida's sojourn in Memphis and the beginning of new challenges that would sharpen her vocation and redirect the course of her life.

· 3 ·

The Lynching at the Curve

THE MURDERS THAT BROUGHT IDA'S LIFE IN MEMPHIS TO A close began with nothing more momentous than a game of marbles. One night in March 1892, a group of black and white boys gathered to play marbles near two rival grocery stores. One black-owned and one white-owned, both stores were located in the heart of a predominantly black neighborhood on the outskirts of Memphis known as the Curve—which took its name from the sweeping curve made by the area's streetcar line as it rounded the corner of the neighborhood's central intersection. Home to a number of white and black enterprises, the Curve was not an unusual place for blacks and whites of all ages to congregate, but on this particular evening a mixed-race gathering that began with child's play turned ugly. A fight broke out among some of the boys, the marbles game having been won by Armour Harris, who was black. The group was then joined by the father of one of the white players, Cornelius Hurst, who whipped the victorious black boy. Soon other adults arrived on the scene, including Harris's father and several friends. When the black men "pitched in to avenge the grown white man's flogging of a colored boy," they were set on by several angry white men.[1] Among them was the owner of the white grocery store, W. H. Barrett.

Also drawn into the fray were two young men who rushed out of the nearby People's Grocery, a black-owned grocery cooperative established in 1889: Calvin McDowell, the grocery's manager, and the store's clerk, William Stewart. Although it is not clear that either man was involved in the scuffle that took place in the Curve that night, both ended up in trouble. Their troubles began the next day, when Barrett led a police officer into the store in search of William Stewart, who he claimed had clubbed him on the head. And when Calvin McDowell came to the door and refused to identify Stewart, Barrett hit him with his pistol. The blow knocked both McDowell and the gun to the floor. An athletic young man who served in the black militia group the Tennessee Rifles, McDowell did not respond meekly. He grabbed Barrett's gun and fired it, narrowly missing both white men. Arrested as a result, McDowell was released the next day on bond and expected to suffer no more than a minor fine. But Barrett took the altercation as an opportunity to create legal trouble for his commercial rivals, persuading a grand jury to indict the People's Grocery owners for maintaining a public nuisance.

So began a race war driven largely by the machinations of Barrett, whose main goal was to reclaim his monopoly over the Curve's black business. A hostile competitor to the People's Grocery since it first opened, Barrett proved relentless in using the unrest at the Curve as an opportunity to undermine the store's business. After his nuisance charges were dismissed with nominal fines, he vowed to "clean out the store," and managed to obtain arrest warrants for two black men who had protested his previous charges against the People's Grocery.[?] One of the two men named on the warrants was Thomas Moss, the president of the joint stock company that owned and operated the People's Grocery; he and his wife, Betty, were among Ida's best friends. In addition to harassing Moss, Barrett also upped the racial tensions around the store by spreading a rumor that a white mob was planning to attack the People's Grocery.

The result was deadly. Anticipating an attack, the men who worked in the store sought assistance from the Memphis police, who refused to intervene because the Curve lay just outside Memphis's city limits. So, after consulting an attorney who told them that in the absence of police protection they were entitled to protect themselves, Moss, McDowell, and Stewart stationed armed guards around the store. Their display of force was soon tested, but not by the white mob falsely rumored of by Barrett. Rather, Barrett came back with nine deputies from the county, who had been dispatched to arrest Moss and the other man named in the warrant. Dressed in plain clothes, the deputies descended on the People's Grocery, where they were driven away by the armed men assigned to protect the store against white vigilantes. Three of the deputies were wounded before the black men guarding the People's Grocery even realized whom they were firing on. Once they did know, they fled—on the heels of the store's terrified patrons. Meanwhile, the uninjured deputies retreated, regrouped, and returned to the store, where they arrested a dozen black men, including Moss, McDowell, and Stewart. Moss would later be described in the white press as the ringleader of the attack on the deputies, and accused of shooting the most seriously wounded of them. But he does not seem to have even been at the store at the time of the attack. Never mentioned in early accounts of the incident, Moss was, by his own testimony and that of his wife, at home at the time of the shooting.

However, in the hysteria that ensued, no effort was made either to establish or to investigate Moss's whereabouts, or those of any of the thirty additional alleged conspirators arrested in the days following the shoot-out. Instead, amid rumors of a massive black uprising, blacks in the Curve were arrested at random, while Memphis whites went on a free-for-all, destroying the People's Grocery and looting its shelves. Four days later, the armed whites who had descended on the Curve were still not satisfied. Their continuing fury was fed by the sensational coverage of the "Curve riot" in Memphis's white press. The city was home to two white newspapers—*The Appeal-Avalanche* and the *Memphis Scimitar*, both of which published accounts of the "negro desperados" that became more fanciful with each retelling. No longer a grocery store, the People's Grocery was described as "a low dive in which drinking and gambling were carried on: a resort for thieves and thugs."[3] According to *The Appeal-Avalanche*, the wounded deputies "had been led into an ambush and subjected to murderous fire by a band of Negroes who were without grievance, and solely activated by race prejudice and a vicious and venomous rancor."[4]

In the face of such press, all eyes turned to the jail where Moss, McDowell, Stewart, and other black men were being held without bail. The white mob that descended on the city jail three days after the shoot-out was hardly unanticipated. Armed, and in many cases inebriated, white men had been patrolling the streets around the jail since the arrests, threatening to "lynch the niggers."[5] Indeed, during the two nights immediately after the shoot-out, the Tennessee Rifles had gathered to guard the jail. Lynchings often began with a raid on the jailhouse, so this black militia group was anxious to protect the men inside the prison, whose numbers included at least one militia member—McDowell. But on the third day of their watch, the militia guard was forced to disperse after the sheriff seized their arms. While Memphis whites remained free to bear arms, the city procured a court order to disarm not only the Tennessee Rifles but also all the city's black citizens—who were also prohibited from buying guns. In the end, no one but the white jailer met the white mob that descended on the prison on March 9, 1892, at three o'clock in the morning. Thomas Moss, Calvin McDowell, and William Stewart were dragged from their cells and marched to a desolate field just north of the city limits. There they were lined up for execution at gunpoint and asked if they had any last words before they died.

Thomas Moss reportedly pleaded for his life, begging to be spared for the sake of "his wife and child and his unborn baby." Once he realized that his pleas were futile, he told his killers to "tell my people to go West—there is no justice for them here."[6] The others recorded no last words. Calvin McDowell evidently perished in a pitched battle with one of the lynchers, whose gun he grasped and held on to until a bullet shattered his closed fist. Another shot killed him, and at some point the mob gouged out his eyes, before leaving all three men stretched out on the ground, partially covered with some brush.

Sketches of Calvin McDowell, Thomas Moss, and the murder scene appeared in The Memphis Commercial *the day after McDowell, Moss, and William Stewart were killed.*

When the trouble began Wells was in Natchez, Mississippi, selling subscriptions to *Free Speech,* and she did not get home until after her friend Tommie Moss had been laid to rest. Before news of the lynchings in Memphis reached her she was on top of the world. Now thirty years old, Ida was doing the work she loved. At long last she felt confident that she could make her living with a newspaper and would never again need to "tie . . . [herself] down to school teaching."[7] On this point she would prove right, her schoolteaching days were over. But the murders of Moss, McDowell, and Stewart would change her life, propelling her on an antilynching campaign that would cost her her newspaper, threaten her life, and sever her ties to Memphis forever. In time, it would also make her the most famous black woman in America.

Tell My People to Go West:
Wells's Last Days in Memphis

Few of these momentous changes were foreseeable by Wells when she arrived back in Memphis a week or so after the lynchings. But she did return to a Memphis utterly transformed. In deep mourning over the deaths of the popular owners of the People's Grocery, the city's once confident black community was shocked "beyond description." Moreover, blacks in Memphis were still at the mercy of mob rule, and lived in fear of their lives. Anticipating black retaliation, the city had secured a court order authorizing the sheriff to "shoot down on sight any Negro who appears to be making trouble." And with this license, whites had flooded the Curve. "They obeyed the judge's orders literally," Wells recalled in her autobiography, "and shot into any group of Negroes they saw with as little compunction as if they had been on a hunting trip." Barred from buying guns, blacks could not even defend themselves; colored men had no choice other than to submit to "outrages and insults for the sake of those depending upon them."[8]

Determined to "sell my life as dearly as possible if attacked," Wells "bought a pistol the first thing after Tom Moss was lynched" and rarely traveled unarmed afterward.[9] But even as she began carrying a pistol in her purse, she realized that the situation in Memphis completely defied self-defense as a remedy. The men who worked in the People's Grocery had tried to defend themselves, and they had ended up not only dead but publicly defamed in scores of white newspapers. Hardworking and responsible young black men, they had lived by all the rules that African Americans were supposed to obey in order to advance themselves and their race. Their deaths revealed the futility of the ambitions long held by Memphis's striving black elite—indeed, it called into question the ideology of racial uplift that had so long fueled Ida's hopes for black progress in the South.

"A favorite with everybody," her friend Thomas Moss was a particularly poignant case in point. Employed full time as a letter carrier—the *Free*

Speech office was on his route—he had worked nights in the black business that he cofounded and co-owned. An eminently respectable man who taught Sunday school, he had died with religious literature from his last class still in his pocket. In short, Thomas Moss was the embodiment of the hard work, self-discipline, and clean living that Southern whites insisted African Americans lacked. Ambitious and enterprising, he had demonstrated the industry and initiative that many black leaders advocated as a form of racial uplift that would earn the race the rights and respect accorded to white people. Yet "he was murdered with no more consideration than if he had been a dog" for the crime of defending his property.[10]

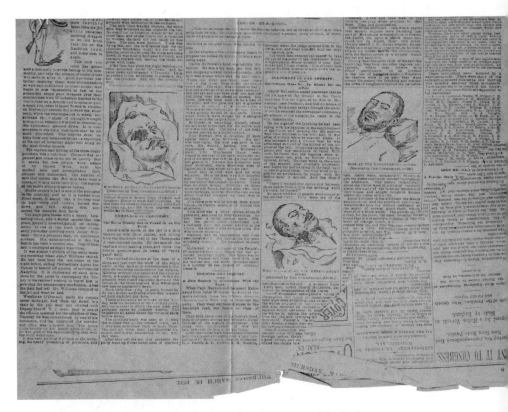

The Memphis Commercial *also featured grisly drawings of the dead men.*

Her worldview utterly transformed by the lynchings, Ida advocated immediate emigration from Memphis. Echoing the dying words of her friend, in her first editorial after his death she told Memphis blacks, "There is . . . only one thing left we can do: save money and leave a town which will neither protect our lives or our property, nor give us a fair trial in the courts." Her advice did not go unheeded. With other black leaders also advocating migration, African Americans left Memphis in droves, clearing out so rapidly that they caused a crisis in the city's economy. With so many blacks either gone or economizing in preparation for departure, business slowed to a "standstill."[11] Throughout the city, vendors found themselves oversupplied with all sorts of goods and waiting in vain for black customers. Indeed, six weeks after the lynching, the African American withdrawal from the city's economy was so noticeable that both the superintendent and treasurer of the City Railway Company, which ran the Memphis streetcar system, visited *Free Speech* to investigate the precipitate drop in their black patronage. They also hoped that the paper would use its influence to get blacks to once again ride the streetcars.

Wells was at work in the *Free Speech* office on Beale Street when the two men arrived. First taken aback by their visit and then confused by their appeal for help, she asked them "what they thought was the cause" of their sudden lack of black passengers. Their reply was disingenuous at best: "They had heard that Negroes were afraid of electricity," they told her, alluding to the fact that Memphis had recently converted from horse-drawn streetcars to cable cars powered by electricity. They wished "to assure our people that there was no danger" and added that Ida should tell her readers "that any discourtesy toward them would be punished severely." Confounded, Wells pressed the men to deal with the real issue keeping Memphis blacks off the streetcars. "Electricity has been the motive power here for over six months," she noted. "How long since you have observed the change? . . . 'About six weeks' . . . Why, it was just six weeks ago that the lynching took place." But the two men refused to acknowledge the connection. "The streetcar company had nothing to do with the lynchings," one of them protested. "It is owned by Northern capitalists."[12]

As far as Wells was concerned, however, City Railway's white Memphis representatives and employees were all implicated in the lynchings. "Every white man of any standing in this town knew of the plan and consented to the lynching of our boys," she told her visitors. Her argument was largely lost on the railroad's representatives, who urged "the colored people to find the guilty ones"—and to return to the streetcars even before that. But their visit did tell Wells that her *Free Speech* editorials were having a powerful effect. One had instructed the African Americans in Memphis "to save their nickels and dimes" so they could leave the city as soon as possible. Wells herself had been walking to save carfare, but she was unaware that many others were doing so as well prior to the City Railway men's appearance in her office. As soon as the two men left her office, she wrote up her exchange with them, encouraging Memphis blacks "to keep up the good work." Likewise, even before the next edition of her paper appeared, she spread the word of a streetcar boycott at the city's two largest churches that Sunday, urging congregants to "keep on staying off the cars."[13] The boycott, however, did not replace migration as the central goal of the Memphis blacks. Anxious to scout out new homes for both herself and others, Ida was among those who hit the road in the months following the deaths of Moss, McDowell, and Stewart. She spent three weeks in Oklahoma that spring, posting several favorable reports of conditions there in *Free Speech*, and also made plans to act on T. Thomas Fortune's suggestion that she "give the East Coast a look-over" before deciding where to resettle.[14]

The migration that took shape in Memphis in 1892 was only one of several such black migration movements that followed the death of Reconstruction. Most notable was the Kansas Exodus of 1879, which saw twenty thousand African Americans from Louisiana, Mississippi, Texas, and Tennessee abruptly leave for Kansas. Largely inspired by black fears for their future in the newly "redeemed" Democratic South, these cotton belt migrants were known as "Exodusters" because they likened the South to biblical ancient Egypt—an opinion Wells would begin to share in 1892. Scourged by the economic exploitation, political oppression, and widespread racial violence that had accompanied the Democrats' restoration in the region, many migrants feared that the Democrats would reinstitute slavery, or at least establish something very much like it. Their flight was urgent, one said, because it would soon be impossible for blacks to leave the South. "The Democrats, as the Slave owners of the South, will fix it," one Exoduster leader noted, "so that . . . not any colored man will be able to Leave the South without a Pass."[15]

The migration had "pull" as well as "push" factors. In particular, the migrants were attracted to Kansas by the promise of cheap land under the 1862 Homestead Act, which had been widely promoted across the South by land developers, and also touted by black leader Benjamin "Pap" Singleton of Tennessee, a proponent of black westward migration. But the defeat of Reconstruction in 1877 was clearly the immediate concern behind the 1879 migration, which saw black migrants fleeing to freedom in Kansas in numbers so large that the movement collapsed at least in part as a result of its own success. Sparsely populated and difficult to farm, the windswept prairie state could not absorb or support the mass migration of impoverished Southern blacks. Not particularly welcome there, many soon found it difficult to secure land or jobs. But while black Southerners lost interest in Kansas, many continued to be interested in leaving the South. Back-to-Africa movements flourished at the turn of the century, which saw a variety of black Southerners earnestly considering resettling in Liberia—although few were able to raise the funds needed to do so.

Like Kansas, Liberia appealed to black Southerners above all as an alternative to where they were. Founded in 1816 by a white organization known as the American Colonization Society (ACS) as a place to resettle American blacks, Liberia had long elicited mixed feelings among black Americans. Few could support the society's desire to return all American blacks to Africa, and prior to 1865 the ACS's ostensibly antislavery goals were called into question by its commitment to beginning this reverse diaspora by returning free blacks to Africa. Moreover, Liberia, although touted by the ACS as a place in which African Americans could flourish in their native habitat, had high mortality rates. Soon notorious as a place where disease and food shortages brought an early end to many who emigrated there, Liberia retained an appeal in the late nineteenth century that spoke to the still more terrifying dangers that blacks faced in the United States. Among those interested in emigrating to Liberia, for example, was a group of blacks from Pastoria, Arkansas, clearly confident that they would be better off almost anywhere else. Titled "A Coloured Application to Git out of Egypt," their 1891 petition to the ACS noted that the only land available to blacks in their community was "6 feet by 4 wide 4 ft. Deep[,] an[d] that not untel . . . dead."[16]

Unlike this Arkansas delegation, however, Wells had not seriously considered migration as a practical or political necessity prior to 1892. Prone to characterizing herself as a Southern girl, Wells had been happy enough to return to Memphis at the end of her 1887 California trip. Willing to brave the shifting political winds of post-Reconstruction Tennessee, she had bought her share in *Free Speech* after conservative Democrats rose to power in Memphis in 1888, ousting the biracial Republican coalition that had long held power there. That year also saw a Democrat take the Tennessee governor's race for the first time since the Civil War. Certainly, the resurgence of Southern Democrats committed to installing a "white man's government" across the South must have troubled Wells long before 1892. Indeed, this unpromising new political climate framed Wells's defeat in her railroad suits, as well as her dismissal from her teaching post by Memphis's lily-white board of education.

Still, until the Memphis lynchings, Wells had advocated meeting white violence with resistance rather than flight. Her *Free Speech* editorials expressed frustration with Republican politics, black leaders, and white racism but did not abandon Southern race relations as irredeemable. Convinced that many of the Reconstruction-era Republicans who still held power and controlled federal offices were more committed to patronage than preserving black civil rights, she had called for new party leadership to "save the country." "Give the young Republicans a chance and relegate some of these chronic office holders to the rear," she had urged party loyalists.[17] Moreover, Ida did not then rule out the possibility of new political coalitions. At a time when the Democrats were increasingly billing themselves as the party of white supremacy and the Republicans had largely abandoned any commitment to racial justice in favor of an alliance with big business, Ida was politically independent. Along with T. Thomas Fortune and other black political mavericks, she called for blacks to rally around specific candidates and issues rather than let party loyalties dictate their votes. The Republicans had always been the lesser of two evils where black voters were concerned. But in the hope that independent voting could gain African Americans greater influence with both parties, Wells and other African American independents insisted that the party did not deserve to take African American votes for granted.

Retrospectively, Wells's hopes for a resurgence of black political power in the South seem quixotic, as we now know that the steady erosion of black voting rights in the late nineteenth-century South would ultimately shut most black Southerners out of politics. Moreover, by the nineteenth century's last decade, it was increasingly clear that the Republican Party was largely content to let the black vote disappear. The 1890 Lodge bill, a measure authorizing the use of federal power to monitor voter registration and elections in the South, was defeated when its Republican supporters abandoned it as part of a deal to pass a higher tariff. Even before the bill died in the Senate in 1891, Ida was worried. "If the Republican party lets this opportunity go by, without doing something in the interest of honest elections," she wrote when the bill was still under consideration, "it deserves to be defeated for years to come."[18]

Still, in the end, it was racial violence rather than the rapid erosion of black political power in the South that drove Wells and other black political exiles out of the region during the 1880s and 1890s. By the early twentieth century, the disenfranchisement strategies pursued by Southern Democrats would triumph, resulting in a wholesale exclusion of blacks from Southern politics that lasted until the passage of the Voting Rights Act of 1965. But as late as the spring of 1892, even to a critical observer such as Wells, black disenfranchisement was not yet a fait accompli.

The Republican Party controlled the Senate until November 1892—when Democrats regained power in the Senate for the first time since the

Civil War. Moreover, prior to their repeal in 1894, the Reconstruction era's federal election laws protecting African American voters remained in place. Although never very effective, these laws gave the federal government the authority to supervise state elections, offering at least statutory support for the Fifteenth Amendment's prohibition against denying any citizen the right to vote on "account of race, color or previous condition of servitude." Neither the Fifteenth Amendment nor the federal election laws offered any protection to the many black Southerners whose voting rights were already giving way to forms of disenfranchisement such as high poll taxes and other racially indirect measures designed to discourage blacks from voting. But the impact of such measures was not always immediately obvious. In Wells's home state, for example, the racially discriminatory impact of the poll taxes and new voting qualifications that Tennessee introduced in 1890 was partially obscured by the fact that the new measures initially decreased both black and white voters.[19] Moreover, while similar measures were in the works across the South, the legal disenfranchisement of the majority of the region's black voters would not be fully accomplished until 1908, with the conclusion of successful disenfranchisement campaigns in Texas and Georgia. In short, the elimination of black voting rights in the South was under way in 1892 but far from complete.

By contrast, that year saw racial violence reach a post-Reconstruction high—1892 saw 239 lynchings. And the Memphis murders taught Wells that there was no practical remedy for the racial terror that sustained Jim Crow. Observing earlier lynchings from farther afield, Wells had previously advocated aggressive self-defense. "Wrote a dynamitic article to the G[ate] C[ity] P[ress] almost advising murder," she noted in her diary on September 4, 1886. The case that had Wells up in arms then was the brutal lynching of a black woman in Tennessee. "A colored woman accused of poisoning a white one was taken from the county jail and stripped naked and hung up in the court house yard and her body riddled with bullets and exposed to view!" Ever the pragmatist, even as Wells expressed her shock and despair, she was thinking about remedies up to and including divine retribution. "Oh my God! Can such be and no justice for it?" No copies of her article exist today, but whatever self-defensive strategy she advised, Wells was left worrying that "it may be unwise to express myself so strongly."[20]

An 1891 editorial in *Free Speech* likely written by Wells helps explain why she might well worry. Likewise "almost advising murder," it praised blacks in Georgetown, Kentucky, who had set their town on fire in the wake of the lynching of a member of their community. "Not until the Negro rises in his might and takes a hand resenting such cold-blooded murders," Ida then wrote, "will a halt be called in wholesale lynching."[21] But events in Memphis in 1892 showed that militant self-defense could be both dangerous and futile—and may well have left Wells feeling a little guilty about her previous editorials. If nothing else, the lynching at the Curve demonstrated that African American attempts at self-defense could generate still more violence, setting the stage for battles the black community could not hope to win. Both during and after the conflict at the Curve, black men in Memphis received no protection under the law. Flight was the best, and arguably the only, option when it came to self-defense.

Accordingly, after the spring of 1892, Wells became a fervent supporter of migration. She did not rule out even Africa as a possible destination for "judicious emigration from lynch-infested districts."[22] Wells's views distinguished her from other leading African Americans of her day, many of whom were adamantly opposed to black migration from the South, irrespective of the destination. The eminent ex-slave leader Frederick Douglass, for example, saw the Kansas migration as "a premature, disheartening surrender" that "would secure freedom and free institutions by migration rather than by protection, by flight rather than by right."[23] But Wells's belief in black self-protection evaporated in the aftermath of the Memphis lynching. "We are outnumbered and without arms," she told *Free Speech*'s readers in an editorial published then. "The white mob could help itself to ammunition without pay, but the order was rigidly enforced against the selling of guns to Negroes. There is . . . only one thing left that we can do; save our money and leave a town that will not protect our lives or our property."[24]

As Wells had come to recognize, violence lay at the heart of the politics of white supremacy that had triumphed in the post-Reconstruction South and was increasingly invoked to suppress all forms of black self-assertion—physical, political, or economic. Brute force played a key role in the achievement of the segregation laws and disenfranchisement measures of the 1880s and 1890s. Moreover, mob violence against black Southerners persisted even with erosion of the political and civil rights that African Americans enjoyed during Reconstruction. Crucial to restoring white supremacy in the post-Reconstruction South, such violence also helped perpetuate white rule. In particular, lynchings and other forms of racial violence served to warn any African Americans who might challenge Jim Crow that there were no legal limits on the power that the region's whites had over black lives. Accordingly, whereas in the years immediately preceding 1885, lynch mobs had targeted as many whites as blacks, in the second half of the decade, African Americans became the primary target of lynching, especially in the South where the practice was all but reserved for blacks.

The racialization of lynching was a product of the resurgence of white political power in the post-Reconstruction South. Just one of many forms of extralegal violence, lynching is difficult to define with precision. Indeed, lynchings are distinguished from other forms of illicit violence less by the character or consequences of the lynchers' assault on the victim than by the contexts in which the violence takes place. In other words, although popular images of lynching usually conjure up a hanging—an image now immortalized by Billie Holiday's famous rendition of the haunting song "Strange Fruit"—other forms of murder and violence can also be called lynching. As was true in Memphis, lynching victims in the Jim Crow South often faced execution at gunpoint. What distinguishes lynchings from all other forms of murder is not any specific type of violence, but the lynchers' claims to justification and social legitimacy.[25]

Lynching has its antecedents in Anglo-American traditions of mob punishment. These typically included the tarring and feathering or flogging of individuals suspected of criminal behavior, and prior to the nineteenth century were not usually lethal. Vigilante justice of this sort proliferated during the American Revolution, when it was used against colonial loyalists and came to be associated with a Quaker patriot named Charles Lynch. A justice of the peace in the town of Chestnut Hill, Virginia, before the Revolutionary War, Lynch headed an informal court that dealt with suspected Tories and horse thieves—who generally sold the animals that they stole to the British—during the conflict. Whatever his Quaker commitment to nonviolence, it did not preclude corporal punishment. Defendants convicted in Judge Lynch's court were tied to a nearby tree and given thirty-nine lashes. Thus the term "Lynch law" was born.[26]

Such popular tribunals became increasingly likely to mete out the death sentence in the nineteenth-century South, where they policed the increasingly volatile borders of the antebellum slave system. A lynch mob shot abolitionist editor Elijah P. Lovejoy in Illinois in 1837, after he refused to be silenced despite repeated attacks on his newspaper. He died guarding a new printing press he had ordered to keep his newspaper going after having lost several presses to previous white mobs. Likewise, both blacks and whites suspected of encouraging slave revolts were also subject to summary justice, which in the early nineteenth century came to be termed lynching. Lynch mobs also went after common criminals, especially in areas where courts were few and far between. But in the post-emancipation South, vigilante justice policed the color line, with courts quiescent if not outright complicit.

Organized by ex-Confederates in Pulaski, Tennessee, during the winter of 1865–66, the Ku Klux Klan, deploying whipping, arson, and murder, dedicated itself to discouraging not only black political participation, but also the education and economic independence of the freed people. Blacks were the Klan's most frequent and numerous victims, but whites were also subject to Klan discipline. Other Klan victims included Northern white women—derisively known among white Southerners as "Oberlin girls"— who traveled South to teach ex-slaves, and white Republicans of both Southern and Northern origins, who were labeled scalawags and carpetbaggers, respectively. Outlawed under the Third Enforcement Act in 1871, the Klan only subsided after a sustained spree of racial violence, which scholars have estimated to include anywhere from four hundred to twenty thousand murders. Deemed as criminal at the time, at least by Republican observers, the Klan's killings were not generally referred to as lynchings. But they helped establish mob violence as a powerful and effective means of suppressing black political participation and maintaining white supremacy—to which white Southerners would return again and again.

Despite this history of politically motivated violence, in the eyes of most late nineteenth-century Americans, the resurgence of racial violence in the South testified neither to political tensions between the races nor even to the Democrats' drive for a "white man's" government. Such possibilities were utterly obscured in a fog of racist ideology that defined lynching as the white South's first line of defense against the naturally lawless and predatory Negro male. This ideology was the product of an era when black men were routinely turned into criminals by an exploitative all-white legal system. A web of racially discriminatory laws was used to make convict laborers out of African American men imprisoned for a host of petty offenses, including crimes as dubious as "vagrancy"—which in the Jim Crow South boiled down to being black and without work.

Moreover, by the 1880s, the criminalization of African American males drew increasingly on Victorian ideas about male sexuality and the evolution of the races. Masculine sexual restraint was thought to be a civilized attribute entirely lacking in "savage" peoples such as the Negro race, whose development lagged behind that of whites. Indeed, this deficiency was both the cause and the effect of black inferiority, according to authorities such as the eminent scholar John W. Burgess, one of the founders of American political science. Burgess taught his students at Columbia University that "a black skin means membership in a race which has never of itself subjugated passion to reason, and has never therefore created any civilization of any kind." The "antithesis of both white men and civilization," black men were alleged to have a special propensity toward rape, as well as a desire for white women. These ideas were a product of the confluence of the ideological needs of white supremacy in an imperial and post-emancipation era and new Social Darwinist notions of race that stressed white middle-class sexual mores as a key element in the race's evolutionary success. Such ideas were still relatively new in the 1890s. Indeed, as late as 1904, rape was described as the "new Negro crime" in *Harper's Weekly* magazine. But the notion of a black rapist seems to have been an instant commonplace to many white Americans. A few months before the 1892 Memphis lynchings, for example, *The New York Times* noted that the offense of rape was "one to which the African race was particularly prone."[27]

As useful as it was compelling, the myth of the black rapist provided a powerful justification for the rising tide of white violence against black men in the late nineteenth-century South, and it was often invoked irrespective of the circumstances in which the violence took place. Nowhere was this clearer than in the aftermath of the Memphis lynchings of 1892, which Memphis's white newspapers soon began to attribute to an allegation of rape, despite the fact that the victims, Thomas Moss, Calvin McDowell, and William Stewart, were never accused of sexual improprieties of any kind. After their arrest, these pillars of Memphis's middle-class black community were denounced in the white press as "desperadoes" from the "tough desperate element of the colored community."[28] Moreover, in the months following their deaths, as whites in Memphis grew increasingly defensive about the lynchings, they began to invoke rape as a justification for the killings. *The Memphis Scimitar*, for example, defended the murders of Moss, McDowell, and Stewart with reference to a noble but ultimately unavoidable contest. "Whenever it comes to the conflict between the races," its editors declared, "the Scimitar is for the grand old Anglo-Saxon every time, no matter what the original cause." And *The Appeal-Avalanche* lost sight of the facts in the Memphis lynchings altogether when confronted with editorials condemning the city in the Boston and Chicago papers. When "an unprotected woman is assaulted," *The Appeal-Avalanche* declared by way of reply, "Chivalrous men in the neighborhood will forget that there are such things as courts."[29]

The blatant falsehoods Memphis's white press used in defense of the lynchings came as a revelation to Wells, who had never previously observed the creation of the racial fictions used to cloak vigilante violence at their point of origin. An avid reader of the black press, she was well aware of the rising tide of white-on-black violence that had swept the South since the mid-1880s. But nothing in her previous experience had prepared her to see upstanding members of her own community first brutally killed and then viciously defamed by local whites.

In Memphis Wells had lived within a relatively sheltered environment, so far as racial violence was concerned. Lynchings were far more common in the isolated rural areas of the South, where blacks were far more exposed, than they were in densely populated urban areas with large black populations. Before the events at the Curve, Memphis had not seen a lynching in decades. Often closely tied to labor struggles between white landlords and black tenants, rural lynchings tended to increase when cotton prices declined. And unlike the events in Memphis, such lynchings typically took place far from any public or African American press scrutiny.

In particular, the link between lynching and rape—which Ida saw so falsely trumpeted in the Memphis case—could rarely be disproved in the aftermath of many rural lynchings. News of such lynchings usually came via brief wire reports that summarized the South's white newspaper accounts of mob violence. Drawn from papers that "praised the vigilantes as peacekeepers against outbreaks of black crime and violence" in general and assaults on white women in particular, the wire reports afforded readers little insight into the circumstances behind the lynchings they chronicled.[30] Instead, as lynchings proliferated during the 1880s, they were generally linked to a rising tide of black sex crimes in ways that began to trouble even black observers.[31]

Indeed, Wells herself had temporized over the causes of lynching before the events in Memphis opened her eyes to what "lynching really was." Like many of her black contemporaries, she condemned extralegal violence against blacks, but was more uncertain about defending black men who were accused of rape. Prior to the Memphis murders, Wells recalled in her autobiography, she had deplored lynching as "irregular and contrary to law and order." But she had never entirely rejected the claimed motives behind it. If "unreasoning anger over the terrible crime of rape led to lynching," she speculated, "perhaps the brute deserved death anyhow and the mob was justified in taking his life"—an attitude that helps explain why her most heated critique of a lynching prior to 1892 focused on a case in which the victim was a black female. Not until the murders of Moss, McDowell, and Stewart did she begin to question the rape allegations against black men that were so frequently invoked in defense of lynching. As she watched the aftermath of their murders unfold, Wells began to suspect that lynching might be little more than "an excuse to get rid of Negroes who were acquiring wealth and property and thus keep the race terrorized and 'the nigger down.' "[32]

Although most directly a product of the mayhem in Memphis, Wells's suspicions about the character of lynching also built on her own experience with rumor and character defamation. As a single woman, whose independence had brought charges of immorality, and as a black woman whose attempt to ride in the ladies' car had branded her a troublemaker, Wells knew from bitter experience that character defamation was a tool Southerners used to fight off challenges to their region's sexual and racial order.

Moreover, her analysis of what "lynching really was" was confirmed when she began to research every lynching that she read about during the violent spring of 1892.[33] She found what had happened in Memphis was not unusual: fully two-thirds of the victims of lynch mobs were never even accused of rape. She also found that many of those accused of rape were charged on the flimsiest of evidence. The very week Moss, McDowell, and Stewart were lynched, for example, another black man was briefly jailed for rape in Memphis, despite the absence of any complaint against him. Discovered in a white woman's room, a Mr. Stricklin was charged with rape "and would have been lynched" but for the fact that the white woman in question insisted on his release.[34] A furniture dealer from whom the woman had recently bought curtains, Stricklin was saved because his customer intervened to explain he had only entered her room to install her new curtains. Although guilty of no crime, Stricklin was fortunate to escape with his life, since the false accusations behind many lynchings often only came to light after their target had already been murdered by an angry white mob—if they came to light at all.

Wells also found that rape accusations that were proved false only after the mob had done its work were sometimes documented in the news reports, alongside the stories of their tragic results. A white correspondent for *The Sun* (Baltimore), for instance, reported that a black man lynched for the rape of a white woman in Chestertown, Maryland, had in fact been innocent. The rapist was known to be a white man who had left town. Indeed, even "the girl herself maintained that her assailant was a white man." But evidently her rapist went unpunished. Once a white man was identified as the true culprit, authorities dropped her rape case altogether, explaining "that they wished to spare the girl the mortification of having to testify in court."[35]

Where such evidence was lacking, Wells conducted her own investigation. More often than not, she found that rape allegations against black men had been triggered by the exposure of consensual relationships between black men and white women. Following up on Associated Press reports about "a big, burly brute" who was lynched in Tunica County, Mississippi, for the alleged crime of raping the town sheriff's seven-year-old daughter, Wells visited and found out that the sheriff's daughter was not seven "but more than seventeen years old." Moreover, on the day of the lynching she had been discovered by her father while she was visiting her alleged rapist—a black man who worked in the sheriff's household—in his cabin. The mortified sheriff "led the mob against him in order to save his daughter's reputation." In Natchez, Wells talked to the mother of a "handsome young mulatto man" who had been "horribly lynched for 'rape'" after he had been seduced by the "beautiful daughter" of his employer.[36] And she also uncovered the story of Ebenezer Fowler, "the wealthiest colored man in Isaquena, Mississippi," who was not even suspected of anything as forcible as rape when he was shot down by a lynch mob in 1885. His crime was "writing a note to a white woman," which proved that "there was an intimacy between them."[37]

Wells's discoveries about lynching enraged her, inspiring her to run a series of antilynching editorials in *Free Speech*. Some focused on local events. She castigated white Memphis, and especially its law enforcement officials, who claimed to be unable to identify the lynchers of Moss, McDowell, and

Stewart, and she continued to encourage African Americans to leave. But Wells also presented her more general findings about lynching, producing an incendiary critique of the interlocking sexual and racial myths white Southerners used to justify the practice. Writing at a time when rape—the "new Negro crime"—was supposedly on the rise in the South, Wells took on the charge that white Southerners most often invoked as unassailable justification for lynching. Not only did her research reveal that most lynchings occurred in the absence of any accusations of rape, it also called into question many of the cases in which rape was alleged. All too often the accused black men were guilty of no other crime than having a sexual relationship with a white woman. Indeed, many of the cries of rape came only after clandestine interracial relationships were exposed.

Wells was not the first African American to doubt the allegations of rape that accompanied many lynchings. Blacks had long questioned many of the trumped-up stories of sexual assault used to justify acts of mob violence, but few had the courage to challenge public opinion on the subject. The black newspaperman J. C. Duke had been chased out of Montgomery, Alabama, in 1888, for publishing an article that attributed a spike in the number of lynchings to "the growing appreciation of white Juliets for colored Romeos."[38] But Wells was the first journalist, black or white, to research the causes of lynching and amass evidence debunking the rape myth so often used as justification.

Enraged by her findings, she addressed the issue in no uncertain terms in an editorial in *Free Speech* on May 21, 1892. "Eight Negroes lynched since the last issue of 'Free Speech,'" she wrote, in a laconic style clearly designed to underscore the routine nature of the violence, "one at Little Rock where the citizens broke (?) into the Penitentiary and got their man; three near Anniston, Ala., one near New Orleans—on the same old racket, the new alarm about raping white women—; and three at Clarkesville, Ga., for killing a white man. The same programme of hanging, then shooting bullets into the bodies was carried out to the letter." Equally routine, Ida emphasized, were the false accusations of rape that accompanied five of the lynchings. "Nobody in this section of the country believes the old threadbare lie that Negro men rape white women," she flatly stated. "If Southern white men are not careful, they will overreach themselves and public sentiment will have a reaction; a conclusion will then be reached which will be very damaging to the reputation of their women."[39]

A mixture of courage and rage fueled Ida's red flag of an editorial. She published this open attack on the morals of white women at a time when—as she herself noted—white Southerners routinely invoked the sanctity of white womanhood as a justification for violence against blacks. Moreover, she was well aware that J. C. Duke had had to leave Montgomery after his editorial allusion to "white Juliets" and "colored Romeos." Duke had taken refuge in Memphis, where Wells had learned enough about his experience to comment on it in an April 1892 article on the "Requirements of Southern Journalism." Reflecting on Duke's experience, she had then noted that outspoken editors might have to be on the "hop, skip, and the jump" in the South. So she must have suspected that her own equally intemperate editorial might endanger her standing in Memphis. However, as before, when she wrote a "dynamitic" article for the *Gate City Press* in the aftermath of a lynching, Wells seems to have been too furious to be discreet: her tersely written editorial crackles with rage. Still, she was not without caution. She sent her editorial to the printer just prior to leaving on a long-planned three-week trip to Philadelphia and New York, and was relaxing on an eastbound train when *Free Speech* hit the newsstands.

The Death of *Free Speech*

As it turned out, Wells's trip east was well-timed. Traveling first to Philadelphia, she attended the African Methodist Episcopal Church's general conference on the invitation of her old friend Bishop Henry MacNeal Turner. Although not much impressed with the deliberations at the conference, Wells enjoyed her reception there. "All the big guns . . . made a lot of fuss over our only woman editor," she recalled in her autobiography.[40] The luminaries she met with included the denomination's leader, Bishop Daniel A.

Payne, who struck Ida as the very "ideal of what I thought a Bishop ought to be," as well as fellow journalist Levi J. Coppin, who edited *The A.M.E. Church Review*, and his wife, Fanny Jackson Coppin, a prominent educator. Wells breakfasted with the Coppins and also enjoyed a tour of Philadelphia's Institute for Colored Youth, led by Mrs. Coppin, the school's principal. Moreover, the trip gave Wells a chance to visit with Philadelphia's well-known black author and activist Frances Ellen Watkins Harper, whom Wells had met and hosted in Memphis the previous year. The sixty-two-year-old Harper offered to return the favor, inviting Wells to Philadelphia, and Wells was happy to oblige. An abolitionist and women's rights activist, Harper was no doubt one of Wells's few female role models. Widely published, Harper wrote not only nonfiction promoting her causes but also poetry and fiction—as Wells had long aspired to do. But as Wells was enjoying her Philadelphia visit, white Memphis was up in arms.

Shortly after her editorial first appeared, it was reprinted on the editorial page of *The Memphis Commercial*, accompanied by a call for Memphis whites to "avenge the insult to the honor of their women." A subsequent editorial published in the *Evening Scimitar*, another Memphis newspaper, went still further. Writing on the assumption that the author of the *Free Speech* editorial was a man, the *Scimitar's* editor threatened to tie "the wretch who has uttered these calumnies to a stake at the intersection of Main and Madison Sts., brand him with a hot iron, and perform on him a surgical operation with a pair of tailors' shears." Evidently ready to make good on these threats, a group of angry whites gathered at the Memphis Merchants' Exchange on February 27, 1892, and marched to the offices of *Free Speech*. Unable to find the paper's editor, they destroyed its printing press and furniture, trashed its office, and left a note saying "anyone trying to publish the paper again would be punished with death."[41]

The *Free Speech* was destroyed. Indeed, no copies of the pink paper have survived the destruction of its archives. Gone too, of course, was the flourishing business that Wells and her business partner, J. L. Fleming, had worked so hard to build. Fleming, to whom Wells's article was first attributed, had managed to leave town one step ahead of the lynch mob, moving to Chicago, where he made an unsuccessful attempt to revive *Free Speech*. Without adequate money or equipment, the paper soon folded, leaving Fleming very bitter. "He blamed me," Wells recorded in her autobiography, "and perhaps he was justified in doing so."[42]

While her newspaper was being gutted, Wells was traveling up the East Coast toward New York. She first learned of the destruction of her paper and the threats against her life from T. Thomas Fortune, the editor of *The New York Age*, who met her train in Jersey City. A longtime correspondent with and supporter of Wells, Fortune had published many of her articles in his paper and had been delighted when she accepted his invitation to visit the New York area. "We've been a long time getting you to New York," he told her at the station, "but now that you are here I'm afraid you will have to stay."[43]

Copies of the morning news, which Fortune brought with him, told the full story. The *Free Speech* had been destroyed and Ida B. Wells had been identified as one of its owners. What was more, once her authorship was discovered, local whites wasted no time letting it be known that her gender would do nothing to protect her should she return. In place of castration, they posed other graphic threats. If they ever saw her again, as Wells recorded, "they would bleed my face and hang me in front of the court house."[44] By telegram, Wells soon assured herself of Fleming's safety and that of her sister Lily—whom Wells arranged to send to California. But she also received additional warning about the threats against her; neighbors, she reported, told her that her "home was being watched by white men who promised to kill me on sight." So despite offers of armed protection from Memphis's black community, Wells decided to stay away, heeding the warnings of those who feared "more bloodshed, more widows, and orphans if I came back."[45]

Indeed, Wells abandoned her home in Memphis without so much as collecting her belongings—never to return. Exactly how she felt as she faced her abrupt relocation is difficult to recover, since her Memphis diary ends in 1891 and none of her personal papers from that time have survived. Coming on top of the earlier loss of her parents in her teens, the recent

Wells, c. 1893

death of her good friend Thomas Moss, and the loss of the profitable paper she had worked so hard to build, along with her home in a city that had fostered many of her hopes and dreams, it must have been devastating. But in her autobiography Wells recorded little sadness or depression. Instead, her losses seem to have motivated purposeful anger, as she once again faced adversity and came out swinging. Offered a one-quarter interest in *The New York Age* in return for her *Free Speech* subscription list, Wells accepted. She also signed on at the *Age* as a salaried weekly contributor. With the help of T. Thomas Fortune and the *Age*'s co-owner Jerome B. Peterson, Wells weathered the loss of her paper—"in which every dollar I had in the world was invested"—emerging even more determined to continue her "fight against lynching and lynchers."[46] She stayed in New York, she notes, less out of concern for her personal safety than because she thought she could better conduct that fight in her new location.

Accordingly, Wells used her displacement to expose the truth about lynching. In New York, "Iola" was reborn as "Exiled," as Wells crafted a new identity as a refugee forced to flee the "Southern horrors" that countless other blacks still experienced. Written under her new nom de plume, her account of the Memphis lynchings and their aftermath appeared in a special issue of *The New York Age* designed to promote her story. Fortune and Peterson printed ten thousand copies of the issue and distributed them nationwide. Now no longer just a Southern girl, Wells addressed a wide audience. Her critique of lynching was equally wide-ranging. Long a critic of segregation, disenfranchisement, and mob violence against blacks, Wells linked them all in her discussion of the Memphis murders, fashioning a compelling new image of lynching as the "Southern horror" that sustained Jim Crow.

· 4 ·

Exile

IDA'S EXILE RESHAPED HER LIFE. IT TOOK HER OUT OF THE South and out of the United States; transformed her from a journalist to a public figure; and launched her lifelong struggle to put an end to lynching. Most transformative, probably, was her first year out of Memphis, which saw her traverse the East Coast and travel to Britain and back in an attempt to find an effective platform for her antilynching crusade. That year, Wells received unprecedented public exposure as she gave personal testimony on the evils of Jim Crow and faced daunting new social challenges as a result. Far from her Memphis social networks, she had to establish herself in a new environment that would soon expand well beyond New York. Often embattled or ill at ease, Wells was under unrelenting public scrutiny as she waged a high-profile battle against lynching. Thirty years old and still unmarried at a time when most of her female contemporaries were raising children, she was subject to a new round of slanderous attacks on her personal life. Such attacks were nothing new and may well have grown less personally hurtful as she grew increasingly used to them. But Wells could not ignore them, since questions about her credibility threatened to compromise the effectiveness of her antilynching work. So Wells's first year in exile saw her struggling to establish both herself and her cause.

Her struggles were compounded by the fact that women lecturers were still a rarity in the 1890s. Indeed, as late as April 1892 Wells sat silent on the platform of a New York antilynching meeting while T. Thomas Fortune and other men described her experiences. However, the 1890s marked the beginning of a new "women's era," when "far less of the world was off limits to women than it had been fifty years earlier."[1] Across the color line, an assertive new generation of educated young women became increasingly active in reform movements, organized women's clubs, and supported women's suffrage. Among black women, Wells helped galvanize this change, breaking new ground as a female speaker in the fall of 1892, when her columns for *The New York Age* began to attract invitations to lecture. Wells had taken elocution lessons in Memphis and had spoken at National Press Association conferences well before 1892. Poised, attractive, and forceful, she proved to be a popular speaker, credited with having "greater power . . . to hold the attention of her audience" than any other woman of her race.[2]

Particularly captivating to those who attended Wells's lectures were her allusions to rape and sex in an era when public discussion of such matters was taboo. This was the late nineteenth century, the Victorian era, a time still known for the sexual reticence of its public discourse. So the boldness with which Wells engaged every aspect of the subject of lynching must have shocked her audiences. Her dissection of the sexual politics that lay behind lynching came at a time when the Comstock law of 1873 barred Americans from disseminating any kind of "obscene literature" by mail—up to and including information on contraception, as the birth control activist Margaret Sanger would find out in 1914.[3]

But Wells was intent on convincing her audiences that lynching was an obscenity, much like slavery: a form of racial violence that clouded both victim and crime in shame. Moreover, she also believed that lynching, like slavery, could be combated only with exposure and public protest. Inspired by the abolitionist movement's successful fight to end slavery, Wells called for "the Garrison, Douglass, Sumner, Whittier, and Phillips who shall rouse this nation to a demand that . . . mob rule shall be put down and equal and exact justice be accorded to every citizen."[4]

Not surprisingly, Wells's approach won her no friends in the South, where the abolitionist movement was still vilified and Wells's antilynching campaign soon became subject to endless derision. But her cause did capture the imagination of reform-minded men and women both in the United States and abroad, mobilizing an antilynching movement that would long outlive Wells herself—as would, alas, the phenomenon of lynching itself. Among her early allies was Frederick Douglass, one of the abolitionist heroes she hoped to emulate. In his seventies but still politically active and very influential, Douglass befriended Wells, hosting her on several visits to Washington and lending his name to the antilynching pamphlets she published. Moreover, he also helped her expand the scope of her antilynching campaign by commending her to British reformer Catherine Impey—who would arrange a speaking tour that would take Wells to Scotland and England.

Never popular among American whites, Wells's antilynching crusade would be most effective in Britain. There she spoke before audiences with a long history of antislavery activism, who would ultimately add influential support to her work. A refugee from racial violence in the New South and a Douglass protégée, Wells appealed to the national pride of British reformers when she asked them to condemn lynching with the same vigor with which they had once condemned slavery. A far-ranging response to events in Memphis, Wells's international antilynching campaign would have only mixed success its first year—although not for lack of effort on her part. Between the spring of 1892 and the spring of 1893, she had one of the busiest and most challenging years in her always busy life, and transformed herself from editor of a small Southern newspaper to the "most noted race woman of her day."[5]

Ida's rise to fame began in June 1893 with the publication of her seven-column story on the Memphis lynchings in *The New York Age*. Fortune's special edition of the *Age* featuring Wells's article received wide circulation, but drew a mixed response among black journalists, who provided Ida with an early harbinger of the often hostile scrutiny she would receive as her reputation grew. As an outspoken black female critic of white racial violence,

Wells threatened male leaders, both black and white. Accordingly, her first critics were black men—who were far more likely to read *The New York Age* than their white counterparts. "She seeks fame and gets notoriety," sniped C. H. Taylor of *The American Citizen* (Kansas City). An open opponent of lynching, Taylor did not disparage Wells's cause. Rather, as a fellow journalist, he seems to have felt eclipsed by her work.[6] He was not the only one. An editorial in *The Indianapolis Freeman* resorted to verse to poke fun at the attention lavished on Wells. "Crown her with flowers / Sprinkle her with perfume," declared an ungraceful but cutting little poem, ". . . Until you carry it ad nauseum." A later issue of the *Freeman* carried an apology that hardly improved on the poem. Although the editors denied implying "that Miss Wells is a fisher of compliments and praise from any source," they undercut their denial by noting that such behavior was all too common among journalists. "We can conceive of women," the editors noted coyly, "and of men too, by the score, bewhiskered, stentorian voiced barnacles of the press, who might cry their eyes out for the compliments that never came . . . but of this somewhat unfortunate young woman, we had thought no such thing."[7]

Potentially more damaging to Wells than any of these sarcastic remarks was a critique coming out of Memphis. It came from some of the black leaders who chose to remain in the troubled city, where racial tensions remained high. They proved willing to turn on Wells to appease white leaders. As a result, in the months that followed her departure in 1892, Wells was denounced by African American leaders who had far more reason to resent Memphis whites than they did Wells. In the wake of the Memphis lynchings, the city's white leaders remained unrepentant about the white-on-black violence involved and instead moved to punish local black men who had been jailed alongside Moss, McDowell, and Stewart for participating in the conflicts that preceded the lynching. During the summer of 1892, Memphis authorities indicted six black men who had supported the owners of the People's Grocery, sentencing them to prison and workhouse terms ranging from eleven months to fourteen years, even as the white men who lynched Moss, McDowell, and Stewart remained unidentified and unprosecuted.[8] Memphis blacks were infuriated by this injustice but too terrified to protest. Public censure from individuals such as Wells had only made Memphis whites more hostile, and further violence was a real possibility, especially since the courts had made it clear that Memphis blacks could not look to the city's courts for legal protection. Increasingly anxious to appease the city's white leaders, some of Memphis's remaining African American leaders even turned their anger on Wells in a vain attempt to restore racial harmony by attacking the city's most notorious exile.

Among them was the Congregationalist minister B. A. Imes, one of the conciliatory black leaders who rose to prominence in Memphis in the wake of Wells's departure. A former ally whose activism Wells had once admired, Imes turned on the *Free Speech* editor after she left, making her the subject of "an indignation meeting for all the colored people in the city." Organized on the heels of Wells's first antilynching article in *The New York Age*, the meeting ended with a resolution to denounce Wells in *The Appeal-Avalanche* (Memphis). The denunciation came in the form of a letter to the Memphis paper, written by Imes and two other black men, who expressed "a most positive disapproval of the course pursued by Miss Ida Wells" and observed that "virtue cannot be encouraged by polluting the minds of the innocent and the pure."[9] Although petty and mean-spirited, their attack on Wells illuminated the dangerous path she trod in speaking out against lynching. A young single woman, she could easily be associated with the immorality she sought to expose. Outside of Memphis, however, Wells's reputation was spared by the powerful allies who helped to defend her and promoted her cause. Among the first to do so were some of Manhattan's and Brooklyn's most accomplished and well-to-do African American women.

"The Best Womanhood of . . . Two Cities"

Long adept at navigating a man's world, Wells sustained her journalistic career in New York with the help of T. Thomas Fortune and Jerome B. Peterson. But her career as a public speaker was not launched by these male editors. Wells made her debut as an outspoken opponent of lynching with the support of a group of black New Yorkers far less inured to the hurly-burly of the public sphere than Fortune or Peterson. In particular, *New York Age* reporter Victoria Earle Matthews and Brooklyn educator Maritcha Lyons, two eminently respectable members of New York's black middle class, reached out to Wells. Appalled by her revelations in *The New York Age*, they decided that the women of New York and Brooklyn should "do something to show appreciation" of Wells's work and "protest the treatment" she had received.[10] Accordingly, they formed the Ida B. Wells Testimonial Reception Committee and began planning an event in her honor.

Although a newcomer to the city, Wells had managed to attract powerful allies whose endorsement would go far toward countering any and all attacks on her reputation. Maritcha Lyons, in particular, was a member of one of New York's most elite black families. The Lyonses traced their free black ancestry back to the eighteenth century, and proudly claimed a mixed-race ancestry that included Native American and English forebears. Although committed to racial uplift, elite black families such as the Lyonses tended to distance themselves from the mass of black New Yorkers—including slave-born Southern migrants such as Wells. The majority cloistered themselves among their social equals in Brooklyn's Fort Greene neighborhood, where they could confine their "social intercourse . . . to people one knows or knows about."[11] Still, the Lyons family's social status did not shelter them from racial discrimination or violence, which may help explain Maritcha's willingness to lend support to a young exile from Tennessee. More than a decade older than Wells, Lyons had nearly lost her life in the New York draft riots in 1863, when armed white rioters gutted her family's Manhattan home. The Lyonses were forced to flee to Providence, Rhode Island, where sixteen-year-old Maritcha was barred from entering public school until her mother successfully sued the state to gain her admission. Despite hostile classmates who refused to sit next to her, Maritcha excelled in school and went on to become an assistant principal in the Brooklyn public school system, but she never forgot that "I had to sue for a privilege which any but a colored girl would have had without asking."[12]

Following in her mother's footsteps, in 1892 Lyons swung into action on behalf of another "lonely, homesick girl"—to borrow Wells's description of herself at that time.[13] Working through church networks, Lyons, together with Matthews and other New York–area black women, raised money to support Wells's writing career. They also organized a lavish public event in her honor. More than two hundred black men and women from New York, Brooklyn, Boston, and Philadelphia gathered to pay homage to Wells in New York's Lyric Hall on October 5, 1892. In doing so they launched Wells on a career as a public speaker that would bring her international renown—and, in some quarters, new enemies.

If Wells's recollections are to be believed, she had no such future in mind when she mounted the speaker's platform to deliver her first "honest-to-goodness address."[14] Instead, facing the impressive gathering, she became terrified and tearful. She had always been something of an outsider to the Memphis black female elite, and had received more support from that city's black male leaders than its women. In New York, by contrast, she was embraced by "the best womanhood of . . . two cities"—Manhattan and Brooklyn. She found the experience both gratifying and intimidating. On the speaker's platform with her were elite New Yorkers such as Maritcha Lyons and Brooklyn's Susan M. McKinney, one of the nation's first black female physicians. Also present was Sarah Garnet. A teacher from a wealthy family, Garnet was the first black woman to reach the rank of principal in the New York City school system, and also well known as the widow of Henry Highland Garnet, one of the leading lights of the antebellum abolitionist movement that Wells revered. Moreover, similarly well-placed African American women from other states also lent their support to Wells as she spoke. Fellow journalist Gertrude Bustill Mossell, a member of black Philadelphia's high society, traveled to New York to honor Wells, as did finishing school graduate Josephine St. Pierre Ruffin, a writer and reformer from a long-established Boston family. Wells spoke with these guests of honor arrayed behind her on the platform. Ida had lectured before, but her nerves were understandable. Nothing in her previous experience had prepared her to speak before so august an assembly.[15] Moreover, her testimonial reception was unlike anything she and quite possibly all of the women assembled there had ever attended.

Lavishly funded and beautifully staged, the event bore the imprint of the black North's female elite, who had no previous record of organizing on behalf of black activists. They were, however, well versed in planning elegant social events. The Ida B. Wells Testimonial Reception Committee decorated Lyric Hall with flower arrangements that included an opulent floral "horn of plenty," and backlit the hall's stage with electric lights that spelled out "Iola."[16] Guests were met by ushers who wore white silk badges bearing the same name, and distributed a program printed on miniature copies of *Free Speech*. Moreover, the reception committee also honored Wells with gifts, presenting her with a gold brooch in the shape of a pen and five hundred dollars to help her start her own paper.

In addition to the gifts, the program featured speeches, resolutions, and music, but at the center of it was Wells herself. To counteract nervousness she planned to read from a prepared text, but was overcome by emotion as she did so. Always comfortable in battle, Wells was almost undone when she had to address a hall full of sympathetic female well-wishers. Recounting the hardships that led to her exile, she mourned "the scenes of struggle, . . . the friends who were scattered across the country." Overwhelmed by a "feeling of loneliness and homesickness for the days and friends that were gone," she spoke through tears at times. But she soldiered on even as her composure wavered, determined to make it through her story even after she had to signal for a handkerchief to dry her eyes and wipe her nose.[17]

The text of Wells's speech at the Lyric Hall does not survive, but her autobiography records that she went on to read the same paper "as the one I read at the first meeting in New York" at other public addresses in the ensuing months.[18] Accordingly, a published transcript of a speech that Wells delivered at Tremont Temple in Boston, in February 1893, can be used to illustrate some of the moments that might have brought Wells to tears. Her speech interspersed a hard-hitting account of the Memphis lynchings with wrenching personal testimony on the domestic sorrows that the lynchings left behind. Her last days in Memphis had been spent with newly widowed Betty Moss and her two young children, and Wells gave powerful voice to that family's bereavement. She recalled witnessing Betty rocking her sleeping infant son, Thomas Moss, Jr., in her arms, her "tears fall[ing] thick and fast . . . on his unconscious baby face" at the thought of "the sad fate of the father he will never see." Still more poignant was her account of how "the

Portrait of Ida, Betty Moss, and the Moss children

baby daughter of Tom Moss, too young to express how she misses her father, toddles to the wardrobe, seizes the legs of his letter-carrier uniform, hugs and kisses them with evident delight and stretches her little hands to be taken up into arms that will never more clasp his daughter's form."[19]

Wells had ample excuse for crying as she recounted events in Memphis for the first time, but she was "mortified" all the same. A woman who prided herself on her composure, she was not given to "public demonstrations" of emotion. Moreover, before her imposing Lyric Hall audience, she had wanted to be at her best to show her appreciation "of the splendid things those women had done." Instead she succumbed to tears—"the woman's weakness in public." Years later, Wells still had "a feeling of chagrin over that exhibition of weakness." Whatever her regrets, her tears could not have been more effective if she had planned them. Her tears, one prominent New Yorker who attended the event told her, "did more to convince cynical and selfish New Yorkers of the seriousness of lynching than anything else could have done."[20]

Moreover, they also marked a high point in Wells's status as an appealing female leader. For black women especially, as Wells's contemporary Matilda Evans would later observe, the "fear of woman unsexing herself was the bug bear" of the era during which Wells rose to fame.[21] Especially when it came to public appearances, middle-class African American women were silenced by ideals of womanhood that made it all but impossible for them to challenge racism and sexism without compromising their own claims to femininity. "Anger and femininity were antithetical" to the Victorian conception of a virtuous woman, making respectable public protest all but impossible. Indeed, advice writers cautioned that women should not even defend themselves from slander or false accusations. "Forever must virtue suffer from the widespread intimations of vice, and honor bow before imputations of shame," lest any display of negative emotion turn ladies into "fishwomen and hucksters." In New York's Lyric Hall, tears took the edge off Wells's angry testimony, eliding such concerns and making her into a womanly and sympathetic figure. Press reports of Wells's lectures even noted her tearfulness, emphasizing approvingly that this "victim" of Southern mob violence was "moved to grief" as she spoke.[22]

Wells's audiences were also moved. In the aftermath of their successful tribute to Wells, Maritcha Lyons and Victoria Earle Matthews decided not to disband the Wells Testimonial Reception Committee. Instead, it became the Women's Loyal Union, New York City's first African American women's club. Likewise, after attending the Wells testimonial, Josephine St. Pierre Ruffin went home to Boston and formed the New Era Club, the first such club in that city. Ruffin also organized similar clubs and speaking dates for Wells throughout New England, calling upon black women in New Haven, New Bedford, Providence, Newport, and other towns to host Wells and organize clubs of their own. In 1894, Ruffin went on to found *The Woman's Era*: a monthly newspaper published by the New Era Club, it was the first black women's newspaper.

In some respects, Wells was an unlikely inspiration for the black women's club movement. Not only did she lack the elite background and social connections possessed by Josephine St. Pierre Ruffin and many of the women who went on to play prominent roles in the movement, but Wells was also far more radical and outspoken than most club women. Not surprisingly, though she would go on to help organize a black women's club in Chicago in 1893, she never found an enduring place in that organization. A catalyst for the women's club movement, Wells could never become a long-term club member herself.

In taking a public stand on lynching and Jim Crow, however, Wells did provide an example of women's leadership that mobilized other African American women to organize on their own behalf. A new site of female activism, these African American women's clubs took shape in an era when disenfranchisement, lynching, and racial discrimination had called into question black men's capacities for race leadership. Early club women, such as Anna Julia Cooper, believed female leaders might well be an improvement on their black male counterparts, many of whom were tainted by the political corruption that marked 1890s politics. A black woman, Cooper noted in *A Voice from the South*, was "always sound and orthodox on questions affecting the well-being of her race. You do not find the colored woman selling her birthright for a mess of pottage."[23]

Yet as the 1890s began, Cooper and her Northern middle-class contemporaries had not found any path to black female political influence. White women had "myriads of church clubs, social clubs, culture clubs, pleasure clubs and charitable clubs," as Cooper noted; and black women likewise had a long history of volunteerism that included organizing mutual aid organizations, community schools, and cultural groups.[24] But in an era when many white women were forming clubs dedicated to pursuing political issues such as civic improvement and women's suffrage, black women were left out. Most white women's clubs did not admit black women as members, and those that did could not be expected to provide them with a platform for race leadership.

Indeed, while Cooper extolled black women's potential for leadership in *A Voice from the South*, she found the prospect of womanly self-assertion difficult to imagine. Feminine delicacy made her "purposely forebear to mention instances of personal injuries to colored women traveling in the less civilized sections of our country"—although she did go on to list such injuries as being "forcibly ejected from cars, thrown out of seats, their garments rudely torn, their person wantonly and cruelly injured."[25] Likewise, Wells's Memphis contemporary Mary Church Terrell, a prominent women's club leader, found such issues too "embarrassing and painful" to describe.[26] Cooper, Terrell, and other middle-class black women of their day often avoided speaking freely about the racial and sexual slights for fear of drawing attention to themselves at a time when "derogatory images and negative stereotypes of black women's sexuality" made black womanhood a fragile ideal. Instead, they adopted what historian Darlene Clark Hine has called "a culture of dissemblance" designed to shield "the truth of their inner life and selves from their oppressors."[27] This ladylike but unsatisfying pose left them looking to others for protection. Drawing upon traditional notions of gender hierarchy, Cooper called for black men "to be a father, a brother, a friend to every weak, struggling unshielded girl."[28]

Wells had a very different vision of female race leadership. Used to defending herself, she had come out of Memphis determined to continue doing so—and carrying a pistol in her purse. Moreover, she must have been somewhat bemused to attract such a groundswell of female support, since her previous challenges to white injustice had never done so. In Tennessee, black men rather than black women had been her major supporters when she sued to secure a seat in the ladies' car. And the limited support she had received from her community in her challenge to the Chesapeake, Ohio, and Southwestern Railroad had left her wondering whether the black elite was willing to support civil rights struggles such as her lawsuits.[29] But her antilynching lectures inspired a different response, leaving Wells still remembering the "kind hearts" of her New York supporters many years later.[30]

The difference, in part, reflected the fact that Northeastern black communities provided far more fertile ground for Wells's brand of activism than did those in Memphis, where black autonomy was more limited and white supremacy more powerful. But her change of scene does not fully explain the unprecedented organization and public activity that she inspired among her Northern peers. Indeed, even the popularity of her lectures does not account for why black female reformers rallied around antilynching. After all, lynching was only one of the many forms of racial violence that Southern whites inflicted on African Americans in the late nineteenth century, and not obviously a women's issue.

Usually a crime against men, lynching was ideologically linked to the indelicate subject of rape—a topic even more "embarrassing and painful" to middle-class blacks than the indignities that segregation imposed upon them. Indeed, even Wells herself had struggled with such fears prior to her exile. In Memphis in 1886, after publishing her first article on a lynching, she worried that "it may be unwise to express myself so strongly," and thereafter remained largely silent on the subject until the Memphis lynchings of 1892.[31] But by the time she moved to New York, Wells had developed a new understanding of lynching that allowed her to engage the subject without embarrassment or regret. A challenge to the rape myths used to justify lynching and silence its critics, her lectures recast lynching as a symbol of the gendered racial terror that was Jim Crow—opening up new rhetorical terrain for black women as a result.

Southern Horrors

Lynching, Wells insisted, was not about rape or even sex: it was about power. Her first pamphlet, *Southern Horrors* (1892), which reprinted her *New York Age* articles, illustrated the narrative strategy she would use to challenge conventional accounts of lynching. Printed with money that her New York supporters collected for her, it began by positioning Wells as a Christian witness to sin and inequity—much like the abolitionists she had always admired. A letter of support from fabled abolitionist leader Frederick Douglass added to Wells's bona fides, as did Douglass's endorsement of her work as an appeal "to the power of a merciful God for final deliverance." Wells published Douglass's letter immediately after her preface, and proceeded with a modesty in keeping with her sex. "It is with no pleasure I have dipped my hands in the corruption here exposed," she assured her readers. "Somebody must show that the Afro-American race is more sinned against than sinning, and it seems to have fallen to me to do so. The awful death-toll that Judge Lynch is calling every week is appalling, not only because of the lives it takes, the rank cruelty to its victims, but because of the prejudice it fosters and the stain it places against the good name of a weak race."[32]

In *Southern Horrors* Wells drew on the traditional moral and religious authority granted to women in nineteenth-century culture as license for her crusade against lynching, which also defended the good name of both black men and women. She countered the attacks on black sexuality often invoked in defense of lynching with questions about the sexual morality of whites, while also using her skills as a journalist to expose the logic of white mob violence. Wells recognized that lynchings were justified by the stories that lynch mobs told about their victims—stories which inevitably sanc-

tioned their deaths. But, as *Southern Horrors* showed, these stories could be
turned around to tell tales on the lynchers. A sweeping exposé of Southern

SOUTHERN HORRORS.

LYNCH LAW

IN ALL

ITS PHASES

Miss IDA B. WELLS,

Price, - - - Fifteen Cents.

THE NEW YORK AGE PRINT,

1892.

Southern Horrors (1892) was Ida B. Wells's first published pamphlet.

sexual politics, the pamphlet documented that white men often used the rape myth to justify killing black men at will and routinely went unpunished for sexual assaults on African American women. It also revealed the shadowy presence of the often licentious Southern white women who hid behind the fury of the mob.

Written in the "simple, plain, and natural" style long cultivated by Wells, *Southern Horrors* supported her stories with "names, dates and facts" designed to attest to their veracity. An early muckraking journalist, Wells had used investigation and eyewitness testimony to inform her early discussions of lynching in *Free Speech*. As a result, she had figures to show that fully two-thirds of the lynch mob's victims had not even been charged with rape, but her argument did not dwell on statistics. Instead, Wells attacked the rape myth, which, she believed, served as the justification for all lynchings—"a concession of the right to lynch a man for a certain crime . . . concedes the right to lynch any person for any crime."[33]

Her work sought to counter images of African Americans as "a race of rapists, who were especially mad after white women" by exposing an underworld of black-white interactions that were criminal only under the South's Jim Crow statutes.[34] Whereas accounts of lynchings by Wells's white contemporaries often featured "graphic descriptions of the murders designed to restage the murders as much as possible," *Southern Horrors* focused on the clandestine interracial relationships between white women and black men that formed the backdrop to many lynchings inspired by rape allegations.[35] Wells's approach was by far more daring. A taboo subject, such relationships were usually ignored by the press even when they ended in mob violence. As a result, the main cause of many lynchings remained shrouded in secrecy. White men, Wells broke this silence to argue, were determined to preserve their side of the color line—by any means necessary.

Indeed, they policed the actions of both white women and black men, since "many white women would marry colored men if such an act would not at once place them beyond the pale of society and within the clutches of the law." Indeed, one such woman, Sarah Clark of Memphis, who "loved . . . and lived openly" with a black man, was "indicted last spring for miscegenation," and went to jail for her crime even though "she swore in court that she was *not* a white woman." Lower-class and unmarried to boot, Clark was not free to choose a black partner or change her racial identity. " 'The leading citizens' of Memphis are defending the honor of *all* white women, *demimonde* included."[36]

Meanwhile, many white women did not share Sarah Clark's willingness to face the consequences of miscegenation, and accused their black lovers of sexual assault rather than face exposure themselves—with tragic results. Wells illustrated this point by citing the testimony of Mrs. J. S. Underwood, the wife of a minister, whose rape accusation led to the imprisonment of her black lover William Offett in 1888. She later recanted, explaining to *The Cleveland Gazette*, "I met Offett at the Post Office. He had a strange fascination for me, and I invited him to call on me." An affair ensued, which Wells also chronicled, quoting Mrs. Underwood's graphic testimony in detail. Offett had accepted Underwood's invitation to call, arriving at her door carrying "chestnuts and candy for the children. By this means, we got them to leave the room. Then I sat on his lap. He made a proposal to me and I readily consented . . . He visited me several times after that and each time I was indiscreet. I did not care after the first time. In fact, I could not have resisted, and had no desire to resist." Only the fear of exposure had caused Underwood to cry rape. A neighbor had witnessed Offett's visits; she also feared that she "might give birth to a Negro baby." With these worries on her mind, she told her husband a "deliberate lie," which sent her lover off to prison for four years.[37] Offett was lucky to be released when the remorse-stricken Mrs. Underwood finally came clean in 1892. The pious Mr. Underwood, who promptly divorced his wife, was gracious enough to secure the innocent man's release.

But many black men who associated with white women were far less fortunate, especially in the South. In 1891, Wells noted, a black boy had been lynched in Tuscumbia, Alabama, for assaulting a white girl in the woods, even though the couple met regularly in those woods. Three black men in South Carolina *"disappeared,"* shortly after a white woman gave birth to what was obviously a biracial child and named three possible fathers.

And in Nashville a black man named Eph. Grizzard was charged with rape for daring to visit a white woman. Arrested, he was taken from jail and "dragged through the streets in broad daylight." With the state's governor, police, and militia all standing by, Grizzard was then put to death. "Knives [were] plunged into him at every step, and with every fiendish cruelty a frenzied mob could devise, he was at last swung out on a bridge with hands cut to pieces as he tried to climb the stanchions."[38]

Similar violence, Wells pointed out, was never used to protect women on the other side of the color line. Indeed, on the very day Grizzard was dragged from his Nashville cell to meet his death, a white man sat in the "same jail for raping eight-year old Maggie Reese, an Afro-American girl. He was not harmed." Likewise, a man in Oklahoma Territory who had "inflicted such upon another Afro-American child that she died," also went unpunished. Wells consistently interspersed her discussion of lynching with brief accounts of white men who raped African American females—many of them prepubescent. And she closed *Southern Horrors* with a brief reference to an equally brutal crime against "poor little thirteen year old Mildrey Brown." Suspected, on circumstantial evidence alone, of poisoning an infant, Brown was "legally (?) hung" in Columbia, South Carolina.[39]

From *Southern Horrors* onward, Wells's work would memorialize black female victims of rape, sexual assault, and lynching. Her discussions of these women usually provided few specifics other than their age, shielding the painful details of the sexual violation they had suffered from public scrutiny. But despite her Victorian discretion, Wells's accounts recovered and publicized these women's sufferings "at the hands of a violent white majority" at a time when assaults on black females went largely ignored.[40]

Moreover, Wells's stories about sexual violence against black women and girls played a crucial role in her analysis of lynching: they underscored that lynching had very little to do with the crime of rape. As she pointed out, the way white Southern men treated black women made it clear that they were "not so desirous of punishing rapists as they pretend. The utterances of leading white men show that with them it is not the crime but the *class*." The region's white leaders were "apologist[s] for the lynchers of the rapists of white women only." "Governor Tillman of South Carolina . . . declared he would lead a mob to lynch the Negro who raped a white woman. So say the pulpits, officials and newspapers of the South. But when the victim is a colored woman it is different . . . nobody is lynched and no notice is taken."[41]

This double standard also proved that the lynch mobs that assaulted black men were not actually policing the crime of rape. Rather, they protected white supremacy and guarded the color line by reserving white women for white men. White men's sexual assaults against black women were neither policed nor punished, but love affairs between white women and black men, if discovered, often resulted in a lynching. "White men lynch the offending Afro-American, not because he is a despoiler of virtue," Wells concluded, "but because he succumbs to the smiles of white women."[42] A powerful indictment of lynching as a crime against black men, Wells's critique of mob violence exposed the racial and sexual double standards that allowed white men to victimize black women with impunity. Moreover, as Patricia Schechter observes, Wells's analysis of lynching "connected the 'private crime' of rape to the 'public' crime of lynching," and in doing so "remapped the authority of the black woman intellectual." Her work demonstrated that neither crime could be limited to the public and private spheres that were thought to divide the concerns of men and women. Instead, "lynching and rape formed a web of racist sexual politics aimed at subjugating Southern blacks."[43]

A radical revision of conventional wisdom, this analysis of lynching made antilynching a women's issue, while also winning her influential allies such as Frederick Douglass. Recently retired from a post as U.S. minister and consul to Haiti, the fiery former abolitionist contacted Wells after reading her work in The New York Age. According to Wells, her articles in the Age had come as a revelation to the legendary "Sage of Anacostia." Until he read them, he told Wells, "he had been troubled by the increasing number of lynchings, and had begun to believe it true that there was an increasing lasciviousness on the part of the Negroes."[44] Wells's exact impact on Douglass is difficult to verify, since he never voiced this belief elsewhere. But he certainly attended one or more of Ida's 1892 lectures, and the high praise he had for them can be seen in a letter she wrote to him in October of that year. As she prepared to reprint her antilynching articles in *Southern Horrors*, Wells asked Douglass to help promote her pamphlet by putting "in writing

"THE SAGE OF ANACOSTIA."

Portrait of Frederick Douglass, c. 1890. A resident of the Washington, D.C., neighborhood of Anacostia, where he settled in 1877, Douglass was often known in his old age as the "Sage of Anacostia."

the encomiums you were pleased to lavish on my article on Lynch Law in the June 25 issue of the *Age*."[45] Douglass did not hesitate to put his praise in writing, supplying a letter that described Wells's discussion of lynching as having "no word equal to it in convincing power."[46]

Convinced himself, Douglass seems to have taken a new interest in lynching after reading Wells's work. Douglass's own first extended discussion of lynching, which he described as "feeble" in comparison to her work, appeared shortly after Wells first began writing for the *Age*.[47] Despite his admiration for her work, however, Douglass never fully embraced Wells's gendered analysis of racial violence. His discussions of lynching left the question of white violence against black women aside in favor of a qualified defense of black men that did not fully link lynching and Jim Crow. Some black men might "be guilty of the peculiar crime so often imputed to [them]," Douglass conceded. But the crime of rape was "easily imputed" and "difficult to disprove," and also the offense that "the Negro is least likely to commit." The glory days of emancipation had proved that black men were not rapists. Even during the Civil War, when "the wives, daughters, the mothers and the sisters of the rebels" were left alone on the plantation, "no instance can be cited of an outrage committed by the Negro on the person of a white woman." If black men had begun to attack white women, Douglass concluded, "the crime is a new one for the Negro, so new that a doubt may be reasonably maintained that he has learned it to any such extent as his accusers would believe."[48]

Wells touches on a similar point in *Southern Horrors*, but much more briefly. As she seems to have realized, defenses of black men that stressed the fealty of the slaves during the Civil War came dangerously close to embracing white Southern nostalgia for the "old-time darkies." Moreover, because they focused on the past rather than the present, they posed little challenge to 1890s discussions of rape as the "new Negro crime." Accordingly, in *Southern Horrors* Wells avoided such pitfalls—and Douglass's Civil War point of reference. Instead, she engaged lynching in the Jim Crow context in which it took place, challenging the rape myth directly while also making sense of the context in which it took shape.

Douglass's admiration and support for Wells suggests that he agreed with her analysis of lynching, even if he chose not to follow her lead. One has to suspect that Douglass's own personal life left him in a compromised position when it came to analyzing the interracial sexual liaisons between black men and white women. To the dismay of many Americans on both sides of the color line, black America's elder statesman had married his white secretary Helen Pitts in 1884, a few years after the death of his first wife, Ana Douglass. The marriage pleased no one but the bride and groom. Half white himself, Douglass jokingly maintained that it proved that he was racially "impartial": "My first wife was the color of my mother and the second, the color of my father." Other African Americans, however, were generally unhappy with his choice. Indeed, according to Douglass, his wife was treated with resentment by virtually all of his black women friends, with the exception of Wells and Sarah Moore Grimke, the wife of Francis Grimke, the radical Presbyterian minister who married the couple.[49]

Wells's acceptance of Helen Pitts helped solidify her relationship with Douglass. As befitted the politics that she outlined in *Southern Horrors*, Wells did not oppose interracial relationships per se, deploring only the coercive, dangerous, and illegal interactions between men and women fostered by Jim Crow antimiscegenation laws. The Douglasses' union, of course, posed no such issues. They "lived together in the holy bonds of matrimony rather than the illicit relationship that was the cause of so many lynchings." Wells admitted that she would nonetheless have preferred it if "Mr. Douglass had chosen one of the beautiful, charming colored women of my race for his second wife." But, following the dictates of her modest rural upbringing, Wells treated Douglass's wife with "courtesy and deference"—or "ordinary good manners"—and soon came to admire and respect Helen Pitts Douglass.[50] As a result of her friendship with both Douglasses, Wells became a regular guest at their Washington home, deepening her bond with her abolitionist hero.

Always good at attracting father figures, Wells relied on Douglass for mentorship and advice right through to his death in 1895. Moreover, starting in the fall of 1892, the two began collaborating on a pamphlet to protest the representation of the Negro at the World's Columbian Exposition in Chicago. Originally scheduled to open in October 1892, the fair celebrated the four hundredth anniversary of Christopher Columbus's discovery of the New World. The precursors of modern-day "expos," nineteenth-century expositions and world's fairs boosted the economic and political achievements of the cities and countries in which they took place with elaborate displays of industrial, scientific, and artistic accomplishments. In the works for more than a decade, the Columbian Exposition was the second world's fair hosted in the United States. Its promoters hoped to build on the popular success of the 1876 Centennial Exposition in Philadelphia, which had drawn more than ten million people.

African American representation and participation in Chicago, however, was an open question. The 1876 centennial had neglected and demeaned African Americans. Barred from any form of participation, Philadelphia's black population was not even eligible for employment on construction crews that built the fairground. The centennial's only representation of African Americans was in a concession variously known as "The South" or "The Southern Restaurant." The brainchild of a white businessman from Atlanta, it featured banjo-playing "old-time plantation 'darkies'" singing odes to "Ole Virginny." Meanwhile the post-emancipation Negro was represented by nothing more than a bronze statue titled *The Freed Slave*. Designed by a white artist, it did not necessarily display freedom as a good thing. According to the novelist William Dean Howells, at least, the statue portrayed "a most offensively Frenchy Negro, who had broken his chain, and spreading both his arms and legs abroad is rioting in declamation of something (I should say) from Victor Hugo; one longs to clap him back into hopeless bondage."[51] Wells was too young for the centennial, but Douglass must have remembered it well. Although not asked to address the crowd during the opening ceremonies, he had been invited to attend and offered a seat in the stands with other dignitaries. But when the day came, he was refused admittance by the Philadelphia police. He remained outside the centennial's grounds until escorted in by Senator Roscoe Conkling of New York.

Accordingly, Douglass was distressed to note that as late as October 1892, when Wells visited him while lecturing in Washington, the Columbian Exposition in Chicago showed little promise of according better treatment to black Americans. Once again, African Americans had been excluded from the event's exhibits, planning, and construction work, and would be required to attend on a special "Colored People's Day." Douglass had been offered a role in the proceedings, but not as a representative of his own people or country. Instead, Haitian officials had invited the former U.S. minister and consul to their country to preside over the Haitian pavilion. Douglass welcomed the invitation, both on its own merits and because he viewed the Columbian Exposition as an international stage on which to air African American grievances. And after attending Wells's lecture, Douglass began to envision a Chicago protest featuring the "Southern horrors" described by Wells. He proposed that they work together to produce a pamphlet offering "an exposition, by paintings, drawing and written accounts of lynchings, hangings, burnings at the stake, whippings, and all southern atrocities" for distribution to visitors to the Columbian Exposition.[52] Wells readily agreed, and the two had begun work on the pamphlet when Wells got sidetracked: in the spring of 1893 a series of events moved her antilynching campaign abroad.

In early 1893, before Wells and Douglass even began to work on the pamphlet, a particularly brutal lynching in Paris, Texas, made international news, and soon had Wells taking her antilynching campaign abroad. A sleepy east Texas community of less than nine thousand, Paris hosted a crowd that exceeded its own population on February 1, 1893, when its residents lynched a black man named Henry Smith, suspected of assaulting a four-year-old white girl. Apprehended by authorities in Arkansas, Smith had tried to escape the vengeance that the townspeople had planned for him, but it only made matters worse. Once captured, he was sent back to Paris for a lynching that was essentially advertised en route. The train carrying Smith "gathered strength from various towns," as "people crowded upon platforms and tops of coaches anxious to see the lynching and the negro who was soon to be delivered to the infuriated mob." By the time Smith reached Paris, ten thousand spectators from as far away as Arkansas had gathered to watch him be tortured and executed. They were not disappointed. With the enthusiastic support of the crowd, Smith's executioners bound him on a scaffold built to stage his death and tortured him with "red-hot irons" for fifty minutes, burning out his eyes and throat and searing off his skin from limb to limb.[53] He died, as one news account noted, "of slow torture in the midst of smoke from his own burning flesh."[54] And when his body finally stopped moving, the crowd set Smith's scaffold on fire and watched his body burn before fighting "over the hot ashes for bones, buttons and teeth for souvenirs."[55]

In Washington when the story of the Texas lynching broke, Wells was horrified and deeply disturbed. She learned of the execution from dispatches that described the violence against Smith in detail, and without editorial disapproval. "Another Negro Burned," reported *The New York Times*, presenting a graphic account of the "awful vengeance of a Paris (Texas) mob." *The Washington Post* emphasized the dead man's alleged crime with a headline proclaiming: "His Victim a Mere Babe." The *Post* followed up with an editorial published a few days later contending that lynching was the appropriate punishment for the crime Smith was alleged to have committed—an allegation the *Post* found "easy to believe."[56] Wells, of course, disagreed. Convinced that African Americans should begin to "investigate every lynching" and thus "have the facts to use in an appeal to public opinion," she hired the prestigious Pinkerton Detective Agency to investigate the events behind Smith's death, instructing the agency to use a man from their Chicago office who could be hoped to investigate the crime without bias.[57] The Pinkerton instead sent out a man from their Kansas office. He did not even investigate the crime, submitting a packet of press clippings on the lynching from Texas papers and a picture of four-year-old Myrtle Vance, Smith's alleged victim.

Stymied by a lack of information, Wells's attempt to mobilize public opinion against lynching hit a low point. In Washington, D.C., to lecture on "Lynchings in the South" in the city's Metropolitan Church, she had been trying for months without success to get her message across to white audiences. Her lectures had not attracted white audiences or white press coverage outside of Boston, a liberal-minded city with a proud abolitionist tradition. And her efforts to get a hearing from the nation's white leaders had proved equally fruitless. Attempts to get her an audience with the Senate Judiciary Committee had failed, as had Frederick Douglass's invitation, delivered in person, to President Benjamin Harrison to attend Wells's Washington lecture—"the President regretted his inability to be present."[58]

Moreover, the murder in Paris, Texas, marked the advent of an even more frightening form of lynching. According to historian Grace Hale, it was "the founding event in the history of spectacle lynching"—a term that Hale coins to describe the turn-of-the-century lynchings that attracted thousands of primarily Southern white viewers.[59] The Paris lynching dramatized just how comfortable Americans were with vigilante justice against African Americans. Women and children had attended the grisly event. A friend of Wells's traveling through Texas not long after Smith's death was shocked to hear it remembered by a white woman and her eight-year-old daughter. "I saw them burn the nigger, didn't I Mamma," proclaimed the little girl, a fact her "complacent mother" acknowledged "as matter of factly as if she had said she saw them burn a pile of trash."[60]

Wells could not have known in the winter of 1893 that the gruesome public burning of Smith was an early portent of many spectacle lynchings. Instead, the unprecedented mass brutality that took place in Texas must have made Wells question the impact of her antilynching campaign. Her appeal to "public opinion" could not transcend its limited audience of primarily Northern blacks, while white Americans seemed more entertained than appalled by Smith's brutal murder.

British public responses were less sanguine, however. *The Times* (London) described Smith's lynching as "the most revolting execution of the age and a disgrace to the State [of Texas]."[61] And, fortunately for Wells, the events in Texas caught the attention of two energetic British reformers. One of them was Catherine Impey, a British Quaker who was the founder and editor of an anti-imperialist journal called *Anti-Caste* (1888–95). A resident of Street, Somerset, a village in the southwest of England that was

British reformer Catherine Impey, on the right, with her sister Nellie

one of the nation's Quaker strongholds, Impey hailed from an antislavery family. Born in 1847, she was raised by abolitionist parents who boycotted slave-grown cotton and sugar and had hosted the slave fugitive William Wells Brown when he lectured in England. Still committed to racial justice long after emancipation had settled the question for many of her countrymen, Catherine honored her family's activist tradition by founding *Anti-Caste*. Unlike most English observers, Impey had followed America's increasingly violent post–Civil War race relations and was well aware of lynching as a distinctive American practice even before Smith's grisly death.

The fall before the Texas lynching, Impey had visited the United States, also investigating "the color question" for her magazine. Among the friends Impey visited on her trip were Helen and Frederick Douglass, who probably introduced her to Wells's work. After staying with the Douglasses in September 1892, Impey went on to attend two of Wells's lectures. She was on hand when Ida introduced an antilynching resolution at the National Press Association meeting in September 1892, and later in the fall Impey made a point of attending Wells's lecture at the November convocation of the A.M.E. Church in Philadelphia. There the British woman introduced herself to Wells and arranged to interview her for *Anti-Caste*. Impey was anxious to give Wells's "lynching stories" greater exposure. Appalled by the "indifference" to lynching she found among American whites, she hoped that the British public would be more willing to censure an "evil . . . so glaring, so terrible."[62]

Not surprisingly then, when the lynching of Henry Smith made international news, Impey immediately thought of Wells. At that time, Impey was visiting with Scottish novelist Isabelle Fyvie Mayo, who wrote under the pseudonym Edward Garrett. Widowed, and slightly older than Impey, Mayo had sympathized with the abolitionist movement as a child, had grown up taking an interest in race relations, and had boarded South Asian students in her Aberdeen home. When news of the Texas lynching reached Scotland, a shocked Mayo asked Impey "why the United States of America was burning human beings alive in the nineteenth-century as the red Indians were said to have done three hundred years before?"[63] Impey could not explain it, but suggested that her new acquaintance Ida B. Wells would be able to do so, at which point Impey and Mayo decided to invite Wells to bring her antilynching message to Britain.

Impey also suggested that they recruit her friend Albion Tourgée as a "follow-up lecturer who could supplement Wells' testimony with that of a 'white American champion of the cause.' " A judge in North Carolina during Reconstruction and counsel for the plaintiff in *Plessy v. Ferguson*, the Ohio-born Tourgée was one of his era's most outspoken white critics of segregation and black disenfranchisement. The author of several popular novels about Reconstruction, during the 1880s and 1890s Tourgée also wrote a regular column for Chicago's leading Republican newspaper, the *Daily Inter Ocean*. Eminent, educated, and fiercely opposed to lynching, Tourgée would have provided excellent support for Wells's crusade, but proved unwilling to travel to England. Perennially strapped for cash, Tourgée sent his regrets, enclosing a grisly postcard of a lynching sent to him by a member of the mob. Wells and Impey would later use it to illustrate their cause.[64]

Wells, by contrast, accepted with alacrity—despite her own uncertain finances. Visiting with Frederick Douglass and his wife when she received Impey's invitation, she was encouraged by Douglass, who told her to go. Moreover, as Wells would later recall, the invitation came as "an open door in a wall." More isolated than Tourgée, whose increasingly unpopular views could at least still command an audience, Wells had not been able to "reach the white people of the country, who alone could mold public sentiment."[65] Impey's invitation offered Wells access to a potentially influential British audience, giving her a chance to replicate the successful transatlantic protest strategies pursued by black abolitionists such as William Wells Brown and Douglass himself.

Moreover, at the same time, Impey's invitation provided Wells with an escape from the only whites whose attention her public lectures managed to secure: her enemies in Memphis. On Wells's mind as she contemplated her British trip was a vicious attack on her published in the December 15, 1892, *Memphis Commercial*. The *Memphis Commercial*, which had evidently been following her lecture tour, described her speaking in Boston before an audience of "thin-legged scholars" and "glass-eyed females." The paper's account of Wells's personal history was even more unflattering. Denouncing her as a "black harlot," *The Memphis Commercial* claimed that her story of exile was false. Wells had not even written the infamous editorial concerning the Curve lynchings; she was merely the "mistress of the scoundrel" who had—presumably, her former business partner Fleming. A floozy peddling the story for her own gain, Wells now toured the East Coast in search of a white husband.[66]

Although *The Memphis Commercial*'s freewheeling attack sounds almost comical today, it posed a serious and demoralizing threat to Wells's reputation. As an unmarried thirty-year-old woman far from home, she was more vulnerable than ever to sexual slander, especially when it came from a hometown source. Fortunately, Wells did not have to face the slander alone. Black women in Boston rallied to support her, founding a local branch of the National Women's Colored League as a platform for their defense of Wells. Electing the energetic Josephine St. Pierre Ruffin as president, they issued a unanimous resolution condemning "the foulest aspersions of one of the daily papers of Memphis" and affirming their "confidence in Miss Wells' purity of purpose and character."[67] Likewise, the black press also came to Wells's defense, lambasting *The Memphis Commercial* for "wantonly and ruthlessly slandering the good name of Miss Ida B. Wells." The white paper's attacks only strengthened Wells's case, the *Topeka Weekly Call* suggested, providing "evidence that the boasted Southern chivalry was a thing of the past."[68]

Not content with these rebuttals, Wells investigated taking legal action against *The Memphis Commercial*. The editors of the Memphis paper had, after all, questioned not only her personal morality but also her professional integrity. Accordingly, Wells fired off a letter to the best-known jurist she knew, Albion Tourgée.

Wells asked Tourgée for a "clear, impartial opinion" on the wisdom of suing *The Memphis Commercial*. She would also need to find legal counsel should the case go forward, she explained. Memphis had only two black lawyers: Thomas J. Cassells, who still resented Wells for replacing him with a more energetic white lawyer in her lawsuit against the railroad; and her former friend Josiah Settle, who had become "the enemy of the *Free Speech*" after one of Wells's articles had criticized a friend of his. Both men "were sycophants," Wells informed Tourgée, with characteristic frankness. They "did not half defend their clients and the *Free Speech* . . . I chided them for it . . . with more zeal than discretion."[69] Already embroiled in the legal case that would lead to *Plessy*, Tourgée told Wells that he "could not afford to do any more gratuitous legal work himself." But he also offered to pass her case along to a colleague, the Chicago lawyer Ferdinand L. Barnett, who had agreed to represent Wells without remuneration.

Although raised largely in Chicago, where his family resettled in 1869, Barnett originally hailed from Tennessee and proved willing to take the case contemplated by a woman from his home state. Trained at the Chicago College of Law—which later became the Northwestern University Law School—Barnett may have been sympathetic to his new client because they shared similar professional histories as well as regional origins. Like Wells, he had been a teacher at one point, and a newspaper editor as well. Indeed, the energetic and politically minded Barnett had founded Chicago's first African American newspaper, the *Conservator*, in 1878—the same year he began his law practice. A passionate "race man," Barnett established the *Conservator* to promote "the welfare of the Negro group"—a statement which also reflected the *Conservator's* status as the first newspaper to capitalize the "n" in the word "Negro."[70] Moreover, he probably also identified with his new client's political views. Like Wells, Barnett had used his paper to attack mob violence against black men and lambaste black politicians who put their own interests over those of their people. Writing in the 1880s, Barnett sounded very much like Ida herself when he bemoaned the lynching of a man charged with an "attempt at outrage" (rape). It was "an attempt, mind you," he noted. "This is a comprehensive term in the south. It embraces a wink by a colored man at a white girl half a mile off. Such a crime is worthy of lynching, but a beastly attack on a colored girl by a white man is only a wayward indiscretion."[71]

Still, Barnett took the precaution of investigating his new client before moving forward with her suit, telling Tourgée he wanted to be sure that there was no "indiscretion" in her past to undermine her potential case. After several inquiries with his Tennessee contacts, Barnett confirmed Wells's good character "with many people from Memphis" and emerged "confident that Wells would be able to prove her case."[72] In the end, however, Barnett and Wells decided not to pursue the suit, fearing it might endanger Wells's antilynching work. Lawyerly in his approach to her case, Barnett was also attentive to Wells's larger political goals—as would also be the case in the closer relationship between Wells and Barnett that would blossom once they finally met. But in the spring of 1893, their rapport was still purely professional. All of Ida's energies were now devoted to moving her antilynching campaign to Britain.

Anti-Caste and Antilynching

Accordingly, April 5, 1893, found Wells aboard the *Teutonic*, a Liverpool-bound steamship. "First voyage across the ocean," she noted in a little travel diary provided by the steamship. "Day is fine and trip so far enjoyable." The journey, however, went rapidly downhill. Wells shared a cabin with Dr. Georgia E. L. Patton, a Meharry Medical School graduate whose final destination was a missionary post in Liberia. Wells had been happy to room with a doctor who could supply medical attention should she take ill on the voyage. But by day three she was reporting: "Seasick. So is Dr. Georgia E. L. Patton. We . . . lie in the two lower berths looking at each other. Ugh." After six more days of "indigestion," the ship finally reached Liverpool, where Wells saw her shipmate off on the final leg of her journey to Africa before traveling to Somerset to recuperate with Catherine Impey.[73]

Though a stranger in a strange land, if Wells was ill at ease in her new environment she left no record of it. Instead, she told a reporter for *The Sun* (London) that being in Britain was like "being born again in a new condition. Everywhere I went I was received in perfect equality with ladies who did so much for me and my cause." Prominent among them was her host Catherine Impey, who shared Wells's activist sensibility.[74] Devoted to temperance—a cause that Wells supported but did not spend much time on—Impey was a "life abstainer" and had been "the leading spirit of the British Women's Temperance Association" until the late 1880s.[75] After that, issues of race had compelled her to withdraw from both the BWTA and its parent organization the British Good Templar Order. In particular, Impey was appalled when the latter chose to reunite with the racially segregated United States Independent Order of Good Templars—the two organizations having previously split in a dispute over the presence of racially exclusive temperance organizations in the United States. The descendant of Quaker abolitionists, Impey had dedicated herself at an early age to working to "remove oppression among the darker races of the world" and was unwilling to be a member of an organization that had segregated American affiliates.[76] So after trying and failing to block the reunification, Impey withdrew. She went on to organize a new temperance organization open to all, and in 1888 she also launched her anti-imperialist monthly, *Anti-Caste*.

A veteran reformer, by 1888 Impey had visited the United States three times. During her travels there, she had developed personal ties to a network of sympathetic American writers and leaders that included many of Wells's friends and allies. When Wells first arrived in Street, the two women must have spent some time just catching up on the health and welfare of common acquaintances such as T. Thomas Fortune, Albion Tourgée, Fanny Jackson Coppin, Frances Harper, and of course Helen and Frederick Douglass. Never married, and affluent enough to pursue her "social reform work" full time, Impey had chosen "a life of independence" and political activism over any domestic alternative—choices that may have provided her with another connection with Wells.

Moreover, Wells must have been gratified to learn that even before her arrival, Impey had already begun to make herself known as a fearless opponent of lynching. Before the 1890s, lynching, which was never practiced in Britain, was known there as a form of " 'frontier justice' committed by isolated communities that lacked access to an effective legal system." As the historian Sarah L. Silkey notes, "British authors related their encounters with lynch mobs as colorful adventure stories about rural American folkways."[77] Even the 1891 lynching of eleven Sicilians in New Orleans, which received widespread coverage in the European press, did not clarify matters. A mob massacre of a group of alleged Mafiosi on trial for murdering the New Orleans police chief, it received attention largely for the diplomatic crisis it provoked between the United States and Italy.[78]

By contrast, Impey's *Anti-Caste* drew attention to racially motivated lynchings as early as the late 1880s. Intent on exposing the evils of racism,

Impey filled her paper with information drawn from a wide variety of international as well as national sources. *Anti-Caste* chronicled lynchings such as the murder of eight black men who were tied to a tree and shot in Barnwell, South Carolina, in 1889.[79] The Barnwell massacre was a naked display of white power designed to suppress black self-assertion in a still "moderately Republican" part of the state. Two of the victims were accused of killing their landlord, and six were charged with the murder of the son of the plantation owner for whom they worked.[80] The Barnwell lynchers were never brought to trial, reported a horrified "Negro Professor at a Southern University" in a letter that Impey published in *Anti-Caste*. "People read of the South and think that they know all about it, but they know nothing of the grievances we have to endure."[81]

Impey committed herself to publicizing the evils of lynching in *Anti-Caste*. Shortly before Wells's visit, she hit upon a dramatic way of doing so. In January 1893, she shocked *Anti-Caste*'s readership by opening the journal with a photograph of a lynching that took place near Clanton, Alabama. A reproduction of the postcard that Albion Tourgée had supplied, it featured a dead black youth hanging from a tree surrounded by a jubilant white mob whose members included a number of small children. Horrifying on its own, the appalling image was all the more shocking as a grisly souvenir manufactured to commemorate the mob violence that had just taken place. Moreover, Impey also reproduced the chilling inscription one of the lynchers had written on the back: "This S-O-B was hung at Clanton, Ala. Friday Aug 21st, '91 for murdering a little [white] boy in cold blood for 35¢ in cash."[82] Impey's use of the image on the postcard dramatized the brutality of lynching to powerful effect. It contrasted the "shameless satisfaction on the faces of the men" in the photograph with the "innocent wonder of those of the children," a spectacle that Impey's caption explained by noting, "The white men are teaching the children how an accused negro ought to be treated,—no trial—no defence."[83] On reading *Anti-Caste* when she got to Britain, Wells was evidently impressed by the result; she went on to include the same photograph and inscription in two of her own publications, *The Reason Why* (1894) and *A Red Record* (1895).

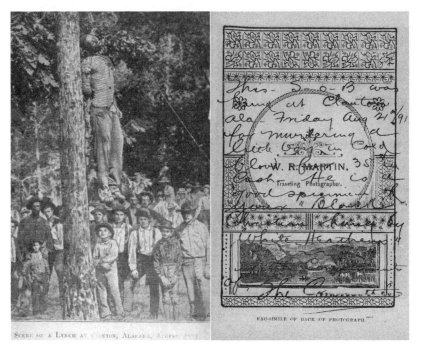

FAC-SIMILE OF BACK OF PHOTOGRAPH.

SCENE OF A LYNCH AT CLANTON, ALABAMA, AUGUST 1891.

Postcard of lynching at Clanton, Alabama, August 1891. On the right is the back of the card, complete with its prolynching message.

A like-minded colleague, Impey also proved an excellent host, whose arrangements helped make Wells well known in Britain. Impey's collaborator Isabelle Mayo was equally supportive and had secured several lecture dates for Wells in Scotland. More affluent and better known than Impey, Mayo would go on to become a member of the Woman's Political and Social Union—a suffragist organization—having already made her name as a writer. Serialized in the religious press, the books she wrote under her pseudonym, Edward Garrett, stressed the womanly ideals of "morality and self-sacrifice," and usually featured, as one reviewer put it, "good, kind, wise women, who seem to be sent into the world to put things straight and lift everyone to a higher plane of existence."[84]

Described by her young American visitor as an "asylum for East Indians," Mayo's Aberdeen home was the first stop on Wells's lecture tour. There, Wells and Impey received a warm welcome from not only Mayo but her boarders, who included two men from Ceylon, a thirty-year-old dentist named Dr. George Ferdinands and a young relative of his who was studying in Britain; and a German music teacher. All "three protégés of Mrs. Mayo threw themselves wholeheartedly into the work of helping make preparations for our campaign," Wells later remembered. The multicultural group spent a "happy two weeks . . . writing letters, arranging meetings, seeing the press, and helping to mail out ten thousand copies of *Anti-Caste*"—Impey having prepared a special issue in Wells's honor, which announced her schedule and promoted her talks. The special issue also announced the organization of the Society for the Recognition of the Universal Brotherhood of Man (SRUBM)—an antiracist organization that "regarded lynchings and other forms of brutal justice inflicted on the weaker communities of the world as having their root in race prejudice."[85]

Picking up where the abolitionist movement left off, the SRUBM reaffirmed the Christian ideal of human fellowship that had once led a British abolitionist to coin the mottos "Am I not a man and a brother?" and "Am I not a woman and a sister?" Likewise, Wells's British lectures consistently appealed to Britain's abolitionist heritage. In her autobiography, Wells recalled presenting British audiences with the "same heart stirring episodes which first gained me the sympathy and support of my New York friends," which "needed no embellishment or oratory from me."[86] But discussions of her visit published in Scottish and English newspapers suggest that she pursued a far more sophisticated and strategic approach to wooing the British public. Working in collaboration with Impey, Wells reframed her antilynching campaign for English audiences, transforming it into a revival of Britain's glorious antislavery movement. Although critical of British imperial regimes in India, Africa, and elsewhere, the Quaker radicals in Impey's circle had long "centered their radicalism on a notion of England's past as a fount of liberty and justice, and on a particular 'English' way of thinking." Wells's antilynching work presented a similar view of Britain.[87]

Whereas her American lectures frequently discussed lynching and Jim

Crow as a betrayal of "American institutions," in Britain Wells presented conditions in the American South as a betrayal of abolition.[88] Wells began her lectures with a description of "how the troubles of the colored people did not end . . . at the close of the Civil War." Since then, "the Negroes had been terrorized into abstaining from voting, and the legislation had all tended toward the social degradation and exclusion of the colored people." Freedom was "mocked in the country that boasts herself the freest in the world," Wells told Scottish audiences in Aberdeen, Huntly, Glasgow, and Edinburgh. During the English portion of her lecture tour, the parallels Wells drew between antislavery and antilynching grew ever more explicit. "England has shown America her duty in the past," she told a Newcastle audience, and "will do so again." And when a Birmingham journalist protested "being expected to give my attention to matters of municipal detail . . . in a civilized country at great distance," Wells defended her decision to protest the Memphis lynching and other "American atrocities" abroad with an eloquent appeal to England's historic role in the antislavery movement. At a time when "the press and the pulpit of our country remains silent on these continuing outrages," African Americans had no recourse but to appeal to the people of Great Britain. "The moral agencies at work in Great Britain did much for the final overthrow of chattel slavery. They can in a like manner pray, write, preach, talk and act against civil and industrial slavery; against the hanging, shooting and burning alive of a powerless race."[89]

Wells's approach was effective, garnering her large and enthusiastic audiences. "Miss Wells has made an impression on the minds of thousands (perhaps ten thousand direct—beside those who read press accounts)," Catherine Impey wrote in an exultant letter to Albion Tourgée. Her arguments inspired " 'leading newspapers of the United Kingdom' to issue 'ringing and outspoken editorials' against lynching." Now a veteran public speaker, Wells clearly captivated her British listeners. Impey struggled to capture the exact character of Wells's appeal: "with great simplicity & directness & with a burning intensity of feelings well controlled—it was the most convincing kind of speaking—it sounded so intensely genuine & real—There was no attempt at oratory—no straining for effects—a persecuted suffering woman came to lay her case before an impartial jury."[90] However, despite a "splendid audience" in Birmingham and "wonderfully interesting meetings" in Manchester, Wells's first British trip was cut short before her appeals to the British public could have the impact that they would later achieve.[91]

After Wells left Manchester, her organizational arrangements collapsed as a result of a bitter conflict between her two hosts that led Mayo to withdraw her support. The falling-out between Catherine Impey and Isabelle Mayo had nothing to do with Wells, though it had its genesis in the "happy two weeks" all three women had spent in Mayo's Aberdeen home. During that time, Catherine Impey had developed strong feelings for Mayo's protégé, Dr. George Ferdinands. As Wells later recalled the story, the British woman was confident that her affection was returned, and therefore shared her feelings with Ferdinands in a letter written shortly thereafter, "taking this advance step because she knew he hesitated to do so because he was of the darker race." He need hesitate no longer, she told him: "she had written her family acquainting them with the state of affairs, and telling them to prepare to receive him as her husband and that she rejoiced to give this proof to the world of the theories she had approved—the equality of the brotherhood of man."[92]

Unfortunately for Impey, her letter came as a complete surprise to Dr. Ferdinands, who "had never dreamed of her in any such connections as her letter indicated." Her declaration to Ferdinands was "a mortifying blunder," Impey later admitted in a letter to her friend Albion Tourgée. She had misinterpreted, she noted ruefully, the young dentist's devotion to "our movement (& myself as its rather careworn founder)" as something more. Meanwhile, Impey's embarrassment was soon compounded when Ferdinands chose to forward the letter to Mayo in Edinburgh, where she and Wells were hard at work "planning for the future." Outraged by the letter, Mayo summoned Impey to Edinburgh to dress her down and demand that she "withdraw from the work" immediately. She also expected Wells to abandon her collaboration with Impey. Wells, however, saw no reason why she and her collaborators could not continue working together as planned.

To be sure, Impey had "fallen in love with Dr. Ferdinands, and had been indiscreet enough to tell him so," but the "incident need not be known by anyone but ourselves" or "harm our work."[93]

Why Mayo refused to consider this solution is unclear. Still furious at Impey, she warned Wells that "Miss Impey was the type of maiden lady who used such work as an opportunity to meet and make advances toward men; that if we went on, she was likely to write such letters to others who might strike her fancy and throw suspicion and ridicule on our cause." And when Wells doubted this prediction, Mayo told her that Impey was a "nymphomaniac." The meaning of this term was initially lost on the sexually naive Wells. But even after Mayo had shocked her by explaining what it meant, Wells remained unwilling to "quit Miss Impey," as Mayo demanded. A longtime political ally to people of color, Impey had made Wells's British trip possible and introduced her to Mayo. Impey might have made a "mistake" in declaring her affections for Ferdinands, but it was a mistake she was unlikely to repeat, Wells concluded. One suspects that Wells was also troubled by the vituperative tone of Mayo's attack on Impey. She "had never heard one woman talk to another as she did," she recalled in her autobiography, "nor the scorn and withering sarcasm with which she characterized her. Poor Miss Impey was no match for her."[94]

In the long run, Wells's sympathy for Impey would cost her Mayo's support—a loss no doubt mitigated by Ida's continuing unease with the tone and character of Mayo's charges, which only became more expansive and vituperative over time. Mayo was a "stern upright Calvinist," according to Wells, and a notably unforgiving one. Her attack on Impey long outlasted their collaboration. Intent on driving Impey out of British and American reform circles, Mayo, between 1893 and 1894, circulated news of Impey's ill-considered letter wide and far, and also publicly accused the reformer of "mental instability."[95] Neither Impey nor Mayo left diaries chronicling the day-to-day interactions that led to their quarrel, leaving questions that cannot be resolved. Did something actually occur between Impey and Ferdinands in Aberdeen, and was Mayo jealous? Or did Mayo's racial liberalism simply not extend to interracial relationships?

At the very least, it is clear that Mayo's defamation of Impey insinuated that a white woman would have to be literally crazy to wish to marry a person of color—a claim that ran counter to Wells's conviction that America's laws against intermarriage helped foster lynching by making consensual relationships between white women and black men illegal. Mayo's reform credentials did not preclude such views, as much of Mayo's fiction suggests that she had what some scholars have termed a "maternalist" approach to reform.[96] The legacy of an abolitionist movement in which benevolent Christian white women campaigned to free powerless slaves, maternalism did not require its adherents to see oppressed people of color as social or racial equals. Instead, especially in the late nineteenth century, it was fueled by a reform ethos that stressed female sexual purity as the source of white women's superiority over both white men and people of color—who were deemed primitive and oversexed in Victorian racial science. Accordingly, a sexually aggressive act such as Impey's pursuit of Ferdinands challenged the image of white women at the core of maternalist reform—calling Impey's mental health into question.

By the time Wells returned to England in 1894, Mayo was actually saying as much. Writing in *Fraternity*, a new magazine published by the SRUBM, Mayo published an article titled "The Female Accusation," in which she contended that false accusations against black men by white women were one of the causes of lynching. Contrary to Wells, she did not trace these accusations back to social sanctions against consensual relationships between white women and black men. Instead, she attributed them to the "morbid peculiarities . . . of women who will 'fancy' anything which will give them a sensation and a little passing notoriety." "These female sufferers of this diseased egotism are not necessarily young and flighty. They are often elderly, dowdy and disappointed," Mayo wrote in a vicious and thinly veiled attack on Impey. Such women caused trouble between the races by imagining that "men fell in love with them" and were one source of the "female accusation" behind many American lynchings.[97] Although focused on Impey, Mayo's charges hint at racist beliefs that may well have troubled Wells, who believed that interracial relationships were a fact of life. Certainly, she cannot have appreciated Mayo's conviction that white women had to be mentally ill to even desire such unions.

Caught in the cross fire, and dependent on both women to facilitate her work, Wells did not challenge Mayo's view of Impey. But she refused to jettison Impey on the grounds that Impey's letter to Ferdinands was a private missive that should have remained that way. Wells's remarkably evenhanded account of the Impey-Mayo conflict in her autobiography reserved its most explicit moral judgment for Dr. Ferdinands. "I often wonder," she wrote, "if he ever realized his mistake in passing on the offending letter instead of destroying it."[98]

Wells's lingering disapproval of Ferdinands's mistake is not surprising given that Wells soon found herself on a ship back to the United States as a result of his actions. Both Wells and Impey had been scheduled to travel to London to lobby on behalf of the antilynching cause at the many annual meetings of reform organizations that routinely took place in Britain's capital city during the month of May. But their plans had to be abandoned when Mayo threatened to withhold the funding she had promised. Wells lacked the funds to disagree, and the result was disastrous. Without Impey's connections, the American reformer was not yet "well known enough to secure entrance . . . at these important meetings." Ironically, only the British Women's Temperance Association, an organization that Impey had abandoned on account of its failure to oppose racial segregation in its U.S. affiliates, opened up its platform to Wells. And when called on to speak at their meeting Wells found that she was expected to talk about temperance. Undeterred, she insisted on speaking about lynching, inspiring at least one of their affiliates to adopt an antilynching resolution. But she also realized her trip was over. "My duty was to tell a story whenever an opening had been made, so when time came for no more meetings it was the appropriate hour for me to return."[99]

Impey, who saw Wells off at Southampton, "blamed herself bitterly for the sudden ending of what promised so well." But Wells never doubted that Impey "had been actuated by any but the purest motives and highest idealism"—an autobiographical recollection that is borne out by the facts that

Wells and Impey remained fast friends through both her trips to England and Impey received an invitation to Wells's wedding in 1895.[100] Though eager not to burn bridges with either of her British sponsors, Wells consistently refused Mayo's demands that she denounce Catherine Impey. Frustrated by Wells's "ingratitude," Mayo would go on to become a public critic of both women.[101] Fortunately, when Wells returned to England in the spring of 1894 she would receive support from a variety of new friends and allies.

· 5 ·

Capturing the Attention of the "Civilized World"

"IDA WELLS, THE COLORED WOMAN WHO HAD BEEN COLLECT-
ing in England to suppress the lynch law in the south, has returned to this
country to visit the world's fair," an *Atlanta Constitution* editorial column
noted on June 21, 1893. "If her funds hold out she will attend to the lynching business later, but she must have a frolic in Chicago first."[1] Although
jarring, this studied insult from a white columnist testified to the success of
Ida B. Wells's British campaign. Before she left for England, both Wells and
her cause went virtually unnoticed in the white press. But after several
weeks of largely favorable coverage in the British press, Wells finally began
to attract the attention of mainstream journalists in her own country.
White Americans could ignore Wells when she addressed black audiences
at home, but when she mobilized antilynching sentiment abroad she became much harder to overlook. Accordingly, Wells spent much of the mid-
1890s working hard to rally international sentiment against lynching.

With this end in view, on her return from Britain she proceeded immediately to Chicago, where the United States had invited "the civilized
world" to come and celebrate "the four hundredth anniversary of the discovery of America" at the World's Columbian Exposition. For Wells, of course,
the exposition was less of a celebration of Columbus's "discovery" than it

was a chance to address the world in her home country. She would soon learn it was more effective to address her home country from abroad. The Chicago world's fair attracted more than 27 million people and was hailed by white visitors as "a new era in the onward progress of [American] civilization." Within the fair's exhibits, however, African Americans were located largely outside that progress. Black American participation in the event was largely confined to a "Colored People's Day," while their African ancestors were displayed in "ethnological" exhibits designed to entertain visitors and document mankind's primitive past. Wells was on hand to protest, along with Frederick Douglass and Chicago blacks such as Ferdinand Barnett. But their protests were largely lost on the fairgoers intent on enjoying such exhibits.

So after the exposition closed in the fall of 1893, Wells looked to Britain again, despite the fact that her six months in Chicago had left her ready to resettle there for good. Willing to brave further collaboration with Mayo to finish the promising work she had begun among British reformers, she set sail for Liverpool once again in early 1894. Her collaboration with Mayo would not last long, but Wells's second sojourn in Britain was otherwise a success, publicizing her antilynching campaign in both England and the United States, where Wells's British lectures and publications were vilified in the white press and challenged by white leaders. Public denigration was the major means by which her American critics sought to silence her. It failed. Indeed, a rising chorus of attacks on her in American newspapers only served to publicize both her cause and career, making Wells a celebrity and transforming lynching into an enduring public issue.

Denounced in *The New York Times* as a "nasty-minded mulatress," Wells was more popular among English audiences, who proved more receptive to her message—and more respectful to Wells herself. The British antilynching movement she gave rise to "rippled back to the United States," fostering a "transatlantic debate that linked the practice to Jim Crow racial segregation, exploitation, and discrimination."[2] Lynching did not end as a result of Wells's efforts, and neither did Jim Crow. But her work would ensure that lynching no longer passed as "frontier justice" in the eyes of the world. Indeed, a long campaign to mobilize federal authority against lynching began shortly after her second British tour—with an unsuccessful U.S. House resolution to investigate the matter. Blocked by Southern politicians, Northern inertia, and the nation's commitment to limit the federal government's judicial authority over the states, federal antilynching legislation would never succeed, but lynching would no longer go uncontested among whites after Wells made her case to the world. Instead, many whites outside the South learned to deplore lynching, and Southern whites learned to deplore Wells.

Storming the White City

Despite the disappointing end to her British trip, Ida's spirits were rejuvenated by an enjoyable ocean voyage home. No doubt relieved to escape the tensions between her quarreling British hosts, she had a far more pleasant time on her return voyage home than she had had on her way over. She remained in good health throughout the trip, having learned how to avoid seasickness from one of her fellow passengers (a "secret" which her autobiography does not divulge). Moreover, she also traveled in good company. The ship had "few if any Americans on board," and thus she experienced little discrimination. Instead, she was befriended by a group of fifteen friendly young Englishmen, who became her primary travel companions.

Like her, they were bound for the Chicago world's fair. Many of them were Quakers, and several were familiar with Wells's work from the English papers. Egalitarian in their outlook, Wells's new friends "were as courteous and attentive to me as if my skin had been the fairest." They helped her speed to her destination, accompanying her "almost all the way to Chicago," and enlivening her journey throughout. Once in the United States, their gentlemanly treatment of Wells caused great consternation among American observers, which did not discourage Wells's English friends in the least. On the contrary, "they seemed to take great pleasure in shocking onlookers with their courteous and respectable attention to me." Wells was equally gratified by these cross-cultural exchanges, reporting that she "enjoyed it hugely, because I had never met any members of the white race who saw no reason why they should not extend to me the courtesy they would have offered to a lady of their own race."[3]

Wells's journey also provided her with a hard-earned break from the grueling speaking and writing schedule she had kept up since leaving Memphis little more than a year earlier—which she would pick up again soon enough. Fun at the fair was, of course, not her objective there—*The Atlanta Constitution's* insinuations to the contrary. Rather, she was anxious to salvage the protest pamphlet she and Douglass had planned. Progress on the project had languished in Wells's absence, despite the fact that Frederick J. Loudin, a black musician and businessman who led the internationally renowned choir the Fisk Jubilee Singers, had lent his support to Wells's and Douglass's fund-raising efforts. As of February, Douglass, Loudin, and Wells had hoped to address the fair's exclusion of African Americans' cultural and economic contributions to the nation with "a carefully prepared pamphlet, setting forth the past and present condition of our people and their relation to American Civilization . . . printed in English, French, German and Spanish."[4] Designed to address an international audience, the pamphlet would be distributed at the fair itself, and simultaneously protest and remedy the lack of African American representation in its exhibits. But an April circular soliciting donations to publish the pamphlet had garnered little support—leaving Loudin and Douglass ready to abandon the project.

Wells, by contrast, returned from Britain more certain than ever that the world's fair provided African Americans with an important opportunity to put "our case before the public," as she told Douglass. Open to the public between May 1 and October 31, 1893, the fair was "in full blast" by the time Ida reached the United States in late June.[5] Determined to have the pamphlet in circulation as soon as possible once her ship docked in Manhattan, Wells "sped through New York," according to *The Indianapolis Freeman*, "like a comet, if not of 'tremendous size' of great velocity," bent on getting there in time "to get out that 'pamphlet.' "[6] By the summer of 1893, Wells was increasingly alone in her unwavering commitment to the project. From 1890 onward, African Americans had protested their exclusion from the fair's planning, staffing, and exhibits to little avail. But even after it opened, there was little consensus in the black community about how African Americans ought to be represented, and whether a protest pamphlet was appropriate.

At issue were disputes about how to best represent the status of African Americans within the nation's body politic. Long before the protest pamphlet idea came up, black leaders were divided over whether the race should be featured in a separate exhibit or represented by a commissioner who would be responsible for securing a proper representation "of the arts, sciences and industries of the colored people of the United States" in the respective exhibit halls.[7] In the end, however, black Americans were shut out of both options by white leaders who offered little support for black participation of any kind, citing disputes within the African American community over black participation as one of their rationales. When a congressional bill was proposed to fund a separate colored exhibit, lawmakers cited black objections to such an exhibit as one argument against the measure. No such appropriation was necessary, they concluded, "in view of the fact that the development of the colored race could not be differentiated from the development of the whole population of the United States."[8]

In practical terms, however, this disingenuous resolution provided blacks with absolutely no representation in the fair. For although the national commission appointed by President Benjamin Harrison to work with Chicago's municipal leaders in planning the event included commissioners from every state and territory, it had no African American members. As a last-minute concession to African American interests, Harrison later added one alternate commissioner, a St. Louis educator named Hale G. Parker. But his appointment was another blow to African American hopes. The principal of St. Louis's public colored school, Parker enrolled his own children in the city's white public schools. Moreover, his own racial identification was somewhat uncertain—or so his critics claimed. "Parker always denied that he has Negro blood in his veins," charged one black paper.[9] Identity aside, Parker had little power to increase black representation at the fair. The American exhibits were chosen by state screening committees whose membership was no more diverse than the fair's national leadership. Accordingly, although officials encouraged African Americans to propose exhibits, virtually all of their submissions were rejected. In the South, where the majority of America's black population lived, such rejections were a matter of policy. Southern officials, as Parker would later explain, did not wish to encourage 'the social equality of exhibits,' " or support the "commercial brotherhood of their producers."[10]

Black women's efforts to secure representation at the Columbian Exposition's Women's Building were equally fruitless. One of the great innovations of the exposition, the Women's Building was the first international exhibit of its kind. "Never before had the United States government positioned women as national representatives at an international event," notes the historian T. J. Boisseau.[11] A result of intensive lobbying on the part of Susan B. Anthony and other female reformers, the Women's Building honored the history and achievement of women in general and American women in particular. Moreover, by late 1890 it offered the last venue available for African American representation at the fair. African Americans hoped that white women, having struggled for representation, would be sympathetic and "a helpful influence for colored women."[12] But the Women's Building Board of Lady Managers, appointed by President Harrison in the spring of 1890, was no more diverse than the rest of the fair's leadership: it was composed of 116 white women from every state in the Union. African American women hoped the board would be willing to remedy his oversight.

Accordingly, they formed two lobbying associations dedicated to adding a black woman to the board: the Women's Columbian Association (WCA) and the Women's Columbian Auxiliary Association (WCAA), which differed only as to whether the board's African American appointment should develop a separate exhibit dedicated to black women or pursue more integrated representation. But once again differences within the black community over what constituted appropriate African American representation provided white fair officials with a pretext for excluding blacks altogether. No black board member would be appointed, announced Bertha

Palmer, the Chicago socialite who presided over the Board of Lady Managers: "the colored people were divided into factions and it would be impolite to recognize either faction."[13] A two-year lobbying campaign led by "representative Negro Women of the United States" did little to change matters. In January 1893, the Board of Lady Managers finally responded to scores of petitions and letters from black women by appointing an African American woman, Mrs. A. M. Curtis, to organize the African American exhibits, but Curtis soon resigned from "a post that was farcical given the few exhibits and the uncooperativeness of the Chief of Installation."[14]

As Curtis's complaint indicated, white women's exhibits predominated in the Women's Building, which emphasized representations of European queens in honor of Columbus's sponsor Queen Isabella of Spain. The representation of women of color was relegated to a mural on "Primitive Womanhood." Lest visitors miss the point, a display of women's "rude arts" featured three types of modern savagery: "the [Native] American, the Negroid, and the Mayolo-Polynesian."[15] Although not the most democratic of figures, the white queen appealed to the fair's organizers as an imperial symbol of the power and freedom modern women enjoyed, especially in comparison to their primitive interiors—African American women included. "We covet not titles or rank in this land of ours, where every woman may be a queen," proclaimed the Board of Lady Managers as it unveiled a portrait of its president, Bertha Palmer, wearing a tiara and carrying a scepter. But "when the women of America choose a leader and representative she is not only a queen, but queenly."[16] Left out of this latter-day understanding of American women as monarchs were, of course, the black women whom Palmer refused to represent.[17]

The actions of Palmer and many other exposition officials ensured a thoroughly white world's fair, which may be another reason why Wells remained adamantly committed to a pamphlet protesting the fair's exclusion of African Americans. The fair's popularity no doubt also contributed. It succeeded beyond its organizers' dreams, attracting a larger audience than any previous world's fair. "Victorian America's equivalent to the modern-day Olympics and Disney World rolled into one," according to historian

Robert W. Rydell, the fair was all the more frustrating to blacks on account of its success.[18] African Americans were "not a part of it," Frederick Douglass complained, while another black fairgoer lamented: "There is a lump which comes up in my throat as I pass around through all this . . . and see little to represent us here."[19] Moreover, the segregationist spirit that shaped the fair only became more obvious as the summer of 1893 approached. As a concession to black protests over lack of representation, fair officials announced that they would hold a special black Jubilee Day on August 25, 1893. Also known as "Colored People's Day," it was the brainchild of a delegation of blacks from Boston, who had appealed to the World's Columbian Exposition authorities to set aside a special day in commemoration of "African American cultural achievements since emancipation." Although not unlike similar days that fair officials had set aside for white ethnic groups, Colored People's Day infuriated many black leaders, who saw it as an insulting and segregationist response to African American demands for representation at the fair.

Wells was among them. She had objected to the idea of a separate day for black people even before she left for England. And on her return she was horrified to find the event designated as "the colored people's day, a day of 'glorious jubilee.' " Among other things, this designation seemed to "certify to the world that the colored people of the United States are content with the treatment accorded to them as citizens of the great Republic in several states of the American Union."[20] Other critics were less decorous: "No 'Nigger Day,' No 'Nigger Pamphlet,' " proclaimed *The Indianapolis Freeman* in March 1893, linking this new plan to the Wells-Douglass pamphlet project in a way that further complicated the challenges that Wells and Douglass faced in soliciting black support for their publication. Both the separate pamphlet and the separate day, the *Freeman* maintained, promised to draw "a lowering and invidious attention to the Negro from 'representatives of the civilized world.' "[21] Blacks would be demeaned in front of foreigners and subject to additional American prejudice as a consequence. Meanwhile, other opponents of the pamphlet questioned whether it was worth the expenditures it would require: "The race have too much in pamphlets and too little in their pockets," *The Bee* (Washington, D.C.) lamented.[22]

Objections to the proposed day were not universal, however. Frederick Douglass supported both the day and the pamphlet—which he saw as having similar ends. Highly annoyed by the *Freeman's* use of the word "nigger," he fired off a letter to the Midwestern paper that admonished both its language and its arguments. "No Brother Freeman, we must not be silent," he thundered. "We have but one weapon unimpaired and that weapon is speech, and not to use this and use this freely, is treason to the oppressed."[23] Although initially ambivalent about Colored People's Day, Douglass had agreed to preside over the August 25 celebration because it also offered African Americans a public forum at the fair. His decision came after several classically trained black musicians, including his grandson Joseph Douglass, managed to persuade him to lend his support to a showcase of young black artists at the fair's Festival Hall during the Colored People's Day ceremonies. In exile at his post in the Haitian pavilion, Douglass clearly welcomed a chance to preside over his own people—if only for a day.[24] As Douglass's biographer William McFeeley notes, America's premier black leader still "had sufficient vanity to look forward to being the center-piece of celebration."[25]

In Britain during most of the debates over Colored People's Day, Wells arrived in Chicago in the summer of 1893 to find blacks divided on that subject, in ways that put the pamphlet plan in jeopardy. Not only was the pamphlet still unfunded, but Wells was also at odds with Douglass for the first time in their acquaintance. While she did not appreciate *The Indianapolis Freeman's* attack on the pamphlet, she joined the paper in opposing any Colored People's Day. By July, the day seemed like an increasingly dubious proposition, fueled by obvious profit motives on the part of the fair's organizers. "Shut out of any other participation in the fair except to spend his money here," Wells noted, the "colored brother . . . had not been doing so very freely." Colored People's Day was nothing more than "a cordial invitation to do so . . . given at the eleventh hour." Moreover, by July, fair officials had announced plans for the event that seemed expressly designed to de-

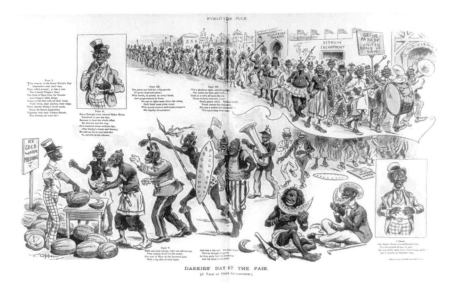

This 1893 cartoon titled "Darkies' Day at the Fair" realized African American fears that the World's Columbian Exposition's Colored People's Day could become a degrading racial spectacle. Published in the world's fair edition of the humor magazine Puck, *it mocked the event with a racist representation of the kinship between black Americans and the various African peoples on display at the fair—who are all portrayed as sharing a common love of watermelon.*

grade black fairgoers. "The horticulture department," Wells further noted, "has already pledged itself to put plenty of watermelons around on the grounds with the permission to the brother in black to 'appropriate' them." The event promised to turn African American participation into a degrading racial show. "The spectacle of the class of our people which will come on that excursion roaming around the grounds munching on watermelon, will do more to lower the race in the estimation of the world than anything else."[26]

Wells's dire predictions about the humiliating spectacle of a "horde" of black people attracted to the Columbian Exposition "by the dazzling prospect of free watermelon" spoke to the class prejudices of the black elite—who tended to see a strict conformity to middle-class behavior as a prerequisite for black racial progress. Douglass's granddaughter Fredericka Sprague, for example, had a similar response. "So, one day has really been found for the colored people at the 'World's Fair,' " she wrote her grandfather, "and the very idea that they are going to the trouble of supplying them with free watermelons is enough to draw every dusky American from his castle and lure him to the Fair ground gates."[27]

Still, African American opposition to Colored People's Day was not just a matter of class anxieties. Wells and other opponents had every reason to believe that the day would be billed as a sideshow. Staged to present the peoples of the world in the context of an evolutionary vision of progress, the fair effectively relegated African Americans to the same level of development as the primitive African peoples on display—an impression that any Colored People's Day festivities might help enforce.

A monument to white American progress, the fair featured an ideal model city, which excluded Africans and other peoples of color. The famous White City showcased American technology and industry in large, classically designed buildings finished with gleaming white paint. Devoted to displaying American manufactures, machinery, transportation, electricity, horticulture, agriculture, and mines and mining, it was flanked by other exhibits displaying the cultures and accomplishments of the peoples of the world—or in some cases the peoples themselves. Set off from the White City, on the midway in the fair's entertainment area, were exhibits styled as replicas of cities and villages from around the world, arranged, as one visitor noted, on "a sliding scale of humanity." At the far end were "the savage races, the African of Dahomey, and the North American Indian."

One of the great attractions on the midway was the sixty-seven Fon people on exhibit. Housed in a replica of a West African village, they were the fair's only major black exhibit and an exotic display of man at his most primitive. Imported, employed, and exploited by a French manager named Xavier Pene, the Fon people hailed from the West African kingdom of Abomey, also known as Dahomey. Scantily clad in clothing designed for their African homeland, the Fon were on hand, as a guidebook to the fair noted, to amuse the public with "war dances, songs, and specimens of savage amusements that made our native Indian seem a 'thing of beauty and a thing of joy forever.' " Black Americans tended to view them as "African savages brought here to act like the monkey." The Fon's well-publicized presence made the issue of African American representation at the exposition especially troubling.[28] Little wonder, then, that black Chicagoans like Wells feared that Colored People's Day would merely confirm the fair's "total exclusion of the negro from all participation except as a part of the ethnological exhibit." A special day would set black Americans apart from other Americans, they maintained, classing them with various African "exhibits."[29]

Anxious to avoid any association with the Fon, Wells and her contemporaries never noticed that the African visitors were subject to their own racist representation. Far from home, the Fon were at a linguistic disadvantage when it came to representing themselves. None spoke English, and only three of them spoke French, so they had to rely on Pene as both their manager and spokesman. Moreover, they were at odds with Pene, who paid them very little and kept them in Chicago far longer than they had agreed to stay—all the while concealing the Fon's dissatisfaction from the press. Nonetheless, four months into their stay, the Africans managed to stage and publicize a successful strike. They prevailed over Pene by shutting down all activity in their village until he agreed to double their previous wages—and supply them with twelve gallons of Claret, five cases of Chicago beer, and two and a half cases of whiskey. They also used the strike to negotiate a return date with their manager, who had hoped to make his popular Dahomey village part of the permanent amusement park that succeeded the fair's midway.

Indeed, the Fon's primitive savagery seems to have been largely staged by Pene, who required "his Negroes [to] dance on the top of the outer wall" of their village and "howl to attract visitors." Once inside, visitors were promised "bizarre exhibitions" performed by half-naked Fon men and women, regardless of Chicago temperatures. The Fon had arrived in Chicago in early May wearing full-length clothing topped by hooded overcoats, but thereafter they were invariably described as wearing loincloths—

even in weather that had them complaining about the cold. The experience cannot have been pleasant: late-season reports on the group describe them as a "blue lipped shivering lot."[30] However, Pene's staging of the Fon as howling naked primitives was not lost on visitors to the fair, who invariably described them as "barbarians, savages or cannibals." Women's rights leader Susan B. Anthony's visit to the Dahomey village made her think twice about the unity of the human species. "I wonder if humanity sprang from such as this. It seems pretty low down, doesn't it? But I don't think Adam knew much more than this."[31]

What African Americans noted, by contrast, were the frequent and unflattering comparisons drawn between the Dahomeans and their own group. A correspondent for *Frank Leslie's Popular Monthly*, who described the Fon as "blacker than buried midnight and degraded as the animals which prowl the jungles of their dark land," was one case in point. "In these wild people," he went on to observe, "we easily detect many of the characteristics of the American Negro."[32] Meanwhile, the humor magazine *Puck* ran a sketch suggesting that African Americans and the Dahomeans were all but identical, and that the Dahomeans might well be the more cultured of the two. Titled "A Sable Surprise," it mocked both men—one African, the other African American—with a report on a surprise encounter between the two. "One was a dude from Dahomey, one was from Illinois," it began, but "if they had changed their costume you [could not] have told which was which."

> The same velvet-black epidermis;—the very same contour of face, with lips that were thick and protruding, and flat noses, broad at the base; with smiles, as they looked at each other permitting their white teeth to show; the tops of their heads scattered over with wool where wool ought to grow . . . They stood contemplating each other, a sight that was funny to see—but that which most paralyzed me—which gave me a shock of amazement, and my large sense of fitness a wrench, was to hear the darky's dialect answered in polished and elegant French.[33]

Meanwhile, in the fair's Food building, a saleswoman for Quaker Oats reinforced these homegrown racial stereotypes. Hired by the cereal company to bring the advertising icon "Aunt Jemima" to life, ex-slave Nancy Green staged one of the exposition's most popular commercial exhibits. Aunt Jemima originated as a Mammy character in a blackface minstrel show staged in 1889, and became associated with pancakes when the businessman Chris L. Rutt used this image of a plantation cook to promote his new invention, a self-rising pancake mix. But not until the 1893 world's fair did Aunt Jemima become a household name. A popular performer, Nancy Green was a stout, dark-skinned woman who held court on top of a giant flour barrel dressed as Aunt Jemima, cooking pancakes for the crowd. "I's in town, Honey," she declared from her barrel-top stage, coining a phrase that became "the catch line of the fair." Tremendously popular, the Aunt Jemima promotion generated fifty thousand orders for pancake mix. Nancy Green's Aunt Jemima was the personification of a product that promised to liberate women from household labor—much like the plantation Mammy of the past. Apparently untroubled by this nostalgia, Green excelled in her role. "Three hundred pounds of affable kitchen wisdom," Green loved to talk about her own slave days, one Quaker Oats executive recalled. "Her stories were no doubt apocryphal but nonetheless entertaining."[34]

Wells never mentioned Nancy Green's popular performance as Aunt Jemima, but she could not have missed her altogether. Fairgoers sported "lapel buttons emblazoned with her likeness" and the phrase "I's in town, Honey" echoed throughout the fair. Moreover, Wells spent much of the fair in the Haitian building, working on the pamphlet with Frederick Douglass. The only site at the fair under the control of an African American, the Haitian building was located a short distance from the Food building and Aunt Jemima. Like the Dahomey village, the public spectacle that Nancy Green's Aunt Jemima offered fairgoers no doubt added to Wells's anxieties about Colored People's Day. Green was a living reminder that African Americans could indeed personify white stereotypes about blacks— much as Wells feared that watermelon-eating black visitors might do. So with these issues in mind, Wells was anxious to get her protest pamphlet in circulation well before Colored People's Day on August 25, 1893.

With Wells and Douglass at odds over the event, *The Indianapolis Freeman* had been gleefully predicting that both "the 'Pamphlet' and the 'Jubilee Day' are dead already." But the *Freeman* underestimated both Wells and Douglass, who managed to agree to disagree about Jubilee Day while continuing to collaborate on the pamphlet. The atmosphere between the two was no doubt strained that summer, which saw Douglass working on his plans for the August 25 ceremony without "any aid from the hotheads," as Wells would later describe herself and other opponents of the Colored People's Day.[35] But Douglass nonetheless set Wells up with a desk in the Haitian building and worked with her as she completed the pamphlet, which featured one chapter by Douglass, three by Wells, and a concluding couple of chapters by two additional recruits, the newspaperman Irvine Garland Penn and Wells's lawyer Ferdinand L. Barnett.

Adding two more authors no doubt helped Wells and Douglass finish up the pamphlet quickly, and Ferdinand Barnett, in particular, was a natural addition. An editor as well as an attorney, he was among the Chicago blacks who had long lobbied for greater African American representation at the exposition. His efforts had been fruitless, so he shared Wells's and Douglass's many reservations about the world's fair   siding with Ida in her opposition to Colored People's Day. A fellow activist and excellent local contact, Barnett was already acquainted with both Wells and Douglass. He had corresponded with Wells about a possible lawsuit just a few months earlier; and he knew the older man through his law partner S. Laing Williams, who, along with his wife, Fannie Barrier Williams, opened his Chicago home to Douglass during his world's fair visit. Meanwhile, I. Garland Penn was a veteran educator who also knew all of his coauthors. The author of an 1891 work titled *The Afro-American Press and Its Editors*, he had included profiles of Douglass, Barnett, and Wells in the book.[36]

Described by Wells as a "creditable little volume," *The Reason Why the Colored American Is Not in the World's Columbian Exposition* exposed much of what the White City sought to hide. A preface by Wells framed the pamphlet's guiding question. "The wealth created by [African American] industry has afforded to the white people of this country the leisure essential to their great progress and civilization," she noted. So "why are not the colored people, who constitute so large an element of the American population and who have contributed so large a share to American greatness, more visibly present and better represented at this World's Exposition?"[37] Frederick Douglass's contribution, which comprised the pamphlet's introduction and its first chapter, turned to history for an answer. The baneful influence of slavery still compromised the nation's character, he explained. The "moral progress of the American people" lagged behind their "material and economic development," making the White City little more than "a whited sepulcher"—a hollow mockery of American values. The nation had fought a great war to end slavery, but African Americans still had few rights that whites were willing to honor. The "people of the South" had no more respect for black life than they did before emancipation—"except perhaps that now they think they can murder with a decided advantage in the point of economy." In the time of slavery, if a Negro was killed, the owner sustained a loss of property. Now he was not restrained by any such loss. Instead, the race was terrorized by "men who count it as no crime to falsify the ballot box and cheat the Negro of his lawful vote." And the nation's leaders stood by "the Negroes' disenfranchisement in clear defiance of the constitution they have sworn to support."[38]

Wells followed up Douglass with three chapters describing the political and economic system that kept blacks subjugated in the South. "Class Legislation" segregated, disenfranchised, and disempowered black Southerners, she explained in Chapter 2, leaving the "entire political, legislative and executive machinery of the country in the hands of the white people." Her two subsequent chapters dealt with the "two great outgrowths" of class legislation: the "Convict Lease System" and "Lynch Law." Both maintained white supremacy. Lynching helped Southern whites drive black men out of politics, while the convict lease system allowed them to profit from the disenfranchised black underclass they created. Instead of educating African American youth, Southern states allowed them to "grow up in ignorance and vice" and then exploited their petty crimes by turning them into convicts who would be worked for "cheap labor, and pay the states a handsome revenue."[39]

Meanwhile, Ferdinand Barnett rounded out the volume with a detailed account of these efforts, which revealed that blacks had been systematically excluded from even working as security guards at the fair, which as of August 25, 1893, employed only two "colored persons . . . whose occupations were of a higher grade than that of janitor, laborer and porter"—and these two were clerks. The exposition was "literally and figuratively, a 'White City,' " Barnett concluded. "Only as a menial is the Colored American to be seen—the Nation's deliberate and cowardly tribute to the Southern demand 'to keep the Negro in his place.' "[40]

The only upbeat contribution to the pamphlet was Irvine Garland Penn's essay on "The Progress of the Afro-American since Emancipation." Penn chronicled the accomplishments of African Americans in business, industry, education, and the arts in an essay that outlined the exhibit that African Americans might have contributed.[41]

Even as she readied these essays for publication, Wells was still hard at work soliciting the funds needed to have it printed. Fortunately, she was able to enlist the aid of Chicago's "representative Negro women," who were still smarting from their dealings with the exposition's Board of Lady Managers. Rallying around Wells much as women in New York and Brooklyn had in 1892, they helped Wells organize a successful series of Sunday afternoon gatherings at black churches. With Douglass presiding at each, Wells presented an eloquent appeal for donations to support the pamphlet, and collected five hundred dollars in short order. While not enough to support the multilingual publishing plan originally envisioned, with additional commitments of fifty dollars from Douglass and Loudin, Wells now had the funds to produce ten thousand copies of her "little book." It featured prefaces in German, French, and English, as a nod to an international constituency.

By the end of August, if not before Colored People's Day, Wells had her pamphlet out, and spent the remainder of the fair on "duty in the Haitian building . . . putting the pamphlet in the hands of the Foreigners." She also made amends with Douglass. Wells sat out Colored People's Day, which was poorly attended, but read newspaper reports of Douglass's speech, which convinced her that the "grand old man" had been right in thinking "it better to have half a loaf than no loaf at all." In an address that was reported "from one end of the country to the other," Douglass spoke before an audience of 2,500. His "full, rich and deep" voice rose in "sonorous tones," the young black poet Paul Lawrence Dunbar remembered. Despite his age, Douglass drowned out catcalls from some white men in the rear of the crowd "as an organ would a penny whistle." "Men talk of the negro problem. There is no negro problem," Douglass thundered. "The problem is whether the American people have honesty enough, loyalty enough, honour enough, patriotism enough to live up to their own Constitution."[42] Douglass also rebuked exposition officials for "ignoring the progress" that African Americans had made in the thirty years since emancipation. The Dahomean villagers had been brought to the fair to "exhibit the Negro as a repulsive savage," Douglass complained, encouraging fairgoers to instead see the Dahomeans as a living measure of African American advancement: "We have come from the Dahomey out of this. Measure the Negro. Not by the standards of this splendid civilization of the Caucasian. Bend down and measure him—measure him—from the depths out of which he has risen."[43]

Wells was profoundly impressed. "The American people had given him his opportunity for scoring its unfairness toward the Negro citizens and he did not fail to take advantage of it in the most fitting way." Douglass's talk, she believed, "had done more to bring our cause to the attention of the American people than anything else which happened during the fair." Accordingly, she "went straight out to the fair and begged his pardon for presuming in my youth and inexperience to criticize him." Douglass readily accepted her apology, and their friendship continued. But both his speech and their pamphlet would turn out to have a limited impact on public perceptions of the fair, which was widely reviewed as the greatest event in the history of the country since the Civil War. Even Douglass's eloquence could not prevent cartoonists from lampooning Jubilee Day as "Darkies' Day at the Fair," and visitors took little notice of the pamphlet. The historian Hubert Bancroft, who wrote the massive *Book of the Fair* that came out at the end of 1893, did not even mention it and dismissed all dissent at the fair as utterly petty. "Among the visitors was a small but demonstrative contingent which seemed to have come to Chicago for no other purpose than to complain," he wrote, "men and women to whom the colossal grandeur of a display contributed by all the nations of earth was as nothing compared with the imperfect cooking of a meal."[44]

Indeed, the only African American to make an enduring political mark at the fair may well have been Booker T. Washington, a conservative black educator who traveled to Chicago from the Tuskegee Institute in Alabama. Still a relative unknown when he attended the fair's International Labor Congress, the thirty-seven-year-old Tuskegee Institute principal offered a model of black leadership strikingly different from the uncompromising militancy favored by Douglass and Wells. A man whose career was built on cultivating the support of important whites, Washington approached them as a "deferential but dignified" leader intent on forging "a partnership with the Southern elite."[45]

A talented fund-raiser, Washington had built the Tuskegee Institute by promoting industrial education as the road to black advancement, and he offered a similar message to his audience at the Labor Congress. "When it comes to business pure and simple and to the exercise of skilled labor," he proclaimed, "the South accords the black man almost the same rights as the white man." Accordingly, African Americans should pursue industrial work and economic power rather than political rights to advance their race. "Friction between the races" would "pass away as the black man gets a hold of the things the white man wants and respects, like the trades and mechanic arts. It is along these lines we are to find the solution to all these problems in the South." Wells and Douglass, who also participated in the Labor Congress, both objected vehemently—with Wells noting that most Southern blacks were landless sharecroppers "who were never allowed to get out of debt" or leave the fields. But Washington's politically accommodationist message appealed to other members of his largely white audience—who commended him to Atlanta's civic leaders as a potential speaker at an upcoming world's fair in Atlanta in 1895. There, Washington would become the first African American to deliver a world's fair opening day address, offering a similar message of racial reconciliation in his now famous "Atlanta Compromise Speech."[46]

Washington's meteoric rise to fame after his appearance in Atlanta gave his message a far more immediate impact on American race relations than did Wells's and Douglass's protests in Chicago. But the months Wells spent at the 1893 fair were not totally wasted. She got to know and like Chicago, and decided to remain there instead of returning to New York City.

The Tennessee exile evidently felt at home among the growing population of black Southern migrants that populated Chicago. Like Wells, more than 40 percent of them hailed from the upper South, mainly Tennessee and Kentucky, and they tended to be "more urban, militant and literate than those who remained in the South." Moreover, as Wells discovered when she sought support for her pamphlet, the city had a sizable and progressive black middle class that supported several churches. And it was also home to Ferdinand Barnett's *Conservator*, which offered Wells a job that may well have seemed more secure than her post at the *Age*—which had recently shrunk from an eight-page paper to a four-page.[47]

Most important, perhaps, Chicago also had Barnett himself, who provided Wells with the most compelling reason of all to resettle there. Wells's autobiography discloses virtually nothing about how or when their professional relationship became personal, but by the beginning of 1894 Barnett had offered Wells "a home of my own" in Chicago.[48] Their courtship was swift. Despite their similar career paths and their legal correspondence during 1892–93, the two do not seem to have met until Wells came to Chicago to work on *The Reason Why the Colored American Is Not in the World's Columbian Exposition*. Once they did meet, however, Wells and Barnett clearly found out they had much in common. At forty, Barnett was ten years older than Wells and far "more easygoing." But he nonetheless shared the fiery young woman's "outspoken and militant" approach to politics. "Once he was threatened with jail because he said in a speech that the American flag was a dirty rag if it didn't protect its citizens," his daughter Alfreda Duster observed, remembering her parents' similarly passionate approach to political issues.[49]

A widower with two young sons, Barnett had lost his wife, Mary Graham Barnett, in 1888, when she died suddenly of a heart attack after only five years of marriage. On his own after that, Barnett was described by one of his contemporaries as a "tall, handsome man" who sometimes wore a Prince Albert coat and a silk hat, "making him the picture (to me) of what a real prince or a king should look." Despite his fine looks and the many "women chasing him while he was a widower," Barnett rarely dated after his wife's death. Although not opposed to remarriage, he had resolved not to marry again until he found someone "meaningful to his life and career." But when he decided Ida "fit that pattern," he did not hesitate to pursue her and

Ferdinand Lee Barnett, c. 1890

marry her. In her early thirties when they met, Wells must have seemed to be a perfect partner: Barnett proposed less than six months after she arrived in Chicago.

Wells proved receptive. Long worried that she would never get married, Ida seems to have been more than happy to meet the highly eligible widower. They got to know each other while working on the pamphlet and were compatible from the outset. Barnett was "always very supportive of whatever she [Wells] got into," while Wells "was always out there scrapping for him." The pair also had good friends in common, such as Albion Tourgée and Frederick Douglass—who one reporter later insisted engineered the Wells-Barnett union.[50] If so, his role cannot have been strenuous. Between the couple's first meeting and their marriage nearly two years later, their relationship had time to blossom—albeit at a distance. Wells would travel back to England in the winter of 1894, leaving Barnett behind.

But his prominence in her thoughts can be seen in one of her publications from that period. Published in *The A.M.E. Zion Quarterly* at the beginning of the year, "Two Christmas Days: A Holiday Story" is Wells's only work of romance. A preachy short story about a former teacher who falls in love with a lawyer, it reaffirms that journalism rather than fiction was Wells's métier. Not particularly compelling, "Two Christmas Days" has only one male protagonist and not much action. But its contents show Wells drawing favorable romantic contrasts between Barnett and previous suitors. A story of love found, lost, and then found again, it features a hero who proves himself by overcoming faults that Wells had encountered in previous suitors—some of whom lacked ambition and discipline. Reformed by love, her fictional hero becomes a hardworking teetotaler—much like Ferdinand Barnett, who was known for not allowing liquor in his home.[51]

Ida had finally found a man she could respect and trust, the story suggests, as does her relationship with Barnett, which continued apace even after she left Chicago. His proposal came sometime before she left, and during her trip the couple sustained a "long distance correspondence courtship." Barnett wooed Wells by writing her letters that met her at every stop on her busy second trip to Britain—and left a lifelong impression. The couple's correspondence does not survive, but Ida often talked about it to her daughter Alfreda, telling her that her "father could write a beautiful love letter." Likewise, Wells herself was a lively and expressive correspondent. So a prolific exchange of letters no doubt helped cement the bond between the two.[52]

Indeed, Wells may have had little time for a more direct courtship during her months in Chicago. With ten thousand pamphlets to distribute, the late summer and fall months saw her spending long hours at the Haitian pavilion right through to the fair's end in October. That fall, she also took on the task of organizing the first black women's club in Illinois. Invited to lecture on "Ladies Day" at a black men's organization named the Tourgée Club in Chicago, Wells advised the female audience to start a club of their own. An enthusiastic, if recent, convert to women's organizations, Wells "told them of the club movement in the East and how women's gatherings in England were very important to the womanhood of that nation."[53] She even went so far as to offer to organize weekly meetings at the Tourgée Club. By September, the Chicago women's club was established, and by the time Wells left for England it had over three hundred members and was still growing.

In the midst of all her other activities and her romance with Barnett, Wells's commitment to antilynching remained urgent. Her English trip had garnered her continuing attention in the white American press, as well as her first commission to write for a white newspaper. That summer, the *Daily Inter Ocean*, a progressive Chicago newspaper that also employed Wells's friend and fellow foe of mob violence Albion Tourgée, hired Wells to investigate the lynching of C. J. Miller.

An African American man from Springfield, Illinois, Miller was put to death on July 7, 1893, in Bardwell, Kentucky—a small town near Kentucky's Missouri border. In the wrong place at the wrong time, Miller had been traveling through Missouri looking for work when nine-year-old Ruby Ray and her nineteen-year-old sister Mary were found murdered near Bardwell. A fisherman who later realized that he might have ferried the likely criminal across the Mississippi River shortly after the crime took place came forward to describe the killer as either "a white man or a very bright mulatto." But this description did not prevent the sheriff in the nearby town of Sikeston, Missouri, from picking up the dark-skinned C. J. Miller as he attempted to hop a freight train. Held in Sikeston without a warrant, Miller maintained "he had never been in Kentucky in all his life."[54] The sheriff ignored his protests, delivering him directly to a train full of beer-drinking whites from Kentucky, who took him to Bardwell, after first trying and failing to confirm his identity with the fisherman. Once in Kentucky, Miller was placed on a platform built by the mob to receive the killer.

Stunned by this turn of events, Miller appealed to the crowd, reiterating that he had committed no crime and had not been in Kentucky when

Lynching of C. J. Miller, at Bardwell, Kentucky, July 7th, 1893.

Captioned "After the Lynching," this drawing illustrated Wells's Daily Inter Ocean *account of the C. J. Miller lynching. The graphically brutal and potentially controversial image was followed by a parenthetical note that read: "The editor apologizes for using this reproduction of a photograph taken at Bardwell, Ky., just before the body of the negro Miller was burned. But in no other way is it possible to give an adequate idea of the inhumanity of the case. Not the least distressing feature is that (as will be seen by the picture) there were so many young people among the witnesses of an act of brutality and savagery."*

the murders took place. With no evidence linking the Illinois man to the crime, even the father of the two dead girls questioned Miller's guilt. "I thought that a whiter man had committed the crime," he told the crowd as they made a fruitless attempt to force Miller to confess, but "the mob refused to listen to reason." The whites who gathered in Bardwell "had spent the day anticipating a lynching," Ida reported, "and proof or no proof they did not intend to go home without a lynching bee." While local officials were still at work confirming Miller's account of his whereabouts—which turned out to be true—Miller was strung up from a telegraph pole and hung. His body was then mutilated and burned. He escaped death by fire, Wells noted with horror, only because "the mob decided to give him the benefit of the doubt and *hang instead of burn him*, as was first intended."[55]

Wells returned to Chicago and published her illustrated account of Miller's death only to receive an equally horrifying telegram headlined JULY 22, MEMPHIS, THE PUBLIC LEDGER. It read, "Lee Walker, colored man, accused of raping white women, in jail here will be taken out and burned by whites to-night. Can you send Miss Ida B. Wells to write it up? Answer. R. M. Martin, with *The Public Ledger*." A cruel and mocking message from one of Wells's many enemies in Memphis, this missive was dispatched one day before Walker was dragged out of jail and murdered. Too bloodthirsty to even take their prisoner to the center of town to lynch him on Main Street, as planned, the Memphis mob hanged Walker from a telegraph pole just a few blocks away from his jail cell. After he was dead they cut him down, burned his body, and dragged his charred corpse to the town's central thoroughfare before stringing his remains up once more, this time to display him in front of the city's courthouse. There the crowd that had collected to watch his death broke the dead man's teeth and cut the fingernails off his body to take home "as souvenirs."[56]

Appalled, Wells included the telegram and a press clipping from *The Public Ledger* (Memphis) reporting the grisly story of Lee Walker's death along with her illustrated account of the C. J. Miller lynching in *The Reason Why the Colored American Is Not in the World's Columbian Exposition*. She also wrote of Walker's lynching in the *Daily Inter Ocean*. But the *Ledger's* telegram to Wells signaled to her the power and limitations of her newfound celebrity. She had become well enough known to figure prominently in the national debate about lynching—and attract personal missives from the lynchers themselves. Yet she could not prevent Lee Walker's death or shield other victims of mob violence. As she wrote in 1894, she could only make the American people "objects of the gaze of the civilized world"; she could only strive to ensure "that for every lynching humanity asks that America render its account to civilization and itself."[57] And by early 1895, this conviction made her leave behind her new job, new friends, and new romantic prospect in Chicago to return to England.

Wells's Second British Tour

The Society for the Recognition of the Universal Brotherhood of Man (SRUBM), the antiracist organization that had taken shape around Wells's visit to Britain, had continued after her departure. Catherine Impey was "practically retired" as a result of Isabelle Mayo's continuing hostility. But Mayo still headed up the organization's Scottish branches and had enlisted Celestine Edwards, a black man from the British West Indian island of Dominica, to replace Impey as the leader of the English SRUBM. She also appointed Edwards to edit the organization's new official publication, *Fraternity*—which replaced Impey's *Anti-Caste*. In September, Edwards moved to pick up Wells's antilynching campaign, with Mayo's enthusiastic support. "Mr. Edwards' arrangements would do you justice," Mayo wrote Wells, relaying the invitation for a second tour, "<u>and</u> you could work unblighted!!"[58]

Wells welcomed the invitation as another "opportunity to spread the truth," even though it meant securing a leave of absence at her new job and dealing with the often difficult Mayo. More cautious this time, Wells negotiated the terms of her visit in advance, asking for "expenses & 2 pound per week—as it was as little as I could come for that at a sacrifice to my business." Moreover, she even negotiated the matter of Impey herself, after receiving a letter from Mayo pressing her to publicly denounce Impey on her return visit. As before, Wells refused, telling Mayo that she "couldn't come . . . if expected to say anything about Miss I.—for I would not be a party to further exposure of her weakness."[59] When Mayo proved dissatisfied with Wells's answer, Edwards stepped in to resolve the dispute, reiterating SRUBM's invitation and assuring Wells that Mayo did not speak on behalf of the organization, which was impatiently awaiting her visit.

Heartened by his support, Wells set sail for England in early 1894. Originally planned for January, her departure was delayed by poor weather, so she did not arrive until March. By then, she must have rued her decision to return. She landed only to find that Mayo had resigned from the SRUBM rather than support Wells's tour. Worse still, the Scottish writer had withdrawn the funds she had guaranteed to cover Wells's expenses. Meanwhile, the SRUBM's support had all but collapsed as well. Edwards, who was scheduled to manage and fund the English leg of Wells's trip with the help of SRUBM's membership, was gravely ill, leaving the organization in disarray. Laid low by a case of influenza that would eventually kill him, Edwards would soon return to his childhood home on Dominica in hopes of recovering his health.

Undeterred and perhaps not entirely surprised, Wells did not even consider leaving. "I have come abroad to give 3 months of my time to work," Wells wrote Frederick Douglass as she scrambled to reorganize her plans, "and I am going to do it."[60] She had been invited to report on her visit for Chicago's *Daily Inter Ocean*, which gave her an unprecedented opportunity to chronicle her antilynching activities as a correspondent for a white newspaper, and Wells was determined to do so. She also had plans to sell *Southern Horrors*—which she and Edwards had repackaged for a British audience under the title *American Atrocities*—and hoped to cover her expenses that way.

Fortunately, her first speaking engagement was arranged in advance and soon led to others. On March 12, Wells addressed an audience of 1,500 at the Pembroke Chapel in Liverpool. Her host was Charles F. Aked, an energetic young Baptist minister who had built one of the largest congregations in that city. On her first visit, Aked had been skeptical of Wells—so much so that he had refused a proposal to let her address his congregation, "because he didn't know me or believe what I said was true." But a visit to Chicago for the world's fair shortly thereafter changed his mind. There, Aked followed "the sensational" newspaper coverage of the Bardwell, Kentucky, lynching. Some weeks later came another report: "the Kentucky mob had lynched the wrong man!" Reading this "under the shadow of the statue of liberty" in Chicago's Jackson Park, Aked realized that "what Miss Wells said was true." Contrite, he was happy to host her on her return visit. And on learning that her arrangements with Mayo and Edwards had fallen through, Aked and his wife opened their home to her. Their Liverpool house became her new "headquarters" and the Akeds her close "friends and ardent supporters." What was more, the couple, Wells remembered, "seemed to know that I did not like, or rather had no confidence in white people, and they set themselves at work to uproot my natural distrust and suspicion. The queen of England herself could not have been treated with more consideration than I was during the course of my stay with them."[61]

Also crucial to the success of Wells's second tour was help from Catherine Impey, who was still working for the SRUBM behind the scenes. Although now marginalized by Mayo's public criticism, Impey's family contacts gave her entrée into important Quaker reform circles. Her cousin Helen Clark would host Wells in Somerset, and Quaker relatives of Clark's organized dates for Wells in Bristol.[62] However, with Edwards ill, Impey in disgrace, and Mayo refusing to have anything to do with her, Wells's reform credentials were once more in question.

Aked had introduced her to his congregation as "accredited to the friends of progress by the Hon. Frederick Douglass." The minister later suggested that Wells write and ask Douglass to supply him with "a letter of introduction in case there was ever any necessity for it."[63] But when Wells passed this request on to Douglass, his reply was frosty. He supplied Aked with a tepid letter and fired off a curt note to Wells. "I see you are already advertised as accredited to England by me," he noted, clearly not happy to be embroiled in a conflict about which he knew very little. "I had not supposed that, being invited to England, you needed my endorsement . . . Will you oblige me by telling me frankly who invited you to spend three months in England and what assurances they gave you of support while on this mission?"[64]

Wells was devastated. "With all the discouragements I have received," she told him in a six-page letter that supplied a blow-by-blow account of her interactions with Mayo, "I have never felt so like giving up since I received your very cool and cautious letter this morning." She had not thought to ask him for a letter before she left, she explained, because it "never occurred to me that I would need letters of introduction as I was coming as I did before—on invitation."[65] By way of proof, Wells enclosed the letter she had received from Mayo outlining the SRUBM's speaking invitation. Wells's letter and its enclosure satisfied Douglass, whose doubts about her mission seem to have been partially fueled by the fact that Wells had borrowed twenty-five dollars from him to help pay for her voyage to England, and was now seeking additional sponsorship, which made him wonder how much other support she actually had for her mission. Moreover, his doubts may have also reflected the endless bad press that Wells received in the United States—much of which described her as a huckster who promoted antilynching for personal gain. But he was reassured by her letter. By May, Douglass was in her corner again, and wrote several letters on her behalf.

Douglass's faith in Wells could only have been confirmed by the reception she received among his old antislavery friends in Britain. The Quaker hosts that Impey had enlisted on her behalf included members of abolitionist families that had once supported Douglass himself. Kinship ties linked many of them to Impey, so they may well have appreciated both Wells's cause and her loyalty to Impey; and they were quick to commend her work to Douglass. Moreover, in doing a favor for Douglass's wife, Helen Pitts, Wells managed to make a particular friend of Ellen Richardson, an elderly Quaker who lived in Newcastle, a port city that was once a hotbed of antislavery sentiment. Richardson's acquaintance with Douglass went all the way back to the 1840s, when Douglass had visited England as a fugitive slave. Richardson and her sister-in-law, Ana Richardson, had raised the money needed to purchase Douglass from the white family who still owned him, thereby securing his freedom. Douglass never forgot their kindness. Neither did his wife, Helen Pitts, who asked Wells to pay a thank-you call on her behalf to her husband's benefactor, should she travel to Newcastle. Wells obliged. Ellen Richardson, very impressed by Wells, sat down that day to send Douglass a favorable account of his protégée.[66] Thereafter, the older woman also followed Wells's tour in the British press, telling Douglass that Wells reminded her of him as a young man. "The child of slave parents and yet can command the attention of high and low," she wrote as Wells was finishing up her visit. "It is astonishing to me how Miss Wells has made her way here—people like her simple earnest way of stating her cause."[67]

Wells "made her way into the hearts of our editors," Richardson told Douglass. Among other things, Richardson must have noticed that British journalists never failed to describe Wells's appearance, which they found both enormously appealing and racially "odd." "She is the very notable product of that mixing of the blood which is proceeding so rapidly in the United States of America," *The Daily Chronicle* (London) noted, going on to explain: "she claims relationship with the red Indian, the negro, and the Anglo-Saxon races. She is under thirty years of age, very vivacious in manner, and decidedly good-looking." Another paper was more succinct, describing Wells as "a good looking mulatto, dressed in uncommonly good-taste."[68]

Wells took her various accolades in stride. Thirty-two years old in 1894, she welcomed the British impression that she was much younger. Indeed, she soon began subtracting several years from her age when she chronicled her "28 years in the South." Moreover, she took little offense at the complimentary British discussions of her exotic appearance, which certainly improved upon American references to her as a "saddle colored Sapphire." However, when one commentator labeled her black blood as a "taint," she objected: "Taint, indeed: I tell you, if I have any taint to be ashamed of in myself, it is the taint of white blood!"[69]

Aware that British fascination with her looks reflected a preoccupation with race mixture that could easily shade into disdain, Wells did not downplay inquiries into her background but instead used them to drive home her point. Blacks had not sought miscegenation, Wells told a British reporter who confessed to being "dead set against it." The color line was routinely violated by white men, whose public disdain for race mixture had not prevented them from creating a mulatto population. Their actions had created the mixed ancestry that the British found so notable in the slave-born Wells. Moreover, "even today . . . the white man is continually mixing his blood with the black; it is only when he seeks to do so honorably that it becomes a crime."[70] A steadfast focus on her antilynching argument also allowed Wells to both capitalize on and transcend the more prurient attention she received.[71]

Wells used the public attention to address the difficulties of denouncing lynching to British audiences. She visited Britain at a time when the "white slavery" of working-class girls in London brothels was a major concern in the nation's news. In England, much like the United States, Wells had to challenge conceptions of lynching as an appropriate punishment for sexual aggression against white women. As a petite and feminine woman of color who had been threatened with lynching herself, Wells was living evidence that would-be lynchers did not limit their racial violence to men. Moreover, her lectures challenged the lynching-for-rape myth with both the story of her exile from Memphis and accounts of white mob violence against other African American women. Indeed, Wells used recent examples of such violence to powerful effect. On March 21, 1894, she told a Liverpool audience that just before she left the United States, she had seen an account of a colored woman who was found hanging from a tree in Little Rock, Arkansas, and had since learned of the still more horrible lynching of another black woman. In Manchester, she listened with tears rolling down her cheeks as a member of her audience read an account of a "woman in San Antonio, Texas, who had been boxed up in a barrel with nails driven through the sides and rolled down a hill until she was dead."[72]

Wells used such powerful stagecraft both to "argue the black female body into consciousness" and to draw attention to lynching as an atrocity that surpassed even the evils of white slavery. A product of the "civil and industrial slavery" that still persisted in the American South, lynching victimized black women as surely as did the domestic violence associated with chattel slavery, Wells argued, reclaiming the abolitionist mantle worn by reformers who had sought to eradicate "white slavery." In doing so, she also offered British reformers the chance to reclaim the glory days of their antislavery campaign.

As during her first visit, Wells missed few opportunities to link antilynching to antislavery and implore her British hosts to once again lead Americans to justice. Appealing to her hosts' sense of national pride, Wells drew unfavorable contrasts between the United States and Britain, while at the same time offering British audiences a short course in American race relations—a set of rhetorical moves she shared with the American readers of her *Daily Inter Ocean* column. Although once "the greatest cotton market in the world," she told both audiences, Liverpool had "redeemed herself from slavery." In Liverpool and other British cities, "a colored person can ride in any sort of conveyance in any part of the country without being insulted; stop in any hotel or be accommodated in any restaurant one wishes without being refused with contempt; wander into any picture gallery, lecture room, concert hall, theater or church and receive only the most courteous treatment from officials and fellow sightseers." Blacks knew no such freedoms in the United States, where they were instead subject to "lynching atrocities" that went unchecked and unpunished. Indeed, Wells was forced to air her people's grievances abroad rather than at home because her race could "not get a hearing in the United States." With the "press and pulpit of the country practically silent . . . the society for the recognition of the brotherhood of man in England and Scotland" offered African Americans their only opening.[73]

Like her abolitionist predecessors, Wells aimed to mobilize the British press and pulpit to address their American counterparts. As she traveled through the English cities of Liverpool, Manchester, Newcastle, and London, her *Daily Inter Ocean* headlines relayed much of the message she sought to get across. "England Sympathizes with the African Race," one noted, while others declared, "Audiences Are Shocked" and "Cordial Receptions from Churches of All Denominations—Horrified at Cruelties Perpetrated."[74] But the progressive readers of the *Daily Inter Ocean* were not the only Americans she wished to reach. So she courted British audiences that could spread the message beyond the confines of her existing readership at home. Again borrowing the tactics of the antislavery movement, Wells appealed to British editors, churches, and reform organizations to denounce lynching.

Thanks to her popularity with British editors, by the time Wells reached London, the press coverage was "beyond all expectation." "I have quite lost count of the number of times I have been interviewed," she told her *Daily Inter Ocean* readers.[75] Featured in *The Daily Chronicle, The Daily News, The Westminster Gazette, The Sun, The Star, The Echo*, and many newspapers in other cities, her work was the subject of interviews, editorials, and lively discussion. Moreover, Wells made powerful contacts among British journalists, including Peter Clayden, the editor of London's second largest paper, *The Daily News*. After attending one of Wells's first talks in that city, Clayden's wife insisted that Wells move into their London home rather than staying at a hotel. There Wells received additional assistance from a network of supporters who gathered in the Claydens' breakfast room every morning to mail out copies of whatever favorable reports on her work had appeared in the British press to the most prominent U.S. politicians, religious leaders, and news organizations. Meanwhile, Wells continued to receive help with publicity from her Liverpool host, successfully enlisting Charles Aked "to introduce her ideas into conservative forums from which she was herself excluded."[76]

As a result of his influence, several important British monthlies condemned lynching without ever mentioning Wells herself. They were swayed by an article that Aked published in the prominent British monthly *The Contemporary Review* in June 1894, which seems to have been written with some help from Wells. Although framed for an English audience and published under Aked's name, "The Race Problem in America" used Wells's statistics and arguments without attribution and included an uncited passage by Wells in its central argument. "The demand of the Negro is for the most elementary justice," Aked wrote, reiterating a statement Wells had supplied to *The Daily Chronicle*: "Make your laws as terrible as you like . . . but prove your criminal a criminal first. Hang, shoot, roast him, if you will—if American civilization demands this—but give him a trial first."[77]

Aked's powerful essay elicited supportive columns in other important British monthlies such as *The Spectator* and *The Economist*, publications that had never covered Wells herself—knowingly, at any rate. As Sarah L. Silkey has pointed out, the "mutual respect and close working relationship" between Wells and Aked rule out any assumption that the minister used her words and ideas without her permission. Wells would name her firstborn son after Aked—a choice that illustrated her abiding admiration for a man whom she clearly never regarded as a plagiarist. "Instead, it would seem," as Silkey suggests, that "Aked lent his name, reputation and white male British identity to give credibility to Wells's ideas, . . . bringing her ideas before an audience that would not have heard them otherwise." His success can be seen in the endorsement his views received in *The Economist*, a journal so conservative that its editors felt the need to reaffirm their support for white supremacy even as they denounced lynching. "Be it understood that we do not write as friends of the negro. The equality of the races does not exist." America should move to eradicate lynching not "for the sake of the negro, but for that of their own countrymen, who cannot be good Republicans with the Lynch Law in their midst."[78]

Ironically, Wells had more trouble garnering antilynching resolutions from British churches and reform organizations than Aked had in securing the support of *The Spectator*. Her work garnered endorsements from the Baptist and Congregational Unions, the British and Foreign Unitarian Association, the Aborigine Protection Society, the British Women's Temperance Association, and the "women members of the society of friends," but many organizations proved unwilling to offer "substantive endorsements for action against lynching." At issue, in some instances, were their ties to their American counterparts. Despite substantial support for Wells among British Unitarians, the National Conference of Unitarians refused to pass an antilynching resolution, with delegates to the denomination's

April meeting contesting Wells's assertions about the complicity of American churches in lynching as "unjust" to their United States brethren. American churches might well be uninformed on the subject, maintained Brooke Hereford, one of the denomination's defenders. "Miss W. says she has sent them [Northern clergy] her pamphlet," he wrote fellow Unitarian William Axon. "What do *pamphlets* amount to these busy days?"[79]

"I find the Christian bodies here less responsive by far than the press has been to the cry of the oppressed," Wells told *The Daily Chronicle* (London) in May. She was clearly troubled to find that even in England she could not escape the influence of American Protestant leaders, who often served as apologists for lynching in the South.[80] Fed up, she lashed out. In an article titled "Mr. Moody and Miss Willard," Wells took on two of America's best-known Protestant leaders, both of whom had strong support in the South. Internationally known evangelical minister Dwight L. Moody, who led a large congregation in Chicago, was a frequent and popular visitor to Britain. To Wells, however, he was an example of the American clergy's failure to speak out against segregation and racial violence. As a young man, Moody had been a leading figure in the religious reconciliation between many of the American Protestant denominations that had divided over slavery. Ironically, it originated during the yellow fever epidemic that swept the South in 1878, killing both of Wells's parents. A moment of spiritual crisis and renewal, the epidemic had reanimated the bonds between Southern and Northern Protestants, as well as fostering generous Northern aid to the South. The reconciliation, however, required Northern Protestants to abandon any criticism of Southern "method[s] of dealing with the Negro." Moody did so. Like most white American clergy, he offered no critique of lynching even as his evangelical tours offered segregated revival meetings in the South.[81]

Equally amenable to such practices was Frances Willard, the immensely popular leader of the Women's Christian Temperance Union (WCTU). Although she hailed from an old Massachusetts family with abolitionist leanings, Willard was an apostle of reconciliation between the North and South. Indeed, she rose to the leadership of the largest women's organization in the United States on the slogan "No North, No South, No Sex, No Sectionalism in Politics." A suffrage slogan, it reflected Willard's commitment to securing women the vote, a cause that she incorporated in the WCTU's platform when she became its president in 1879. Her organization pursued both suffrage and temperance, but largely along racial lines designed to accommodate their white Southern members. Many branches of the organization were segregated, and, as historian Edward Blum notes, "the WCTU generally remained silent regarding racial violence." In addition, WCTU leaders "nourished disenfranchisement by actively arguing on its behalf." Not surprisingly, as a result, the WCTU held limited appeal among African American women, many of whom rejected its segregationist policies and its "antipathy toward the cause of race justice."[82]

Wells targeted Moody and Willard, however, not because of the specifics of their careers, but because both were well-known figures who had become frequent subjects of discussion on her British tours. On her first trip, when Wells had told British audiences that white religious leaders remained silent on the topic of lynching, they often asked, but "what about Rev. D. L. Moody and Miss Frances Willard?" And in reply, Wells had answered that, as far as she knew, Moody and Willard had never challenged lynching or Jim Crow. She could remember notices of Moody's revival sermons during her Memphis days "that said Negroes who wished to attend his meetings would have to go into a gallery or that a special service would be set aside for colored people." And likewise, she read an 1890 interview with Willard published by *The Sun* (New York) in which Willard had "all but condoned lynching."[83]

On her return trip, Wells was still fielding the same questions, this time from critics who refused to believe her. Wells chose to discuss Willard and Moody in *Fraternity*, which also reprinted Willard's interview from *The Voice* (New York). Her article took particular aim at Willard, since Moody's support of segregated congregations paled next to the opinions Willard had expressed in her interview. In it, Willard supported the disenfranchisement of black men and also deplored the dangers that they posed to white women. "The colored race multiplies like the locusts of Egypt," she had told *The Voice.* "The grog shop is its centre of power. The safety of women, of childhood, of the home, is menaced in a thousand localities at this moment, so that men dare not go beyond the sight of their own roof-tree."[84]

Willard had been under fire in the black press since her *Sun* interview—with little apparent effect. Willard bemoaned the WCTU's lack of success building a large colored constituency, but often in racist terms unlikely to attract black members. If anything, she was even more tolerant of lynching than Wells accused her of being. Willard told a February 1893 national meeting of the WCTU that she was eager to organize the colored people in the organization, particularly now that "a lurid vengeance has devoured the devourers of women and children." Willard's remarks underscored her unshakable conviction that interracial sex was the cause of lynching, as well as her belief that "an average colored man is loyal to the purity of white women; but when under the influence of intoxicating liquors the tendency of all men is toward a loss of self control, and the ignorant and vicious, whether white or black, are the most dangerous characters."[85]

Yet Willard's views did not make her an easy target. She was immediately defended by Lady Henry Somerset, who published a flattering interview with Willard on May 21, 1894, in *The Westminster Gazette.* A close friend of Willard's, Somerset hosted her at her Reigate Estate, just outside of London, during much of 1893 and 1894. The two women answered Wells's charges by sitting down in Somerset's garden for a cozy exchange that underscored Willard's antislavery lineage. "Your family for generations back were all Abolitionists," Somerset said to Willard, suggesting any charge that the American leader did not support racial justice had to be absurd. "Your father and mother were educated in the famous Abolition College, founded by the Congregationalists in Oberlin, Ohio." But when their discussion moved to the present day, Willard revealed how far removed she was from her family's abolitionist past by disavowing the idea that a Northerner such as herself could have any influence on Southern matters. "State rights prevail with us," she told Somerset, "and prevent action by the National Government." Talking to a Northern woman such as herself about lynching "is really much the same as though London had been held responsible for atrocities in Bulgaria." Willard also insisted that "neither by voice nor pen have I ever condoned, much less defended, any injustice toward the coloured people."[86]

This careful disclaimer aside, however, Willard had no real defense against most of Wells's charges. Largely in agreement with the racist views held by many of the WCTU's white Southern members, she was not willing to denounce disenfranchisement—or even lynching. Instead, she explained that her opposition to black voting arose from her belief that the franchise should be limited to the educated and should never have been expanded to include "alien illiterates" such as immigrants or blacks. Politics had no place for "the plantation Negro who can neither read nor write, whose ideas are bounded by the fence of his own field and the price of his own mule." And when it came to lynching, Willard stood by her claim that black men menaced the safety of women and children in "a thousand localities," adding: "I had been told by the best people I knew in the South—and I knew a great many ministers, editors, and home people . . . If this be not true, then the well-nigh universal testimony of white people in the South is unworthy of credence."[87]

Quick to capitalize on Willard's weak rejoinder, Wells responded by noting the simultaneously defensive and self-satisfied tone that marked Willard's interview with Somerset. "The interview published in your columns to-day hardly merits a reply, because of the indifference to suffering manifested," Wells wrote in a letter that *The Westminster Gazette* published the next day:

> Two ladies are represented sitting under a tree at Reigate, and, after some preliminary remarks on the terrible subject of lynching, Miss Willard laughingly replies by cracking a joke. And the concluding sentence of the interview shows the object is not to determine how best they may help the negro who is being hanged, shot, and burned, but "to guard Miss Willard's reputation."

Wells's answer was effective in the short run. The British papers sided with her against the "two prominent white women" who seemed to have "joined hands in an effort to crush an insignificant colored woman."[88] Somerset's close friendship with Willard undercut the effectiveness of her defense of Willard, and Wells's British friends rallied around her, organizing a breakfast in her honor with sixteen members of Parliament.

Subsequently invited to dinner at the House of Commons by William Woodall, a Liberal member of Parliament, Wells spent her last days in London in a triumphant round of parties and meetings with British reformers. On the last night of her stay came the final victory. On the eve of her departure, Wells's English friends and supporters founded an organization called the British Anti-Lynching Committee. Designed to carry on her work after her departure, it was made up of a diverse coalition of reformers, whose ranks included twenty Liberal members of Parliament as well as several members of the British nobility. Led by the Duke of Argyll, it would investigate "lynching and mob outrages in America," with the aim of giving "expression to public opinion in condemnation of such outrages in whatever way may seem best calculated to assist the cause of humanity and civilization."[89]

Wells left Britain having made a lasting impact. Over the next year and a half the Anti-Lynching Committee would send letters of protest to the governors of all the Southern states, while also flooding those officials with more than two thousand newspapers, petitions, and other documents containing antilynching material. It also corresponded with black editors across the South gathering information on lynching, and at one point planned to send a subcommittee to the United States to investigate further—a proposal that was greeted with howls of outrage from American politicians in both the North and South. In the end, only one member visited, but the committee had made its point. Far more prominently placed than Wells, the British Anti-Lynching Committee would exert enough pressure on American state leaders to ensure that the impact of Wells's British antilynching campaign outlived her visits there and gave her cause an unprecedented new visibility at home.

After three months and 102 public appearances in Britain, Wells brought her antilynching campaign back home. While her British backers were anxious to see her "follow up the advantage which their moral support had given," Wells was utterly exhausted. In desperate need of rest, she booked the most leisurely and roundabout voyage to the United States she could find, traveling to Canada via the Gulf of St. Lawrence and then taking a train to New York. She may also have been in no hurry to return to her native land or travel with other Americans on an ocean liner bound for the United States, having had "many a set-to with the ubiquitous Americans living abroad."[90]

"Home, did I say?" she had written Helen Pitts Douglass in April 1894, after supplying Douglass with the date of her passage home from Britain: "I forgot that I have no home." On the road for over two years, and more welcome in Britain than in the United States, Wells had come to question whether any African American could claim to be at home "in the land of the free and home of the brave."[91] But soon Wells would prove herself wrong by making an enduring home for herself with her faithful correspondent Ferdinand Barnett, who was waiting for her in Chicago.

· 6 ·

"Although a Busy Woman, She Has
Found the Time to Marry"

IN OUTLINING THE STORY OF HER MOTHER'S LIFE, ALFREDA Duster described the years that followed Wells's second British tour with a string of terms that captured the activist character of her parents' union: "Marriage—Family—and continued Work against Lynching." Wells would marry in 1895 and thereafter give birth to four children, whose arrivals slowed rather than stilled her antilynching campaign. Committed to eradicating lynching and promoting black civil rights, she struggled to balance her political activism with the demands of motherhood—which she found to be a "profession by itself, just like lecturing or teaching."[1] Her domestic responsibilities made her different from any male black leader of her generation and made it difficult for her to sustain her place on the national scene—or build an enduring following. Although the best-known black female leader of her day, Wells would never become the heir to Frederick Douglass—as some of her supporters had once predicted. Married in the spring of 1895, she had her first child a year later, and thereafter juggled her activism with domestic responsibilities that kept her closer to home.

Motherhood, however, was not the only issue limiting Wells's future prospects as a leader. Gender made Wells an unlikely successor to Douglass in an era when men predominated not just in politics, but in all organizations and movements. In making her mark as an antilynching activist, Wells had challenged conventional assumptions about male leadership, inspiring contemporaries to brand her "our noble Joanna of Arc"—after the teenage warrior who led French armies to victory in the fifteenth century.[2] Remembered for cutting her hair, donning armor, and mastering the martial arts, Joan of Arc was as much an icon of gender transgression as she was of female leadership—a point the Wells–Joan of Arc comparison underscored. Moreover, the comparison invoked a transitory moment of female leadership, which in Joan's case ended up with a heresy conviction and death at the hands of her enemies. Especially within the context of nineteenth-century gender conventions, the French leader was remembered as a saintly martyr who gave her life to liberate her people rather than as an example of a woman who could lead men. So images of Wells as a modern-day Joan of Arc likewise presented Wells as a persecuted figure whose leadership would be brief and who posed no permanent challenge to male leadership.

Wells would escape any heresy trial, but both her marriage and the public furor that greeted her when she returned from her second British tour must have helped cement the image of her leadership as a fleeting aberration. Moreover, when Douglass died not long after she returned from her second British trip, Wells was in no position to fill his shoes. Her second British tour was a resounding success, insofar as it subjected lynching to new scrutiny in the United States. It fostered antilynching bills, Congressional debate, and Southern embarrassment, all of which combined to promote the passage of antilynching laws in several states, and scrutiny of the practice throughout the nation. But the success of Wells's antilynching campaign did not win her the support of American whites. Instead, she returned home from England as notorious as she was famous, and continued to be discussed in derisive terms even in Northern publications such as *The New York Times*. Influential without ever being popular, Wells correctly read articles defaming her as a "negro adventuress" as evidence that "the work had done great good."[3] As she recognized, abuse from *The Appeal-Avalanche* (Memphis), *The Atlanta Constitution*, *The Telegraph* (Macon, Ga.), and *The Washington Post* indicated that she was receiving attention from people who once had ignored both Wells and lynching, but now felt compelled to acknowledge both.

Widespread white hostility, however, would also ensure that Wells would never succeed Douglass. Instead, she would remain a persecuted Joan figure, even after Douglass died early in 1895, leaving black America with no obvious successor. A variety of regional leaders represented the race, and Wells was well-known enough to be vilified in the national press, but no post-emancipation black leader had emerged who could match Douglass's national recognition, popularity, or authority. Part of the problem was that the late nineteenth century was not an auspicious time for black leaders. Violence took the lives of some of the leading black political leaders of the post-emancipation era, while the elimination of the black vote through much of the South during the 1880s and 1890s effectively eradicated electoral politics as a continuing source of black leadership. Moreover, independent and uncompromising black leaders such as Douglass did not, and indeed could not, flourish in the Jim Crow South, which further compromised any prospects for the emergence of a black leader with a national following. In 1895 more than 90 percent of black people still lived in the South, but even Southern-born "Afro-American agitators," such as Ida B. Wells and T. Thomas Fortune, generally ended up moving north.

Most politically effective as an agitator rather than as an established race leader, Wells remained an agitator all her life. In 1895, with her antilynching campaign still going strong, Wells did not jockey to replace Douglass. Instead, she continued to focus on using her formidable skills as an orator and journalist to combat lynching, and worked to build an antilynching coalition that depended on international rather than national leadership. No real Joan of Arc either, Wells never embraced the role of martyr—despite the storm of criticism she received. Instead, she welcomed support from other black women, who once again spoke up in her defense. In 1895, when Wells's antilynching campaign was vilified by a Missouri editor who slandered both Wells and black women as a group, a national organization of black women's clubs was formed to rebuff such assaults. An agitator even among her allies, Wells would not always see eye to eye even with her female defenders. But she was heartened to see her work inspire a new sense of activism among black women even as she entered into a marriage and family life that would test her own ability to remain fully committed to such work.

"Practical Negro Advancement"

Possibly most problematic for Wells's antilynching campaign in the long run was not her marriage or family life, but rather the black leader whom many whites anointed as Douglass's successor. An accommodationist rather than an agitator, Booker T. Washington, the principal of the Tuskegee Institute in Tuskegee, Alabama, would quickly bypass other potential leaders in the mid-1890s to replace Douglass as the leading voice of his race. A Southerner, Washington rose to national prominence on claims that he spoke for the blacks of his region. A man whose career took shape within the political constraints of the Jim Crow South, Washington recognized that whites rather than blacks were his most crucial constituency, and crafted a folksy and nonconfrontational leadership style that brought him widespread national recognition and support among whites. Whereas the African American activists T. Thomas Fortune and Wells—and Douglass himself—had provided post-emancipation black America with a moral leadership that challenged racial injustice, the Alabama educator advocated a program of black economic development tailored to fit the Jim Crow regime.

In the spring of 1894, while Wells was in Britain protesting lynching, Washington proposed a far more conciliatory approach. "Practical Negro Advancement," he told a black audience in Washington, D.C., would not come from "stump speeches" or black political agitation (in what may have been a veiled dig at Wells). Instead, the accumulation of wealth by African Americans would bring with it the "rights, political and otherwise, to which they are entitled. The accumulation of property would not only earn blacks the right to vote, Washington maintained, it would give them the power to

Booker T. Washington,
c. 1890

end lynching. If "ten colored businessmen in any of the small towns in the South, whose aggregate deposits in the leading bank of the town amount to $100,000 . . . heard that some colored man was going to be lynched one night," Washington maintained, they could prevent mob violence by going to the president of the bank and threatening to withdraw their deposits the next day. No "lynching would occur that night . . . nor any other night. The president and directors of the bank don't propose to have it weakened and perhaps ruined simply to gratify the thirst of a mob for blood."[4]

Washington's advocacy of black self-help and industrial education reassured whites in both the North and the South that the Negro problem was largely the responsibility of the Negro. Unlike Douglass and Wells, the educator from Alabama did not rebuke the white South for using a combination of disenfranchisement, economic exploitation, and racial violence to all but reenslave African Americans. Nor did he ask white Northerners to intervene in Southern affairs. Instead, he maintained that African Americans did not "command respect" among whites because they did not "amount to anything."[5] Instead of appealing to Northern whites for help, blacks needed to embrace hard work and a modest education designed to prepare them for industrial jobs. Not surprisingly, Washington's message proved far more attractive to white Americans than Wells's demands for equal rights and protection from white violence.

Washington's doctrine of accommodation proved immensely popular among whites, who acclaimed him black America's spokesman in the fall of 1895, not long after Douglass's death. Before then the little-known head of a small educational institution in a backwater state, Washington catapulted to fame as a spokesman for blacks after receiving tremendous white acclaim for a speech he delivered on September 16, 1895, at the opening of Atlanta's Cotton States and International Exposition—the South's own world's fair. In what would become known as his Atlanta Compromise Speech, Washington never even acknowledged the racial violence that had driven Wells and many other black Americans north. Instead, he counseled blacks to remain in the South and abandon any pursuit of social or civil equality in favor of bettering themselves by working in the South's fields and factories. The segregated black audience who caught Washington's speech from the balcony of the Exhibit Hall might have questioned whether blacks could prosper in a region where segregation barred most African Americans from well-paying jobs. But he offered whites an alluring vision of a profitable New South, built on the backs of a tractable and politically powerless black labor force.

Indeed, Washington's speech was a welcome contrast to the "dreadful assertions" made by Ida B. Wells, one local white woman noted after attending his lecture. "I thought yesterday as I listened to the dignified, logical and splendid speech of that negro man how different would be the influence should he take the lecture platform."[6] Her words would prove prophetic. Washington would soon have a distinctive influence on his race. His Atlanta Compromise Speech in 1895 ushered in an era in African American history sometimes known as Booker T. Washington's age of accommodation.

From the latter half of the 1890s to his death in 1915, Washington was the nation's best-known and most widely respected black leader. He advised several presidents and controlled most of the white philanthropy and political patronage allotted to his race as well as much of the black press. The moderate face of black leadership, he was so prominent among whites that his compromising politics have sometimes obscured the historical record embedded in the complaints of his more radical black contemporaries. But the uphill battles against lynching and Jim Crow waged by Wells and other black activists during this period should caution us against thinking about African American accommodation as a reality. Even Washington, as it turned out, did not fully support his own program. Throughout his career he secretly funneled money into African American legal challenges to Jim Crow segregation and discrimination, while offering no public comment on these issues.

Moreover, even as Washington was courting favor among whites, Wells was still using the protest tactics pioneered by the abolitionists to draw public attention to an unpopular cause. Uncompromising in her politics, Wells was incapable of the diplomacy, duplicity, or racial deference practiced by Booker T. Washington, whose accommodationist leadership made her antilynching campaign more necessary than ever.

"The Problem of the Civilized World"

Indeed, Wells entered the most influential phase of her antilynching campaign in the year or so leading up to her marriage—just as Washington rose to fame. Whereas Washington looked to white Americans for support, as Wells toured the United States "talk[ing] about lynching from one end of the country to the other," she had to rely on British and African American allies. Not surprisingly, she was in constant contact with her most devoted ally, Ferdinand Barnett, who supported and encouraged her work, even as it delayed their nuptials. Wells's American tour saw her "trying to organize antilynching leagues [and] antilynching societies," a task which Barnett helped by founding the Illinois Anti-Lynching League, an organization which feted Wells on her return to Chicago in August 1894.[7] Wedding plans would not prevent her from completing the American phase of her antilynching crusade. Designed to capitalize on the British antilynching movement she had started, her coast-to-coast American tour could not wait. Partners in politics, and soon to be partners in life, the couple did not announce their engagement until a few weeks before they married on June 27, 1895.

A forceful counter to Washington's accommodationism, Wells's antilynching crusade achieved its successes without ever generating widespread public support for herself or her followers. Much like the abolitionists, who challenged the morality of slavery without ever amassing a large following, Wells and her supporters managed to stir up enough "discussion, agitation and censure" to create social change despite generating little public enthusiasm. If nothing else, between 1893 and 1897 Wells's antilynching movement shamed some state leaders into legislative attempts to curb vigilante violence in their states. During those years North Carolina, Georgia, South Carolina, Ohio, Kentucky, and Texas all passed antilynching laws designed to protect prisoners in police custody and/or to punish participants in mob violence, while other states considered such measures. Lynching did not come to an end in these states or anywhere else, but these rarely enforced, and sometimes overturned, state laws, together with an unsuccessful attempt by Senator James Blaine of Vermont to sponsor a congressional investigation into lynching, signaled the beginnings of a public outcry that simply did not exist before Wells's British tour.

Arguably, what influence the antilynching movement gained stemmed largely from the animus it inspired. When Wells returned to the United States in the summer of 1894, she found herself even more unpopular among American whites than she was when she left. A few days after her return to New York, *The New York Times* denounced her as "a slanderous and nasty-minded mulattress, who does not hesitate to represent the victims of black brutes in the South as willing victims." Not surprisingly, white Southerners were still offended by what one editor called Wells's "outrageous libels on the women of the South." Her antilynching campaign, he predicted, would only "pave the way for more lynch law." His prediction seemed accurate enough, at least in Memphis, where *The Memphis Scimitar* responded to the campaign by calling for Wells to be "tied to a stake at Main and Madison streets, and branded on the forehead with a hot iron."[8]

No longer neglected by the white press, Wells might well have wished she was. But after her second British tour, she no longer pursued her antilynching campaign alone. She came home with a powerful new ally in the form of the British Anti-Lynching Committee, an energetic organization of elite British men and women whom her white countrymen could not dismiss as easily as they did Wells.

The committee made its debut with an international press release issued on August 1, 1894, which announced its intention to respond to the "appeal for help" that its members had received from the "negro population in the United States."[9] Thereafter, it began a crusade against lynching and mob violence that soon had American politicians and the American press in an uproar. During Wells's second visit, British congregations and reform organizations had repeatedly fired off antilynching resolutions to American news organizations and political leaders. And after her departure, the British Anti-Lynching Committee joined in, flooding American newspapers and political officials with antilynching correspondence. Following Wells, who had long stressed the importance of investigation in exposing the true causes of violence, the committee also sent out letters investigating recent lynchings in several American states. "It appears almost incredible that such lawlessness can occur in communities supposed to be civilized," Anti-Lynching Committee secretary Florence Balgarnie wrote Alabama governor Thomas J. Jones on October 6, 1894, addressing a lynching that had taken place in his state two months earlier. By October the committee had already sent out similar letters, "modified according to circumstances," to the governors of Arkansas, Tennessee, Mississippi, Louisiana, Texas, and Florida.[10]

Most state governors took offense. But, in so doing, they also drew public attention to lynching. Governor Jones of Alabama, for example, responded to the Anti-Lynching Committee in a widely circulated letter. Issued under his secretary's name, Jones's missive charged that just as American reformers did not inquire into "the eviction laws in Ireland, or the oppression of the natives in Egypt or India," British reformers had no business in investigating American affairs. "A similar communication from the authorities of another country would be treated as an international incident which no government in England would overlook or fail to resent." Likewise, other state governors in both Northern and Southern states, whether or not they received letters of inquiry about lynching in their own states, were near-unanimous in denouncing the committee's censures as "a meddlesome interference."[11]

The Southern governors' positions were generally echoed in the nation's leading newspapers. *The Washington Post*, for example, described the British Anti-Lynching Committee as a "Committee of Impertinence," while *The Atlanta Constitution* issued a sarcastic call for "a committee over here to protest against the wholesale slaughter of darkies in Africa whenever John Bull gets after them." Meanwhile, *The New York Times* blamed lynching on its victims, noting "it is a peculiar fact that the crime for which negroes have frequently been lynched, and occasionally been put to death with frightful tortures, is a crime to which negroes are particularly prone."[12] Moreover, critiques of the Anti-Lynching Committee that appeared in Britain's conservative newspapers were widely referenced, reprinted, and endorsed in the American press—while support for the committee in the liberal British press received no coverage of any kind.[13]

In the South, however, neither rationales nor indignation could entirely address the unease created by the Anti-Lynching Committee's activities. Short of capital since the Civil War, the Southern states had been especially hard hit by the Panic of 1893—a series of bank failures that marked the beginning of an economic depression that lasted through 1896. Export prices for cotton declined steadily throughout this period, leaving the leaders of many Southern states anxious to attract foreign investors. Always ambivalent about their largely black labor force, by the mid-1890s Southern officials were also interested in attracting European immigrants, whose labor, they believed, would strengthen their economy. Accordingly, the British Anti-Lynching Committee's relentless attention to racial violence worried many Southern editors and state officials.

Indeed, such fears were strong enough to prompt many Southern whites to denounce antilynching as a plot designed to sabotage the Southern economy. Other critics, by contrast, maintained that antilynching was a capitalist plot. Censured for the racial violence in his state, Governor William Northern of Georgia maintained that British opposition to lynching had been drummed up to support "the enforced development of the western country, largely mortgaged to English and New England capitalists." These crafty conspirators had entered into the business of "slandering the southern people, as a result of worries that they could lose their investments, should western immigration be diverted south."[14]

These wild theories about the true sources of British antilynching sentiment may have amused Wells, who would have loved to have had the support of generous British and American capitalists during her British travels. Certainly they amused a British reporter for *The Daily Chronicle* (London), who noted that *The Sun* (New York) simultaneously reported that Wells was "destitute of funds" and employed by the "interests of a Western land boom." Did American politicians, this writer wondered in a pointed critique of the corruption that ran rampant in Gilded Age politics, believe that absolutely everyone was under the control of "a trust or a syndicate with dollars in it"?[15] Especially in the South, Wells was routinely represented as either an "enterprising missionary" or the clueless "agent" of unspecified conspirators, long after she returned from Britain.[16] By and large, Wells ignored these preposterous allegations. If nothing else, she may have seen no need to: in the fall of 1894, Southern whites provided ample evidence that everything that Wells said was true.

Such evidence included a new mass lynching in Millington, Tennessee—just fifteen miles from Memphis—on August 31, 1894. Six black men accused of burning down several barns in the area were arrested. In the custody of two deputies and handcuffed together in a wagon bound for the county jail, they were assaulted by a white mob armed with shotguns. They died in their shackles, shot en masse; unprotected by the deputies, who later claimed that "they had been waylaid, and their prisoners forcibly taken from them and killed."[17] The mass murder of six unarmed men, who could do little to defend themselves other than jump out of the wagon and die in a heap bound together by heavy iron manacles, was an embarrassment to the white South. One white newspaper in Ohio noted: "If Ida B. Wells had desired anything to substantiate the charges against the south that she has been rehearsing, nothing more serviceable could have come to hand."[18]

Indeed, even the Southern press was at a loss when it came to defending the Millington massacre. None of its victims was charged with rape, and no real evidence could be found to suggest that they were even guilty of arson. Moreover, if they had been, as Wells fumed in an interview given the following day, "there is no other place in the world where a capital offense is made of burning barns."[19]

Under closer scrutiny than ever before, whites in Memphis publicly rued the Millington murders. Taking a far different tone than it had after the murder of Wells's friends just two years earlier, *The Memphis Scimitar* lamented, "Every one of us is touched with blood guiltiness in this matter unless we prove ourselves ready to do our duty as civilized men and citizens." Moreover, even though his state had never prosecuted lynchers in the past, Governor Peter Turney of Tennessee announced that he would now move "to put an end to these 'crimes against civilization' in Tennessee."[20] State officials also convened a grand jury that indicted thirteen white men for their complicity in the Millington lynching. Among them were the two deputies who delivered the prisoners to the mob.

The show of public outrage displayed in Memphis reflected a new embarrassment about lynching on the part of white citizens there. But in the end, it was just a show: little had actually changed. "The south has made many such demonstrations," predicted a cynical writer for the black newspaper *The Cleveland Gazette*. In staging a trial, the "Memphis grand jury and courts are simply exercising a little extra care in working the same old Southern bluff or blind."[21] The *Gazette's* predictions proved spot-on: by January an all-white jury had refused to convict any of the Millington lynchers, leaving their crimes forever unpunished.

At the time, however, Wells took satisfaction in the signs of change she saw in Memphis. If not for her antilynching campaign, she believed "Memphis would have been just as self-satisfied and complacent over the murder of the six colored men in 1894, as it was in 1892."[22] Only after "the attention of the civilized world" focused on lynching in America did "the people of Tennessee feel the absolute necessity for a prompt, just and vigorous arraignment of all the murderers connected with the crime." As early as November 1894, Wells was also aware that the Memphis murderers were unlikely to be punished. But whatever doubts she may have had about whether the lynchers would receive justice in Southern courts, she was happy to see them arraigned. "Lynching is no longer 'our problem,'" she concluded: "it is the problem of the civilized world."[23]

If nothing else, the British Anti-Lynching Committee's scrutiny had prompted several state governors to make public statements opposing mob law—statements they were under some pressure to uphold, at least so long as Wells could keep the attention of the civilized world. That fall, Wells had little difficulty in doing so. The British Anti-Lynching Committee's scrutiny and condemnation of racial violence elicited a steady stream of largely negative press focused on the impropriety of any English interference in American affairs. But at the same time, lynchings received far more negative press than they ever had before, and were subject to new, if largely unsuccessful, attempts to convict both the lynchers and the lawmen who turned prisoners over to them.

Hard to prevent, lynching was even harder to punish. Southern whites, as one potential juror in the Millington case put it, were unwilling "to convict any white man for killing a —— nigger."[24] Indeed, the state-level antilynching laws that were proposed, and in some cases even passed during the

1890s, all grappled with the issue of how to create effective penalties for lynching. Georgia, South Carolina, Kentucky, and Texas passed laws to penalize state officials who failed to protect prisoners, while South Carolina, North Carolina, and Ohio made the lynch mob liable for damages to the families of their victims. However, these laws proved no easier to enforce than the many existing laws that lynch mobs broke when they bypassed the legal system in the name of vigilante justice. Still, the new laws may have contributed to the slow decline in the number of American lynchings that began in the mid-1890s. As Wells noted, public support for mob violence among American politicians had "encouraged Lynch Law, and upon the revolution of this sentiment we must depend for its abolition."[25]

But she still had trouble attracting white support as she traveled across the country during the fall of 1894 and winter of 1895. Ida's first lecture after her return from England was at the Bethel A.M.E. Church in downtown Manhattan, where she addressed an enthusiastic audience of more than three hundred people, including "many whites."[26] How many of them were press, however, remains an open question. When Senator Henry W. Blair of New Hampshire—one of the last surviving Radical Republicans in Congress—proposed in August 1894 House Resolution 214, which called for a federal investigation into lynching, it went largely unsupported outside the black community. Only African Americans petitioned in favor of the resolution, which died in committee. Wells had managed to win over some influential white reformers, such as the clergyman and editor Lyman Abbott and the women's rights activist Susan B. Anthony, but her white American allies were too few and far between to sustain her lecture tour.

After New York, Ida traveled to Chicago and spent a month there resting and organizing her cross-country tour. But while she was feted by a standing-room-only audience at the African Methodist Church's Quinn Chapel, she still had trouble securing white audiences. It was not for lack of a national reputation. Wells did attract the attention of the owner and director of the Slayton Lyceum Bureau. Mr. Slayton, a white man, attended Wells's talk at Quinn Chapel and was impressed enough by her skills as an "effective public speaker" to offer her a job. He could guarantee her "four engagements a week at fifty dollars a night, over and above expenses." But she was "to leave out any talks on lynching"—"the American people will not pay to hear you talk about lynching." Not surprisingly, Wells refused. But Slayton's prediction proved accurate. Between the summer of 1894 and the following spring, Wells traveled "from the Atlantic to the Pacific" speaking out against lynching before audiences that were still largely black. She earned, as she noted in her autobiography, "every dollar of my expenses connected with the trip with addresses delivered to my own people."[27]

Wells's antilynching campaign continued to meet with suspicion even among liberal white reformers. She attended gatherings of Protestant ministers in Kansas City and San Francisco but was unable to persuade either to issue any strong resolution against mob violence. In Kansas City, Southern sympathizers walked out of a meeting of the city's Ministers' Alliance, which was considering such a resolution, after a debate that included many "unkind, ungentlemanly and unchristian remarks." In San Francisco, Wells could not even command a hearing. Along with the other women at a meeting of California ministers, she was "excluded from the room" while a male minister discussed the subject, "relating some thrilling instances of negro depravity which he did not consider it proper for ladies to listen to."[28]

Further north, Wells was gratified to see Boston's William Lloyd Garrison, Jr., honor the activist memory of his famous abolitionist father by supporting her antilynching campaign. Enlisted by Moncure Conway, a Virginia-born abolitionist who had lived largely in England since the Civil War, Garrison led a meeting launching the Massachusetts Anti-Lynching League at Faneuil Hall in August 1894. But support for Wells was not universal even among Massachusetts radicals. Thomas Wentworth Higginson, who numbered among the "Secret Six" of abolitionist radicals who had funded John Brown's raid on Harpers Ferry, objected to Wells's approach. She was not hard enough on rape, he argued, explaining: the "condemnation of lynching . . . was in no way impaired by linking it with the condemnation of another offense closely associated with it in the public mind as often affording the occasion for lynching and always its argumentative excuse."[29] Higginson's remark underscored the most serious problem that Wells faced in attempts to mobilize whites against lynching. Her antilynching argument was rejected by the one audience that might have been able to lend it the most authority: white women reformers.

White female reformers such as the Women's Christian Temperance Union leader Frances Willard both resisted and resented Wells's insistence that lynchings had little to do with rape or sex. Indeed, Willard continued to challenge Wells on these points long after their initial conflict in London. The Negro rapist was "a cause of constant anxiety . . . among the white women and little girls" of the South, Willard told the national meeting of the WCTU in Cleveland in late 1894, which Wells also attended. In a speech that equated sex between white women and black men with rape, Willard once again publicly denounced Wells's argument that white women often initiated sex between the races as "unjust, and save in the rarest exceptional instances, wholly without foundation." Moreover, Willard also rejected Wells's claim that black women were frequent victims of sexual violence in the New South. "The bleaching of the black race which was the ever-present bar sinister of the olden time in the slaveholding States has largely ceased," the white reformer insisted.[30]

The conflict between Wells and Willard was far more than a failure of empathy or understanding on the part of Willard and other white members of the WCTU. Under Willard's leadership, the WCTU had become a major player in the turn-of-the-century "social purity" campaigns that sought to protect white women from sexual predators of all kinds, and especially those of the lower races. The organization's largely white membership had a pointed interest in "the racial politics of rape," at least when it came to defending the purity of the white race—and for that reason was uneasy about denouncing lynching. These members of the "woman movement" subscribed to a race-based "evolutionary republicanism," which advocated the linked goals of temperance, social purity, and white women's suffrage as a means of "safeguarding the development of the Anglo Saxon . . . race."[31] Much like Scotland's Isabelle Mayo, Willard and other white members of the WCTU saw white female reformers as uniquely qualified for moral leadership of the world's peoples by virtue of the racial and sexual superiority possessed by white women—a conviction that made it difficult for them to believe that white women would ever seek out sexual relationships with African American men. White women were supposed to be passionless and pure representatives of the highest morality the human race had to offer. Their enlightened influence could inspire men to turn their backs on alcohol and the weaknesses of the flesh.

Unintimidated by Willard's critique, Wells stood her ground one more time. In her own appearance before the Cleveland convention, she maintained that all her statements could be documented, unlike Willard's ridiculous assertions "that it was unsafe for a white woman to venture out of doors in the South." Declaring her respect for Willard and her temperance work, Ida maintained that she found some of Willard's "positions on the lynch question untenable." Defending her own integrity as a journalist, she noted: "We have to give the facts. *In giving them no imputation is cast upon the white women of America, and it is unjust and untruthful for any one to so assert. I wish it were possible not to make such allusions, but the Negro race is becoming as careful as to its honor as the white race.*" Accordingly, Wells called for the WCTU to endorse "a strong set of resolutions condemning lynching." Wells's speech received nearly unanimous support from the organization's black members.[32]

The organization's largely white membership, however, favored Willard over Wells. "No anti-lynch resolutions passed the WCTU national convention held here last and this week, notwithstanding Miss Wells' short address (longer time was not given to her)," reported *The Cleveland Gazette*. Instead, the WCTU passed a toothless antiviolence resolution that deplored "lawless acts" in general, while also condemning the "unspeakable outrages which have so often provoked such lawlessness."[33]

Moreover, after the meeting, Willard attempted to cover up the conflict between black and white women in the organization with a series of personal attacks on Wells that seem to have been informed by a disdain for black people of Wells's class. "They are a pathetic people when educated," she wrote in her diary in 1896 after visiting a black school in the South. Unwanted in America, their life here was bound to be "grievous." "If I were in their place I'd make a beeline for Africa."[34] Not surprisingly, she had little sympathy for Wells, who refused to migrate anywhere. Instead, Willard was threatened enough by Wells to write letters denouncing her to a variety of prominent white reformers. She told her "good friend" Albion Tourgée that Wells was a "percussive personality" who "lacked the balance and steadiness that are requisite in a good reformer." On this point, however, Willard got no support from Tourgée, who instead spoke out in defense of Wells. Addressing the Wells-Willard squabble in his regular column in the Chicago Daily Inter Ocean on November 24, 1894, Tourgée, writing in his characteristically emphatic style, underscored that all Wells's charges against Willard and the WCTU were "literally true." The organization led by Willard had been "absolutely silent" about lynching until confronted by Wells and her British allies, and "it had not yet uttered any vigorous protest."[35] Undeterred by Tourgée's sharp rebuke, Willard sought out other allies, calling on some of America's most prominent reformers to chastise Wells.

Descended from abolitionists, the WCTU leader was "devoted to the cause of the colored people," maintained a flattering February 1895 letter, ostensibly written by Frederick Douglass. Signed by a distinguished group of reformers including Wells supporters Lyman Abbott and William Lloyd Garrison, Jr., it contained a barely veiled attack on Wells: "We feel that for any person or persons to give currency to statements harmful to MISS WILLARD as a reformer, is most misleading and unjust."[36] Published by Willard's friend Lady Somerset in an English newspaper, the letter, as it turns out, did not have the support of all its signatories. Garrison had endorsed its vague and general statement of support for Willard without knowing anything about what had happened during the WCTU's November conference. Moreover, once he knew more, he was "horrified at this 'apology for southern outrages.'"

Likewise, Frederick Douglass, who died a day after he signed the letter, had also been unaware that his endorsement of Willard condoned the WCTU's temporizations on the subject of lynching—as well as Willard's attack on Wells. "Any impeachment on this or any other matter was an insult to his memory," Helen Pitts Douglass told Florence Balgarnie, after the

British woman wrote her to find out whether Douglass had knowingly lent support to the temperance leader's attack on Wells. Although private, Mrs. Douglass's letter was in accord with her late husband's last public comments on Willard, which were highly critical. A little more than a year before he died, Douglass had presented a fiery antilynching lecture that denounced "the good Miss Frances Willard, of the W.C.T.U." as a "Northern woman, of Southern principles." Also published as a pamphlet titled *The Lesson of the Hour: Why Is the Negro Lynched?* (1894), Douglass's lecture indicted Willard and several other white American leaders for defaming the black man as a "moral monster, ferociously invading the sacred rights of woman and endangering the home of the whites."[37]

Despite such rebuttals, Willard's attempts to discredit Wells continued until Willard's death in early 1898. With the help of Lady Henry Somerset, who continued to lead the British WCTU, Willard launched another assault on Wells at an international gathering of WCTU affiliates held in London in 1895. Under fire among their British WCTU affiliates for failing to take a strong stand against lynching, the WCTU leaders issued a resolution criticizing mob violence, followed by a contradictory one endorsing the American WCTU's stance on lynching and segregation. Somerset charged "Miss Ida Wells, the colored agitator against lynching" with having made "unfair attacks upon Miss Frances E. Willard and other temperance leaders in the United States, charging them with being unsympathetic with the Negroes in the United States." Willard seconded this critique and "regretted . . . that Miss Wells by her attitude had stirred up the black blood to strife"—a point echoed by several American members of the WCTU.[38]

Only the secretary of the British Anti-Lynching Committee, Florence Balgarnie, spoke up on Wells's behalf. In tears by the end of the proceedings, Balgarnie maintained that "the Women's Christian Temperance Union of America had acted the part of the apologist for, rather than that of a denouncer of, the outrages perpetrated on Southern Negroes." Although accurate, Balgarnie's statement was met with "a systematic series of objections" from a hostile audience that eventually forced the secretary to sit down.[39]

However, Wells had other British allies. "The American ladies, led by

The American
temperance leader
Frances Willard,
c. 1880–98

Miss Willard, appear to complain that Miss Wells had not sufficiently minced words in telling of these shocking outbursts of lawlessness," noted *The Daily News* (London)—which was still edited by Wells's London host, Peter Clayden.[40] Equally critical of Willard was Wells's old friend Catherine Impey, who had withdrawn from the WCTU in the 1880s to protest the segregationist practices of its Southern branches. Impey was appalled by Willard's attempt to characterize the segregated branches of the WCTU as the benign product of the organization's conviction that "coloured women, as a class, much prefer to affiliate with those of their own race." The segregation within its Southern branches, Impey wrote, had nothing to do with the preferences of its black members; it was a consequence of the spirit of "caste segregation" that prevailed among Southern whites. Worse, that spirit was sanctioned by the WCTU leaders, who took no responsibility for preventing Jim Crow within its ranks—much as "the national government of America repudiates the responsibility of Lynching, &c."[41] None of these critiques, however, posed a serious challenge to Somerset's and Willard's leadership of the WCTU.[42]

Despite Willard's continuing animus against her, Wells devoted little time to their quarrel after 1894. Still lecturing, Wells was also completing a new pamphlet, A Red Record: Tabulated Statistics and Alleged Cases of Lynching in the United States, 1892–1893–1894 (1895). Filled with facts and figures on lynching drawn from the Chicago Tribune's annual compilation of lynching statistics, A Red Record juxtaposed the empirical data she presented on her subject with Willard's penchant for hearsay. Willard kept insisting that "colored men have been lynched for assault[s] on women," Wells noted, but her own data showed that in many cases "the facts were plain that the relationship between the victim lynched and the alleged victim of his assault was voluntary, clandestine and illicit."[43]

Addressed to the "student of American sociology," A Red Record marshaled the research-based social analysis advocated within this emerging scientific field to challenge Willard's more traditional assertion of a moral female authority that came from within. Wells's longest antilynching work, A Red Record was written in accordance with the methodology advocated by the sociologists of her day, who urged researchers to address social problems by analyzing "all available pertinent facts about the past and present."[44] It was also an extended rebuttal to Willard in which Wells insisted that "virtue knows no color line, and the chivalry which depends upon the complexion of skin and texture of hair can command no honest respect."[45]

Wells was ahead of her time. Still in school when she published A Red Record was a new generation of black leaders including the future Harvard Ph.D., W.E.B. Du Bois, who would soon look to the social sciences for the "emancipation of the American Negro." Hoping to expose and controvert race prejudice and document racial discrimination, Du Bois devoted much of his early career to ambitious studies of African American communities, in the hopes that a scientific knowledge of the race could be applied to the "social and economic advancement of the Negro People"—an approach he would later reject as useless.[46]

Far less committed to the scientific method than Du Bois, Wells did not expect as much from it, and closed A Red Record with a call for activism that displayed her lifelong conviction that the only remedy for injustice was agitation and public action. She called upon readers to "disseminate the facts contained in this book," mobilize their churches and civic associations to denounce lynching, challenge the idea of a "white man's government," "and support [Senator] Blair's anti-lynching resolution."[47] But her call to action would go largely ignored among whites until the 1930s, when the Texan Jesse Daniel Ames led a revolt "against the crown of chivalry which has been pressed like a crown of thorns into our head." Lynching, Ames and the other women in the Association of Southern Women for the Prevention of Lynching at long last realized, policed not only the South's black population, but Southern white women as well. White women were not protected but rather held in thrall by the discussions of black-white rape that became "the folk pornography of the black belt." As the historian Jacquelyn Dowd Hall explains: "the fear of rape regulated white women's behavior and restricted their interactions with the world. The ideology of chivalry helped construct white womanhood: it shaped white women's identities and options even as it guarded caste lines."[48]

Both ahead of her time and unpopular with most white women, Wells never breached those lines, as her battle with Willard showed. Indeed, she could not even persuade her good friend Susan B. Anthony, the former abolitionist and preeminent women's rights activist, to reject Willard's leadership of the WCTU or challenge the segregated women's suffrage associations in the South. A supporter of Wells's antilynching campaign, Anthony hosted Wells when she spoke in Rochester, New York, late in 1894. Committed to black equality, Anthony fired her secretary during Wells's visit—after the woman "refuse[d] to take dictation from a colored woman." But she supported Willard's position on segregation within the WCTU, telling Wells that "for the sake of expediency, one often had to stoop to conquer on the color question." Anthony had repeatedly done so herself, she confided to Wells. For instance, she always asked longtime suffrage activist Frederick Douglass to stay home when the Equal Suffrage Association met in the Southern states, so his presence would not prevent white Southern women from joining the ESA. And she refused to organize black women's branches of the ESA below the Mason-Dixon Line for similar reasons. Do "you think I was wrong in so doing?" Anthony asked Wells. Wells's answer was an uncompromising "yes."[49]

Despite such differences, Wells considered Anthony to be "a dear good friend," who never held Wells's "youth and inexperience" against her. "She gave me rather the impression of a woman who was eager to hear all sides of the question." Moreover, Wells seems to have realized that her differences with Anthony, when it came to making compromises on the color question, had to do with their very different understandings of the role of women in reform. Anthony was willing to support the Frances Willards of the world because she believed that once women got the ballot all society's wrongs would be righted. "The wrongs, injustice, inequality, maladministration of the law" that plagued American society would give way to a new "millennium"—which would make the short-term compromises required to achieve it worthwhile. But Wells, by contrast, believed no such thing. "Knowing women as I do, and their petty outlook on life," she told Anthony, "I do not believe that the exercise of the vote is going to change women's nature or the political situation."[50]

On this subject, perhaps, the young Wells had a knowledge born of experience that Anthony did not. Certainly, she knew that cross-racial alliances between white women and black women would come no more easily than similar alliances between men, and that white women's conceptions of womanhood often excluded black women.

Indeed, by the spring of 1895, Wells was exhausted by her efforts to create such alliances. She had traveled from the "Atlantic to the Pacific," and "done all that one human being could do in trying to keep the matter before the public in my country and in trying to find that righteous public sentiment which would help put a stop to these terrible lynchings." "Physically and financially bankrupt," she returned to Chicago, to take another position on which she and the strong-minded Susan B. Anthony would disagree. Wells had been long considered by Anthony and others to be "married to a cause."[51] But on June 27, 1895, Wells finally "found the time to marry"—as one report on her wedding noted.[52] Moving at long last on an event that had been postponed three times to accommodate the bride's speaking engagements, Wells joined hands in matrimony with Ferdinand Lee Barnett at Chicago's Bethel Church, becoming Mrs. Ida B. Wells-Barnett.

"The Opportunity to Help Unite Our People"

The Wells-Barnett wedding was squeezed into a busy schedule that had Ida crisscrossing the Midwest "delivering addresses nightly" up to within a week of her wedding day, which did not prevent it from being the social event of the season in Chicago's black community. Since the bride had no family in Chicago and no time to organize a wedding, the event was organized by the Ida B. Wells Club, which issued five hundred invitations to the "leading colored people from all parts of the country." The audience it drew was impressive. In attendance was the entire Illinois Republican Women's Committee—a white organization that Ida had been working with. And the wedding also attracted a popular audience of "fully two thousand people [who] thronged the streets and the vicinity"—making it impossible for many invited guests to enter the church.[53] Even the bridal party had to fight its way through the packed streets surrounding the church. But the ceremony went off without a hitch, and began with Ida giving herself away, by walking "the length of the church down the left aisle" on her own, dressed with characteristic flair in "satin en train, trimmed with chiffon and orange blossoms."[54]

For Ida, the wedding was a homecoming as well as a new beginning. Her two youngest sisters, Annie and Lily, traveled from California to serve as bridesmaids—"beautifully attired in lemon crepe."[55] Moreover, Wells invited them to live at her new home in Chicago after the wedding; both did so until they married and set up households of their own. Among other things, Wells's marriage to Barnett offered her a home to replace the one she had lost in Memphis, complete with family members from whom she had become separated, as well as new in-laws and stepsons. But Wells's desire to create a home for herself and her younger sisters did not go unchallenged. As Wells remembered it at any rate, the news of her wedding inspired a "united protest from my people. They seemed to feel that I had deserted the cause, and some censured me rather severely in their newspapers for having done so."[56]

The most enduring critic of the marriage seems to have been Susan B. Anthony. Several years after Ida became Mrs. Wells-Barnett, Anthony repeatedly bit out her friend's married name in disapproving tones, prompting Wells to ask her, "Miss Anthony, don't you believe in marriage?" Wells's

Susan B. Anthony, c. 1890

reaction helps illuminate her hopes for her marriage. Obviously she did not share Anthony's opinion that marriage was not appropriate for "women like you with a special call to do special work." Nor was she willing to avoid marriage, as Anthony had, for fear that it would mean "dropping the work to which I had set my hand." Rather, Wells listened quietly as Anthony rebuked her for taking "divided duty."[57] Now a mother with an eleven-month-old baby at home, Wells could hardly contest the older woman's assertion that she was giving neither her baby nor her work her full attention.

But according to her autobiography, Wells was unmoved by Anthony's rebuke. Instead, she could not help reflecting that her marriage had enabled her "to carry on her work" at a time when she had become discouraged. Marriage offered her, she remembered in a curious turn of phrase, "the opportunity to help unite our people so that there would be a following to help in the arduous work necessary."[58]

Wells's view of why she married underscored that for her and most other black women reformers, marriage eased the economic strain involved in serving as the leader of a struggling community that was hard put to support reformers. Although never well off herself, Anthony was able to rely on speaking fees and the generosity of wealthy friends to sustain her work, something Wells found almost impossible to do—especially since she had siblings to support. Whereas Anthony was an immensely successful fundraiser who received thousands of dollars in donations and bequests from the middle-class white women who supported her cause, before she married Wells struggled mightily to support herself on the fluctuating income she received as a journalist. Wells did not marry Barnett for financial reasons, but she did come into the marriage in need of a helpmeet.

An exiled traveler who spent most of her young life perennially short of cash, Wells did not even have a real home when she and Barnett married, which may help explain Wells's expression "unite our people." Certainly, among other things, the new home she created with Barnett would offer her a refuge from the overwhelming round of activities that had come to characterize her public life. Only after she married, she recalled in her autobiography, did she finally reach a "place" where she could "rest quietly without feeling that I must be either on the train or traveling through the country to some place of meeting where I was scheduled to speak."[59]

Neither Wells nor Barnett ever saw their marriage as a traditional one. Rather, both of these high-powered individuals entered into their marriage looking for an accomplished partner who would be able to provide support for their work. Ida kept her own name, adopting the hyphenated name of Ida B. Wells-Barnett at a time when married women typically adopted their husband's surname. She "didn't want to lose the identity of Ida B. Wells," her daughter Alfreda Duster later explained, "because it was on that basis she'd made all her trips to Europe" and "done all her antilynching work . . . [and] her writing." Happily, Barnett also valued his new wife's professional profile. Much like Ida, he entered into their marriage looking for an accomplished partner who would be able to provide support for his work. The first black woman to graduate from the University of Michigan, Mary Graham Barnett served as the city editor at Barnett's *Conservator* in Chicago until her death in 1888.[60] Forty-one when he remarried, Barnett told an acquaintance, "When I do think of marriage it will be to a *woman*—one who can help with my career."[61] And in Wells, Barnett found such a woman. Shortly before they married, Wells took the responsibility for the *Conservator* off his hands. She bought out Barnett and the paper's owners, becoming the paper's manager and editor, which left Barnett free to become in 1896 the first African American assistant state's attorney in Illinois.[62] Barnett would hold that position for fifteen years, while making a national reputation for himself as an expert on writs of habeas corpus and extradition.

Likewise, Barnett supported his wife's professional career. He clearly never expected his new wife to become a homemaker. He came into the marriage with an established household that included both of his parents. Indeed, during his years as a widower, Barnett had relied on his parents to supply much of the help he needed as a single parent. His eighty-five-year-old father, Ferdinand Lee Barnett, Sr., had domestic talents, having spent much of his life working as a cook on the steamboats that traversed Lake Michigan; while his mother, Martha Brooks Barnett, who was fifteen years younger than her husband, had "taken over" the care of her widowed son's children after his first wife died. So Barnett had little need of a wife to look after his two sons. Instead, even after he married Wells, his mother seems to have continued to raise his sons, occupying a position of authority in the Barnett household that posed a challenge for Wells. Once the younger couple began to have children of their own, Barnett resolved the situation by moving his parents and his teenage sons into a separate house of their own. "My father . . . had two homes," Alfreda recalled. "His mother and the two boys . . . lived not too far from the house, and so he would get a chance to see both his families."[63]

Meanwhile, the home that Barnett shared with Wells, as Alfreda recalled it, "was almost a business." Her mother was "busy all the time and not tied down by house work and cooking." Ida "didn't like to cook," so Barnett, who had learned to love working in the kitchen while assisting his father in the steamship galleys, took over much of that responsibility.[64] He also employed household help to assist with the other day-to-day domestic chores, leaving Ida free to catch up with the evening papers while her husband prepared dinner. Work dominated the couple's daily life. Once the family had finished dinner "or even before," their house would fill up with people, there to discuss professional or political matters. Ferdinand Barnett, in particular, had the "habit of carrying on his business at home," his daughter noted. Even though he had a law office downtown, he treated his home as an "extended office."[65] And while Ida was sometimes unhappy with the number of guests that her quiet husband brought home, she was "also liable to bring home somebody." She knew "all the outstanding people of the day," and hosted many visiting speakers and distinguished guests, as well as leading youth groups that met in her home.[66]

By all accounts, the Wells-Barnett union was busy and eventful from the very beginning. Ida took charge of the *Conservator* offices less than a week after her wedding, while Ferdinand abandoned the newspaper business altogether, taking on a challenging new job as Illinois's first African American assistant state's attorney. Moreover, even as she took over the *Conservator*, Ida was back on the lecture circuit less than two months later, denouncing lynching at a talk in Buffalo, New York. In the interim, exhaustion and the challenges of settling into a new household kept Wells-Barnett in Chicago—although far from idle. An active member of the Illinois Republican Women's central committee, she served as the president of the Ida B. Wells Club between 1894 and 1898, and wrote regularly for white newspapers in Chicago as well as for her own publication. Pleased to note that marriage had not slowed Wells-Barnett down, *The Indianapolis Freeman* reported that she was "still giving hammer blows to the lynching industry."[67] In addition, even as they were settling into married life, both Ida and her new husband also had to contend with a terrifying race riot in Spring Valley, Illinois, a coal town one hundred miles south of Chicago.

The spring and summer of 1895 saw racial hostilities building in the economically depressed town. For more than a year, a bitter labor conflict had divided the Spring Valley Coal Company and its unionized labor force, which was composed largely of Italian immigrants and white Americans. After the end of an unsuccessful miners' strike in 1894, the company had added racial conflict to the mix when it replaced the striking miners with black workers. The African American strikebreakers immediately became the target of the labor strife that had divided the town. On August 3, 1895, an Italian miner was robbed and beaten by a group of men that the white community assumed to be African American. The following day, a white mob assembled to demand that the coal company fire its black workers by way of retribution. When the company's manager refused, several days of rioting ensued. White miners, armed with "miners pick, clubs," and "old rusty guns," drove all the blacks they could find out of town, injuring more than a dozen people as they pulled men, women, and children out of their homes and chased them into the woods outside Spring Valley. A mass meeting of more than one thousand miners then assembled on August 6 to adopt a resolution ordering the city's African American inhabitants "to leave the city and carry off their effects" by five o'clock the following day. The next day the group gathered to enforce this order. With the town mayor and law enforcement officers looking on, the white miners force-marched out of town all the African Americans who had not already fled or been forced to leave. "Women and children were driven from their homes, were abused and insulted and their trunks and belongings were dragged about and despoiled."[68]

African Americans throughout Illinois and beyond were outraged. Both Barnetts attended a mass meeting at Chicago's Quinn Chapel on August 6, where black Chicagoans considered taking the law into their hands and dispatching a group of armed men to defend Spring Valley's black population. Cooler voices, including Ida B. Wells-Barnett and her husband, counseled against black vigilantism and organized a Quinn Chapel Committee to provide aid to Spring Valley's black refugees. The committee collected $1,400 to send a delegation to Spring Valley to investigate the riot, provide support for Spring Valley blacks, and sue the town. But in the end the committee had to complete its mission in Chicago, since Barnett and the two other black men charged with visiting Spring Valley found the town impossible to reach. No trains stopped there during the day—the only safe time for African American visitors to arrive. And when Barnett looked into the possibility of reaching the town by taking an earlier train that stopped in a nearby town, he found that the two towns nearest to Spring Valley were both municipalities that blacks were not allowed to enter.[69] However, the Quinn Chapel Committee was able to offer valuable support to the refugees, all the same. In addition to providing financial relief, the committee's advice that they bring criminal charges against the attackers resulted in several convictions. Those convicted were all recent immigrants, arguably a result of anti-immigrant sentiment among the rural Americans who heard the case, but still they set a precedent for organized resistance to lynching in Illinois that would stand for many years to come, with the Barnetts usually leading the charge.

"Our Noble 'Joanna of Arc'"

Ida continued to make news on the national scene even after she sequestered herself in Chicago. With the British Anti-Lynching Committee still campaigning against lynching on her behalf, and Willard still complaining that Wells was unfair to white women, marriage made Mrs. Wells-Barnett no less a target for slander. Wells had long been denounced in the Southern press as an opportunist and a liar, and just as she got married, her antilynching campaign elicited an attack on black women as a group that was offensive enough to provoke hurt, anger, and a new spirit of activism among African American women across the nation.

In June 1895, J. W. Jacks, president of the Missouri Press Association, sent an indignant response to one of British Anti-Lynching Committee secretary Florence Balgarnie's censures. Jacks's letter was largely an attack on African American women, written by a Southern apologist who claimed to be an expert on the Negro race. "Our laws mete out the same punishment to both white and colored people for the same crimes," Jacks told his British interlocutor. But whereas the chastity of white women was such that it would cost "as much as a man's life to rob her of her virtue by seduction," black women had nothing to lose. "Out of some 200 in this vicinity," he wrote, "it is doubtful if there are a dozen virtuous women." Black women had nothing but disdain for sexual restraint, Jacks maintained, insisting that one such woman had told him that "a certain Negro woman" was ostracized by her peers for not letting "any man except her husband, sleep with her."[70]

Only one of a number of nasty attacks on black women published in the 1890s, Jacks's letter is less important for its content than for the militant reaction it elicited.[71] Instead of broadcasting the letter to a British audience, as Jacks had hoped, Wells's friend Florence Balgarnie passed the letter to a black women's club leader, Josephine St. Pierre Ruffin, editor of The Woman's Era. A Wells supporter since the Ida B. Wells testimonial reception in New York in 1892, Ruffin had sided with Wells and Balgarnie in their 1895 battle with Willard.[72] Ruffin was appalled by Jacks's letter and reluctant to reproduce its contents in her publication. So, instead of reprinting any portion of it in The Woman's Era, she sent copies of the letter to her subscribers and solicited their responses.

The reaction was dramatic. Black women were "suddenly awakened by the wholesale charges of the lack of virtue and character," a distressed Margaret Murray Washington (Booker T. Washington's wife) wrote back; while

Fannie Barrier Williams later claimed that "it stirred the intelligent black women as nothing had ever done."[73] Acting on this outrage, Josephine St. Pierre Ruffin called together the first National Conference of Colored Women of America, which met in Boston in August 1895. Wells was unable to attend, but in her absence, the conference resolved "that we, the representative women of the Negro race in the United States, have witnessed with great admiration the noble and truthful advocacy of Mrs. Ida B. Wells Barnett, defending us against the lying charges of rape, and we take this opportunity of congratulating her upon her recent marriage, and are glad to hail her, in the face of her assailants, as our noble 'Joanna of Arc.'"[74]

A tribute to Wells's career as an outspoken black female leader, the conference saw new expressions of militancy among the middle-class club women who responded to Ruffin's call. "There was a time when our mothers and sisters could not protect themselves from such beasts," one of its founders commented, "but a new era has begun and we propose to defend ourselves."[75] Likewise, the conference convener, Josephine St. Pierre Ruffin, noted that black women could no longer continue to be reduced to "mortified silence" by charges of a "delicate and humiliating" nature.[76] Accordingly, the conference participants formed a permanent organization "pledged to correct the image of black women."[77]

Led by Margaret Murray Washington, the National Federation of African American Women "united 36 women's clubs in twelve states." A year later, the NFAAW merged with the National League of Colored Women, a rival coalition of black women's clubs that came together in 1895 under the leadership of Mary Church Terrell. A prominent Washington, D.C., club woman, Terrell was the daughter of the wealthy black businessman Robert Church, who had funded Wells's escape from Visalia, California, more than ten years earlier. Old acquaintances, she and Ida would remeet at the inaugural meeting of the new organization produced by the merger, the National Association of Colored Women (NACW), in Washington, July 14–16, 1896. Wells-Barnett must have welcomed a second chance to enjoy the national movement she had inspired, especially since it included some of the most influential women in the country. "A famous gathering of famous women," it included Harriet Tubman, Frederick Douglass's daughter Rosa Douglass Sprague, and many others, such as longtime Wells supporters Victoria Earle Matthews and Josephine St. Pierre Ruffin.[78]

Ironically, however, Wells-Barnett would never have any real opportunity to assume a leadership role in the organization that she inspired. The different clubs in the NACW were led by powerful regional leaders, and although Ida's national reputation, powerful personality, and central role in the club movement's origins made her a logical candidate for NACW leadership, both her personality and personal history effectively barred her from ever being considered. For all that Ida's outspoken campaign against lynching and Jim Crow helped inspire a new sense of activism among black women, the NACW's highly respectable leadership would not follow in her controversial footsteps.

Instead, leadership struggles within the NACW focused largely on which one of the handful of privileged and powerful women who dominated the various black women's clubs in different parts of the country would be chosen to lead the national organization. Would it be Boston's Josephine St. Pierre Ruffin, or Washington's Mary Church Terrell, who had led the National League of Colored Women? And finally there was the first president of the short-lived NFAAW, Margaret Murray Washington, whose power base was in the South. An advocate of self-help among women, Washington had risen to national prominence along with her husband.

In 1896, Mary Church Terrell won out, becoming the first president of the NACW. Although longtime acquaintances, Wells and Terrell were not close friends, and the gulf between them dramatized the class differences between Wells and the leading club women. A decade earlier, Wells had been very taken with the fair-skinned, elegant "Mollie" Church when she had a chance to spend some time with her in Memphis. "She is the first woman of my own age I've met who is similarly inspired with the same desires hopes & ambitions," she had enthused in her diary after spending a morning with Church in 1887.[79] But the two had little opportunity to become friends. While Ida began teaching at sixteen, the daughter of the South's first black millionaire attended Oberlin and spent little time in Memphis thereafter. After marrying a Harvard-educated lawyer, Robert Herberton Terrell, she settled in Washington, where as one of the wealthiest and best-educated black women in the country, Terrell rapidly became a leading member of Washington's black elite.

In 1896, Terrell won the NACW presidency largely on the strength of her position as the head of the Colored Women's League of Washington— a federation of 113 women's clubs in D.C. and the surrounding area that amounted to more than half of the two hundred clubs in the NACW. The other leading contenders for the post, including Josephine St. Pierre Ruffin and Margaret Washington, were appointed vice presidents—and Washington also become the editor of the organization's newsletter, *National Association Notes*. The new organization's Joan of Arc, by contrast, was given far more minor responsibilities. Wells-Barnett chaired the resolutions committee during the meeting, graciously approving a resolution endorsing the work of the WCTU put forward by members of the League of Washington Women rather than jeopardize the fragile coalition of women's clubs that were joining to create the NACW. She also received an appointment to the editorial board of Josephine St. Pierre Ruffin's *Woman's Era* and a few other little assignments, such as serving as secretary on the committee charged with publishing the new organization's minutes.

She left the meeting unfazed, however, since the most notable milestone in Wells-Barnett's life during 1896 had nothing to do with the NACW. That year, she was "not too busy to find the time to give birth to a male child."[80] Born exactly nine months after his parents' wedding, and named after Wells-Barnett's British mentor, Charles Aked Barnett testified to Wells's decision to ignore "the advice of certain people who advised the use of whatever contraceptives were available back in the 1890s." She had no interest in preventing a pregnancy, she later explained to her daughter Alfreda. "She really enjoyed her family, and she felt that people who deliberately did not marry and did not have children were losing the rounding-out possibility of their lives."[81] The oldest of her mother's eight children, Wells

Wells-Barnett and her first child, Charles Aked Barnett

entered motherhood with a confidence born of the experience of "having had the care of small children from the time that I was big enough to hold a baby."[82] On the road with her firstborn within months of his birth, she initially juggled motherhood and work with great success.

Barnett supplied a nurse to accompany his wife and child to the Washington meeting of the NACW. Just two months later, Wells-Barnett was back on the road again, lecturing in support of suffrage on behalf of the Illinois Republican Women's central committee. The committee could not afford to supply Wells-Barnett with a full-time nurse but agreed to hire nurses to help out at each of her public events. So the fall of 1896 saw Wells-Barnett traversing Illinois with her six-month-old. In doing so, she became, as she noted in her autobiography, "the only woman in the United States who ever traveled throughout the country with a nursing baby to make political speeches." But her nursing baby occasionally raised his voice in an "angry protest" of his own when he heard his mother's voice on the lecture podium.[83]

Wells-Barnett had her second child, Herman, in November 1897, and would give birth to two daughters thereafter: her namesake Ida arrived in 1901, and her youngest, Alfreda, in 1904. But Herman's birth marked the point when Wells-Barnett began to be convinced that "the duties of a wife and mother were a profession in themselves, and it was hopeless to expect to carry on public work." Not only did a second child make the balancing act that Wells-Barnett performed in the year after the birth of her first child increasingly impossible, but her view of motherhood had begun to change.

Wells-Barnett had entered her marriage believing that something had smothered "the mother instinct" in her—perhaps a youth spent raising her siblings, or her "early entrance into public life," or both, she mused. But with the birth of her sons, that instinct blossomed and reshaped her life. "I had to become a mother," Ida noted in one of the most sentimental passages in her largely unsentimental autobiography. "I realized," she wrote, "what a wonderful place in the scheme of things the Creator has given women." Having children, she then understood, provided women with "one of the most glorious advantages in the development of their own womanhood."[84]

As she began to see motherhood as both a womanly vocation and a profession, Ida pursued both with her characteristic intensity. Accordingly, in 1897 she gave up her editorship of the *Conservator* and abandoned "her public work" to dedicate herself to raising her children. As a mother, Ida admitted, she chose to emulate the "Catholic priest who declared that if he had the training of a child for the first seven years of his life, it would be a Catholic for the rest of his days." A firm believer in her own values and

Protestant religious faith, Wells-Barnett stressed her desire to be there for the "training and control of her child[ren]'s early and most plastic years."[85]

By all accounts, Ida achieved her goal. "I know I still carry with me, the admonitions of my mother and father about various things," her youngest daughter Alfreda admitted more than fifty years after Wells-Barnett's death.[86] But motherhood did not preclude activism. Despite her decision to dedicate herself to her children after Herman's birth, for example, Wells-Barnett delayed giving up the presidency of the Ida B. Wells Club until she had led a successful battle to establish black Chicago's first kindergarten.

Wells-Barnett's interest in making sure that Chicago had a kindergarten that was open to black children was in accord with most progressive education theories of her day. Developed in Germany, kindergartens were an "experimental" innovation in the 1890s, designed to ease children into the daily discipline of school. They were generally private institutions established by "educated and elite women with leisure time." Chicago had several, including one in "what was then the Negro district." Known as the Armour Institute, it was accessible to blacks, but "its waiting list was such that there was little hope for the many colored children who needed this training."[87] So Wells held her presidency of the Ida B. Wells Club until 1899 in order to lead a successful campaign for weekly kindergarten classes at the Bethel Church. Open to black children throughout the city, the classes were led by two young black women with kindergarten training, who had previously been unable to secure work in the city's white kindergartens.

More controversial than it might seem, Wells-Barnett's kindergarten initiative probably won her some enduring enemies. Many black Chicagoans rejected the idea of a segregated school of any kind, fearing it would block black children from admission to the Armour kindergarten. Although no foe of integration as a principle, Wells-Barnett had no patience with this argument. Her long experience teaching in black schools in the South had left her convinced that African Americans could and should take responsibility for educating their own children if need be. "Here were people so afraid of the color line that they did not want to do anything to help to

supply the needs of their own people," she said of the kindergarten's detractors.[88]

As strong-minded in motherhood as she had been before her children
arrived, Wells-Barnett struggled with both her resolve to remain home and
its consequences, finding herself on "divided duty"—much as Susan B. Anthony had predicted. At least in theory, the black women's club movement
offered her one venue where motherhood and activism were often combined. Founded on the motto "The battle for womanhood is the battle for
race," the NACW would place an increasing emphasis on "individual home
life" and the belief that proper child care was the "chosen kingdom of
women."[89] But Wells-Barnett's interest in the club movement would dimin-
ish as the movement's scope became more domestic. As much as she reveled
in the experience of motherhood, Ida remained both unwilling and unable
to limit her political concerns to the domestic realm. Always acutely conscious of the constraints of sexism as well as racism imposed on black
women, she was not willing to leave political matters in the hands of the
men of her race.

Moreover, Wells-Barnett found no real place in the NACW, which
held its second meeting in Nashville, Tennessee, in 1897. The choice of
venue effectively, if not deliberately, barred Wells-Barnett from attending—
she was still unwelcome in Tennessee. And in 1899, when the NACW held
its third meeting in Chicago, Wells-Barnett was not invited. Wells-Barnett
would blame Terrell for this slight, but in fact it seems to have been initiated by Fannie Barrier Williams. A leading member of Chicago's black
elite, in 1893 Williams had supported Wells-Barnett's pamphlet on the
world's fair. The two women had other connections as well, since Fannie
Barrier Williams was married to S. Laing Williams, an attorney who was
Barnett's law partner throughout the 1890s. But the relationship between
the Barnetts and the Williamses went downhill as the latter couple became
increasingly closely affiliated with Booker T. Washington, whose accommodationist politics won no favor with the Barnetts. As rival leaders within
Chicago's female black community, Fannie and Ida developed a deep personal enmity. Speaking in her official capacity as the leader of the Illinois

Portrait of Mary Church Terrell, c. 1900

Federation of Women's Clubs, Williams told Mary Church Terrell that Chicago women would not participate in the meeting if Wells-Barnett was invited.

In a decision that Ida later described as "a staggering blow," Terrell acquiesced, leaving the antilynching activist off both the NACW's program and the local arrangements committee. Deeply hurt, Ida never forgave Terrell, even after Terrell explained that she had only omitted her name on the request of several "women in Chicago." Suspicious of Terrell's political ambitions, Ida remained convinced that Terrell had excluded her from the meeting's activities in order to ensure her own reelection as president of the NACW—using "the narrow minded attitude of my own home women to ignore me lest I might become a contender for the position she wanted again."[90]

Although Terrell never saw Ida as a real challenger for her own position, in ousting Wells-Barnett she killed two birds with one stone. She placated Fannie Barrier Williams, who led a large group of Chicago club women, while also undermining Josephine St. Pierre Ruffin's bid for the leadership of the NACW. The only leading club woman to display consistent public support for Ida in her battle with Frances Willard, Ruffin was the most serious challenger to Terrell's reelection in 1899—she had the support of New England club women and would have had Ida's support had Terrell not managed to keep Wells-Barnett from attending the meeting. Ruffin was troubled by the increasingly accommodationist and domestic tenor of the NACW under Terrell's leadership, complaints which Wells-Barnett would surely have seconded. But in Ida's absence, Ruffin had little support from women outside her own region, and Terrell won her reelection easily.[91] Moreover, under Terrell's leadership the NACW would continue to embrace a "politics of respectability" that marginalized activists such as Ruffin and the even more outspoken Ida B. Wells-Barnett—who both parted company with the NACW after 1899.

When she discussed women's suffrage with Anthony, Ida described women as "petty"—a comment that reflected how hard it was for her to marshal the patience, social background, or diplomatic skills necessary to flourish within the genteel world of female reformers.[92] But personality was not the only issue. Ida's political agenda also led her to seek out the masculine sphere of influence rather than limiting herself to the domestic sphere allotted to women.

No matter the joys of motherhood, Wells-Barnett remained aware that women's sphere had a very limited influence over the men who controlled the fate of black America. In contrast to Susan B. Anthony, who remained ever confident that "when the women get the ballot all that will be changed,"[93] Wells-Barnett had little confidence that women had inherently better political values than men—an attitude that may have been reinforced by her experience in the NACW—and she understood the importance of masculine power in a society where male dominance was not limited to the political sphere, but extended into the home as well. Wells-Barnett supported women's suffrage, but believed that women's political influence would be limited by their preoccupation with the domestic sphere. "Many women would not vote," she told her daughter, and those that did "would be influenced by their husbands."[94]

Accordingly, as the new century turned, Ida B. Wells-Barnett increasingly abandoned the black women's club movement in favor of continuing to agitate against lynching with none of the delicacy or discretion that the NACW deemed appropriate. Active in the short-lived Afro-American Council, which grew out of the ashes of the Afro-American League in 1898, Wells-Barnett was preoccupied with organizing that group's 1899 meeting in Chicago, even as NACW members were scheming to limit her influence at their own.

Succeeded by the Niagara Movement, the Afro-American Council was one of the precursors of the NAACP, and Wells-Barnett would be far more active in these efforts to create a national organization to protect black civil rights than she ever was in the NACW—becoming one of the founding members of the NAACP. But in the end neither Ida B. Wells-Barnett nor her husband would find a comfortable home in the black political world of early twentieth-century America. Consolidation of white political power in the New South combined with continuing racism in the nation at large to force African American leaders to tread an increasingly careful political path. But caution was never one of Wells-Barnett's strong suits: she was always more successful as an agitator than as a leader. Instead, the turn of the century saw first Booker T. Washington and then the young W.E.B. Du Bois rise to power, eclipsing Ida's brief moment of national leadership.

· 7 ·

Challenging Washington, D.C.—
and Booker T.

NO LONGER AT THE HELM OF THE *CONSERVATOR* OR WRITING regularly for any other paper, Ida Wells-Barnett hoped to make motherhood her primary occupation as the nineteenth century came to a close. But with mob violence continuing to take the lives of African Americans, Ida never managed to remain home long. Over the new century's first decade Wells-Barnett would have two more children and would embrace a vision of motherhood that accommodated work outside the home. A "mother," she would begin to insist, "should teach her sons to cook" so that they "could have a dinner while mother was taking care of the business of the world."[1] Ida's approach to motherhood underscored that even a growing family would not distract her from the terrible problems that black Americans faced during a time now known as "the Nadir" of African American history.[2]

A pioneering black historian born during that era, Rayford Logan named the turn-of-the-century "the Nadir" because it marked the bitter end of the nation's post–Civil War "road to reunion." With the war long behind them, white Americans in the North and the South were content to reduce blacks to a second-class citizenship maintained by "Exploitation, Disenfranchisement, Segregation, Discrimination, Lynching, Contempt."[3] Decided in 1896, the Supreme Court case *Plessy v. Ferguson* ended African American hopes of federal action against the South's separate-car laws. Instead, the high court sanctioned state laws providing blacks with "separate but equal accommodations." The now famous ruling received little media attention at the time, since *Plessy* merely sanctioned what was already well established across the South. But Justice John Marshall Harlan, who dissented from the decision, predicted that it would "become quite as pernicious as the decision made by the tribunal in the *Dred Scott* case"—the 1856 Supreme Court ruling that held that blacks "had no rights which a white man is bound to respect."[4] His prediction proved accurate. *Plessy v. Ferguson* underscored that African Americans were no longer under the protection of the Reconstruction-era constitutional amendments that had once given them the franchise and promised them "equal treatment" under the law. Not overturned until the *Brown v. Board of Education* decision in 1954, for almost a half century *Plessy* provided powerful legal precedent for racial segregation not just on trains, but in schools, businesses, and a huge variety of other facilities throughout the South, and weakened black civil rights in the North as well.

Abandoned by the courts, by the late 1890s African Americans had also lost any claim on their onetime ally, the Republican Party. Republican support for racial justice had been declining since Reconstruction; by the 1890s, white Republicans did not even bother to protest the disenfranchisement measures enacted by Southern Democrats that all but eliminated the black vote throughout their region. Disenfranchisement, in turn, left African Americans unrepresented in the federal government, which lost its last black congressman in 1901.

As a result, African Americans entered the new century needing aggressive national representation more desperately than ever. The continuing racial violence and civil rights losses that African Americans suffered during the late 1890s exposed the futility of pursuing African American racial uplift through accommodation, as advocated by Booker T. Washington, the most widely recognized black leader of the Nadir. Indeed, by the end of the twentieth century's first decade, even white progressives had begun to question Washington's lack of public support for black civil or voting rights. Meanwhile, African American agitators such as Wells-Barnett struggled to rally protection for black citizenship rights.

Not surprisingly, then, the new century's first decade saw Ida consistently involved with African American attempts to organize national action against lynching and Jim Crow—even as she struggled to meet the demands of a growing family. Before the decade was half over her two boys would have two sisters, Ida and Alfreda. But even with four children at home, Wells-Barnett found public work impossible to avoid, given the climate of the Nadir. Both she and Ferdinand Barnett were increasingly anxious to see united action among African Americans across the nation to protect the interests of blacks as a group. Just as slavery had only been defeated through national action, the racial injustices of lynching and Jim Crow required a national response—and federal action. If nothing else, white Southerners' reactions to Wells-Barnett's antilynching campaign had underscored that white supremacy would never be reformed from within.

Accordingly, from 1898 onward the Barnetts worked with other black activists to challenge both federal inaction and Booker T. Washington's leadership. Above all, these challenges took the form of a long struggle to establish a viable national civil rights organization, which finally culminated in the establishment of the National Association for the Advancement of Colored People (NAACP) in 1909. The NAACP's unsuccessful predecessors included the Afro-American Council, organized in 1898 and soon compromised by Washington's powerful influence; and the Niagara Movement, founded in 1906 by a resurgent group of Washington opponents. Underfunded and internally divided, the Niagara Movement was also short-lived. But it did help give rise to a new alliance among former Niagara Movement members and white progressives: the NAACP.

Wells-Barnett was an active member of these organizations and a founding member of the NAACP—the only enduring civil rights organization to come out of these efforts. Yet she would not last long in any of these organizations, all of which brought together fragile coalitions of moderates and radicals. Uncompromising in her radical politics, she was also at a gender disadvantage when it came to navigating the highly contested black politics of the Nadir. One of the few black women involved in any of the early civil rights organizations, she found little room for herself in these male-dominated initiatives, which tended to set aside their leadership roles for men. Far too opinionated to play a purely supporting role in any organization, Wells-Barnett had an outspoken, aggressive personality that ran contrary to the womanly ideals of her day. Easily dismissed as a troublemaker, she was never fully appreciated for her political acumen and repeatedly edged out of any leading role in the civil rights initiatives that she helped launch. Among them was the NAACP, which went on to initiate a long fight for federal antilynching legislation that built directly on the antilynching tradition she had created.

In 1930, when Wells-Barnett wrote her autobiography, she wondered whether the NAACP would have become "a live active effort in the lives of our people" had she managed to stay active in it—a question that at once underestimated and overestimated her own powers of influence, while ignoring the growing power of the NAACP. Even though she sustained no enduring ties with the NAACP—or any of the national black civil rights organizations that emerged during her lifetime—Wells-Barnett would nonetheless help shape twentieth-century civil rights activism by pioneering a well-defined protest agenda of her own.

"The Protection of Washington"

The end of the nineteenth century saw Wells-Barnett continue to lobby for federal protection for black civil rights at a time when such protection seemed ever more elusive. The Republican Party had regained the presidency in 1896 with the election of William McKinley, whose victory initially seemed auspicious to the Barnetts and blacks who campaigned on his behalf. Critical of lynching during his campaign, McKinley had even deployed troops to prevent mob violence during his years as Ohio governor. However, once in the White House, McKinley provided no more support for black rights than his Democratic predecessor Grover Cleveland, as proved painfully evident in 1898, when McKinley failed to protest the lynching of one of his own appointees in South Carolina.

Initially, the new president seemed as if he might fulfill the hopes of his black supporters. During his first year in office, he appointed several black officeholders, including Frazier B. Baker, who became the postmaster of Lake City, South Carolina, in the fall of 1897. Patronage appointments, post office jobs were controlled by federal authorities and routinely used by both Republican and Democratic presidents to reward their party's political allies. A sop to the North's black voters for their loyalty in the 1896 election, McKinley's appointment of Baker was also designed to solidify African American support for his administration. South Carolina legislators objected, but since their state no longer had any white Republicans worthy of patronage, McKinley had no trouble ignoring their protests.[5] Unfortunately, he also went on to ignore the assaults on Baker that followed, up to and including the one that took his life—issuing no public comment of any kind on the death of his appointee.

Lake City's new postmaster was under attack from the moment he took his post. Local whites protested his appointment by riddling his house with buckshot and bullets shortly after he arrived. But Baker refused to be driven from his post: "being a government official, he felt confident in the protection of Washington," he told reporters.[6] His confidence was misplaced. On February 22, 1898, Baker was killed by a mob of one hundred white men who converged outside the small building that housed his home and the local post office. After torching the building, they opened fire on Baker, his wife, and their four children as the family fled the burning building. The volley of bullets that killed Baker also killed his youngest child, a three-year-old girl, who was in her mother's arms; Baker's wife, son, and two older daughters managed to survive, but only his son escaped crippling bullet wounds.

Clearly a political assassination designed to reject the appointment of an African American postmaster in the Palmetto State, Baker's murder underlined the ever declining status of blacks in American politics. Along with

Isaiah Loftin, another black postmaster shot in the arm in Hoganville, Georgia, the same month Baker was appointed, Baker was a victim of what *The New York Times* described as the South's "war on Negro officials," which Republican officials chose to ignore.[7] "The Lake City Coroners' Jury found that Postmaster Baker came to death at the hands of persons unknown to the jury," reported the *Chicago Tribune* in April 1898, also noting: "That jury ought to take the day off and get better acquainted with the leading citizens of the town."[8]

As a political supporter of McKinley and a mother of her own young children, Wells-Barnett was outraged by the lethal attack on Baker and his family. Even before the jury's all too familiar conclusion was announced, she swung into action, mobilizing a mass meeting of Chicago blacks in March 1898 to protest Baker's death and seek support for his surviving family members. At the meeting, Ida also raised money for a trip to Washington to pressure McKinley to initiate a federal investigation into the Lake City murders. Successful in doing so, she was soon on the road again, with another "nursing baby"—Charles's younger brother, the five-month-old Herman Barnett.

As it became increasingly clear that McKinley would issue no public comment on Baker's death, Wells-Barnett may well have rued ever campaigning for him. But once in Washington she was able to draw on her political connections to schedule a personal meeting with the president—which she attended in the company of seven Illinois congressmen and a state senator. By that spring, McKinley was recruiting both black and white Americans to fight in the Spanish-American War, in which the United States supported Cuba's struggle to gain independence from Spain. Accordingly, Ida made the war the center of her argument. "Justice Like Charity" should "begin at home," her petition to McKinley maintained: before the United States fights "barbarism in Cuba," it should attend to the "slaughter" of African Americans at home by punishing Baker's murderers and taking federal action against lynching.[9]

Ida's petition did not secure justice for Baker and his family, but the relentless pressure she and other African Americans put on McKinley did result in the first federal proceeding against a lynch mob. In 1899, the federal court in Charleston, South Carolina, tried thirteen Lake City men for participating in a conspiracy to deprive Frazier Baker of his civil rights. Tried before an all-white jury, in a proceeding notable for witness perjury and the defense lawyer's "naked appeal to the racist sensibilities of the . . . jury," the case ended in a mistrial. But the federal prosecutor's eloquent closing argument gave new hope to black activists. Lynching, he told the jury, "outraged justice"; if Southerners were going to embrace mob violence over sanctioned justice meted out to criminals in the courts, they might as well "shut down the school houses, burn the books, tear down the churches and admit that Anglo Saxon Civilization is a failure."[10]

Beyond bearing testimony to the effectiveness of Wells-Barnett's anti-lynching crusade, the federal prosecutor's judgment against lynching had little practical consequence. The government did not retry the case, and black postmasters soon became "relics of another era, at least in predominately white communities."[11] Moreover, Wells-Barnett's attempts to secure restitution for Baker's widow and orphaned children also failed. A bill for a one-thousand-dollar grant to the family, introduced by Congress's only remaining black legislator, North Carolina congressman George White, struck Wells-Barnett as far too little. But both White's bill and Wells-Barnett's efforts to secure a more adequate one were derailed when the United States declared war on Spain, giving Congress a new set of responsibilities.

However overshadowed by war, to Wells-Barnett and other black activists the shootings of the postmasters Loftin and Baker underscored that African Americans could not depend on the federal government to protect their rights. They must instead "organize for self protection," making more necessary than ever the kind of national black civil rights organization envisioned by T. Thomas Fortune when he founded the Afro-American League in the 1880s. Accordingly, in 1898, both Barnetts supported the founding of the Afro-American Council—which sought to revive the league. And even before then, the Barnetts and other African American activists greeted the Spanish-American War as an opportunity for blacks to advance their national civil rights by serving their country in war.

Such hopes now seem quixotic. But as the Spanish-American War began, "blacks recalled that the fighting ability of the Black soldiers in the Union army had been a compelling reason for granting freedom and equality to blacks."[12] Another war might serve the same end. Blacks were among the first to volunteer to serve in Cuba, and both Barnetts supported such efforts. Ida "eagerly assisted" in the mobilization of the Eighth Regiment in Springfield, Illinois, even moving down to Springfield with her children to support the troops and staying with the regiment until "it was mustered in to service."[13]

Likewise, Wells-Barnett did not let family obligations keep her from attending the September "race meeting" that founded the Afro-American Council. As Herman was now old enough to be weaned, she left both boys with their grandmother and traveled to Rochester, where the meeting was held. There she stayed with Susan B. Anthony and dutifully heard out the older woman's strictures against the "divided duty" of motherhood. Very happy to be a mother, and used to disagreements with Anthony, Wells-Barnett ended up "not sorry that I had gone."[14] The meeting had brought together a group of black leaders—also assembled in Rochester for a ceremony to commemorate Frederick Douglass—and promised to fulfill black hopes for a strong national civil rights movement.

The gathering got off to a rocky start. Looking back rather than forward, a frustrated T. Thomas Fortune began by assailing the group for failing to support his previous attempts at a national civil rights organization. Plagued by health problems, family troubles, and financial woes, Fortune was also increasingly compromised by his friendship with Booker T. Washington—who had deep pockets. Although never entirely loyal to Washington, Fortune often served as his informant, and sided with the conservative black leader often enough to make his own politics increasingly unpredictable. Formerly a staunch radical, Fortune had become a loose cannon. Among the leaders of the group that gathered to found the new civil rights organization, he questioned whether African Americans were even "ready" for such an organization.[15]

Dismayed by her old friend's attitude, Wells-Barnett moved to block

Fortune from any leadership role in the Afro-American Council. She pressed him on whether he "planned to accept the presidency" of the new organization, given his reservations about its prospects. Fortune demurred, and Wells-Barnett felt that she had made a crucial intervention. The A.M.E. Church leader Bishop Alexander Waters, who was an enthusiastic proponent of the new initiative, was elected president instead. And Wells-Barnett herself "was once again launched in public movements," accepting the position of the new organization's secretary and becoming deeply embroiled in its efforts to combat mob violence.[16]

Later that fall her work at the council was propelled into high gear by a race riot in Wilmington, North Carolina. One of the few remaining Republican strongholds in the South, Wilmington was an anachronism that the state's Democrats could not tolerate. The city had elected a Populist and Republican coalition in 1896, preserving both Republican rule and black voting rights in North Carolina well into an era when both blacks and Republican officeholders were a thing of the past in much of the South. So, in the fall of 1898, North Carolina Democrats organized to drive "men of African origin" out of state politics. Across the state, white newspapers launched smear campaigns demonizing black men as rapists who preyed on innocent white women. When Alexander Manly, the editor of *The Daily Record*, North Carolina's only black newspaper, contested these claims, he only added fuel to the fire. Like Wells-Barnett before him, Manly suggested that white women were not "any more particular in the matter of clandestine meetings with colored men, than are white men with colored women." Also like Wells before him, he was driven out of town. Moreover, Manly's challenge to the sexual purity of white women became a rallying point for restoring white supremacy in Wilmington.[17]

That November saw the state legislature restored to the Democrats. Tactics included sending armed white men clad in red shirts through African American neighborhoods in southeastern North Carolina to suppress the black vote. North Carolina's "Red-shirts" had embraced the campaign tactic first used by Senator Benjamin Davis Tillman to restore white supremacy in South Carolina in 1876. Moreover, after the election, a white mob rounded off the Democrats' coup d'état by expelling the city's Republican officials—who would not be up for reelection until the following year. They forced Silas P. Wright, the city's white Republican mayor, to resign, along with the rest of the biracial city council. Led by Alfred Moore Waddell, a Democrat and former congressman who appointed himself the city's new mayor, the mob also shot or drove out of town the city's remaining black leaders. At the end of the day, ten African Americans were dead in a bloody race riot that mob leaders had delayed until after the election "so that their district would not lose its congressman as punishment." Its "object lesson," as one white observer noted, was crystal clear: the eradication of blacks from North Carolina politics.[18]

With the city's remaining blacks under siege in the days after the riot, one black woman wrote a desperate letter to President McKinley. Why was he leaving Wilmington's loyal African Americans "to die like rats in a trap"?[19] McKinley offered no response and extended no federal protection to Wilmington's remaining black population. Nor did he respond to similar pleas from African Americans across the nation, including those issued by the members of the Afro-American Council, which reconvened on December 29, 1898, to show the world that in the absence of federal and state protection, "we (10,000,000) African Americans have decided by the assistance of God to help ourselves."[20]

Although dedicated to black self-protection, the council rejected Booker T. Washington's philosophy of substituting economic self-help for political agitation. The Wilmington race riot underscored the dangers of such an approach. The city was home to a hardworking black middle class, whose economic achievements had not earned them the white respect that Booker T. Washington claimed would come with wealth. On the contrary, Wilmington's most prosperous African Americans were leading targets of the rioters' assault. And blacks throughout the city had been completely unable to protect the fruits of their labor in the face of the political violence that stripped them of their property and their citizenship rights.

Horrified by events in Wilmington, Afro-American Council secretary Ida B. Wells-Barnett gave a powerful and widely quoted speech on "Mob

Violence and Anarchy," which criticized both Booker T. Washington and President McKinley. The former, she said, had "made the great mistake of imagining that the black people could gain their rights merely by making themselves factors in industrial life"; while the latter was "much too interested . . . in the decoration of Confederate graves to pay any attention to Negro rights." Now an opponent of McKinley's imperialist Spanish-American War, she also noted: "We are eternally opposed to expansion until this nation can govern at home."[21]

Wells-Barnett's comments at the Afro-American Council meeting presaged a growing disaffection with the Tuskegee principal's accommodationist course, which would soon divide and destroy the organization. Harsher than Ida's were the words of John P. Green, a delegate who maintained that McKinley had not spoken out on the riots only "because he was advised to remain silent by certain 'colored men' whose names he could give." There were enough Washington loyalists on the council to ensure that Green's thinly veiled critique was greeted with "hisses, groans and boos."[22] But disaffection with Washington only escalated in 1899, dividing the council into "radicals" who opposed him and "conservatives" who supported him. Still on the fence about Washington's leadership, Wells-Barnett spoke at a pro-Washington rally in Boston earlier that year. But by the time the council met again in August 1899, she had joined the ranks of his opponents.

Wells's final break with Washington followed the lynching of Sam Hose in Georgia that spring. A young black farmer in Palmetto, a farming community just outside Atlanta, Hose allegedly shot and killed his employer, the white landowner Alfred Cranford, after the two men fought over a debt on April 13, 1899. Also accused of raping the farmer's wife, Mattie Cranford, and injuring the couple's infant son, Hose received no mercy when he was captured and delivered into the hands of a white mob ten days later. He was burned alive before two thousand white people, who "fought over pieces of his flesh for souvenirs."[23]

When Hose's charred knuckles appeared on display in an Atlanta store owner's window, Atlanta University scholar W.E.B. Du Bois turned aside from scholarship in favor of activism. Thirty-one years old and en route to the offices of *The Atlanta Constitution* with a cautiously worded letter protesting Hose's lynching, the Harvard-educated scholar was stopped short by his chance encounter with this gruesome trophy of a black life cut short. Raised in Massachusetts and prepared to spend a life challenging racism from within the groves of academia, Du Bois realized, after seeing Sam Hose's knuckles on display, that "one could not be a calm, cool and detached scientist while Negroes were lynched, murdered and starved."[24]

Hose's lynching had a different but equally lasting effect on activists such as Wells-Barnett and her pastor Reverdy Ransom, who presided over Chicago's Bethel Church. Although inured to lynchings, both were appalled when Booker T. Washington refused to issue any public comment on Hose's death. By 1899, Washington was the best-known black leader in America. But when white reporters "questioned [him] regarding the Georgia lynching he had nothing to say." His "position and hopes in the interest of the Tuskegee Institute," he told them, made him feel constrained to keep silent. "I think I can be of more service to the race," he added, by "helping to lay the foundation for an education which will be a permanent cure for such outrages." Moreover, although Washington stated that he was opposed to "mob violence under all circumstances," he also described the lynch mob's black victims as sexual predators, explaining, "as a rule the men guilty of these outrages are ignorant individuals who have had no opportunity to secure an education and moral restraint."[25]

Both Washington's failure to denounce the Hose lynching and his assumption that Hose was in fact guilty of the crimes with which he had been charged were deeply disappointing to Ida. Moreover, an investigation into Hose's death sponsored by Wells-Barnett, Ransom, and other blacks in Chicago soon called the dead man's guilt into question. Louis Levin, the white private detective they hired, reported in June that Hose had killed Cranford only after his employer had drawn a gun on him during their quarrel. He also noted that Hose had fled the scene after exchanging shots with Cranford, rather than going to assault Mrs. Cranford and her infant son. Hose was not guilty of rape or any crime against Cranford's family.

"Sam Hose was burned to teach Negroes that no matter what a white man does to them, they must not resist," Wells-Barnett wrote in *Lynch Law in Georgia* (1899), a pamphlet she published that month, which reprinted Levin's report. Hastily put together, it chronicled both Hose's lynching and those of eleven other men lynched in Georgia between March and April 1899—including Elijah Strickland, a black preacher, lynched one day after Hose for alleged but unspecified "complicity in his [Hose's] crime." Ida's pamphlet used prose condensed from *The Atlanta Journal* and *The Atlanta Constitution* to both describe the crimes and illustrate white Southern attitudes toward lynching. Both papers reported the deaths of Hose and the other black men in enthusiastic, almost pornographic, detail, making Wells-Barnett's case for her. Subtitled "A Six-Weeks' Record in the Center of Southern Civilization, as Faithfully Chronicled by the *Atlanta Journal* and *Atlanta Constitution*," her pamphlet contained few words by Wells-Barnett other than a preface imploring her readers to "Consider the Facts."[26]

In June 1899, Washington finally broke his silence. In a letter published in *The Birmingham Age-Herald* and several other newspapers, he denounced the recent lynchings in the South as bad for both blacks and whites. The letter pointed out that most lynchings were not linked to rape allegations, but still counseled African Americans to repudiate the Negro rapist as a "beast in human form."[27] Not surprisingly, Wells-Barnett lost all faith in Washington after that. Intent on establishing an antilynching bureau at the August 1899 meeting of the Afro-American Council in Chicago, she issued no public critique of Washington then. But a letter reporting on the council's meeting that she wrote for *The New York Age* contained a disparaging reference to Washington. Whatever she said was suppressed by the paper's editor, T. Thomas Fortune, who told Washington that he had "a sassy letter" of complaint from Wells-Barnett. Ida, Fortune noted dismissively, was like "a bull in a China shop."[28]

Fortune's derisive dismissal underscored the vast personality difference between Wells-Barnett and Washington. A shrewd manipulator of his public image, Washington rose to power by carefully appealing to American whites. Although never as apolitical as he seemed, he maintained his white Southern support by avoiding public agitation of any kind. Relentlessly upbeat about the future of race relations in the South, "he seldom even referred to race prejudice," which he described as "something to be lived down rather than talked about."[29] Even Washington's involvement with the Afro-American Council took place behind the scenes, since he was unwilling to advertise his involvement with an organization he did not fully control. Although in Chicago when the council met there in 1899, Washington did not attend any of its sessions—lest he end up associated with radical resolutions or speeches that might alienate his white supporters. Instead, Washington met privately with council president Bishop Alexander Waters and some of the organization's more conservative members in his hotel room. Washington would become ever more two-faced over the course of his career, balancing his public accommodationism with secret support for legal challenges to disenfranchisement and segregation.

By contrast Wells-Barnett remained blunt and outspoken, rarely concealing her opinions for long, even when she had considerable incentive to do so. While not unlike that of her mentor Frederick Douglass, Wells-Barnett's forthright political style was increasingly anachronistic next to the accommodationist approach perfected by Booker T. Washington. Driven out of the South for speaking too freely, Wells-Barnett, with her assertive temperament, proved a liability even in the largely Northern organizations she helped to found. Both black and female, she was expected to be cautious, deferential, and discreet, and consistently failed on all counts. In 1898, for example, she delivered a blistering critique of Governor John R. Tanner of Illinois for failing to protect the black strikebreakers brought into the Illinois coal mining towns of Virden and Prana. Delivered in Chicago's Quinn Chapel, her speech startled many of her listeners, since her husband, for all practical purposes, worked for the governor—who had the power to oust Ferdinand Barnett from his lucrative position as Illinois's first black assistant state's attorney. Barnett managed to keep his job, but the *Illinois Record* reported that during Wells-Barnett's speech, "Barnett, her husband, was twitching and pulling his whiskers as she spoke," while other listeners whispered, " 'Oh! his job . . . is gone.' "[30]

Likewise, Wells-Barnett's gender made it hard for her to maintain her influence in the Afro-American Council. During the organization's early years, Ida ran the council's antilynching bureau and served as the council's national organizer, a position she used to protest lynching and organize against the disenfranchisement schemes used by white Southerners. But in 1900 she also began to critique Booker T. Washington, who had preempted W.E.B. Du Bois's 1899 attempt to establish a National Negro Business Bureau within the Afro-American Council by establishing his own National Negro Business League. The Atlanta University professor did not respond to the slight himself. On the job market at the time, and willing to believe the rival organization was T. Thomas Fortune's idea, he hoped to have Washington's support in finding a new post. But Wells-Barnett was far less cautious. Washington was unwilling to support any movement he "did not inaugurate," Ida charged in an article published in the *Conservator*. Never in favor of supporting council initiatives that he could not control, the Alabama educator had stolen Du Bois's idea, establishing an "organization of which he will be president, moderator and dictator." Washington responded with equal, if far more covert hostility. "Miss Wells is fast making herself so ridiculous that everyone is getting tired of her," he noted in a private letter to his secretary, Emmett Scott.[31]

Wells-Barnett's open defiance of Washington marked the beginning of the end of her influence within the Afro-American Council. She was unable to attend the 1901 meeting because she would soon deliver her third child—her daughter Ida, who was born shortly after the council met. But that meeting saw Washington and his supporters taking advantage of her absence. Wells-Barnett was not reelected to her position as the organization's national organizer; since Du Bois was also absent, Emmett Scott replaced him as head of the National Negro Business Bureau—which he went on to merge with Washington's National Negro Business League. Reporting on the meeting's events, Scott flatly asserted he was "glad Mrs. Barnett was not there to complicate the situation."[32]

Still, for a time, the council's antilynching bureau provided support for Wells-Barnett's ongoing crusade against mob violence, allowing her to set up an office on Princeton Avenue and publish another antilynching pamphlet. Titled *Mob Rule in New Orleans* (1900), it solicited support for anti-lynching work from "friends and members" of the council and highlighted the July 26 massacre of Robert Charles, a black laborer in New Orleans. Originally from rural Mississippi, Charles had settled in New Orleans in 1896, arriving in the city at a time of heightened racial tensions.[33] In the economic depression that followed the Panic of 1893, many local employers had replaced white workers with poorly paid rural blacks and Italian immigrants, making both groups unpopular in the always color-conscious city.

On July 23, 1900, Charles was accosted by three members of the New Orleans police with explosive results. A thirty-four-year-old man, Charles was sitting on a stoop with his roommate Leonard Pierce. The two men had tried to pay a call to a couple of women Charles knew. Finding them either unavailable or not at home, they were waiting to try their luck one more time when they were spotted by several patrolmen, who began to interrogate them "as to who they were, what they were doing, and how long they had been there."[34] Literate and politically active, Robert Charles followed the news in his region closely. In 1898 Louisiana legislators had passed a new state constitution that included demanding new educational and property qualifications for voting, which were largely limited to black men as a result of a "grandfather clause" that protected the voting rights of men whose fathers and grandfathers had been eligible to vote in 1867.[35] Moreover, the brutal lynching of Sam Hose in 1899 had infuriated Charles; he had begun to consider moving to Liberia to escape the political discrimination and racial violence that plagued blacks in the United States.

A disaffected man who was acutely aware of the injustices faced by his race, Charles refused to answer the barrage of questions he and Pierce received from New Orleans police, at which point the officers decided to arrest both men. When Charles objected, one officer began to beat him with a billy club and all three policemen drew their guns. Armed himself, Charles drew his own gun and returned fire after one of the officers shot him in the leg. He then escaped, having shot and wounded the man who had shot him. Tracked down at his home later that day, Charles defied the officers again, shooting two dead and once again eluding arrest. With two officers killed and one wounded, the New Orleans Police Department was offering a $250 reward for the apprehension of Charles "dead or alive."[36] The result was a massive four-day manhunt that ended with a mob of twenty thousand armed whites laying siege to Charles, who had holed up in a downtown New Orleans house. Defiant to the end, Robert Charles held off the mob for "several hours," picking off his would-be captors from a second-story window with his Winchester as they tried to enter the building. An excellent marksman, he killed seven white men and wounded twenty, leaving his hiding place only after the mob set fire to the house. Charles died in a fusillade of bullets that left him "perforated from head to foot," while several other New Orleans blacks also perished in the manhunt that led to his death. Anxious to punish someone for Charles's defiant behavior, white New Orleans terrorized the city's African American population as long as Charles remained at large, lynching seven black people at random and wounding many more.[37]

Despite the carnage, Charles was celebrated as a hero among New Orleans blacks, who respected his decision to "die with his face to the foe." Without funds to hire a detective to investigate the events that led to Charles's death, Wells-Barnett put together *Mob Rule in New Orleans* using the same techniques she had used to produce *Lynch Law in Georgia*. Much of the pamphlet was drawn from local press accounts, and it included detailed accounts of the deaths of the black New Orleanians who were murdered as the mob searched for Charles, crimes that went unpunished and were reported without censure or regret. Among the dead was a seventy-five-year-old man who was shot on his way to work and a woman who died in her bed when the mob peppered her family's house with bullets. Simply by their blatant siding with the lynch mob rather than its victims, Southern reporters supplied Ida with a critique of lynching. The beating of "Esther Fields . . . a Negro washerwoman" who "ran into the arms of the mob, and was beaten into insensibility in less time than it takes to tell it" could not be pinned on Charles.[38] Rather, it showed that white violence against black people was indiscriminate and largely unprovoked.

When it came to defending the actions of Robert Charles himself, however, Ida sought out evidence. Outnumbered and outgunned, Charles had fought white authorities with far deadlier force than any other black victim of a Southern lynch mob and was described in the white press as a "Negro desperado," a "ravisher," and "a fiend in human form."[39] Faced with these stereotypes, Ida wrote to Charles's former friends and associates in an attempt to understand the man who had defied the power of the New Orleans police. What she learned was that Charles had no criminal record, and was described by his friends as a "law-abiding, quiet, industrious, peaceable man."[40]

An autodidact, Charles left behind a room full of "well-worn textbooks, bearing his name written in his own sprawling handwriting, and well-filled copybooks found in his trunk," which the white press took as sinister evidence of his hostility toward whites. Charles had "burnt the midnight oil," *The Times-Democrat* (New Orleans) maintained, and "was desirous of improving himself intellectually in order that he might conquer the hated white race." But to Ida, who was self-educated herself, Charles's books and papers had a far more obvious explanation. They suggested that Charles had been a man who spent "the hours after days of hard toil in trying to improve himself, both in the study of textbooks and in writing."[41] Far more familiar than *The Times-Democrat* with the black emigrationist literature found in Charles's room, Ida was quite sure that "nothing ever written in the *Voice of the Missions* . . . suggest[s] that a peaceable man should turn lawbreaker, or that any man should dye his hands in his brother's blood." What provoked Charles was not such literature but rather the fact that he had been accosted by the police without "any warrant or other justification," and then had a price posted on his head that authorized whites "to kill Charles at sight." "The white people of this country may charge that he was a desperado," a black acquaintance of Charles who was unwilling to supply his name told Wells-Barnett in August 1900, "but to the people of his own race, Robert Charles will always be regarded as the hero of New Orleans."[42]

Charles's heroism, however, received little recognition from black leaders other than Wells-Barnett. Terrorized, African American leaders in New Orleans were willing to label him "a demon," a "devil in embryo," and a "lawless brute." He became a suppressed memory best summed up by New Orleans jazz pioneer Jelly Roll Morton, who noted many years later: "I once knew the Robert Charles song but I found it was best for me to forget it, and that I did in order to go along with the world on the peaceful side."[43] Even in the North, Wells-Barnett's attempt to rehabilitate Robert Charles as an icon of manly black self-defense was quixotic. In a nation where white supremacy reigned increasingly uncontested, Charles had few avowed fans even among his own people—as Morton's comment makes clear.

Mob Rule in New Orleans never received wide circulation. Wells-Barnett's antilynching bureau received almost no funding from the always hard-pressed Afro-American Council, forcing Wells-Barnett to issue a limited printing of *Mob Rule* that asked its readers "to pass this pamphlet on to another." Ironically, the underfunded pamphlet also solicited contributions for the bureau's work, which was grinding to a halt as a result of its money problems. By 1902, the bureau "had no funds in the treasury to pay postage much less the printer," despite Ida's pleas.[44]

Antilynching was no longer a priority for the council. Under the direction of its major funder, Booker T. Washington, it was now devoting its resources to mounting quiet legal challenges to disenfranchisement laws such as Louisiana's grandfather clause. Intent on preserving his publicly accommodationist stand on black political rights, Washington kept these cases quiet, making the council seem moribund. Moreover, Bookerites on the council also quashed calls for a more activist organization—further eroding the council's support among Northern blacks. In 1902, the increasingly divided organization elected T. Thomas Fortune president in an election so irregular that Wells-Barnett and several other longtime members rejected it as a Bookerite coup. Ida resigned her position in protest, while Boston radical William Monroe Trotter proclaimed that the council was now "Booker T. Washington's in everything but name."[45] In gaining control, Washington all but killed it. Not only would Wells-Barnett never return to the council, but, along with William Monroe Trotter and W.E.B. Du Bois, she and Ferdinand Barnett were soon attacking what Du Bois called "the Tuskegee Machine."

MOST CULTURED NEGRO IN THE UNITED STATES.

PROF. WILLIAM E. BURGHARDT DU BOIS.

This embellished portrait of Du Bois appeared in the Chicago Tribune *on June 18, 1903, shortly after the publication of* The Souls of Black Folk. *Then thirty-five years old, and a professor at Atlanta University, W.E.B. Du Bois had completed undergraduate degrees at Fisk and Harvard Universities before going on to do postgraduate work at the University of Berlin and returning to Harvard to complete his doctorate. In 1896, Du Bois received a Ph.D. in history from Harvard University, becoming the first African American to receive that institution's highest degree.*

Today Du Bois is Washington's most famous critic, thanks to his magisterial rebuke of Washington's assumptions in *The Souls of Black Folk* (1903), but he was not Washington's first or most influential critic. Although his 1903 essay "Of Mr. Booker T. Washington and Others" presented an influential challenge to Washington's leadership, it was anticipated by both Wells-Barnett and Trotter, who both broke with Washington before Du Bois. Wells had been butting heads with Washington since he had failed to speak out on the Sam Hose lynching in 1899, and by the beginning of 1903 her critique of Washington's accommodationism had expanded to include a discussion of the practical limits to his doctrine of industrial education. Blacks "who followed Booker T. Washington's idea of an industrial education," Wells-Barnett told a meeting of the Chicago Political Equality League on January 17, 1903, "have found that the trade union will not permit the negro to be a member and refused to allow him to work outside them. In the half a dozen unions which admit colored men, they find again that color is a handicap, since they are the first laid off and the last put to work."[46] Not surprisingly, both Wells-Barnett and her husband promoted the Du Bois critique of Washington in *The Souls of Black Folk*.

In particular, Ida commended the book to white women reformers such as Jane Addams, the founder of Hull House, the Chicago settlement house, and Celia Parker Woolley, a Unitarian minister who was active in the Chicago Women's Club. In some respects more open to Wells-Barnett's activist brand of reform than the black women of the NACW, these progressive reformers had rallied in support of Wells-Barnett's successful attempt to end a 1903 campaign by the *Chicago Tribune* to segregate the city's schools. And that year also saw Woolley beginning to consult with Ida on her plans to establish an interracial settlement house, later established as the Frederick Douglass Center. Accordingly, Ida and her husband were among the blacks Woolley turned to when she convened "a gathering of the literati at her home near the university [of Chicago]" to discuss *The Souls of Black Folk* in the spring of 1903.

With the other blacks and whites at the meeting all but "united in condemning Du Bois's views," the Barnetts were at the center of a lively discussion in which they supported the part of the book the rest of the group opposed—"that chapter which arraigns Booker T. Washington." It was a learning experience for Wells-Barnett and her husband. They "saw, as perhaps never before, that Mr. Washington's views on industrial education had become an obsession with the white people of this country." Their opposition to his views created a "warm session," but in the end the Barnetts emerged content that they had given their audience "an entirely new view of the situation." Moreover, Ida left planning to organize another gathering— "a meeting of our best-brained"—to promote Du Bois's work.[47]

Meanwhile, in Boston, William Monroe Trotter, who would eventually become a close friend of both Barnetts, was waging a campaign against Washington that dated back to the 1890s and had shaped his professional career. Born in Ohio in 1872 but raised in Boston, Trotter was a decade younger than Wells and sixteen years younger than Washington. Like Du Bois, he was a member of the generation of blacks born after slavery. The son of an ex-slave who served in the Massachusetts Fifty-fourth Regiment, he grew up in a middle-class home. His father, James Trotter, prospered after the war, allowing his son to attend Harvard University, where he excelled. William graduated from Harvard magna cum laude in 1895—the same year that Booker T. Washington told blacks, "We must start from where we are, at the bottom."[48]

Like his fellow Harvard graduate W.E.B. Du Bois, Trotter was by his upbringing and education ill-suited to follow Booker T. Washington's accommodationist leadership. Both men were members of a new class of blacks that Du Bois referred to as the "talented tenth," "the best and most capable" members of their race. Like other American leaders, they had been "schooled in the colleges and universities of the land"—and were living testimony that the most promising black Americans need not settle for an industrial education. On the contrary, Du Bois argued, blacks needed "leaders of thought and missionaries of culture among their people . . . The Negro race, like all other races, is going to be saved by its exceptional men."[49]

One such man, Trotter had little in common with the unschooled rural Southerners that Washington claimed as his constituency. Having excelled in the white schools he had attended from grade school through college, he was equally successful in business. An insurance agent and mortgage broker, he settled with his wife in a spacious home in Boston, where the Trotters' "sitting room window" overlooked "the country as far as Blue Hill" and his "bedroom window over the bay down to . . . Deer Island."[50]

Yet Trotter's success did not leave him feeling content or secure. Disturbed by worsening race relations in both the North and the South, as well as black leader Booker T. Washington's failure to challenge the erosion of black civil rights, by the late 1890s Trotter had become convinced "that pursuit of business, money, civic or literary position was like building a house upon the sands, if race prejudice and persecution and public discrimination for mere color was to spread up from the South and result in a fixed caste of color."[51] He also believed that Booker T. Washington's accommodationist leadership was a major source of the growing white disdain for black civil rights in both the North and South.

As the new century opened, Trotter abandoned business for activism, helping to found the Boston Literary and Historical Association, which became "a forum for militant race opinion." Moreover, along with another young black radical, George Forbes, he began a newspaper: *The Guardian*

William Monroe Trotter in 1905

(Boston), which began publication on November 9, 1901, and soon became Trotter's lifework. It was dedicated to "an extended attack on the person, prestige and racial policies of Booker T. Washington."

Written with a personal animosity that brought his own character into question, Trotter's attacks on the Alabama educator were as freewheeling as they were sustained. His paper derided Washington as a man with "leonine jaws ... mastiff-like rows of teeth," a "great cone" of a forehead and "dull and characterless eyes," whose "medium size frame" bore "every evidence of high living." When Washington's daughter, Portia, was expelled from Wellesley College in 1902, the *Guardian* reported the news in gleeful tones. Washington's children were "not taking to higher education like a duck to water," Trotter's paper noted, and "while their defect in this line is doubtless somewhat inherited, they justify to some extent their father's well known antipathy to anything higher than the three R's for his 'people.' "[52]

But not all of Trotter's attacks on Washington were below the belt. With the Afro-American Council claiming to represent the race as a whole, and Washington controlling the council and much of the black press, Trotter was hardly the only black radical to chafe under the Tuskegean's "iron hand."[53] Instead, Trotter was able to mobilize a radical revolt among Du Bois and other disaffected black Northerners who had yet to break with Washington. The revolt began in 1903 when Trotter and other Boston radicals attended the Afro-American Council's annual meeting in Louisville in 1903. Speaking before a council now firmly under Washington's control, they proposed a resolution calling for President Theodore Roosevelt to ask Congress to reduce the political representation of Southern states that denied blacks the vote—an idea that other black radicals such as Wells-Barnett had long supported. And they also floated other, less specific measures, such as an endorsement of the statement that "agitation is the best means to secure our civil and political rights." Led by Fortune, the council rejected all their proposals, with Washington telling the gathering, "An inch of progress is worth more than a yard of complaint."[54]

Now determined to challenge Washington publicly, Trotter made a special point of attending the meeting of Boston's National Negro Business League on July 30, 1903. Hosted by the Columbus Avenue African Methodist Episcopal Church, the meeting attracted a crowd of two thousand and featured addresses by T. Thomas Fortune and Booker T. Washington. Trotter arrived with a list of nine bitterly sarcastic questions that he planned to ask from the floor. Designed to heckle Washington, they included queries such as: "Are the rope and the torch all the race is to get under your leadership?" But before Trotter could ask a single question, the meeting degenerated into chaos. Fortune's remarks were interrupted when someone threw a bag filled with cayenne pepper at him, which reduced him to coughing and wheezing his way through his text. And when Washington was introduced, pandemonium broke out. As the Alabama educator began to speak, "someone in the rear of the hall shouted: 'We don't want to hear from you Booker T. Washington. We don't like you.'" Soon Washington's friends and enemies were scuffling and trying to shout each other down.[55] Standing on a chair to roar out his nine questions, Trotter went largely unheard. One man was stabbed in the melee, and Trotter and his sister Maud were arrested when they tried to prevent the police from arresting another member of the crowd.

In the end, Trotter silenced only himself. Washington got a chance to deliver his speech after the Boston police dragged the protesters out of the church. Still, what came to be known as "the Boston riot" helped galvanize black resistance to Washington outside of Boston. In particular, W.E.B. Du Bois, whose challenge to Washington's leadership in *The Souls of Black Folk* had been more scholarly than activist, was at long last moved to take a "strong side."

Previously unwilling to be drawn into Trotter's war on Washington, Du Bois enjoyed a cordial relationship with both men prior to the riot. Washington had chosen to ignore Du Bois's strictures against him in *The Souls of Black Folk*, and Du Bois and Trotter had an acquaintance that went back to their college years at Harvard. Indeed, Du Bois's first news of the riot came when he visited Trotter in Boston after teaching at Tuskegee's summer session. Du Bois arrived to find his host in jail—Trotter having received a thirty-day sentence for his role in the riot. Du Bois initially assumed that the irrepressible Trotter had brought his fate upon himself, but he soon came to believe that the riot had been "precipitated by a Washington man." Moreover, he also realized that he could no longer "occupy the middle ground, and appease the *Guardian* on one hand, and the Hampton-Tuskegee idea on the other." Accordingly, he published a letter in the *Guardian* which affirmed his faith in Trotter, and described him as the victim of "a petty & dishonest attack."[56]

Du Bois's public support for Trotter ended his relationship with Washington. Not content with sending Trotter to jail, Washington also sponsored a libel suit against Trotter and the *Guardian's* co-owner George Forbes, and attempted to destroy their newspaper by funding a series of unsuccessful new black newspapers in Boston—all designed to depose the *Guardian* as that city's black paper. Equally merciless to the now disloyal Du Bois, Washington laid siege to the faltering finances of the university that employed the young scholar by writing to "all his white philanthropist friends" denouncing Atlanta University as a school unworthy of their support.[57] But Washington's attacks only made his opponents more vocal.

The Parting of the Ways

The spring of 1904 saw Ida B. Wells-Barnett join W.E.B. Du Bois in denouncing Booker T. Washington at a symposium on "The Negro Problem from the Negro Point of View" sponsored by the monthly magazine *The World Today*, which Washington attended. Ignoring all other subjects, Du Bois and Wells-Barnett took on Washington's leadership as one of the major problems that African Americans faced. In an essay titled "The Parting of the Ways," Du Bois abandoned the respectful and measured tone he had used in *The Souls of Black Folk*. Sounding every bit as vituperative as Trotter, he presented a dismissive parody of Washington's ideas and politics: "As to voting, what good is it after all?" It "does not pay as well as the grocery business and breeds trouble."[58]

Writing on "Booker T. Washington and His Critics," Wells-Barnett also blasted the Tuskegean, taking aim at the folksy humor Washington used to ingratiate himself with white audiences. Washington, she charged, routinely demeaned the very people he was supposed to lead, using darky jokes to entertain the "cultured body of women at the Chicago Women's Club." " 'Well John, I am glad to see you are raising your own hogs,' he began, before descending into dialect: 'Yes, Mr. Washington, ebber since you done tol us about raisin' our own hogs, we niggers round her hab resolved to quit stealing hogs an gwinter raise our own.' " Self-aggrandizing as well as disdainful of the hardworking farmers who struggled to make a living in the South, Wells-Barnett noted, Washington's story went so far as to suggest that "the Negroes of the black belt as a rule were hog thieves until the coming of Tuskegee."[59]

Moreover, rural black Southerners were not Washington's only targets. His speeches also derided the labors of the "northern teachers who endured ostracism, insult and martyrdom, to bring the spelling-book and the Bible to educate those who had been slaves." Both Wells-Barnett and Washington were educated by such teachers. But unlike the Tuskegean, Ida revered the abolitionist tradition that such teachers represented. Crucial to the advancement of the race, they had also provided Wells-Barnett with her strongest connections with the white reformers of her era, such as Albion Tourgée and Catherine Impey. Unlike younger black leaders such as Du Bois and Trotter, Wells-Barnett was old enough to have seen the talented tenth first take shape, and looked back to the glory days of Reconstruction as its site of origin. Indeed, she resented Washington's work for denigrating the educational achievements of "the Freedmen's Aid Society, the American Missionary Association and other such agencies which gave the Negro his first and only opportunity to secure any [of the] kind of education which his ambition and intellect craved: They have given us thousands of teachers for our schools in the South, physicians to heal our ailments, druggists, lawyers and ministers."[60]

Worse still was that Washington's program ignored the pioneering work of such whites largely because he chose to speak to another class of whites. A revival of "the South's old practice of slavery in a new dress,"

Washington's "gospel of work is not a new one to the Negro . . . It was the only education the South gave the Negro for the two centuries she had absolute control over his body and soul. The Negro knows that now, as then, the South is strongly opposed to his learning anything else but how to work."[61]

Wells-Barnett's article spoke to the concerns that Washington's critics increasingly shared about the very future of the race under his leadership. The turn of the century saw the Tuskegee Institute grow richer and richer and its principal ever more powerful, at a time when whites were cutting back on all other education offered to African Americans, including grade school. His ideas were cited as the "inspiration" for the New Orleans school board's decision to "cut the curriculum for Negro children down to the fifth grade," and also had Mississippi's governor advocating abolishing black public schools altogether in favor of "training blacks to perform manual labor." Moreover, industrial education was Washington's answer to everything, including problems that it could not solve, such as lynching—a subject on which "Mr. Washington says in substance: Give me money to educate the Negro and when he is taught how to work, he will not commit the crime for which lynching is done." Such appeals were especially galling, since Ida believed that even Washington knew that "lynching is not invoked to punish crime but color."[62]

While Wells-Barnett and Washington's other critics had no objection to industrial education per se, they were horrified to see Washington fill Tuskegee's coffers by offering it as the universal panacea for all the problems faced by the race. Industrial education could never take "the place of political, [civil] . . . and intellectual liberty," Wells-Barnett told Washington, and African Americans were not willing to be "deprived of [the] fundamental rights of American citizenship to the end that one school for industrial training may flourish."[63]

Though new leadership was desperately needed in the African American community, none such could be expected to emerge from the Afro-American Council or any other existing organization in which Booker T. Washington had supporters—as Du Bois found out when he tried to lead a challenge to Washington at a January 1904 New York meeting of black leaders assembled by millionaire Andrew Carnegie. Trotter was barred from the meeting altogether, and Du Bois's attempt to create a committee of independent black leaders to address the race's problems was soon so compromised by Bookerites that Du Bois felt forced to resign.[64]

After 1904, however, Du Bois and several other radicals began to organize against Washington in secret, calling together a quiet gathering of anti-Bookerites at Niagara Falls, New York, in the summer of 1905. Participants were invited to support an "organized, determined and aggressive action on the part of men who believe in Negro freedom and growth." They ended up staying in Fort Erie, Ontario—on the Canadian side of the falls—which was the only place Du Bois could find an affordable hotel willing to host a Negro conference. Fifty-nine men were invited, and twenty-nine came, creating a new national black organization, the Niagara Movement, dedicated to securing full citizenship rights for black people.

Women were not invited to join the organization until the following year, leaving Ida out, and Ferdinand Barnett was not included among the movement's founders. Already a Republican appointee, Barnett would be nominated for a municipal judgeship by Chicago's Republican Party later that summer. So he was in no position to participate in the potentially controversial meeting—if invited. As Barnett may well have suspected, his Republican support was already contested by the Tuskegee machine.[65] But Barnett's friend and fellow radical Dr. Charles E. Bentley was among the Niagara Movement's organizers and later mobilized both Barnetts in support of the movement's Illinois chapter, among the organization's more successful branches. During its first year it managed to get an African American appointed to the new charter committee of Chicago—helping preserve the schoolchildren in Chicago from another attempt to segregate the schools there. In addition, the Illinois Niagara Movement members led a successful battle to ensure that the racist play *The Clansman* received no press, and supported Barnett's run for municipal judge. By 1907, Ida was listed as a member.

Barnett's judgeship would prove elusive. The Republican judicial slate

Some of the founders of the Niagara Movement commemorated their 1905 meeting with a photograph taken in front of the falls. W.E.B. Du Bois is among the men in the middle row, sitting second from the right.

swept the state elections in November 1906. Barnett, the only black candidate in the race, defeated his Democratic opponent by five hundred votes, although he received twenty thousand votes fewer than any of the other Republican candidates. The judgeship seemed to be his. But citing an "error in the police returns," a few days later the election officials reversed the results, declaring Barnett to have lost by 304 votes, a margin that only increased after he demanded and received a recount.[66] Understandably suspicious, Barnett charged "wholesale fraud," claiming "the judges and clerks refused to count a large number of the ballots, but unlawfully, incorrectly and fraudulently marked them as defective"—an allegation that seems likely.[67] Unpopular among whites in both parties, his election was particularly unpopular among members of the Illinois judiciary, who were not anxious to see a black man take the bench.[68] In the end, the most appropriate assessment of the whole debacle came from Senator Tillman of South Carolina. A visitor to Chicago that fall, the white supremacist senator was amused by the contested election. South Carolina's record on race relations might not be stellar, he chortled, but "we never yet have stooped to the infamy of electing a negro and then counting him out after the election."[69]

Both Barnett's defeat and Tillman's comment came at a time when Wells-Barnett and other black reformers in Chicago had become increasingly frustrated in their attempts at creating enduring interracial alliances with white reformers such as Celia Parker Woolley, who was now heading up the Frederick Douglass Center. A mission very close to Wells-Barnett's heart, the center was designed to be a place where "white and colored could meet and get to know each other better."[70] It opened in 1905 in a building located on Wabash Avenue, which was "then the dividing line between Negro and white neighborhoods." Organized along the same lines as Jane Addams's Hull House, it was designed to move middle-class reformers into impoverished urban communities to live and work among the people they hoped to reform (although the Douglass Center was located in a middle-class black community on the border of the black belt, at some remove from the slums that had begun to emerge in the heart of Chicago's South Side).[71] It offered South Side residents a variety of lectures and classes, as well as services such as a kindergarten, a summer day camp, and an athletic club. In addition, the center served as a meeting place for black women's clubs and other community organizations.

Both Barnetts were among the volunteers who lectured and taught classes at the center, until it became clear to Ida that Celia Woolley assumed that whites would ultimately be in charge. Ida and other black women had raised much of the money needed to support the center, but once it was up and running, Woolley turned to other white women to supply the leadership for the club's organizations. For example, when Woolley decided to organize a women's club to support the center, she consulted Ida on how to set up its bylaws, but made it clear she "wanted a white woman" to lead the club.

Ida ignored the slight, but she grew still more disappointed with Woolley when she dragooned her into serving as the vice president of the club and asked her to organize the election of a white president whose summer vacation plans did not permit her to campaign for the job. Determined to support the Frederick Douglass Center, Ida continued to cooperate with Woolley for a time, but her distrust of the white reformer only grew. When Woolley publicly denigrated a lecture that Ida delivered at the center on "What It Means to Be a Mother," her remarks came as "a dash of cold water to Ida," who lost all confidence in Woolley thereafter. "From that time on," Wells-Barnett noted in her autobiography,

> Mrs. Woolley never failed to give me this impression that she did not propose to give me much leeway in the affairs of the center . . . I felt at first that she had been influenced by other colored women who, strange to say, seemed so unwilling that one of their own race should occupy a position of influence, and although I was loath to accept it, I came to the conclusion before our relations ended that our white women friends were not willing to treat us on a plane of equality with themselves.[72]

Wells-Barnett's conflicts with other reformers only grew more frequent over the course of her life. Often seen as a measure of her difficult personality, they should also be seen as a measure of a personality made more difficult by the racial and gender mores of her era. Not the only black Chicagoan to feel slighted by Celia Woolley, Ida struggled with the challenges of interracial cooperation when whites did not always respect their black collaborators. Woolley, for example, also alienated Julius Taylor, the editor of the black newspaper *The Broad Ax* (Chicago). Although supportive of the center, Taylor was troubled by Woolley's condescending attitude toward the African Americans she sought to help, and even declared that Wells-Barnett should not have accepted the position as vice president that Woolley forced on her: "She is a lady of too much prominence to accept such a minor or unimportant position in any women's club."[73]

Wells-Barnett also proved too prominent to work with Mrs. Plummer—the Frederick Douglass Center Women's Club president whose election she organized. In the fall of 1906, after a vicious antiblack riot in Atlanta resulted in the death of between ten and twenty-five African Americans, Mrs. Plummer was quick to embrace white accounts of the riot that described it as retribution for black sexual violence against white women. African Americans could prevent tragedies such as the Atlanta riot, she instructed a Douglass Center audience, by driving out "the criminals among you." Ida was appalled, and told her so. Plummer bristled. Dismissing Wells-Barnett's expertise on lynching, Mrs. Plummer told her "that every woman I know had told me that she is afraid to walk out after dark . . . your mouth is no more a prayer book than that of any other of my friends who have talked with me about this subject."[74]

Wells-Barnett's exchanges with Woolley and Plummer suggest that her strong personality was at odds with the demeanor demanded of a woman of her race in interracial settings. Neither Woolley nor Plummer expected to be criticized or challenged by a black woman. Ida's temper, which she described as "always my besetting sin," made it difficult for her to navigate her way through her conflicts with overbearing white reformers, even when she tried "to learn to take my friends as I found them"—as her more mild-mannered husband often advised. Ida took Ferdinand's advice with reference to the Douglass Center and did her best to weather her conflicts with Woolley and Plummer. But the Douglass Center's founder remained adamantly opposed to allowing Wells-Barnett any leadership role at the center—a position which soon put the two women at odds. In 1907, Wells-Barnett was nominated by the center's women's club to replace Plummer as president—after the other woman declined to run for a second term. When Woolley refused to support her nomination, Ida's temper got the best of her. She "left the Douglass Center never to return."[75]

"Under the Shadow of Abraham Lincoln's Tomb"

Wells-Barnett's affiliation with the NAACP was even shorter-lived. Founded in 1909, the NAACP opposed lynching with an energy previously equaled only by Wells-Barnett, and like her the organization used lynching "to draw attention to other racial inequities." Moreover, Wells-Barnett loomed large in the events leading up to the founding of black America's first enduring civil rights organization. The NAACP first took shape around the antilynching protests inspired by a race riot that took place in Springfield, Illinois, on August 14, 1908—on the Barnetts' home turf. Although hardly Illinois's first race riot, the Springfield riot made it clear that the race problem was no longer limited to the South. The hometown and burial place of Abraham Lincoln, Springfield would celebrate the centennial year of the Great Emancipator's birth in February 1909, but that summer the town seemed poised to kill off the very people Lincoln had helped free. Moreover, whereas earlier race riots in Illinois had been prompted by labor strife in the state's mining towns, the Southern bugaboo of alleged rape was at the center of the 1908 conflagration in the state capital.

Springfield's growing black population had already come under scrutiny earlier that summer when a white mining engineer had died following a scuffle with a black man whom he found in his daughter's bedroom. And then, on the morning of August 14, came the news that the white wife of a streetcar worker had charged a young black man with rape. With two black men charged for sexual assaults on white women in the town jail, a mob of angry whites began to assemble.[76] That evening the mob found that both prisoners had already been spirited out of town by Springfield's sheriff, who hoped to avoid any violence. However, the rowdy crowd only became more enraged and marched into town to attack Harry T. Loper, the white restaurant owner who had lent the sheriff his car to transport the prisoners. After destroying Loper's cafe, the vigilantes moved on to lay waste to Springfield's African American community.

The instigator was a middle-aged white woman named Kate Howard, who told the crowd of angry men swarming the jail, "Come on and I will show you how to do it. Women want protection and this seems to be the only way to get it." The mob followed her lead, attacking the town's black businesses and homes with shouts of "Curse the day that Lincoln freed the nigger" and "Niggers must depart from Springfield."[77] By the time five thousand Illinois National Guard troops restored order late the next day, ten people were dead and eighty injured. Most of Springfield's black population had been driven out of town and the mob's rampage had damaged more than $200,000 worth of property.

Among the first to condemn the riot were assistant state's attorney Ferdinand L. Barnett and his wife, Ida B. Wells-Barnett. The couple, the *Chicago Tribune* noted, "expressed themselves forcibly regarding the Springfield uprising."[78] In the days that followed, the Barnetts' protests were echoed by other concerned citizens across the North, both black and white.

Indeed, the Springfield riot became a cause célèbre among white reformers after it captured the imagination of William English Walling, a muckraking journalist who had just returned from czarist Russia, along with his wife, the Russian revolutionary Anna Strunsky. Both Walling and Strunsky had witnessed pogroms in Russia and attributed these murderous anti-Jewish riots to czarist tyranny, so they were shocked to see similar vicious race hatred on display in Lincoln's hometown. In Chicago on the eve of the Springfield riot, they traveled to Springfield the next day to investigate and were horrified to find that Springfield whites were unrepentant. The son of a Kentucky slaveholder, Walling was a socialist who rejected his past and was troubled by the fact that many members of the mob hailed from the South. Kate Howard, the "notorious 'Joan of Arc'" of the Springfield riot, had taken her inspiration from a recent visit to Texas and Arkansas, where she had "observed enviously that enforced separation of the races helped teach the negro where he belonged." The Southern spirit of white supremacy was moving North, Walling concluded, where it threatened "American civilization" with "either a rapid degeneration or another profounder and more revolutionary civil war."[79]

Published as "The Race War in the North," Walling's anguished call to arms appeared in the liberal magazine *The Independent*. His broad-ranging critique of white racial violence echoed many of Wells-Barnett's discussions of lynching. Indeed, Walling seems to have drawn on her work: his article even employed the kind of parenthetical grammatical commentary Wells-Barnett often featured in her antilynching pamphlets—such as bracketed question marks and exclamation points[!]. But whereas Wells-Barnett always had trouble mobilizing white reformers, Walling's call to arms spurred several white reformers into action.

Among them was Mary White Ovington, a reformer and journalist, who then lived in a settlement house in Manhattan's San Juan Hill district—a black neighborhood located in the area that now houses Lincoln Center. Keenly interested in race relations, and far more sympathetic to Du Bois than to Booker T. Washington, she shared Walling's despair over the state of American race relations, and was excited by his challenge "to white and colored to battle, as the abolitionists had battled, for the full rights of the Negro." She wrote to Walling, proposing an organization dedicated to that cause. Accordingly, the NAACP first took shape in Walling's New York apartment, in a January 1909 meeting attended by Walling, Ovington, and Henry Moskowitz. The three envisioned a biracial organization dedicated to securing black civil rights, and set about enlisting national support. One of their first recruits was the New York journalist and publisher Oswald Garrison Villard. The son of the railroad magnate Henry Villard, Villard was the owner of both the *New York Evening Post* and *The Nation*. A descendant of reformers on his mother's side, Villard was also the grandson of the renowned white abolitionist William Lloyd Garrison.

Villard helped Walling draft a national "Call" to action. Signed by sixty-nine prominent reformers and published in the *Post* and *The Nation* on February 12, 1909, the centenary of Lincoln's birthday, it challenged Americans to take "stock of the nation's progress since 1865."[80]

Wells-Barnett was among the signers of "The Call," and one of the three black speakers at the National Negro Conference meeting held in New York that spring to establish the new organization. In a speech titled "Lynching, Our National Crime," Wells-Barnett presented a succinct history of lynching. "First: Lynching is color line murder. Second: Crimes against women is the excuse, not the cause. Third: It is a national crime that requires a national remedy." She called for federal action and the establishment of "a bureau for the investigation and publication of the details of every lynching."[81] The NAACP would take on lynching as one of its major issues in its early years—following Ida's proposed program almost to the letter.[82] But Wells-Barnett would find no role in the organization.

An interracial gathering of white reformers and Niagara Movement activists, the three hundred men and women who assembled in New York's Charity Hall that spring cobbled together an alliance sustained by compromises on both sides of the color line—and effectively excluded the uncompromising leadership of figures such as Ida B. Wells-Barnett and William Monroe Trotter. Many of the white reformers who attended the meeting had followed the Negro problem largely through the speeches and writings of Booker T. Washington and "expected to meet a belated people who would arouse their pity."[83] Instead, they encountered a group of opinionated and accomplished black radicals, who were adamantly opposed to the white reformers' plans for enlisting Booker T. Washington's support. One black woman—probably Wells-Barnett—rejected such proposals with an "almost tearful earnestness born of bitter experience—'They are betraying us once again—our white friends.'" Washington himself had declined Oswald Garrison Villard's invitation to attend the meeting, and also discouraged his supporters from attending, leaving the floor to his opponents. He was more interested, he told Villard, in "progressive, constructive work" than "agitation and criticism."[84]

Still, the absent Washington hovered over the meeting "like Banquo's ghost," as Wells-Barnett later recalled.[85] His leadership offered a conservative alternative to the more radical path advocated by most of the African Americans attending. Convinced that the fledgling organization needed Washington's endorsement to survive, Villard was anxious to establish an agenda that Washington would not oppose—with or without the support of other blacks at the meeting. "If you want to raise money for anything for the Negro in New York, you must have Washington's backing," he maintained. Wealthy and well connected, Villard spent enough time in elite circles to be well aware of Washington's close ties to powerful industrialists; far less familiar with America's black leadership, he was surprised and annoyed to find "the whole colored crowd" who attended the meeting "bitterly anti-Washington."

Shortly after midnight, the conference's final session appointed a forty-person steering committee, made up of a carefully chosen list of people whose selection, according to Mary White Ovington, "suited nobody." But it did allow the National Negro Conference — which changed its name to the NAACP in 1910—to begin its inaugural year. Booker T. Washington was left off the organization's steering committee, as were black "extremists" such as Ida B. Wells-Barnett and William Monroe Trotter. Dominated by whites, the Committee of Forty included only a few black leaders: "middle-of-the-roaders" such as Mary Church Terrell, and the anti-Washingtonian W.E.B. Du Bois, who had been a diplomatic presence at a meeting only "somewhat less noisy than bedlam."[86]

Among those unsatisfied with the new organization's leadership was Ida B. Wells-Barnett, who was stunned to find herself omitted from the committee charged with designing the program and structure of the new organization. Her name had been on the original list submitted to the nominating committee appointed to select the group and she had thought she had the support of W.E.B. Du Bois—the nominating subcommittee's sole black member. So when her name was not read during the meeting's final session, Ida got up and left the meeting. She was prepared "to put the best possible face on the matter," she said in her autobiography, but she seems to have left in a characteristic fit of temper. As she left, other participants in the meeting were still contesting her omission from the Committee of Forty, and she was soon called back into the building as a result. But even after nominating-committee chair Charles Edward Russell "illegally" added Wells-Barnett to the Committee of Forty shortly after the meeting ended, the damage was done.

Wells-Barnett returned from the National Negro Conference meeting feeling betrayed by Du Bois, who had taken her name off the leadership committee so he could add that of Niagara Movement activist Charles Bentley—and better represent that organization. Du Bois also believed that Wells-Barnett was not crucial to the Committee of Forty—and was indiscreet enough to say as much to her. "I knew that you and Mr. Barnett were represented by Celia Woolley at the Douglass Center and that you would be represented through her," he told Wells-Barnett after the meeting.[87] This explanation no doubt only added to Ida's bitter feeling against Du Bois. By 1909, she was no longer affiliated with the Douglass Center, and she had little reason to trust Woolley to represent the interests of black women (although Woolley was among those who lobbied to see Wells-Barnett added to the committee).

Indeed, Wells-Barnett's experiences with the white women at the Douglass Center may explain why she left the National Negro Conference meeting more resentful of New York reformer Mary White Ovington than she was of Du Bois. In *Crusade for Justice* Wells-Barnett recalled that shortly after she made her precipitous first exit from Charity Hall, "Miss Mary Ovington, who had taken a very active part in the deliberations, swept by me with an air of triumph and a very pleased look on her face." Ovington was none too enthusiastic about Wells-Barnett's leadership: she would later characterize Ida and other black radicals as "fitted for courageous work, but perhaps not fitted for the restraints of organization." In turn, Wells-Barnett saw Ovington, who would go on to serve the NAACP as executive secretary, board member, and for a time chairman, as a woman who was largely indifferent to the problems faced by black women. A fervent admirer of Du Bois, Ovington "basked in the sunlight of the adoration of the few college-bred Negroes who have surrounded her," Wells-Barnett noted with rancor. "But [she] has made little effort to know the soul of the black woman; and to that extent has fallen short of helping a race which has suffered as no white woman has ever been called upon to suffer or understand."[88]

However, neither Ovington nor Du Bois was responsible for the omission of black radicals such as Wells-Barnett and William Monroe Trotter from the Committee of Forty. It was Villard. Still hoping for Washington's endorsement, Villard had made sure that most of his detractors were excluded from the committee. "It is not to be a Washington movement, or a Du Bois movement," he had assured Washington, even before the meeting began. Likewise, he later admitted to Ovington that "the whole meeting was rigged up in advance—which it naturally had to be."[89]

A powerful man with little patience for grassroots leadership, Villard found the opinionated black radicals at the meeting "trying" and "was unreceptive to having more than a few African-Americans on the Committee of Forty." Married to a Georgia-born wife who "insisted that her husband invited neither black people or Jews to their home," Villard expected African Americans "to be humble and thankful or certainly not assertive and aggressive."[90] He cannot have enjoyed Wells-Barnett's behavior at the meeting. Indeed, during its early years even Du Bois's status in the organization was precarious. But Du Bois had the support of energetic white progressives such as Ovington and Walling, who viewed the accomplished African American professor as indispensable to the organization both "as organizer and as symbol."[91]

No such arguments could be made on behalf of Wells-Barnett. While "long time friends of the Negro" such as white progressive John Milholland admired Wells-Barnett for her many years of antilynching work, some of the other young reformers who attended the meeting scarcely knew who she was. Her antilynching campaign had never reached them, and by the end of the century's first decade, Wells-Barnett's credentials for race leadership were becoming increasingly outmoded. She lacked the illustrious education of a Du Bois and the powerful institutional base of a Washington—and she was a wife and a mother in an age when few prominent professional women had domestic responsibilities. In the end, it is hard to know which of her handicaps was most decisive. But together they ensured that Ida B. Wells-Barnett no longer loomed large in discussions of the race's most prominent leaders.

In some ways, the shift was a measure of the changing times in which she lived. Nineteenth-century black America had had more room for leaders such as Wells-Barnett. Slavery had created a generation of leaders such as her mentor Frederick Douglass, who educated themselves and whose major credentials for leadership lay largely in their personal experience and charisma. Among them were women as well as men—most notably Sojourner Truth and Harriet Tubman. But by the early twentieth century, the slave society that had given birth to such leaders was gone forever, and the possibilities for black leadership were increasingly limited to a more conventional range of individuals. Not unlike the white leaders of their era, the black professionals who inaugurated the Niagara Movement were educated men who rarely thought to include women in their race's leadership class. Women were only admitted into the Niagara Movement as an afterthought, and the movement's leaders subscribed to a gendered understanding of leadership that erased the ways in which Wells-Barnett's antilynching campaign had reshaped the agenda of black radicalism during the 1890s.

Meanwhile, the biracial coalition that cobbled together the NAACP had even less room for black female leaders such as Wells-Barnett. Conservative members of the Committee of Forty such as Villard would have preferred to leave the organization's policy decisions "to a coterie of distinguished white men." But when the group reconvened in New York in 1910 to establish its permanent organization, white radicals such as Walling successfully insisted that the organization's permanent staff include "a colored leader of nationwide prominence." They selected Du Bois for the task, launching him on a new career as the NAACP's director of publications and research—a post that also made him the editor of its journal, *The Crisis*. By contrast, Wells-Barnett, who had hoped that the new organization would provide an opportunity to revive the antilynching bureau she once ran under the auspices of the Afro-American Council, received no such appointment. Invited to attend the 1910 meeting, all expenses paid, she came. And she even took a position on the NAACP's executive board, where she helped launch *The Crisis* by arguing that the NAACP should develop its "own organ" rather than relying on "already established" publications to represent "our cause."[92] But with *The Crisis* in Du Bois's hands, she never found a role in the NAACP. Ill-suited to "the restraints of organization" in an era when those restraints fell particularly hard on black women, Wells-Barnett became increasingly distrustful of biracial organizations in the last decades of her life.

But she was no happier in the national organization of black women that she helped found. She revisited the National Association of Colored Women in 1910 on behalf of the NAACP. But at that organization's meeting in Louisville, Kentucky, Wells-Barnett soon found herself at odds with Margaret Murray Washington in a debate over the editorship of the NACW's periodical *National Notes*. Still perhaps hoping to find a national platform for her views, she led an unsuccessful attempt to challenge Mrs. Washington's control over the publication—which was both published and edited by Mrs. Washington and printed by Tuskegee Institute students at no cost to the NACW. In doing so, Ida had the support of NACW members who complained that the publication appeared somewhat sporadically and never published submissions containing any criticism of Booker T. Washington. But her motion that the NACW take over the magazine and open its editorial leadership to election was overruled and tabled by the chair of the meeting—and Wells-Barnett was hissed off the floor when she challenged the decision. Disappointed by "that spirit which seems to dominate every organization we have," Wells-Barnett withdrew from the NACW.[93]

She remained a committed activist, but the last two decades of her life would see her largely confining her talents to local black organizations, where her uncompromising character was less of a liability.

· 8 ·

Reforming Chicago

ON NOVEMBER 9, 1909, A BLACK MAN NAMED WILLIAM "FROG" James was arrested in Cairo, Illinois, a river town at the southern tip of the state. A tall, burly teamster, James was charged with the rape and murder of Annie Pelley, a young white woman who worked as a salesgirl in a local department store. James may have been guilty: after Pelley's body was discovered in an alley, bloodhounds followed the scent on the piece of cloth used to strangle her to his home, where the police found a handkerchief made of the same fabric—or so the news reports claimed. But the case against James never made it to any court of law. Two days later he was dead, hanged from a steel arch that graced the city's main intersection. He died at the hands of a mob of some ten thousand people, who even turned on the gaslights that illuminated the arch to better enjoy the spectacle. The crowd included several hundred women, some of whom helped string James up, as well as countless armed men, who riddled James's body with hundreds of bullets after the rope used to suspend his body broke. After hanging and shooting James, his executioners dragged his corpse to the alley where Pelley had been found and set it on fire. But before they torched his body, members of the mob removed his heart and other organs to preserve as souvenirs. They also cut off his head—which they mounted on the fencepost nearest the scene of his crime.

Their carnage, however, did not end with James's death and decapitation. Intent on finding another "suitable victim," James's killers marched on the jail looking for Arthur Alexander, a second black man also charged in the Pelley case.[1] When they could not find him they bludgeoned open the cell of Henry Salzner, a white man awaiting trial for killing his wife with an ax. After hanging Salzner, the mob left to track down Arthur Alexander. Alexander died the next day.

The Cairo lynchings caught Ida B. Wells-Barnett in a rare moment of despondency. Her hopes for reviving her antilynching bureau with the support of the NAACP had been crushed. A little more than a year after the Springfield riot, she still had no organizational support to bring to bear against racial violence in Illinois. Though she led a mass protest meeting of Chicago blacks, she balked when her husband urged her to go to Cairo to investigate. "I don't see why I should have to go and do the work that others refuse," she told Ferdinand over dinner as the couple discussed the case one evening in late November.[2]

Her usually mild-mannered spouse, however, was anxious for a report on events in Cairo, so he pressed the issue. Cairo would be the first real test of Illinois's 1905 antilynching law, which held officers of the law responsible for any violence against prisoners in their custody. Since Cairo sheriff Frank Davis had handed Frog James over to the mob, the new law should have cost Davis his job.[3] But now, weeks after the lynching, it seemed as if he would receive no lasting penalty, Barnett explained to his wife, as the family finished their evening meal. Governor Charles Deneen of Illinois had been reluctant to even suspend the sheriff from his post while the matter was investigated—as the new law required. He had done so only after black protesters demanded he "do his duty," and now seemed ready to reinstate him almost immediately. Barnett worried that the Illinois antilynching law was going to be proved a dead letter. "You will have to go to Cairo and get the facts with which to confront the Sheriff," he told his wife.[4]

Ida was not persuaded. She "had already been accused very strongly by some of our men of jumping in ahead of them and doing work without giving them a chance," she told her husband. For once, she was willing to "let them attend to the job." Moreover, she did not have the legal expertise needed to contest Davis's reinstatement, and was busy raising her children and leading the Negro Fellowship League—a new community organization that she created in 1908. Moreover, the forty-seven-year-old mother of four may have also felt too exhausted to go. In her autobiography Ida noted that although her husband urged her to leave that very night, she made no move to do so. Instead, she ended their argument by picking up five-year-old Alfreda and carrying her off to her bed, where she sang both her daughter and herself to sleep.

She was woken a little later that evening by Charles, her eldest, who told her, "Mother, if you don't go nobody else will." That the lanky thirteen-year-old had been following his parents' argument surprised her. Moreover, it moved her, providing Ida with the impetus she needed. "From the mouths of babes and sucklings," she reflected, with her usual activist understanding of the Scriptures. She left the next morning, buoyed by the support of her family. "Intensely interested in her mission," all four of the children accompanied their father when he saw her off at the train station.[5]

The abiding political support that Ida received from her family helps us understand the last two decades of her life. During these years, Wells-Barnett remained as politically active as ever, while staying much closer to home. Always uncomfortable in the confines of national organizations such as the NACW and the NAACP, Wells increasingly shifted her attention to community activism; Chicago and Illinois became the major sites of her reformist energies.

Wells-Barnett's Illinois-based activism was also a response to the increasingly pressing social problems faced by black communities throughout the state. They were especially severe in Chicago, which was becoming a major destination for the first waves of the Great Migration of black Southerners to the urban North that would reshape the nation during the first half of the twentieth century. Only 30,000 in 1900, Chicago's black popula-

A 1909 portrait of Ida B. Wells-Barnett and her four children. On her right is her thirteen-year-old, Charles, and on her left is his brother, Herman, twelve. Eight-year-old Ida sits in the middle of the photograph, behind the baby of the family—the five-year-old Alfreda.

tion expanded exponentially thereafter, rising to 44,000 by 1910, reaching 109,000 ten years later, and hitting the quarter of a million mark in 1935. With the flood of migrants came a host of social problems. The rural black Southerners who sought work within the city's booming industrial economy were excluded from labor unions and many factory jobs—except when called upon to serve as strikebreakers. Moreover, as their numbers grew and the labor market became increasingly racially divided, race relations declined. Unwelcome in most white neighborhoods, the migrants were crowded into dilapidated and inadequate housing on the South Side, where they were likewise excluded from many of the city's social services.

Black Chicago's social problems soon preoccupied Ida. She repeatedly challenged the color line, helping to fight off several school segregation plans and contesting discrimination against blacks in stores and other public facilities. And although she never abandoned her national fight against lynching and racial violence, after 1910 Wells-Barnett grew increasingly concerned with addressing the problems faced by black migrants in her own region.

Consequently, Wells-Barnett figured less and less prominently on the national scene, a development that has led some to characterize the older Ida as a "lonely warrior" who ended her career in isolation.[6] While such characterizations capture Wells-Barnett's increasing alienation from the national organizations that she had helped found, most notably the NAACP and the NACW, her isolation should not be exaggerated. During the 1910s and 1920s she did not so much work alone as turn to a more community-based political work, while at the same time sustaining an immersion in the life of her family that often fostered such work. At no point in her long and busy professional life did Ida spend much time working alone, and her later years were no exception. Instead, she drew on a variety of social and political networks that began in her own household and extended across Illinois, which would prove far more susceptible to Ida's influence than the national scene.

"Mob Violence Has No Place in Illinois"

Ida's trip to Cairo provided her with one of the rare unqualified victories of her political life. She arrived to find Cairo's blacks united in the belief that Frog James had committed the murder with which he had been charged, and therefore supporting Sheriff Davis's reinstatement. Davis was a popular Republican officeholder who had won the respect of Cairo blacks by employing several African American deputies. James, on the other hand, "was a worthless fellow"—or so the town's leading A.M.E. minister told Wells-Barnett. The first challenge Wells-Barnett faced in Cairo was to convince the town's black leaders that the sheriff should be punished for permitting mob violence, despite the low character of the victims. Cairo blacks, she told the minister, could not condone the lynching of "any fellowman who was a member of the race." If they did so, "the time might come when they had to condone that of other men higher up, providing that they were black."[7]

Ida began by enlisting the help of Will Taylor, a black pharmacist whom she knew from Chicago. With Taylor's help, she spent her first day in Cairo talking to the town's "colored citizens." By that evening, the two had assembled a well-attended community meeting where Wells-Barnett explained "that it would be endangering the lives of other colored people in Illinois if we did not take a stand." At issue was not Frog James's crime or personal character, she maintained, but whether "Mr. Frank Davis had used his great power to protect the victim of the mob; if he had at any time placed him behind the bars of the county jail as the law required; and if he had sworn in any deputies to help protect his prisoner."[8]

Wells-Barnett's probing inquiries raised questions that even the black men who had worked as Davis's deputies could not answer in the affirmative. Davis claimed that he had attempted to protect James by removing him from the town jail and hiding him in the woods outside town the night before the lynching. But in doing so, Davis may well have made James all the more accessible. The mob, after all, had had little trouble tracking him down in the woods, and wresting him from Davis and the one deputy that he had enlisted to help him. Moreover, both lawmen surrendered James to the mob without ever firing a shot; Davis had even managed to keep his gun.[9] By the meeting's end, Ida had succeeded in reversing black Cairo's support for Davis. She left with a resolution against him, signed by many who had previously supported reinstatement.

Armed with the resolution, Wells-Barnett spoke against Davis at a hearing held in Springfield later that week. "Not another Negro face was in evidence," leaving her to "represent the colored people of Illinois" on her own—although a local black lawyer named A. M. Williams later joined her. As the only nonlawyer speaking to an audience that included Governor Charles Deneen, Ida was grateful for Williams's support and advice. The hearing pitted her against Davis's lawyer, a former state senator who was also one of the "biggest lawyers in southern Illinois."[10] Ida presented the facts she had gathered in Cairo along with a brief on the legal barriers to Davis's reinstatement written by Ferdinand Barnett. The day ended with Governor Deneen requesting both sides to negotiate an "agreed statement of fact" on the case that he could consult before rendering any decision. Although "not a lawyer," as a journalist Wells-Barnett was utterly confident that she knew "a statement of fact when I saw one," and had no trouble holding her ground against her high-powered opponent as they haggled over the details to be included.[11]

Much to the surprise of everyone involved, Ida's understanding of the case prevailed. Her research convinced Governor Deneen that "Davis did not do all in his power to protect the prisoners." In denying Davis's petition for reinstatement, Deneen also issued a powerful public condemnation of lynching: "Mob violence has no place in Illinois," he wrote. "It is denounced in every line of the constitution and every statute. Instead of breeding respect for law; it breeds contempt. When such mob violence threatens the life of a prisoner in the custody of the Sheriff, the law has charged the Sheriff under the penalty of the forfeiture of his office, to use the utmost human endeavor to protect the life of his prisoner. The law may be severe: whether severe or not it must be enforced."[12]

An outstanding victory for Wells-Barnett, Deneen's ruling all but ended lynching in Illinois. Thereafter, Illinois sheriffs took to calling in additional deputies and support rather than give in to the mob whenever racial violence loomed. Racial violence continued, but it was no longer completely unopposed by state officials, whose vigilance helped Illinois "put lynching legally in its past."[13]

Moreover, Ida's work on the Cairo lynching helped her find new supporters. Propelled to Cairo by the encouragement of her family, Ida returned to Chicago rejuvenated, and resumed "the work that others refuse." The NAACP had supplied no aid to her work in Cairo. Instead, she had had to depend on the local black community. On her return to Chicago, Wells-Barnett continued to so do, turning to her fledgling community organization, the Negro Fellowship League, rather than the NAACP, to support her.

In some respects an unlikely outlet for Wells-Barnett's wide-ranging reform commitments, the league originated as a Bible study class. However, Wells-Barnett had always understood the Scriptures as a source of political inspiration, and so too would the young men who joined the class that Ida agreed to teach after she and her daughters joined the Grace Presbyterian Church in 1904. Ida's commitment to Grace Church underscored how raising a family had changed her day-to-day life. During her Memphis years, Ida had never committed to any one Protestant denomination, but she wanted her children brought up the same way she had been—"in a Christian home under the influence of a Sunday School and Church." Accordingly, prior to 1904, the entire Barnett family attended Ferdinand's longtime church home, the Bethel A.M.E. However, after their pastor, the radical minister Reverdy C. Ransom, left to found an urban mission in the heart of the South Side, the Barnetts sought out a new church; Ida could not abide Ransom's replacement, Abraham Lincoln Murray—a man who stood accused of making advances to one of his married female parishioners. So she and her husband sought out new places of worship, and ended up attending different churches. Ferdinand and the boys began to attend a Baptist church, while Ida and the girls joined Grace Presbyterian. Why the couple attended different churches is not clear, although Ferdinand Barnett may not have shared his wife's flexibility when it came to matters of denomination. Ida embraced Grace Church even though she "was not Presbyterian by doctrine." As she explained in her autobiography, "Since all Christian doctrines agreed on a standard of conduct and right living it mattered very little to me what name we bore."[14]

The Negro Fellowship League

At Grace Church, Wells-Barnett found not only a "new church home" but a new base for her political activism. Her Bible study classes were "delightful," attracting a group of twenty-five to thirty young men, "ranging from eighteen to thirty years of age." Ida and her pupils "discussed the Bible lessons in a plain commonsense way and tried to make the application of their truths to our daily life." Not surprisingly, such discussions eventually led to activism. Troubled by the Springfield riot in 1908, members of the class began to meet in the Barnett home to discuss "what we can do."[15] Encouraged by their teacher, they founded the Negro Fellowship League (NFL), which favored political debate over Bible study. Dedicated to social change, the NFL also began to admit women, at which point "it gradually became quite the thing" for its members "to bring their lady friend." Eight or nine years old when these meetings began, young Alfreda Barnett was a regular participant, and remembered being "thrilled" by the opportunity to spend time with the "big kids," whose meetings became increasingly activist over time.[16] NFL members supported Ida's mission to Cairo as well as both Barnetts' interest in the small but growing population of black men imprisoned at Joliet Penitentiary—the northern Illinois prison that served the Chicago area.

Casualties of the Great Migration, many of these men were rural Southerners whose legal troubles had begun as they struggled to make their way in an overcrowded and increasingly unwelcoming city. For much of its history, Chicago had been a place where most whites hardly knew that "there were a thousand Colored people" in their midst—and expressed little racial hostility as a result.[17] Before the Great Migration black Chicagoans were less segregated than the city's Italian immigrant population. They lived in African American enclaves scattered across eight or nine neighborhoods—most of which were otherwise white. But when thousands of rural blacks began to pour into Chicago during the 1910s, the city's relatively tranquil race relations began to change. White Chicagoans proved unwilling to house the black newcomers, so most of the migrants were forced into a narrow, thirty-block stretch of dilapidated housing on the South Side—already Chicago's seediest black neighborhood. As the migration continued, the South Side, along with one other black neighborhood on the West Side, would increasingly become the only areas open to African American residents. With residential segregation came other attacks on black civil liberties that contemporary observers likened to "the hardening of Jim Crow patterns in the South."[18] Among them was the relentless policing of the young black Southerners who came to Chicago looking for work. Many had trouble finding work or a place to stay, and often ended up in jail as a result.

Assistant State's Attorney Ferdinand Barnett encountered many such migrants, and often "brought home some of these boys he believed were innocent" as well as young men "that he had gotten out of jail" but "didn't have any place to go." For her part, Ida began to visit the state prison at Joliet after receiving invitations from prisoners there. She found that "some of them came from good homes" and most "had been well educated." Moreover, she relayed the inmates' problems to the young men in the Negro Fellowship League, encouraging them "to begin practical studies which would bring us in closer touch with those members of our race who were swelling the criminal records."[19] Long worried about the special dangers the American justice system posed to young blacks, Ida hoped the league could help the young black men arriving in the city daily from the rural South.

As hardworking, "consecrated" young men whose families hailed from the South, the organization's members, Wells-Barnett believed, were ideally situated to provide guidance to more recent migrants struggling to survive in Chicago—if they could raise the resources to do so.[20] Such help was desperately needed. The uneducated and impoverished rural migrants were shunned by the "better class of our people," and unwelcome at most social service agencies. "While every class is welcome in the Y.M.C.A. dormitories, Y.W.C.A. homes, the Salvation Army and the Mills hotels," Wells-Barnett lamented, "not one of these will give a Negro a bed to sleep in or permit him to use their reading rooms or gymnasiums."[21]

"Only one social center welcomes the Negro and that is the saloon," Wells-Barnett declared in 1910 at a meeting of the Congregational Union at the Palmer House, an elegant Chicago hotel. An affluent white organization, the union hosted a lecture by Dr. James G. K. McClure, a Presbyterian clergyman. McClure described Chicago's African American social problems as the failings of an inferior race and "The White Man's Burden." Ida's rebuttal was heated. "The statistics we have heard tonight," she explained, do not mean "that the Negro race is the most criminal of the various in Chicago. It does mean that ours is one of the most neglected groups." At issue was the Chicago environment that many black migrants encountered: the only accommodations and amusements open to blacks were located on State Street—in the heart of the city's vice district. "Here they found only saloons, buffet flats, poolrooms, and gambling houses . . . With no friends, they were railroaded into the penitentiary."[22]

For once, Ida profited from her outspokenness. In the Palmer House audience was Mrs. Victor Lawson, the wife of the owner of *The Chicago Daily News*. Although she and her husband were among the YMCA's major donors, the Lawsons had been unaware that it did not serve blacks. After verifying Ida's claims, they withdrew their funding from the Y and offered to support Wells-Barnett in establishing a facility that blacks could use. Delighted, Ida proposed a league reading room and social center that would serve as a "sort of lighthouse . . . on State Street." There, NFL members would "be on the lookout for these young people and extend to them a helping hand." Such a place, Ida told the Lawsons, could become "self-sustaining," once it got off the ground.[23]

The Lawsons agreed, and with their support Wells-Barnett rented a building on State Street and opened the "Negro Fellowship League Reading Room and Social Center for men and boys" on May 10, 1910. The league's new home was in a neighborhood "so questionable" that some NFL members refused to visit the place. Likewise, "the secretaries whom we employed were averse to visiting the poolhalls, saloons, and street corners to find and invite young men and distribute cards." But Ida regarded the center's location as ideal. "State Street needed them," she told reluctant members of the league.[24]

Ida was untroubled by the raucous neighborhood. When a noisy craps game disrupted the league's very first Sunday program, Ida marched out and introduced herself to "dirty disreputable men seated on the ground" enjoying "a bucket of beer." Asking them to be "a little more quiet," she invited them to join the NFL Reading Room. Embarrassed by this gentle rebuke, the gamblers disbursed and NFL events were "never again disturbed or molested." Ida claimed the NFL was a damper to crime, leading to fewer police patrols and even one fewer brothel—its proprietor relocated, finding the NFL chorus's weekly performances of "Sunday school and church hymns . . . too much of a reproach to her conscience."[25]

Staffed by one employee and a roster of volunteers, the NFL's reading room was open from 9:00 a.m. to 10:00 p.m., and housed a "selected library of history, biography, fiction and race literature especially." It offered visitors a place to read, study, write letters, and pursue a "quiet game of checkers, dominoes or other games that would not interfere with those who wished to read." Nonalcoholic refreshments were available—or as the NFL's announcements noted, "the young ladies of the League will have charge of the punch bowl, and hope to be able to give every visitor a glass of refreshing lemonade."[26] Visitors were also encouraged to attend weekly lectures by a variety of prominent speakers, ranging from white reformers such as Jane Addams and Mary White Ovington to black intellectuals such as William Monroe Trotter, Garland Penn, and the historian Carter G. Woodson. Free and open to the public, these events attracted local people as well as league members. For example, Lucius C. Harper, who would later become editor of the *Chicago Defender*, long remembered the league from his youth on the South Side. He and friends were "loitering about the corner of 31st and

State St." one night when a league member on his way to hear a speech by Woodson invited them to attend. Harper went "just to pass the time away" and developed a lifelong passion for black history.[27]

The NFL soon expanded its activities to meet the needs of black newcomers, offering men's lodgings on the building's second floor, where visitors could secure a bed for fifty cents a night, and even making food available to those in need—vouchers were offered for meals at a restaurant across the street. The NFL also began helping migrants find jobs, opening an employment bureau that placed 115 men during its first year alone.

During that first year, Wells-Barnett also realized her goal of using the league to protect black men from injustice, mobilizing members to block the extradition of Steve Green, a fugitive from Crittenden County, Arkansas. Arrested in Chicago on August 14, 1910, Green had fled his home state earlier that summer after a lethal altercation with his former landlord, Will Saddler. The conflict began when Saddler and three other men tracked Green down to force him to continue working Saddler's land. Having found better-paying work elsewhere, Green was not interested. But he soon found himself looking down the barrel of Saddler's gun. "Green didn't I tell you that if you didn't work my farm this year there would not be enough room in Crittenden county for you and me to live," the aggrieved Saddler told Green, before shooting him three times at close range.[28] Badly wounded but still mobile, Green grabbed his own gun and fled, killing Saddler as he made his escape.

Now a fugitive from justice as well as a lynch mob, Green made it as far north as Chicago before he was caught and held for extradition. Convinced that he would be "burned alive" if returned to Arkansas, he ate ground glass when the extradition order went through.[29] But his suicide attempt failed, and Green was put on a train for Crittenden County in the custody of an Arkansas lawman who told him, "Steve, you are the most important 'Nigger' in the United States: there will be a thousand men at the station when we get there and we will have a rope and coal oil ready to burn you alive."[30]

Reading about Green's case in the morning papers just as he was to depart, Wells-Barnett contacted black attorneys Edward H. Wright and

W. G. Anderson to obtain a writ of habeas corpus on the fugitive's behalf. The lawyers telegraphed and telephoned news of the writ to sheriffs in all the towns on the railroad line, catching up with Green in Cairo, Illinois, where the local sheriff arrested him and sent him back to Chicago. Ida had managed to snatch him from the mob's waiting hands. Back in Chicago he slept at the NFL and managed to dodge subsequent extradition attempts until Arkansas abandoned his case as "hopeless." "He is one Negro who lives to tell the tale that he was not burned alive according to the program," Ida reported in *Crusade for Justice*.[31]

Green's successful escape was featured in the first issue of the NAACP's magazine *The Crisis*, although W.E.B. Du Bois's discussion of the case never managed to mention Wells-Barnett. In the NFL, Ida had clearly found a far more congenial organization than the NAACP. "Lifted to seventh heaven" when the league's reading room and social center first opened, Ida promoted its activities tirelessly for nearly a decade.[32] With all of her children now in school, she was free to work at the league on a daily basis. Accordingly, for the first three years of its existence, Ida staffed the NFL employment bureau, oversaw all of its programs, and between 1911 and 1914 also managed to publish an NFL newspaper, *The Fellowship Herald*.

Chronically underfunded, the NFL never achieved the large membership Ida hoped to attract. Between forty and fifty men used its facilities and services each day, and its lodgings were often full. But with only a secretary on the payroll, the league could not do much work "among the people in the neighborhood." Moreover, the NFL's funding declined dramatically after the YMCA opened a new facility for African Americans on Wabash in 1913. Committed to funding the league only for its first year, Victor Lawson transferred his donations back to the Y.[33] Despite the work being done at the NFL, he preferred to support the YMCA's staff of white social service professionals over the headstrong Wells-Barnett—whose expenditures and programs did not always meet with his approval.[34]

Lawson's withdrawal left Ida in desperate need of funding. Convinced "that the YMCA would never take over the work that we were doing," and worried that the Y's annual membership fee of twelve dollars was more than many migrants could afford, she was unwilling to consider closing the NFL.[35] Ida tried to solicit support for the NFL center from the Sears Roebuck mogul Julius Rosenwald, but managed to offend the leader of the committee Rosenwald sent to visit the NFL almost immediately. Mr. Sachs opened his meeting with Wells-Barnett by repeating a joke that he had heard Booker T. Washington deliver earlier that week. It was a folksy and not particularly funny story about an old man who did not mind that his "wife had left him," but for the fact that "she had left the chicken coop door open and all the chickens had gone home too." Not amused, Ida not only "didn't laugh" but compounded her offense by explaining that blacks questioned Washington's leadership precisely on account of such jokes. Would Chicago Jews admire the prominent Rabbi Hirsch, she asked, "if every time he appeared before a gentile audience he would amuse them by telling stories about Jews burning down their stores to get insurance?" Having made her visitor silent and red in the face, she then went on to answer the question herself: "I am sure you would not, and a great many of us cannot approve Mr. Washington's plan of telling chicken-stealing stories on his own people in order to amuse his audiences and get money for Tuskegee."[36]

"Needless to say, the conversation ended there," Wells-Barnett noted in her autobiography, with no apparent regret.[37] But as usual, she paid a high price for her outspokenness. Six months behind on the rent, she attempted to turn the NFL over to the Methodists, but when church officials questioned the absence of "leading people of the race" in the league she changed her mind. An organization of workingmen, NFL leaders included an elevator man, a redcap, and a ragpicker. Wells-Barnett had found that elite Chicago blacks did not want "to know . . . men of this type" and had little interest in working with them. Deciding to retain her leadership over the NFL, she slashed expenses dramatically by the simple expedient of moving the organization to a much more modest facility—a little storefront on State Street.

With no major donor after 1913, Wells-Barnett was obliged to provide much of the organization's operating budget herself—which she accomplished by taking work as an adult parole officer and dedicating her monthly salary of $150 to cover the NFL's expenses. Wells-Barnett was appointed to her new job by municipal court chief justice Harry Olsen, who appreciated what the NFL was doing for migrants with legal troubles and was anxious to see it stay open. Though Wells-Barnett's work as a parole officer meshed well with her objectives for the NFL, her daily life became grueling. Between 1913 and 1915, Ida was stretched thin by long days in court, followed by nights at the NFL, where she met with her probationers. Forced to all but abandon her home life, Ida gave up her annual summertime trips to the country in favor of sweltering summers working in Chicago.

Still, despite Ida's workload, the NFL was a growing concern. In 1913, Illinois passed the Municipal and Presidential Voting Act, and as a result Wells-Barnett was soon hard at work organizing black women to vote. A product of years of activism by Illinois suffragists, the limited suffrage bill was designed to avoid any conflict with the state constitution. It allowed Illinois women to vote in municipal and presidential elections, and in some but not all state contests as well—providing female suffrage for all state offices not specifically designated in the state constitution as requiring a vote by male electors. A tremendous victory despite these limitations, the new law made Illinois among the very first states to allow female suffrage of any kind. A lifelong supporter of women's suffrage, Wells-Barnett had been active in the Republican Party for many years, and had even founded the Women's Second Ward Republican Club in 1910 "to assist men in getting better laws for the race and having representation in everything which tends to represent the city and its national government."[38] After the passage of the 1913 law, she wasted no time, especially in the Second Ward, which had a majority black population but no black elected officials. Working with Belle Squire, a white columnist for the *Chicago Tribune*, Ida organized the Alpha Suffrage Club (ASC).[39] With Ida presiding, the group met weekly at the Negro Fellowship League "to study political and social questions." They also canvassed the neighborhood block by block asking women "to register so that they would help put a colored man on the city council."[40]

Committed to nationwide female suffrage as well, women of the ASC also raised money to send Wells-Barnett to the National American Woman Suffrage Association (NAWSA) parade in Washington on March 13, 1913. There, Ida made the national news one more time. As a concession to its Southern membership, the NAWSA imposed a segregation policy on its state suffrage affiliates. In deference to Southern sentiments about black suffrage, male or female, NAWSA required all black suffragists to march at the end of the parade in one unit rather than appearing in their state delegations. Though the NAWSA policy conflicted with the policies of the Illinois Equal Suffrage Association, whose president, Grace Wilbur Trout, had approved an integrated state delegation, when the Illinois delegation assembled, Trout told them that the parade's organizers had advised them "to keep the delegation entirely white" and that she intended to honor their request. A heated argument ensued. With the support of Belle Squire and Grace Brooks, another white Illinois suffragist, Ida insisted, "I shall not march at all unless I can march under the Illinois banner." But Trout and other members of the Illinois delegation proved unwilling to "go against the law of the national organization," and they carried the day.[41]

Mortified, Wells-Barnett promptly left the group, seemingly to join the other African American suffragists—as instructed. But she had not given up. When the Illinois delegation marched down Pennsylvania Avenue, Ida stepped out from the crowd that had assembled to watch and "walked calmly out to the delegation and assumed her place." A news report noted, "There was no question about her eligibility and she finished the march."[42] Any objections that her presence might have inspired among Southern women were overshadowed by the crowds of men that mobbed the procession, almost bringing it to a halt. But Wells-Barnett's transgressive appearance in the parade was captured by the *Chicago Tribune*, which ran a photograph of her marching alongside Squire and Brooks in the Illinois delegation—a little smile on her face.[43]

Among those who took inspiration from the photo may well have been Chicago's black women voters, who turned out in large numbers in the 1914 elections, coming only 167 votes short of delivering one of the Second

Wells-Barnett marching with other women suffragists in a parade in Washington, D.C., 1913

Ward's primaries to William R. Cowan, an independent black candidate for alderman. Thereafter, Republicans of both races courted the Second Ward's black female voters. By 1916, the Alpha Suffrage Club had two hundred members and had become a force to be reckoned with. Led by Ida, that year they helped elect Chicago's first black alderman: Oscar De Priest, who would have a long and successful political career, but prove no longtime ally to Ida.

Indeed, Ida's involvement with municipal politics would prove the undoing of her municipal job as a parole officer in 1915. That year, she committed the Alpha Suffrage Club to support the candidacy of William Hale "Big Bill" Thompson, only to withdraw her support later after Judge Harry Olsen announced his candidacy. Continuing to support Thompson would have required her to discredit Olsen, to whom she owed her job as parole officer. Ida could not do it: "All my life I have been the victim of ingrates," she noted in her autobiography. "I have constantly affirmed that I agree with the old time Spartans in spirit, anyhow, when they put ingrates to death."[44] Ida attempted to change her course gracefully, even securing

Thompson another well-connected black community leader to help his campaign. Still her wavering loyalties cost her her job. Big Bill Thompson won, partially thanks to Wells-Barnett's initial efforts, but he did not forgive her for her last-minute defection. Less than six months later he appointed a white parole officer to replace her.

While Ida's reduced daily workload must have been something of a relief to the entire Barnett family, it also meant that the "Negro Fellowship Reading Room and Social Center had again to fall back on what we could make from our employment office." That income would keep the NFL open for five more years—although on a shoestring, since "nobody who applied for a job was ever turned away."[45] Moreover, the NFL's expenditures included securing legal support for African Americans who ran afoul of the Illinois justice system—although much of it was supplied pro bono by Ferdinand Barnett.

Their work bridged the growing class divide that separated Chicago's established black professionals and the young black men who languished in local prisons such as Joliet. The "common people" who populated the NFL, Ida noted, were willing "to give their mite to help a man who they believed to be innocent." But Chicago race leaders were far less good-hearted. In particular, she claimed, "all of our leading politicians, doctors, lawyers, and prominent people" refused to support "Chicken Joe" Campbell, a Joliet prisoner who was put on trial for the rape and murder of the prison warden's wife.[46] Though Campbell eventually won the support of a number of local churches, as well as Robert S. Abbott, editor of the *Chicago Defender*, Campbell's cause was indeed ignored by the Chicago NAACP—an organization whose members included some of Chicago's most prominent black citizens.

Campbell came to Ida's attention in the spring of 1915 after Chicago papers reported he had been confined to solitary in complete darkness for fifty hours on bread and water. She immediately wrote a scathing letter to local newspapers and also sent an NFL lawyer to Joliet to represent the defendant. "Is this justice? Is this humanity? Can we stand to see a dog treated in such a fashion without protest?" Campbell was one of several Joliet prisoners suspected of setting a fire that resulted in the death of the prison warden's wife. There was no evidence of rape, the body having been burned in the fire; Campbell was nevertheless charged with rape and murder, largely because, Ida suspected, he was "the only colored man around." "Sweated and tortured to . . . confess," he maintained his innocence once he secured a lawyer.[47] And thereafter the Barnetts and the NFL saw him through his trial and three appeals, the last of which resulted in his sentence being commuted from death to life in prison.

Other legal battles brought more decisive victories. In 1918, just after Campbell's final appeal, Ida was able to secure a pardon for J. K. Smith, another Joliet inmate. Smith had been falsely convicted of kidnapping a child who turned up two years later in the custody of a Chicago couple, who then stood trial for the same crime. "A poor man, without friends," he finally secured his release with an appeal to Ida B. Wells-Barnett, who collected the legal papers needed to secure his pardon.[48]

The NFL challenged racial discrimination outside the justice system as well.[49] In 1913, led by Ida, the league banded together with other black organizations in Chicago to defeat a bill that would have segregated the city's streetcars and Pullman cars. The lone woman on the delegation, Ida spoke on behalf of both the NFL and the city's black women's club. The group spent a day at the state legislature, where they succeeded in denouncing the bill so vigorously that "the author of the measure . . . declared he was sorry that he had presented the bill and had never met such a brilliant array of colored people in his life."[50]

Some of the NFL's efforts had mixed results. In 1915, the NFL combined forces with the NAACP to seek an injunction against the screening of D. W. Griffith's *The Birth of a Nation*, an epic silent film about Reconstruction still infamous for its racist depiction of the freedmen, who were played by leering white men in blackface. But the municipal court refused their request and Griffith's film ended up running "for many weeks in Chicago," a fiasco that Ida blamed on poor preparation on the part of the NAACP lawyer who presented black Chicago's case. Wells-Barnett and the league also lent their support to successful battles against other discriminatory measures ranging from a federal bill outlawing interracial marriage inspired by prizefighter Jack Johnson's notorious union with a white teenager to a weekly segregated social hour hosted by Chicago's Wendell Phillips High School.

Despite its financial woes, the NFL was clearly Ida's longest-lasting and most satisfying organizational commitment. The league's freewheeling agenda seems to have been largely at her disposal. Acting within her capacity as president, Wells-Barnett challenged everyday racial slights as energetically as she did more serious injustices. Her small battles ranged from a letter to the editor of the *Chicago Tribune* rebuking the paper for referring to a recently deceased black Civil War veteran as an "aged darkey" to publicly lamenting the lack of African American speakers at the 1914 dedication of Illinois's Eighth Regiment, a black military unit.[51] She also secured the immediate dismissal of a Marshall Field's department store salesclerk who told her, "I don't have to wait on a black 'nigger' like you."[52]

Ida's "everyday resistance" to Jim Crow in all its incarnations was an irrepressible part of her personality rather than a product of her organizational or political commitment.[53] Despite sharing similar political views and affiliations, Ferdinand Barnett was nowhere near as combative as his wife in daily life. Ferdinand's "aggressiveness and his work on civil rights were mostly with his pen," noted the couple's daughter Alfreda Duster. By contrast, Ida's militant spirit permeated her daily life. Alfreda remembered her mother as "walking the halls" of her grade school, always ready to intervene if her children had any trouble with their teachers. And Barnett family lore included comical examples of Ida's unflagging opposition to Jim Crow, such as the story of the time when she got tired of waiting to be served at Marshall Field's, a store many black people avoided "because you knew they wouldn't treat you right." Unwilling to leave empty-handed, Wells-Barnett simply picked up her purchase—"a pair of men's underpants . . . put them over her arm, and walked toward the door. Immediately, a floor walker stopped her, and so she was able to buy them." Ida's story of this "funny incident" became a part of family history. Years later Alfreda was still amused by the image of the ever-militant "Ida B. Wells-Barnett with a pair of men's underpants dangling over her arm." "She was only five foot three or four, and she had grown plump in her fifties," Alfreda said, thinking about how her mother must have looked as she marched out of the store, "but she walked as if she owned the world. She floated."[54]

In short, the spirited and often impulsive activism that often got Ida into trouble in organizational settings flourished within the Negro Fellowship League. In part, the league afforded her greater freedom because she was its only well-known leader, and supplied much of its funding. But at issue was not just the lack of other contenders to lead the NFL. Rather, the working-class blacks who supported the league were far more open to Ida's leadership than the largely middle-class race leaders she had worked with in the past. A child of ex-slaves with roots in the rural South, she lacked the elite pedigree, college degree, and social standing that characterized many of the leaders of the NAACP and the National Association of Black Women's Clubs. But she was well versed in the challenges faced by the NFL center's working-class men. Long accustomed to working with men, she had raised her brothers, supervised her stepsons, and now had two teenage sons of her own. Self-educated and self-made herself, she also understood the class aspirations that inspired league members to take "courses in law and medicine while they earned their daily bread at the post office." Indeed, the NFL helped sponsor community-wide essay contests that nourished the intellectual aspirations of ordinary black Chicagoans, taking pride in the fact that NFL members regularly excelled in such competitions.

The NFL and the NERL

NFL members also allowed Wells-Barnett to ally their organization with other radical organizations, most notably William Monroe Trotter's National Equal Rights League. A Niagara Movement member, Trotter had founded the NERL (originally called the Negro-American Political League) in 1908 to lobby the federal government to protect black civil rights.[55] Like Wells-Barnett, Trotter had little patience for white moderates—who were equally impatient with him. Combative, arrogant, and outspoken, he had alienated Oswald Garrison Villard at the NAACP's very first meeting in 1909. Much like Ida, Trotter never secured a post in the organization, even though he was one of the leaders of the anti-Washington movement that led to its founding. Unlike Wells-Barnett, however, Trotter did not turn to community organizing as a result. A Harvard graduate who attended white schools throughout his youth, Trotter was one of black Boston's intellectual leaders rather than a community activist. Indeed, Trotter ran the NERL as a one-man show. The organization had no headquarters, staff, or budget, just a mailing list and a public forum provided by Trotter's newspaper, the *Boston Guardian*.

A fiery militant all his life, Trotter directed his equal rights activism toward the federal government, enlisting the support of the NFL to broaden his base. Starting in the fall of 1913, the two organizations collaborated in protesting new regulations mandating the segregation of federal offices under President Woodrow Wilson. Trotter and Wells-Barnett traveled to D.C. to present Wilson with a petition signed by approximately twenty thousand, but their protest had no effect, inspiring Trotter to return the following year and make the national news by publicly berating President Wilson. Although Trotter was widely chided for his "insolence," it met no criticism from Wells-Barnett, who afterward established a Chicago branch of the NERL. Moreover, she and Trotter went on to form an enduring political partnership. Though highly independent, opinionated, and aggressive people, they were in accord when it came to politics. Indeed, their collaboration suggests their difficulties with other race leaders of their day were as much a matter of politics as they were of personality.

Much of their work together combined organizational forces to protest the spread of Jim Crow laws and practices in their era's municipal, state, and federal institutions. For example, the NERL lent support to Ida's battle against Jim Crow streetcars in Chicago, while the two organizations combined to fight a bill prohibiting interracial marriage in D.C. and cosponsored a letter-writing campaign against a national immigration bill that would have banned African immigration. Tellingly, neither was ever willing to join forces with what was becoming the nation's foremost civil rights organization: the NAACP.

Still headquartered in New York, the NAACP by 1914 had six thousand members and fifty branches. Du Bois remained the editor of *The Crisis*, and the only African American on staff. But he had managed to push the organization toward a militant integrationism that was not incompatible with the politics pursued by Trotter and Wells-Barnett. Moreover, the NAACP had also escaped the controlling imprint of Booker T. Washington, whose influence declined rapidly in the half decade prior to his death in 1915. Still neither Trotter nor Wells-Barnett proved responsive to Du Bois's attempt to make the NAACP "the battle line" for all race work. Both distrusted Du Bois and were not impressed by the NAACP branches in their cities. The Boston NAACP was dominated by Bookerites in its early years, while the Chicago NAACP was home to many of the middle-class black leaders whom Ida had clashed with in the past.

"A Far More Dangerous Agitator Than Marcus Garvey"

Instead, as World War I loomed, Trotter and Wells-Barnett soldiered on as "individual sharp shooters fighting their own effective guerrilla warfare"—to borrow a phrase from Du Bois.[56] As maverick black radicals, however, both would become even more isolated after the United States officially entered into what was then called the Great War on April 6, 1917. Passed on May 17, 1917, the Selective Service Act recruited African Americans into a segregated and widely racist army. Moreover, many African Americans were ambivalent about lending their support to a war dedicated to protecting democratic freedoms abroad, when they had yet to secure such freedoms at home. "You white folk are going to war to fight for your rights. You all seem to want us to go," an anonymous letter writer who wrote the federal government on behalf of the "Black Nation" noted. "If we was to fight for our rights, we would have a war among ourselves. The Germans has not done us harm and they cannot treat us any meaner than you all has."[57] Such complaints inspired surveillance rather than sympathy among government officials, who soon had the Bureau of Investigation (later to become the FBI) looking for German spies working to undermine the loyalty of black citizens. And when German agents could not be found, African Americans who spoke out on behalf of black civil rights became subject to federal scrutiny.

Not surprisingly, Ida and her husband attracted the attention of the bureau after they protested a vicious race riot that rocked East St. Louis, Illinois, on July 2, 1917. In her autobiography, Ida misremembered the riot as occurring in the summer of 1918. It occurred a year earlier and introduced her to the stark contradiction that African Americans faced when they were first recruited to support the "war for democracy." Like many black families, the Barnetts supported the war effort from the start. Ida's sons Herman and Charles both enlisted, as did her stepson Ferdinand, Jr. Moreover, Ida led the NFL's 1917 campaign to prepare "Christmas kits" containing sweets and other seasonal gifts for "our boys" in the 183rd Brigade, a black brigade stationed at Camp Grant, Illinois.[58] But the East St. Louis riot was a wrenching challenge to the patriotic loyalty of African American families across the nation.

The first of a series of race riots that took place during and immediately after World War I, the East St. Louis riot left thirty-nine blacks and nine whites dead and leveled much of the city's black downtown. The violence erupted in the wake of an unsuccessful strike at the Aluminum Ore Company, a factory that supplied airplane parts to the U.S. military. Although most of the non-union workers the company recruited to break the strike were white, the strike took place at a time when East St. Louis Democrats accused the city's political and industrial leaders of importing "Southern blacks to supply employers with non-Union labor and the Republican party with votes." Although these charges had no basis in fact, they ensured that St. Louis blacks became the focus of its white population's economic and political frustration. That frustration turned deadly one

East St. Louis during the July 1917 riot

evening in July when blacks in downtown St. Louis, defending themselves from the white gangs who regularly shot up their neighborhood, fired on two white men cruising their neighborhood in a "big black touring car."[59] The two men in the car were not white gang members, but white policemen, who were both fatally wounded. The next morning, vengeful whites stormed the black section of East St. Louis, first beating and then killing black residents in a festival of violence that lasted all day.

The most destructive race riot of its era, it inspired protests in black communities across the country, including a fiery speech by a young Caribbean radical named Marcus Garvey, who maintained that "Monday [July] 2nd, will go down in history as one of the bloodiest outrages against mankind for which any class of people could be held guilty."[60] Garvey was a Jamaican who had come to the United States in 1916 on a fund-raising tour for the establishment of an industrial school in his home country. After giving talks across the country, including an address before the NFL, the radical black separatist decided to prolong his visit. Appalled by events such as the East St. Louis riot, in 1918 he established a chapter of his Jamaican organization, the Universal Negro Improvement Organization, in Harlem to promote racial uplift, racial unity, and political independence among American blacks. For Garvey, the East St. Louis riot was proof that "white people are taking advantage of black-men today because black-men all over the world are disunited."[61]

Ida B. Wells-Barnett and Ferdinand Barnett would prove sympathetic to Garvey's call to unite "the masses of our people and endow them with racial consciousness and unity." But they never embraced his belief in a separate black nationality. For them, the state of Illinois, rather than black American political affiliations, was at fault in East St. Louis. After protesting earlier episodes of mob violence in Springfield and Cairo, the Barnetts were bitterly disappointed that their state had once again done nothing to protect its black citizens. Indeed, several Illinois National Guard members stationed in the city had either watched or joined the mob. At an NFL meeting on the riot, Ferdinand Barnett warned Chicago blacks that it was now clear that self-defense was the only option. "Arm yourselves with guns and pistols," he told them. "Don't buy an arsenal, but get enough guns to protect yourself . . . and when trouble starts let us not hesitate to call upon our Negro militia men to defend ourselves."[62]

After a speech underscoring her long-standing belief that mob violence should be combated with investigation and protest, Ida was sent on a fact-finding tour. She arrived in East St. Louis the next day to find the city's black population all but gone, and the militia accompanying a few female refugees who had returned to pick up clothing and other necessities. Braving an outbreak of smallpox among the refugees, Ida got a vaccination and traveled with them. Her investigation revealed that trouble had been brewing in East St. Louis well before the riots. Local blacks had even visited the governor a month before asking for protection against simmering labor conflicts. Wells-Barnett lobbied the governor to bring the rioters to justice, but the state's investigation instead focused on the black men who had organized in their own defense. Sixteen were tried and convicted; all received sentences of no less than fifteen years. And while seventy-five whites were also tried, few were convicted and only ten received a sentence of longer than five years. The governor reported that justice had been served.

Published as *The East St. Louis Massacre: The Greatest Horror of the Century*, Ida's investigation was quickly censored by the military. But her account of the riot, which included interviews with riot victims documenting the violent participation of both the National Guard and the East St. Louis police, helped spur a congressional investigation. The Barnetts also took on the defense of Leroy Bundy, a black dentist charged with the murder of the two police officers—largely on the evidence that he had called for East St. Louis's blacks to use armed self-defense to protect their neighborhood from the white gang violence that preceded the riot. Working with the NFL and the *Chicago Defender*, the Barnetts saw Bundy through several trials and appeals before he was finally acquitted in 1920. A drain on the Barnetts' financial resources, the Bundy trial further strained their relationship with the NAACP, which had offered to represent the black men charged with participating in the riot but had failed to provide counsel for Bundy. Unlike the Barnetts, most of Chicago's race leaders were very nervous about antagonizing state and federal officials at a time when the black community's national loyalties were under scrutiny. Indeed, while Ida was in East St. Louis, a delegation of black men led by Congressman Oscar De Priest and attorney Edward H. Wright visited the Illinois governor to assure him they held him blameless. "The Barnetts were radicals," Ida said they told him, and "he need pay no attention to resolutions which we had published in the papers."[63]

Wartime pressures on African Americans to abandon criticism of the government would further marginalize the Barnetts, who refused to "forget our special grievances." As radical as ever, early in the war they were labeled subversive by the Bureau of Investigation and the federal office of military intelligence. Ida's pamphlet, *The East St. Louis Massacre*, caught the attention of the Department of War as a source of "inter-racial antagonism," while her husband was labeled rabidly "pro-German." An initial investigation into Barnett's activities, however, went nowhere because Chicago Bureau of Immigration agents "failed to find a single black person willing to admit to having heard Barnett speak."[64]

But the Barnetts were soon under investigation again in the wake of another riot. Stationed at Houston's Camp Logan in mid-July, the Third Battalion of the Twenty-fourth Infantry was an African American unit that had remained on active duty ever since it was first organized during the Civil War. Composed of experienced soldiers, the regiment endured a long hot summer of segregation, racial epithets, and harassment at the hands of the Houston police that ended with one hundred black soldiers taking up arms against local whites on August 27, 1917. The conflict began after the police assaulted and then arrested two black soldiers in downtown Houston. By the time word of the arrests got back to camp, one of the soldiers was rumored to be dead. One hundred of his fellow soldiers took up arms and marched on downtown Houston, killing fifteen whites and injuring a dozen others. The U.S. military's response was swift and severe, and made no allowances for the violence against the African American soldiers that had precipitated the riot. While white soldiers were disciplined, all of the black soldiers involved received court-martials, and thirteen were sentenced to death in hasty military trials without appeal. Black protests on behalf of the Houston rioters were muted. "We simply dare not start to try to express our feelings and those of our people as a result of this affair," wrote the editor of the normally outspoken *Cleveland Gazette*; while *The Baltimore Afro-American* was censured into silence by the Justice Department after referring to the soldiers as "martyrs."[65]

But Wells-Barnett, who also saw the soldiers as martyrs, refused to be silenced. The army had executed the leaders of the Houston riot, she believed, "to placate Southern hatred." Accordingly, Ida encouraged the NFL to hold "a memorial service for the men whose lives had been taken and in that way utter a solemn protest," a plan that failed when Ida could find no black church willing to host the event. So Ida settled for distributing buttons that she had ordered for the service. Emblazoned with the words "In

Memorial MARTYRED NEGRO SOLDIERS," they caught the attention of the Secret Service. But when confronted by two Secret Service agents, Ida stood her ground. "I am not guilty of treason," she told them when they threatened to arrest her for disloyalty. She also refused to let them confiscate her buttons. "The government deserves to be criticized," she told them. "I'd rather go down in history as one lone Negro who dared tell the government that it had done a dastardly thing than save my skin by taking back

A 1917 photograph of Ida B. Wells-Barnett wearing her button commemorating the MARTYRED NEGRO SOLDIERS *executed for their participation in the Houston Riot*

what I said." And, true to her word, she continued "disposing of the buttons to anyone who wanted them."[66] Ida also modeled her button in a photograph that shows her much as she must have appeared to the Secret Service agents. Gray-haired, sweet-faced, and a little plump, Ida wore her button on a dress made of silk and lace. Adorned with a strand of pearls, she was the very image of a respectable middle-aged black woman.

Ida featured as a "known race agitator" in military intelligence thereafter, and was refused a passport when she was selected to represent the NERL at the National Colored Congress for World Democracy in Versailles in 1919. The applications of other NERL members were also denied. William Monroe Trotter, who had also refused to "close ranks" during World War I, traveled to France on seaman's papers, working his way across the Atlantic incognito as a cook on a small freighter. He missed much of the peace conference as a result, never securing admission to the National Colored Congress or gaining an audience with President Woodrow Wilson. Present at the Versailles peace conference, however, was NAACP representative W.E.B. Du Bois, who attended without difficulty.

By 1918, the NAACP had garnered recognition as the most prominent voice of the Negro, while both Wells-Barnett and Trotter were losing influence. In part, the shift was a result of the success of the protest tradition that Trotter, Wells-Barnett, and other black radicals had nurtured during Booker T. Washington's accommodationist reign. Their fights against segregation and lynching had become central to the NAACP. Moreover, Wells-Barnett's pioneering work among South Side blacks in the NFL met a similarly ironic fate. Among the organizations that displaced the NFL was a branch of the YMCA dedicated to serving South Side blacks that originated at least in part as a result of her call for the establishment of social service organizations in Chicago's black neighborhoods. And the state of Illinois also moved to remedy some of the social problems addressed by the NFL, establishing a free employment agency that made the NFL's service obsolete.

After 1916, the NFL faced even more serious competition from yet another philanthropic agency. "It seemed that the Urban League was brought in to supplant the activities of the Negro Fellowship League," Ida complained in *Crusade for Justice*. A new branch of a national organization founded in New York in 1911, the Chicago Urban League was, of course, not established to displace existing social service agencies. Rather, like the NFL, it was dedicated to serving the needs of rural black migrants to the urban North. When its organizers won the support of "almost every organization among the women's clubs," a far broader base of support than her own organization had ever achieved, Ida was quick to see it as a threat.[67] Conceivably the NFL and the Urban League could have collaborated, but Ida ignored the Urban League's attempts to enlist the support of local black leaders, and soon found her own organization overshadowed. A well-organized and efficient institution, the Urban League was run by a staff of full-time social work professionals. An interracial organization that emphasized social service work over political protest of any kind, it soon won the support of Chicago's white business leaders and philanthropists, as well as many of Chicago's leading black citizens. It also had none of the NFL's public sector liabilities: whereas the federal government regarded Ida's activities at the NFL as subversive, the Urban League received funding for its employment bureau from the Department of Labor. Housed in the venerable Frederick Douglass Center, which became its permanent home after Celia Parker Woolley's death in 1918, the Urban League quickly became one of black Chicago's leading organizations.

"Chicago Disgraced"

The NFL was on its last legs when a thirteen-day riot rocked Chicago during July 1919. The conflagration was one of twenty race riots that erupted in cities and towns across the country during a period later christened "the Red Summer of 1919" by NAACP leader James Weldon Johnson. The Red summer took place in an era of global upheaval that saw the Bolshevik revolution transform Russia into a Communist society. In the United States, the postwar period ushered in America's first "Red scare," along with a rising tide of racism and xenophobia. Blacks, immigrants, and radicals of all nationalities became the target of suspicion and hostility. Both the Red scare and the Red summer were products of the social and economic conflicts of the era, which saw rising unemployment, renewed labor conflicts, and a national wartime housing shortage.

In Chicago, white soldiers came home to a labor market made newly competitive by the Great Migration, which had all but tripled the city's black population. The postwar housing shortage that plagued much of the country was particularly acute in Chicago. By 1919, the city's South Side and West Side black neighborhoods were overflowing, leaving African Americans little choice but to seek housing in white neighborhoods. They were met with intense hostility. Like many whites across the country, white Chicagoans were determined "to reaffirm the Negroes' prewar status on the

Aftermath of the Chicago riot of July 1919

bottom rung of the nation's social and economic ladder"—and maintain the racial boundaries that kept their communities white.[68] But in protecting such boundaries, they confronted an African American community made newly militant by the war. Many black veterans came home unwilling to settle for second-class citizenship in "a white man's country," and resolved to take up arms to defend themselves against white violence.

The worst of the urban riots that swept the country that summer, the Chicago riot came as no surprise to Wells-Barnett. Throughout the war, white Chicagoans had policed their city's racial boundaries with force, attacking African American families that tried to escape the dilapidated and overcrowded housing on the South and West Sides. And by June 1919, the violence had escalated into a rash of antiblack bombings that prompted Ida to lead delegations of concerned citizens to see Mayor William Hale Thompson. When two separate attempts to gain an audience with him failed, she published a letter in the *Chicago Tribune* imploring the city "to set the wheels of justice in motion before it is too late, and Chicago be disgraced by some of the bloody outrages that have disgraced Saint Louis."[69]

After a career spent fighting mob violence, Ida could see what was coming. But she was in no position to stop it. By the end of World War I, Ida's influence in Chicago had ebbed. Black politicians and organizations such as the Urban League had become the major liaisons between the black community and city, eclipsing Ida's tiny NFL. Moreover, in an era when all radicals were suspect, Ida was persona non grata in municipal circles—and described in one military investigator's report as "a far more dangerous agitator than Marcus Garvey."[70]

Not surprisingly, then, Ida's complaint got no response; less than three weeks later, a sunny summer day turned deadly. After several days of temperatures in the nineties, on July 27, 1919, Chicagoans of both races crowded the shores of Lake Michigan. The riot began when a group of black boys began playing in the waters between the black-only Twenty-fifth Street Beach and the white beach beginning at Twenty-ninth Street. As they drifted close to the Twenty-sixth Street breakwater, a white man standing on the shore began to throw rocks at them. One missile struck the black teenager Eugene Williams in the forehead, causing him to lose consciousness and sink. Unable to save their friend from drowning, the other boys called for help, and as both blacks and whites converged on the scene, the conflict quickly escalated. The rioting lasted for five days, killing thirty-nine people and injuring 537 more before several regiments of the state militia finally managed to restore order. The rioters also burned many Chicago homes to the ground, leaving more than a thousand people homeless.

"We lived at 3234 Rhodes, and riots started . . . only . . . what you might call a stone's throw from our house," Wells-Barnett's daughter Alfreda later recalled. Her mother went "out every day . . . to see the people involved." One of her stepbrothers, who looked white, had to stay inside during the upheaval—"in order to be alive." But Alfreda felt safe. Her mother still "kept a gun in the house all the time," and "vowed as in Memphis . . . that she wasn't going to die by herself. She wasn't afraid of dying, she was going to take two or three of them with her." But fortunately, the riot did not "come close to the [Barnett] house," which was protected by a "von Hindenberg line" organized by the "colored men east of State Street to repel the [white] hoodlums . . . reported to be coming over to annihilate Negro citizens." In all other respects, however, the Chicago riot was an extremely disheartening experience for Wells-Barnett. Ida found herself at odds with other members of a "Protective Organization" founded by local clergymen, who did not share her opposition to leaving the investigation of the riot in the hands of State Attorney General Edward J. Brundage. Brundage had been in charge of the investigation into the East St. Louis riot, and had been woefully ineffectual there. But the ministers ignored her protests. After she resigned from the group, one even murmured, "Good riddance." She left with angry tears streaming down her face.[71]

Ida was also sidelined by the local NAACP, which remained cautious and conservative. Walter White, the recently appointed assistant national secretary to NAACP head James Weldon Johnson, traveled from New York to investigate the riots, and found the Chicago branch reluctant to take much action. White also got an earful from Ida when he visited Ferdinand L. Barnett's office. Furious at the NAACP, Ida "launched into a tirade against every organization in Chicago because they have not come into her organization and allowed her to dictate to them," White later recalled.[72] In the end, the city drew on the Urban League to mediate its relationship with the South Side and supply much of the manpower for the city's investigation into the riot. The woman who had pioneered the investigative approach to racial violence, Wells-Barnett, had lived to see the day when, in Chicago at least, such work had become the province of organizations rather than individuals; and investigations into racial violence were commissioned by municipal authorities rather than left to muckraking journalists.

The Elaine Massacre

When a wave of renewed racial violence against black sharecroppers in the Arkansas Delta in the fall of 1919 attracted little official investigation, Wells-Barnett was drawn back into the fray. The pitched battles that took place in Elaine, Arkansas, pitted black sharecroppers against local whites and federal troops brought in to quell the "race war." The conflict and its casualties remain hazy to this day. State officials and the local papers covered up the activities of the military and white civilians, describing the Elaine riot as a "negro uprising."[73] However, both NAACP representative Walter White and Ida B. Wells-Barnett recorded a series of extraordinarily brutal white attacks on blacks in Phillips County, where Elaine is located, during October 1919. At issue was not a "black uprising," but the organization of the Progressive Farmers and Household Union among the county's sharecroppers earlier that year. The union united sharecroppers across the county in a push for fair compensation for their crops. It addressed the long-standing grievances of black agricultural laborers across the Delta, who were ruthlessly exploited by white landowners. Charged exorbitant rates and refused a fair market price for their shares, sharecroppers saw little profit from their crops even at the end of World War I, when cotton prices reached an all-time high.

The stage for the Elaine massacre was set early that fall when union members—many of whom were World War I veterans—insisted on marketing their own crops in the nearby town of Helena, Arkansas. "We helped you fight the Germans," organizer Robert Hill stated, "but we want to be treated fairly." Facing opposition from the planters, they secured a lawyer "to sue for their fair share of the largest cotton crop in Southern history," and paid a high price for their ambition.[74] On September 30, 1919, a group of armed men arrested Ocier Bratton, a white accountant who was working on the case for his father's law firm in the nearby town of Ratio, Arkansas. Meanwhile, in Elaine, another group of whites fired on a meeting of union members and their families at the Hook Spur Church. When the black men guarding the meeting fired back, killing one man, the shoot-out became a "negro uprising."[75] Thousands of armed whites descended on Elaine. Among them were 536 troops dispatched by Governor Charles H. Brough of Arkansas. Ordered to disarm both blacks and whites and shoot blacks who refused to surrender their weapons, the troops seemed to have joined forces with the white vigilantes. Armed with military weaponry that included seven machine guns, Arkansas whites overpowered and outnumbered the Phillips County blacks who chose to defend themselves.

All told, five whites died in Elaine, alongside an unrecorded number of blacks—later estimated by Walter White at two hundred and by the *Arkansas Gazette* reporter Louis Sharpe Dunaway at 856. Both estimates suggest nothing short of a massacre, as does the eyewitness testimony from the riot. One white teacher later reported having seen "twenty-eight black people killed, their bodies thrown into a pit and burned," as well as the bodies of sixteen African American men strung up on a bridge outside Helena. Two days after the shooting, other Elaine residents noted, "the stench of dead bodies could be smelled two miles."[76] However, the black corpses remained unreported and unacknowledged in the local presses' accounts of the violence. Instead, papers in Arkansas and other states reported only white casualties, describing the Elaine riot with headlines that blared: "Wholesale Murder of White People May Be Part of Plot Against the South."[77]

Arkansas authorities arrested over one thousand black men, women, and children, holding them in a makeshift "stockade" in Helena, while a committee of local whites "investigated" their crimes. The investigation was largely an exercise in labor discipline. To secure his release, each black man had to get a white to vouch for him "as being a 'good nigger.' The white man was usually a planter or employer, who would 'vouch' only after the Negro had given assurance and 'guarantees' as to work and wages." Even after labor discipline was over, however, 122 black men remained incarcerated on charges of "murder, rioting, conspiracy, etc."[78]

The Elaine riot eventually received national attention as a result of the struggles of those prisoners, twelve of whom stood trial for murder. By early December, six were sentenced to death after hasty trials. Among the African Americans to protest the Elaine riot and its aftermath was Wells-Barnett, who challenged the justice of these verdicts. Speaking on behalf of both the National Equal Rights League and the Negro Fellowship League, Ida questioned the crime committed by men "who had defended themselves when fired upon." She also issued an appeal, published in the Chicago Defender, encouraging black organizations across the country to pool their resources to fund the defense of the twelve prisoners facing capital charges. "Send me the money and I will show you what we can do," Ida concluded, as feisty as ever. "You furnish me with the sinews of the war and I will fight your battles just as I have done for twenty-five years."[79]

But a lot had happened in twenty-five years. Ida was no longer the only African American fighting her people's battles against racial violence. Fair-skinned, with blue eyes and blond hair, Walter White began his fact-finding tour of Arkansas a few days after the riot. His appearance allowed him to pass for white, a fact that he exploited. Armed with a press pass from The Chicago Daily News, White posed as a white reporter. His ruse allowed him to secure interviews with Governor Brough, sharecroppers' union attorney Ulysses S. Bratton, and a local black attorney. But his fact-finding trip ended abruptly when local whites got word of a "damned yellow nigger down here passing for white," forcing White to hop a train just one step ahead of a gathering mob.[80] But he was able to piece together the story of the massacre, which he publicized in *The Crisis*, *The Nation*, *The Chicago Daily News*, and other publications. Moreover, White also reported the massacre to the Justice Department, and quietly mobilized NAACP branches across the country to provide legal defense for the Arkansas prisoners, rendering Ida's later attempts on their behalf largely redundant.

An increasingly powerful organization, by 1918 the NAACP was emerging as the national civil rights organization that Ida and other late nineteenth-century black activists had once been so anxious to organize. But the NAACP's cautious approach to defending the Arkansas prisoners left little room for old-school black agitators such as Wells-Barnett. She learned of the NAACP's campaign to free the prisoners when the *Defender's* managing editor told her that the organization did not want the paper to publish a subscription list for Wells-Barnett's legal defense fund, "since the NAACP was already doing all the work necessary in the matter." The editor also suggested that she simply turn over the money she had already collected to the NAACP, but Ida, with her donors' support, used the funds "to make an investigation and find out just what the NAACP had done."[81]

So in January 1920 Ida returned to the South for the first time in almost thirty years. No less intrepid than Walter White, she sneaked into the Helena prison with the condemned men's mothers and wives on visitors' day, posing as a visiting cousin from St. Louis. To the prison guards looking on, the plump and graying fifty-eight-year-old lady was indistinguishable from any of the other "insignificant colored women who had been there many times before." So they took no notice as she spent "nearly all day Sunday" quietly interviewing the prisoners and encouraging them to fight for their release. Still at home in the religious culture that permeated the rural black South, she shared a message of hope with them that came out of her perennially activist reading of the Bible. "Pray to live and ask to be freed," she told them, after hearing them sing mournful spirituals. "The God you serve is the God of Paul and Silas who opened their prison gates, and if you have all the faith you say you have, you ought to believe that he will open your prison doors."[82]

After she returned to Chicago, Ida published the prisoners' testimony in a pamphlet titled *The Arkansas Race Riot* (1922). But how much influence her pamphlet and prison visit had on the legal status of the prisoners is an open question. The NAACP's small national legal staff, working together with local defense attorneys, secured their release in 1925 with a pathbreaking challenge to Arkansas law, leading to the reversal of the state's violation of the condemned men's constitutional rights by the U.S. Supreme Court. A significant legal victory for the NAACP as well as the prisoners, the case opened up later state convictions to new constitutional challenges. Wells-Barnett, however, did not even acknowledge the NAACP's efforts, instead crediting the success of the prisoners' legal battle to local attorneys "engaged by the colored people themselves." Seemingly unaware that these local men were among the several attorneys retained by the NAACP in its five-year struggle to free the prisoners, she recast their release as a community struggle won at least in part as a result of her encouragement. One of the prisoners visited her in Chicago after his release to tell her "how much he felt indebted by my efforts," she noted. "Mrs. Barnett came and told us to quit talking about dying . . . and pray to him [God] to open our prison doors, like he did for Silas and Paul," he told the Barnett family. And "after that . . . we never talked about dying any more, but did as she told us, and now every last one of us is out and enjoying his freedom."[83]

His gratitude should not be discounted, for it suggests that Wells-Barnett's visit did bring a crucial message of hope. But Ida's recollection of the legal representation that secured the release of the Arkansas prisoners as having been funded by individual contributions rather than by the NAACP reveals how little she would ever come to appreciate the patient campaign for racial justice that the NAACP began during her lifetime. Still heir to the radical spirit of Frederick Douglass, Ida rejected incremental approaches to social change as adamantly as the abolitionists who came before her had once rejected gradualist approaches to the abolition of slavery. But no Civil War would come along to end lynching and Jim Crow during her lifetime. Instead, Ida was left to approach old age with nagging questions about whether her long career as an activist had had any lasting impact.

· 9 ·

Eternal Vigilance Is the
Price of Liberty

WRITTEN DURING THE LAST FEW YEARS OF HER LIFE AND STILL unfinished when she died in 1931, Ida B. Wells-Barnett's autobiography, *Crusade for Justice*, is tinged with a bitterness that has helped shape perceptions of her life. *Crusade for Justice* opens with Ida explaining that she decided to record her story after a young woman told her that while she knew that Wells-Barnett was known as a "heroine" and a "martyr," she had no idea what the older woman had done to merit this reputation. "Won't you please tell me what you have done?" she asked her. Ida claims to have taken no offense at the young woman's request, since "the happenings about which she inquired took place before she was born." But the four-hundred-page autobiography that Wells-Barnett wrote by way of reply reveals that as she got older she was increasingly troubled to find her long public career was all but forgotten before it had even reached a close. Diagnosed with gallstones in 1920, shortly after the demise of the Negro Fellowship League, she survived what was then a difficult surgery, only to spend the following year bedridden and depressed, wondering whether she "had anything to show for all those years of toil and labor."[1]

In the end, she rallied. "It seemed to me that I should now make some preparation of a personal nature for the future, and this I set about to accomplish," she writes in one of the more cryptic passages in her autobiography. Unfortunately, her text does not go on to illuminate the ambitions that shaped the last decade of her life. Instead, the complete narrative of her life ends around 1920, followed only by an unfinished chapter, which discusses her 1927 challenge to the American Citizenship Federation, a Chicago organization dedicated to defending the ideals of "liberty and patriotism." The organization's high ideals did not prevent it from holding a fund-raising dinner at the Drake Hotel, which did not admit colored people, while also inviting the editor of the city's foremost black newspaper: Robert Abbott of the *Chicago Defender*. When the organization realized that the African American newsman would not be able to gain admission to the Drake, Abbott was asked to return his invitation, and the dinner proceeded as planned. But when Ida got wind of the story she was furious. "Eternal Vigilance is the price of liberty," she begins a chapter dedicated to detailing the protests that she lodged with Abbott, the *Defender*, the Drake Hotel, and the American Citizenship Federation. She may have lodged complaints elsewhere as well, but we will never know: her chapter ends in the middle of a sentence.[2]

A fitting coda to an activist life, Wells-Barnett's last chapter ended her life as she lived it, still fighting the battles others refused, and often alienating other African American leaders as a consequence—such as Robert Abbott, who did not welcome her intervention into a matter that he had chosen not to protest. Ida contested his choice, insisting that African Americans could never lose sight of "the preservation of our liberties." Now involved in many "social agencies and activities," blacks had become dangerously quiet on the subject of racial injustice. She wondered "if we are not too well satisfied to look at our wonderful institutions with complacence ... instead of being as alert as the watchman on the wall." As usual, both the Scriptures and black America's long freedom struggle guided her reflections. The great abolitionist Wendell Phillips had preached that "eternal vigilance is the price of liberty"; and in Isaiah 62:6–9 the Lord calls for Jerusalem to be secured by "watchmen on the walls" who "never hold their peace day or night."[3]

Wells-Barnett remained among freedom's watchmen all her life, but she questioned the vigilance of the African American leaders who followed her. In part, her questions reflected her doubts about the emergence of an increasingly organized and powerful African American leadership class, who staffed these "social agencies" and other "wonderful institutions." Wells-Barnett had fought to create these institutions, but she was uneasy about whether they fostered the aggressive and uncompromising leadership needed to secure and protect black civil rights. She worried that black civil rights leaders had become content to "draw . . . salaries" instead of engaging in a relentless battle against injustice. Wells-Barnett was activist by lineage and temperament as well as political leanings. For her, institutions were never radical enough. The "restraints of organization" always involved compromises that she could not easily reconcile with her profound commitment to moral, political action—to "do something" about every injustice.[4] Forged in the crucible of slavery and emancipation, Wells-Barnett's uncompromising leadership had come to seem outmoded over the course of her life, leaving her both eclipsed and abandoned by civil rights organizations she had helped create—such as the NAACP.

The NAACP and the NACW

Still, Ida would overcome her hostility to the NAACP long enough to rally around its campaign to pass a federal antilynching measure known as the Dyer bill in the early 1920s. But she remained otherwise an outsider to the nation's largest civil rights organization, even as it embarked on a long campaign to secure federal legislation against lynching that essentially picked up where her antilynching struggle had left off. The Dyer bill would have mandated federal fines on counties in which lynching occurred. It was designed to make Southern officials who tolerated mob violence accountable for the results—much as the Barnetts had done when they helped to block the reinstatement of Cairo sheriff Frank Davis in 1909. Defeated in the Senate in 1922, the Dyer bill never became law, but the NAACP's role in shaping and supporting the bill testified to the enduring impact of Ida's antilynching campaign.

Now the nation's foremost civil rights organization, the NAACP had appropriated the "template for antilynching activism" that Wells-Barnett pioneered in the 1890s. Much like the short-lived antilynching bureau that Ida had once led under the auspices of the Afro-American Council, the NAACP used investigation, exposure, and relentless publicity to combat mob violence and lobby for antilynching legislation. Moreover, the association also followed Wells-Barnett's lead in rallying around lynching as a protest issue all the more powerful because it could be used to "draw attention to other racial disparities." As one historian of the NAACP comments, "at a time when the public refused to honor voting rights, integrated education, equal employment opportunities, open housing, access to public accommodations, or social equality, the NAACP could gain a hearing by showing how violence threatened generally held Judeo-Christian and democratic values."[5] Although made without reference to Wells, the comment applies equally to the international antilynching campaign that Ida led in the 1890s, and underscores that her impact on the national civil rights organization cannot be easily overstated.

Indeed, although the NAACP would remain a male-dominated organization for many years to follow, NAACP leaders such as Walter White also followed Ida's playbook when it came to mobilizing female leaders and women's organizations in support of its antilynching campaigns. As we have seen, Wells-Barnett single-handedly transformed lynching into a women's issue. Her antilynching struggle built on her keen insights into the rhetorical challenges and gender politics involved in confronting lynching as a form of racial injustice. Women could be more effective than men, Ida realized early on, when it came to challenging the rape myths that were so often invoked in defense of mob violence. For so long as lynching supposedly protected the virtue of white women, black men could not address the subject without running the risk of sounding self-interested, self-defensive—or both. But black and white women alike could give effective testimony on the evils of burning black men alive in the name of chivalry.

Accordingly, the NAACP enlisted first black women and later white women to support its antilynching initiatives. By the 1930s, it had an interracial coalition of women working on this issue that included the first antilynching group to come out of the white South. Organized in 1930 by the Texas native Jessie Daniel Ames, the Association of Southern Women for the Prevention of Lynching (ASWPL) censured the lynchers on their home ground, appealing to Southern white men to abandon lynching "as a menace to private and public safety, and deadly blow at our most sacred institutions." Moreover, unlike the white female leaders of Wells-Barnett's day, ASWPL members refused to allow the "perpetrators" of lynching's "atrocities to hide behind their skirts."[6] Antilynching legislation remained perennially elusive all the same, but the practice of lynching declined steadily over the course of the twentieth century—at least in part as a result of such vocal and widespread opposition.

With the NAACP putting lynching at the top of its agenda even during Wells-Barnett's lifetime, the world's first antilynching crusader might well have felt more sanguine about whether she had anything to show for her life's work. But during the last decades of her life, Wells-Barnett got virtually no public credit for her leadership in defining antilynching as a civil rights cause—or for pioneering protest strategies to draw public attention to mob violence. In many ways the living link between the abolitionist tradition represented by her mentor Frederick Douglass and the twentieth-century civil rights activism of the NAACP, Wells-Barnett was written out of the black protest tradition by a new generation of reformers who appropriated her ideas while rejecting her leadership. As a result, she became deeply suspicious both of the biracial coalition of reformers who led the early NAACP and the middle-class black men who were becoming increasingly prominent in that coalition over time. Her interactions with the NAACP had always been fractious, and her disappointment with the organization only grew in 1919, when Walter White provided no support for her demands for a more thorough investigation into the riot that had devastated black Chicago.

Not content to leave the "preservation of our liberties" to the NAACP or any other organization, Ida would spend the final decade of her life still on watch, but increasingly isolated. No longer at the helm of the NFL, she struggled to find a new forum in a world increasingly unsuited to her leadership style. She did not succeed. But for Ida, "eternal vigilance" was not about success. Sixty years old in 1922, she never considered retiring from public life, even as she bemoaned her diminishing public influence and recognition.

As a result, Ida's last decade was busy. With the exception of her

Taken during World War I, this 1917 photograph showcases the whole Barnett dynasty. Standing on the far left is Hulette Barnett, the wife of Albert Barnett (one of Ferdinand's sons from his first marriage). To her left is Herman Barnett, alongside his stepbrother Ferdinand and siblings Ida and Charles. On the far right is their other stepbrother, Albert Barnett, and sister Alfreda Barnett. Seated are Ferdinand Barnett and Ida B. Wells-Barnett, and Hulette and Albert Barnett's four little girls, Beatrice, Audrey, Hulette, and Florence.

daughter Ida, who lived with her parents even as an adult, the Barnetts' children were out of the house by the mid-1920s, but visited frequently. Ida welcomed her first grandchild in 1921, when her son Herman had a son of his own. A "fondly hovering" grandmother, she would live to see the birth of three more.[7] Her sister Annie Fitts and her husband lived nearby, and were also frequent callers, along with their children. Moreover, Ida kept a close eye even on her children's adult lives. She saw her youngest daughter, Alfreda, married in 1925, and was plagued with worries about Herman, a lawyer who worked in his father's office but was perennially penniless due to a weakness for gambling. Ida's seventy-year-old husband, by contrast, was as hardworking and self-sufficient as ever and continued to make his family's private household public by bringing clients home for dinner.

For Ida, hosting such guests was more of a challenge than ever. With federal provisions for Social Security yet to be enacted and Ida no longer bringing in an income, the Barnetts' finances could no longer cover the kind of regular help that had long freed Ida from domestic chores. Now in charge of household tasks she had long been happy to avoid, Ida deeply regretted "the loss [of her] ability and resources to keep the place clean, to keep the house in repair, et cetera"—all of which became more pressing when her husband brought home guests.[8] But Ida did not let her domestic responsibilities take over her time. When she could afford it, she still hired local girls to help with housework, and in 1925 she and Ferdinand would conserve their meager resources and reduce their domestic responsibilities by resettling, along with daughter Ida, in a five-room apartment on East Garfield Boulevard.

Even before then, however, Ida kept up her public work. Her interest in the Dyer bill brought her briefly back into the fold of the NACW in 1922. When the organization met in Richmond that year, shortly before the bill's defeat, Wells-Barnett was on hand to rally support for the measure but found herself completely overshadowed by James Weldon Johnson—a well-known writer, educator, and musician who served as general counsel for the NAACP. Invited to address the NACW on the Dyer bill, Johnson was introduced by a Virginia club woman, Addie Hunton. In doing so, Hunton offered a review of the history of the antilynching movement that credited the origins of the "agitation" against lynching to *Richmond Planet* editor John Mitchell, Jr.—who wrote a number of late nineteenth-century antilynching editorials but was far less prominent than Wells-Barnett. Worse, Hunton went on to laud Johnson and other members of the NAACP for being the first to pick up Mitchell's torch. In beginning his own talk, Johnson "was gracious enough to say that one of the national association's number in the person of Ida B. Wells Barnett had done some work against lynching," but Ida was not mollified. Even the NACW's own members' contributions to antilynching work had begun to be overshadowed by the NAACP's claims to leadership on the issue, she complained, noting with characteristic sarcasm that "the club women seemed to be happy to cast their own organization as a tail to the kite of the NAACP."[9]

Possibly in the hope of changing the NACW's direction, Wells-Barnett ran for president of the organization at its next biannual meeting in 1924, only to see the powerful and popular club woman Mary McLeod Bethune win 658 of the 700 delegates' votes. Ida's landslide defeat was not surprising given that she had never been a regular or particularly popular participant in the association's organizational life. But she may well have been dismayed to find her once meteoric leadership so completely obscured even in a national organization she had helped usher into being. Like the NAACP, the NACW was dominated by middle-class professionals who had little patience for old-fashioned radicals such as Wells-Barnett. Although no longer as conservative as it was during its early years, the NACW, like the NAACP, embraced painstaking litigation, diplomatic lobbying, cautious leadership, and the careful cultivation of white allies, in preference to noisy protest. Moreover, neither organization showed any interest in commemorating the work of their more controversial and combative founders—leaving Ida increasingly unremembered even in her own lifetime. Like most organizations, both the NACW and the NAACP generated organizational histories that focused on the contributions of members who remained within the fold rather than on the impact of former members whose contributions were fleeting or oppositional.

Wells-Barnett in her sixties

The Watchman on the Wall

Wells-Barnett had spent her life largely outside the fold of any enduring organization, and by the 1920s she had begun to pay the price. Her response
was a last-ditch flurry of initiatives that culminated in an unsuccessful campaign for the Illinois state senate in 1930. The impetus for her quest for

public office grew out of her continuing involvement in women's club work, local affairs, and municipal and state politics. The president of the Ida B. Wells Club in 1924, she took on a variety of club responsibilities thereafter, which included involving the club in legal defense work, similar to work taken by the NFL.[10] She also became active in the Metropolitan Center, founded by the People's Community Church of Christ, a new nondenominational church suited to Wells-Barnett's long-held lack of interest in the niceties of denominational doctrine. There, she founded and led another women's club, the Women's Forum, in 1926. Between 1926 and 1927 she also used these organizational ties to support the Brotherhood of Sleeping Car Porters' drive to unionize Chicago's Pullman Company employees.

A national business headquartered in Chicago, the Pullman Company supplied sleeping cars and staff to railroads across the country, employing an army of black maids and porters. Underpaid, they made their living largely from tips, and were at the mercy of company policies that required them to supply all passengers with unvarying and obsequiously servile domestic service (until 1927, company policy even dictated that all Pullman porters were to be addressed as "George"). With a third of the company's traveling labor force living in Chicago, by 1925 the city had become the battleground for a prolonged unionization struggle. Among the challenges the brotherhood faced as it struggled to establish itself in a company town was gaining an audience with Chicago's black leaders. Largely middle-class and ambivalent about trade unions, many of Chicago's black leaders hoped to sit out the struggle between the Pullman Company and its employees.

As usual, Ida took a more radical position. Committed to trade unionism and distressed that the brotherhood had received little support from the local press or Chicago's black leaders, in 1926 she invited A. Philip Randolph, the union's founder and president, to tell "his side of the story" to her Women's Forum.[11] Further meetings with other black women's clubs followed, allowing Randolph to educate club women, and ultimately their husbands, on the issues at stake in the brotherhood's labor struggle—which included securing porters the right to be addressed by names other than

George. As a result, by 1927, the brotherhood was able to gain the support of the Chicago Citizens' Committee, which included many members of the city's black elite.

That year also saw Wells-Barnett lending her support to investigating and protesting conditions among the thousands of African Americans displaced by the Mississippi flood of 1927. Caused by unusually heavy rains that spring, the flood was a natural disaster of catastrophic proportions that killed more than five hundred people and drove a half million more out of their homes. With twenty thousand square miles of the Delta under water, the summer saw Mississippi blacks fleeing the state in droves, while planters attempted to retain their labor force by impressing black men into work gangs. Even the Red Cross aid supplied to the black refugees was minimal, and disease ran rampant in the makeshift camps that housed them. Working with the Ida B. Wells Club, Wells-Barnett fired off a protest to Secretary of Commerce Herbert Hoover, and once again plunged into Republican politics.

Whether Hoover received or responded to the protest is unclear, although he did go on to form a flood relief commission that met with Ida's approval. Meanwhile, Ida's outrage over the treatment of the flood victims seems to have inspired her to take a renewed interest in Republican politics. With an eye to local politics, she founded the Third Ward Women's Political Club. Fueled by her distaste for the corrupt political scene in Prohibition-era Chicago—where bootleggers and politicians collaborated to keep Chicago's vice districts in business—the club aimed to mobilize women to use their votes to shape local politics, while also training them to run for office. Naturally, one of the first women to run was Ida herself, who competed for a spot as a delegate to the 1928 Republican National Convention. Positioned as an independent candidate seeking representation from the First Illinois Congressional District, she never had a chance. Her opponents included Oscar De Priest and Daniel M. Jackson, two well-known and well-connected black politicians who prevailed easily over Wells-Barnett.

However, the defeat did not discourage Ida from remaining intensely active in Republican politics. An energetic member of the Illinois Republican National Committee, she campaigned for Hoover for president. In particular, her efforts targeted the state's black women, many of whom had yet to vote in a presidential election. Victorious in Illinois and many other states, Hoover won the election, but like many of the Republican presidential candidates the Barnetts had supported, proved a disappointment in office. He endorsed his party's plan to rebuild itself in the South by way of "lily-white" organizations designed to pose no threat to the region's racial status quo.

Turning back to state politics in 1930, Wells-Barnett made one last quixotic effort to secure a political office, competing in the primary for the state senate seat in the third senatorial district. At least in part, Ida's campaign seems to have been inspired by white Republican Congresswoman Ruth Hanna McCormick's successful campaign for the Republican nomination for the U.S. Senate in 1929. A former ally of black Chicagoans, McCormick had snubbed the entire membership of the Illinois Federation of Colored Women's Clubs when she employed Washington, D.C.'s Mary Church Terrell to run her campaign's outreach to female black voters. Illinois's black club women's response is recorded in an NACW resolution regretting that McCormick could "find no Negro woman in the state which must elect her, [to work] on her campaign." Black women must represent themselves, Wells-Barnett seems to have been reminded, when McCormick abandoned her Illinois allies. But at the same time, McCormick's nomination also testified to the viability of female candidates for Senate seats, although she lost the general election in 1930. Inspired by the prospect, Ida launched her own bid for a seat in the state senate in January 1930, just a few months after McCormick's nomination.

Quixotic from the very beginning, Wells-Barnett's campaign received no endorsements from local politicians or political parties. She ran in a black majority district, against competition that included the senate incumbent, Adelbert H. Roberts. In office since 1924, Roberts was the first African American to be elected to the Illinois senate. Formerly a member of the Illinois assembly, he had also served as a clerk for Chicago's municipal court and had supported Ferdinand Barnett when he protested the East St. Louis riot. His real competition was not Ida, but another black man: the lawyer Warren B. Douglas, who had the support of U.S. Senator Charles Deneen of Illinois—Barnett's former boss and mentor. Undeterred, Ida collected the five hundred signatures required to compete in the primary, and once again competed as an independent, with fitful support from independent organizations such as the Abraham Lincoln Republican Club. Not surprisingly, she did not manage to secure any endorsements from past political allies, such as Charles Deneen and Edward Wright. Both had loyalties to the most established candidates in the race, and may well have had doubts about a campaign funded largely out of the Barnetts' increasingly modest household budget.

Among Ida's few surviving diaries is a "day book" from that era, in which Ida recorded brief notes on the events of her day and the expenses she incurred. It spans a five-month period between January and May 1930, and records just how strained the family budget was during Ida's Illinois senate campaign. As her book opens in January 1930, Ida looks back on the Christmas season, noting that her daughter "Ida had no coat . . . neither did [H]erman . . . so we went nowhere all holiday week. Can't understand why my folks have no money."[12] Ida seems to have been unwilling to consider an obvious explanation: her campaign expenses loomed large in the budget deficit she repeatedly bemoans in her diary—as her careful record of expenditures makes clear. Ida spent five dollars on petitions that she needed to circulate and submit in order to get her name on the ballot, and seventy-five dollars more on printing thirty thousand cards and letters to promote her campaign, all at a time when she was reduced to paying a girl to help her clean the house "25 cts on account." Tight finances also required the would-be senator to interrupt her campaign for wash days, and make excuses to friends who wished to call. "I wish I c[oul]d have them stop with me" she writes at one point, "but the house is too dirty & no money to clean." Ever supportive, and perhaps less perturbed by the messy house, Ferdinand Barnett sponsored the *New Deal Paper* that his wife published to promote her campaign, printing and distributing twenty thousand copies "at his own expense."[13]

In the end, it was all for naught. Ida never made it past the primary, receiving only 752 votes of the more than ten thousand cast. When Adelbert Roberts's victory was announced, Ida took her defeat coolly, noting cynically in her day book that the incumbent Roberts had the "veteran machine behind him," which "always wins because the independent vote is weak and unorganized and its workers are purchasable." What Wells-Barnett hoped to achieve given these odds is not entirely clear, but Ida was never one to avoid a contest because she had no hope of winning. Looking ahead, she hoped to "profit by the lessons of the campaign," and made a note to "conference with my backers" as soon as she got a chance.[14]

Perhaps she already had another election in mind. We will never know for sure, since her day book does not go past May 1930, and Ida would die suddenly less than a year later, on March 14, 1931. Four months shy of her sixty-ninth birthday, Wells-Barnett was taken ill after a Saturday morning spent shopping in Chicago's downtown Loop area. She died four days later of "uremic poisoning"—a condition now usually known as kidney failure. She left behind a shocked and grieving family, headed by her husband, Ferdinand Barnett, who would survive his wife by only five years, dying in 1936.

In the middle of a chapter of her autobiography when she died, Ida was also still contesting racial injustice, as usual. After her senate race, she lent her support to a concerted effort to block the Supreme Court nomination of Judge John J. Parker of North Carolina—a man who believed that "the participation of the negro in politics is a source of evil and danger for both races."[15] Opposed by the Illinois Women's Republican Club, the Brotherhood of Sleeping Car Porters, a Chicago political group known as the Douglass Civil League, the NAACP, and many other black organizations across the country, the Parker nomination threatened to put an end to African Americans' hopes for recovering their rights in the highest court of the land. But his nomination did not survive the flood of anti-Parker petitions and telegrams that came to Washington from African Americans across the country. As Wells-Barnett had long hoped, in states where African Americans had the vote, the franchise gave them the power to defend themselves. Southern blacks had yet to regain the voting rights that Ida's father once enjoyed, but a half century of black migrants fleeing the South had combined to create an increasingly powerful black vote north of the Mason-Dixon Line. With African American voters holding the balance of power in upcoming elections in Illinois, Kansas, Ohio, and Indiana, Northern Republicans had to pay attention to black opposition to Parker. His nomination was defeated in the Senate, 41 to 39, in a vote widely recorded as an important victory for the NAACP. But Ida B. Wells-Barnett played her part in Parker's defeat and, one hopes, welcomed it as a victory for the "eternal vigilance" she had so long committed to battles to preserve African American liberties.

Notes

Introduction: "If Iola Were a Man"

1. *Daily Inter Ocean*, June 28, 1895.
2. Ibid., 4, 6. Wells quotes these white justifications for lynching in Ida B. Wells, *Southern Horrors* (1892), reprinted in *Southern Horrors and Other Writings: The Anti-Lynching Campaign of Ida B. Wells, 1892–1900*, ed. Jacqueline Jones Royster (Boston: Bedford Books, 1997), 59.
3. Ibid., 52.
4. Ida B. Wells, *Crusade for Justice: The Autobiography of Ida B. Wells*, ed. Alfreda Duster (Chicago: University of Chicago Press, 1991), 69.
5. William McFeely, *Frederick Douglass* (New York: Norton, 1991), 376.
6. Wells reprints letters from Douglass in *Southern Horrors* (1892) and *A Red Record* (1895), which are reprinted in *Southern Horrors and Other Writings*; he also collaborated on her third pamphlet, Ida B. Wells, Frederick Douglass, Irvine Garland Penn, and Ferdinand L. Barnett, *The Reason Why the Colored American Is Not in the World's Columbian Exposition* (1893), ed. Robert Rydell (Champaign, Il: University of Illinois Press, 1999).
7. Timothy Thomas Fortune to Booker T. Washington, September 25, 1899, in *The Booker T. Washington Papers*, vol. 5, eds. Louis R. Harlan et al. (Champaign: University of Illinois Press, 2000), 220.
8. Alfreda Duster, "Introduction," in Wells, *Crusade*, xxx; Steven Hahn, *A Nation Under Our Feet: Black Political Struggles in the Rural South from Slavery to the Great Migration* (Cambridge, Mass.: Harvard University Press, 2005).
9. Typescript draft preface version of *Crusade for Justice*, complete with deletions that

are cited here, n.d. The Ida B. Wells Papers, Box 1, Folder 11, University of Chicago Library, Special Collections.

10. Duster, "Introduction," xxx; Wells, *Crusade*, 415.

1: Coming of Age in Mississippi

1. Ida B. Wells, *Crusade for Justice: The Autobiography of Ida B. Wells*, ed. Alfreda Duster (Chicago: University of Chicago Press, 1991), 4.

2. Ibid., 5.

3. J. G. Deupree, "The Capture of Holly Springs, Mississippi, Dec. 16, 1862," *Publications of the Mississippi Historical Society* 4 (1902): 58.

4. "The emancipated slaves own nothing," said former Confederate general Robert V. Richardson shortly after the Civil War, "because nothing but freedom has been given to them." Quoted in Eric Foner, *Nothing but Freedom: Emancipation and Its Legacies* (Baton Rouge: University of Louisiana Press, 1983), 3.

5. Federal Writers' Project, *Slave Narratives: A Folk History of Slavery in the United States from Interviews with Former Slaves*, "North Carolina Narratives" (Washington, D.C., 1941), vol. 11, part 1, 361, www.gutenberg.org/files/22976/22976-h/22976-h.htm.

6. Wells, *Crusade*, 8.

7. Ibid., 9–10.

8. Alfreda Duster, interview by Studs Terkel, recorded September 2, 1971, Chicago Historical Society.

9. Wells, *Crusade*, 8.

10. Duster, interview by Studs Terkel.

11. Rust College was renamed Shaw University in 1870, became Rust University in 1882, and reassumed the name Rust College in 1915.

12. Wells, *Crusade*, 9.

13. Ibid.

14. Ibid.

15. The black leader Tyler Williamson was shot and fatally wounded in one such election. Ruth Watkins, "Reconstruction in Marshall County," *Publications of the Mississippi Historical Society* 12 (1912): 172.

16. Wells, *Crusade*, 9.

17. Eric Foner, *A Short History of Reconstruction* (New York: Harper & Row, 1990), 184.

18. An anonymous account of the shooting attempt is cited "on good authority" in Watkins, "Reconstruction," 179. Exactly in what year it took place is not clear in Watkins or documented elsewhere.

19. Foner, *A Short History*, 245.

20. Wells, *Crusade*, 16.

21. "History of Rust College," quoted in Linda O. McMurray, *To Keep the Waters Troubled: The Life of Ida B. Wells* (New York: Oxford University Press, 1998), 13.

22. Ida B. Wells, *The Memphis Diary of Ida B. Wells*, ed. Miriam DeCosta-Willis (Boston: Beacon, 1995), 78; for discussion of the "consecrated teachers" at Rust, see Paula J. Giddings, *Ida: A Sword Among Lions* (New York: HarperCollins, 2008), 30.

23. Wells, *Crusade*, 21.

24. Ibid., 10.

25. On yellow fever, see Edward J. Blum, "The Crucible of Disease: Trauma, Memory, and National Reconciliation during the Yellow Fever Epidemic of 1878," *The Journal of Southern History* 69, no. 4 (November 2003): 791–820; and Jo Ann Carrigan, "Privilege, Prejudice, and the Strangers' Disease in Nineteenth-Century New Orleans," *The Journal of Southern History* 36, no. 4 (November 1970): 568–78.

26. Hodding Carter, "A Proud Struggle for Grace, Holly Springs, Mississippi," in *A Vanishing America: The Life and Times of the Small Town*, ed. Thomas C. Wheeler (New York: Holt, Rinehart and Winston, 1964), 72.

27. Wells, *Crusade*, 11.

28. Ibid.

29. Ibid., 12.

30. Ibid., 15.

31. Ibid., 16.

32. Ibid.

33. Ibid., 17.

34. "Speech of Senator Benjamin R. Tillman, March 23, 1900," *Congressional Record, 56th Congress, 1st Session*, 3223–24, reprinted in *Document Sets for the South in U. S. History*, ed. Richard Purday (Lexington, Mass.: D.C. Heath, 1991), 147.

35. Wells, *Crusade*, 18.

36. David Levering Lewis, *W.E.B. Du Bois: The Biography of a Race* (New York: Holt, 1993), 69.

37. In her long quest to publicize her mother's life story, Duster at one point began to fictionalize her mother's autobiography, adding details that nevertheless seem to be drawn from stories that her mother had told her.

38. Wells, *Crusade*, 22.

39. Ida B. Wells, "A Story of 1900" (1886), in *Memphis Diary*, 183.

40. Ibid., 183, 184.

41. Wells, *Crusade*, 22.

42. Ibid., 21.

43. Wells, *Memphis Diary*, 24.

44. *Fisk Herald*, January 3, 1886, 5.

45. Wells, *Memphis Diary*, 64.

2: Walking in Memphis

1. Linda O. McMurray, *To Keep the Waters Troubled: The Life of Ida B. Wells* (New York: Oxford University Press, 1998), 20.
2. Ida B. Wells, *The Memphis Diary of Ida B. Wells*, ed. Miriam DeCosta-Willis (Boston: Beacon, 1995), 136, 158.
3. Ibid., 26, 61, 59.
4. Ibid., 55, 66, 100.
5. Alfreda Duster, "Last copy of 1st 56 pages of Biography I Wrote," Chapter 3, n.d., Ida B. Wells Papers, University of Chicago, Box 7, File 3, University of Chicago, Special Collections, 1.
6. Amy G. Ritchter, *Home on the Rails: Women, the Railroad, and the Rise of Public Domesticity* (Chapel Hill: University of North Carolina Press, 2005), 45.
7. Ida B. Wells, *Crusade for Justice: The Autobiography of Ida B. Wells*, ed. Alfreda Duster (Chicago: University of Chicago Press, 1991), 18.
8. Ibid., 19.
9. Anna Julia Cooper, *A Voice from the South* (New York: Oxford University Press, 1990), 91.
10. Wells, *Crusade*, 19.
11. *The Chesapeake, Ohio and Southwestern Railroad v. Ida Wells*, Agreed Statement of Facts (March 1885), Tennessee State Library and Archives, 11.
12. Barbara Young Welke, *Recasting American Liberty: Gender, Race, Law, and the Railroad Revolution, 1865–1920* (Cambridge: Cambridge University Press, 2001), 324.
13. Ibid., 328; *Hall v. Decuir* (1877), quoted ibid.
14. Welke, *Recasting American Liberty*, 278.
15. Joseph Cartwright, *The Triumph of Jim Crow: Tennessee Race Relations in the 1880s* (Knoxville: University of Tennessee Press, 1976), 106.
16. *The Chesapeake, Ohio and Southwestern Railroad v. Ida Wells*, Declaration (January 23, 1884), Tennessee State Library and Archives.
17. *The Memphis Daily Appeal*, December 25, 1884, cited in Wells, *Crusade*, 19.
18. Wells, *Crusade*, 19; and Alfreda Duster, interview by Studs Terkel, recorded September 2, 1971, Chicago Historical Society.
19. Wells, *Crusade*, 19.
20. Ibid., 20.
21. Wells, *Memphis Diary*, 57.
22. Ibid., 66; "Discrimination Case Still Pending," *The Cleveland Gazette*, December 11, 1886, 2.
23. Robert T. Shannon, *Report of Cases Argued and Determined in the Supreme Court of Tennessee* (Louisville, Ky.: Fetter Law Book Company, 1902), 85: 616.
24. Wells, *Memphis Diary*, 141.

25. *Plessy v. Ferguson* (1896), in *Plessy v. Ferguson: A Brief History with Documents*, ed. Brook Thomas (Boston: Bedford/St. Martin, 2007), 44.
26. Barbara Y. Welke, "When All the Women Were White, and All the Blacks Were Men: Gender, Class, Race, and the Road to *Plessy*, 1855–1914," *Law and History Review* 13, no. 2 (Fall 1995): 312.
27. Wells, *Crusade*, 20.
28. Ibid., 21.
29. Wells, *Memphis Diary*, 141.
30. Ida B. Wells, writing as "Iola," "Functions of Leadership," *The Freeman* (New York), February 7, 1885, reprinted in *Memphis Diary*, 179.
31. Wells, *Memphis Diary*, 57.
32. *The Indianapolis Freeman*, December 2, 1893.
33. Wells, *Memphis Diary*, 80.
34. Ibid., 38.
35. *The Bee* (Washington, D.C.), quoted in *The Freeman* (New York), "Among the People," December 12, 1885.
36. Wells, *Memphis Diary*, 80.
37. Ibid., 130.
38. Ibid., 83, 127.
39. Ibid., 44.
40. Ibid.
41. Ibid., 74, 64, 96.
42. Ibid., 82, 52, 101.
43. Ibid., 91, 93.
44. Ibid., 95.
45. Ibid., 97, 96, 95.
46. Wells, *Crusade*, 25, 26.
47. Wells, *Memphis Diary*, 96.
48. Ibid., 99.
49. Ibid., 105, 106.
50. Wells, *Crusade*, 31.
51. Wells, *Memphis Diary*, 98.
52. On black middle-class sexual mores see Christina Simmons, "African-Americans and Sexual Victorianism in the Social Hygiene Movement, 1910–40," *The Journal of the History of Sexuality* 4, no. 1 (1993): 51–75.
53. Wells, *Memphis Diary*, 37.
54. Ibid., 88.
55. Ibid., 37.
56. Ibid., 131.
57. Ibid., 131, 133.

58. McMurray, *To Keep the Waters Troubled*, 67.
59. Wells, *Memphis Diary*, 138.
60. Ibid., 56.
61. Ibid., 39.
62. Ibid., 60.
63. Ibid., 53.
64. Wells, *Crusade*, 31.
65. Wells, *Memphis Diary*, 35.
66. Ibid., 36.
67. Ibid., 35–36.
68. Wells, "A Story of 1900" (1886), as reprinted in ibid., 182–84.
69. Ibid., 184.
70. Wells writing as "Iola," "Functions of Leadership" (1885), reprinted in ibid., 178.
71. Wells writing as "Iola," quoted in *The Freeman* (New York), September 12, 1885.
72. Wells writing as "Iola," "Woman's Mission," *The Freeman* (New York), December 26, 1885; Wells writing as "Iola," "The Model Girl: A True Picture of the Typical Southern Girl," *The New York Age*, February 18, 1888.
73. Wells writing as "Iola," "Woman's Mission"; Wells writing as "Iola," "The Model Girl."
74. Wells writing as "Iola," "The Model Girl."
75. Wells, *Memphis Diary*, 78.
76. Wells writing as "Iola," "Our Women: The Brilliant Iola Defends Them," *The Freeman* (New York), January 1, 1887.
77. Wells, *Crusade*, 44.
78. Ibid., 2.
79. Ibid., 32.
80. *Weekly Pelican* (New Orleans), August 13, 1887, quoted in *The New York Age*, August 24, 1889.
81. *The Indianapolis Freeman*, August 24, 1889.
82. Wells, *Crusade*, 33.
83. Ibid., 36.
84. Ibid., 37.
85. Ibid., 36.
86. Ibid., 43, 44.
87. Ibid., 39.
88. Ibid., 41, 38.
89. McMurray, *To Keep the Waters Troubled*, 127.
90. Wells, *Crusade*, 41.
91. Ibid.

3: The Lynching at the Curve

1. Ida B. Wells, *Crusade for Justice: The Autobiography of Ida B. Wells*, ed. Alfreda Duster (Chicago: University of Chicago Press, 1991), 48.
2. Ibid.
3. Ibid., 49.
4. *The Appeal Avalanche* (Memphis), March 7, 1892.
5. Dennis Brindell Fadin and Judith Bloom Fadin, *Ida B. Wells: Mother of the Civil Rights Movement* (New York: Clarion Books, 2000), 41.
6. Wells, *Crusade*, 51.
7. Ibid.
8. Ibid.
9. Ibid., 62.
10. Ibid., 55.
11. Ibid., 53.
12. Ibid., 54.
13. Ibid., 55.
14. Ibid.
15. Henry Adams quoted in Nell Irvin Painter, *Exodusters: Black Migration to Kansas After Reconstruction* (New York: Norton, 1992), 193.
16. Quoted in Michele Mitchell, *Righteous Propagation: African Americans and the Politics of Racial Destiny after Reconstruction* (Chapel Hill: University of North Carolina Press, 2004), 42.
17. *Free Speech* quoted in *The Bee* (Washington, D.C.), April 13, 1889.
18. *Free Speech* quoted in *The Indianapolis Freeman*, June 7, 1890.
19. Michael Perman, *Struggle for Mastery: Disfranchisement in the South, 1888–1908* (Chapel Hill: University of North Carolina Press, 2001), 59.
20. Ida B. Wells, *The Memphis Diary of Ida B. Wells*, ed. Miriam DeCosta-Willis (Boston: Beacon, 1995), 102.
21. Quoted in *The Weekly Avalanche* (Memphis), September 6, 1891.
22. Ida B. Wells, writing as "Iola," "Judicious Emigration," *The Indianapolis Freeman*, November 1896.
23. Frederick Douglass, "The Negro Exodus from the Gulf States," *The Journal of Social Science* 11 (May 1880): 14. Douglass reiterated his views in 1892 when he reprinted much of this address in *The Life and Times of Frederick Douglass* (1892), 530.
24. Wells, *Crusade*, 52.
25. Christopher Waldrep, *The Many Faces of Judge Lynch: Extralegal Violence and Punishment in America* (New York: Palgrave Macmillan, 2002), 14.
26. On the story of Charles Lynch, see Philip Dray, *At the Hands of Persons Unknown:*

The Lynching of Black America (New York: Modern Library, 2003), 21. Other useful overviews of the history of lynching include Waldrep's *The Many Faces of Judge Lynch*; W. Fitzhugh Brundage, ed., *Under Sentence of Death: Lynching in the South* (Chapel Hill: University of North Carolina Press, 1997); Stewart E. Tolnay and E. M. Beck, *A Festival of Violence: An Analysis of Southern Lynchings, 1882–1930* (Champaign: University of Illinois Press, 1995); and Margaret Vandiver, *Lethal Punishment: Lynchings and Legal Executions in the South* (New Brunswick, N.J.: Rutgers University Press, 2006).

27. Rape is described as the "so-called 'new' negro crime, by which is meant the crime against white women" in "The Negro Problem and the New Negro Crime," *Harper's Weekly*, June 20, 1903, 1050. This description is reiterated in "Some Fresh Suggestions about the New Negro Crime," *Harper's Weekly*, January 23, 1904, 120, which notes that "the assault of white women by colored men may fairly be described as the 'new' negro crime"; *The New York Times*, "Mob Law in Arkansas," February 23, 1892, 4.

28. Ida B. Wells, *Southern Horrors* (1892), reprinted in *Southern Horrors and Other Writings: The Anti-Lynching Campaign of Ida B. Wells, 1892–1900*, ed. Jacqueline Jones Royster (Boston: Bedford Books, 1997), 65; *The Appeal-Avalanche* (Memphis), March 22, 1892.

29. *The Appeal-Avalanche* (Memphis), May 30, 1892.

30. Jacqueline Goldsby, *A Spectacular Secret: Lynching in American Life and Literature* (Chicago: University of Chicago Press, 2006), 65.

31. Wells, *Crusade*, 72.

32. Ibid., 54.

33. Ibid.

34. Wells, *Southern Horrors*, 56.

35. Ibid., 56, 61.

36. Wells, *Crusade*, 65.

37. Wells, *Southern Horrors*, 58.

38. Ibid., 53.

39. Ibid., 52.

40. Wells, *Crusade*, 59.

41. Wells quotes the *Evening Scimitar* in *Southern Horrors*, 52; Wells, *Crusade*, 62.

42. Wells, *Crusade*, 67.

43. Ibid., 61.

44. Ida B. Wells quoted in *The American Citizen* (Kansas City), July 1892.

45. Wells, *Crusade*, 62.

46. Ibid.

4: Exile

1. Jean V. Matthews, *The Rise of the New Woman: The Women's Movement in America, 1875–1930* (New York: Ivan R. Dee, 2004), 35.
2. "Miss Ida B. Wells Will Deliver a Lecture" (advertisement), *The Bee* (Washington, D.C.), October 29, 1892.
3. The 1873 Comstock law ("an Act for the Suppression of Trade in, and Circulation of, Obscene Literature and Articles for Immoral Use") imposed a federal ban on the circulation of not only erotic literature, but sexual aids and information of any kind—including literature discussing birth control. Margaret Sanger describes the suppression of her women's magazine under this law in "Comstockery in America," *International Socialist Review* (1915), 46–49.
4. Ida B. Wells, "The Lynch Law in All Its Phases" (1893), reprinted in Mildred I. Thompson, *Ida B. Wells-Barnett: An Exploratory Study of an American Black Woman, 1893–1930* (Brooklyn, N.Y.: Carlson Publishing, 1990), 186.
5. *The Indianapolis Freeman*, June 24, 1893.
6. *The American Citizen* (Kansas City), August 12, 1892.
7. *The Indianapolis Freeman*, July 16 and August 20, 1892.
8. *Detroit Plaindealer*, June 17, 1892; *The Indianapolis Freeman*, July 30, 1892.
9. *The Appeal-Avalanche* (Memphis), June 30, 1892.
10. Ida B. Wells, *Crusade for Justice: The Autobiography of Ida B. Wells*, ed. Alfreda Duster (Chicago: University of Chicago Press, 1991), 78.
11. Craig Steven Wilder, *A Covenant with Color: Race and Social Power in Brooklyn* (New York: Columbia University Press, 2001), 116.
12. Dorothy Sterling, *We Are Your Sisters: Black Women in the Nineteenth Century* (New York: Norton, 1997), 189.
13. Wells, *Crusade*, 79.
14. Ibid.
15. Ibid., 78, 79.
16. Ibid., 79.
17. Ibid.
18. Ibid., 82.
19. Wells, "The Lynch Law in All Its Phases," 176.
20. Wells, *Crusade*, 80.
21. Quote in Darlene Clark Hine, "The Corporeal and Ocular Veil: Dr. Matilda Evans and the Complexity of Southern History," *The Journal of Southern History* 70 (February 2004): 26.
22. Patricia A. Schechter, "'All the Intensity of My Nature': Ida B. Wells and African-American Women's Anger in History," *Radical History Review* 70 (October 1998), 57.

23. Anna Julia Cooper, *A Voice from the South* (New York: Oxford University Press, 1990), 139.
24. Ibid., 85.
25. Ibid., 91.
26. Mary Church Terrell, *A Colored Woman in a White World* (Amherst, New York: Humanity Books, 2005), 29, 335.
27. Darlene Clark Hine, "Rape and the Inner Lives of Black Women in the Middle West: Preliminary Thoughts on the Culture of Dissemblance," *Signs* 14 (Summer 1989): 917.
28. Cooper, *Voice from the South*, 32.
29. Wells, *Crusade*, 21.
30. Ibid., 80.
31. Ida B. Wells, *The Memphis Diary of Ida B. Wells*, ed. Miriam DeCosta-Willis (Boston: Beacon, 1995), 102.
32. Ida B. Wells, *The Reason Why the Colored American Is Not in the World Columbian Exposition* (1893), reprinted in *Southern Horrors and Other Writings: The Anti-Lynching Campaign of Ida B. Wells, 1892–1900*, ed. Jacqueline Jones Royster (Boston: Bedford Books, 1997), 50.
33. Ibid., 61.
34. Wells, *Crusade*, 71.
35. Jacqueline Goldsby, *A Spectacular Secret: Lynching in American Life and Literature* (Chicago: University of Chicago Press, 2006), 65.
36. Ida B. Wells, *Southern Horrors* (1892), reprinted in *Southern Horrors and Other Writings: The Anti-Lynching Campaign of Ida B. Wells, 1892–1900*, ed. Jacqueline Jones Royster (Boston: Bedford Books, 1997), 53, 55.
37. Ibid., 54.
38. Ibid., 59.
39. Ibid., 71.
40. Alison Piepmeier, *Out in Public: Configurations of Women's Bodies in Nineteenth-Century America* (Chapel Hill: University of North Carolina Press, 2004), 147.
41. Wells, *Southern Horrors*, 58.
42. Ibid., 54.
43. Patricia Schechter, "Unsettled Business: Ida B. Wells against Lynching or How Antilynching Got Its Gender," in *Under Sentence of Death: Lynching in the South*, ed. W. Fitzhugh Brundage (Chapel Hill: University of North Carolina Press, 1997), 301.
44. Wells, *Crusade*, 72.
45. Ida B. Wells to Frederick Douglass, October 17, 1892, Frederick Douglass Papers, Library of Congress, Manuscript Division.
46. Frederick Douglass's letter, October 25, 1892. The letter appears at the beginning of *Southern Horrors*, 51.

47. Frederick Douglass, "Lynch Law in the South," *North American Review* 155 (July 1894): 17–24.

48. Ibid., 23.

49. Francis Grimke, "The Second Marriage of Frederick Douglass," *The Journal of Negro History* 19, no. 3 (July 1934): 324–29.

50. Wells, *Crusade*, 73.

51. Robert W. Rydell, *All the World's a Fair: Visions of Empire at American International Expositions, 1876–1916* (Chicago: University of Chicago Press, 1987), 28, 29.

52. *The Indianapolis Freeman*, November 26, 1892.

53. *The New York Times*, February 2, 1893.

54. *The Sun* (New York), February 2, 1893.

55. Wells, *Crusade*, 84.

56. *The New York Times*, February 2, 1893; *The Washington Post*, February 2, 1893; *The Washington Post*, February 5, 1893.

57. Wells, *Crusade*, 84.

58. "Invited to Attend a Lecture on Lynching," *The Washington Post*, January 29, 1893.

59. Grace Elisabeth Hale, *Making Whiteness: The Culture of Segregation in the South, 1890–1940* (New York: Random House, 1999), 207.

60. Wells, *Crusade*, 85.

61. *The Times* (London), February 8, 1893, 5.

62. Catherine Impey, "To My Dear Friends," March 21, 1893, Albion Tourgée Papers, quoted in Linda O. McMurray, *To Keep the Waters Troubled: The Life of Ida B. Wells* (New York: Oxford University Press, 1998), 186.

63. Wells, *Crusade*, 85.

64. Tourgée quoted in Mark Elliott, *Color-Blind Justice: Albion Tourgée and the Quest for Racial Equality from the Civil War to Plessy v. Ferguson* (New York: Oxford University Press, 2006), 239, see also 241; Catherine Impey, "A Lynching Scene in Alabama," *Anti-Caste* 6 (January 1893): 1.

65. Wells, *Crusade*, 86.

66. *The Memphis Commercial*, December 15, 1892.

67. *The Cleveland Gazette*, February 11, 1893. See also *The American Citizen* (Kansas City), February 25, 1893; McMurray, *To Keep the Waters Troubled*, 177–78.

68. *Topeka Weekly Call*, January 8, 1893, M 181.

69. Ida B. Wells to Albion Tourgée, n.d., Ida B. Wells Papers, Box 10, Folder 6, University of Chicago Library, Special Collections.

70. Christopher Robert Reed, *Black Chicago's First Century* (Columbia: University of Missouri Press, 2005), 207; "Do You Know?" *Chicago Defender*, July 10, 1943.

71. Davis, *The Negro Newspaper*, quoted in McMurray, *To Keep the Waters Troubled*, 238.

72. Ferdinand Barnett to Albion Tourgée, February 23, 1893, Ida B. Wells Papers.

73. Ida B. Wells, "The 1893 Travel Diary," in *The Memphis Diary of Ida B. Wells*, ed. Miriam DeCosta-Willis (Boston: Beacon, 1995), 162.

74. Vron Ware, *Beyond the Pale: White Women, Racism and History* (London: Verso, 1992), 177.

75. G. R. Simpson, "Notes," *The Journal of Negro History* 10, no. 1 (January 1925): 104.

76. Ware, *Beyond the Pale*; Sandra Stanley Holton, "Segregation, Racism and White Women Reformers: A Transnational Analysis, 1840–1912," *Women's History Review* 10, no. 1 (2001): 5–25.

77. Sarah L. Silkey, "Redirecting the Tide of White Imperialism: The Impact of Ida B. Wells's Transatlantic Antilynching Campaign on British Conceptions of American Race Relations," in *Women Shaping the South: Creating and Confronting Change*, eds. Angela Boswell and Judith N. McArthur (Columbia: University of Missouri Press, 2006), 100.

78. "The Lynching at New Orleans," *The Times* (London), March 17, 1891, p. 5.

79. *Anti-Caste* 3, no. 1 (January 1890): 3, cited in Caroline Bressey, "A Strange and Bitter Crop: Ida B. Wells' Anti-Lynching Tours in Britain, 1893 and 1894." Centre for Capital Punishment Studies, *Occasional Papers* 1 (December 2003), www.wmin.ac.uk/law/pdf/CBressey.pdf.

80. Terence Finnegan, "Lynching and Political Power in Mississippi and South Carolina," in *Under Sentence of Death: Lynching in the South*, ed. W. Fitzhugh Brundage (Chapel Hill: University of North Carolina Press, 1997), 197.

81. *Anti-Caste* 3, nos. 7 and 8 (July and August 1890): 4, quoted in Bressey, "A Strange and Bitter Crop."

82. Ida B. Wells-Barnett, *A Red Record: Tabulated Statistics and Alleged Causes of Lynching in the United States, 1892–1893–1894* (1895), www.gutenberg.org/files/14977/14977-h/14977-h.htm.

83. Carolyn L. Karcher, "Ida B. Wells and Her Allies Against Lynching: A Transnational Perspective," *Comparative American Studies* 3, no. 2 (2005): 141.

84. McMurray, *To Keep the Waters Troubled*, 190.

85. Wells, *Crusade*, 89. *Anti-Caste* 3, nos. 7 and 8 (July and August 1890), quoted in Bressey, "A Strange and Bitter Crop."

86. Wells, *Crusade*, 90.

87. Sandra Stanley Holton, "Segregation, Racism and White Women Reformers: A Transnational Analysis, 1840–1912," *Women's History Review* 10, no. 1 (2001): 7.

88. See, for example, Ida B. Wells, "The Lynch Law in All Its Phases," 171—a speech she delivered in Boston.

89. Wells, *Crusade*, 99, 100.

90. Carolyn L. Karcher, "The White 'Bystander' and the Black Journalist 'Abroad': Albion W. Tourgée and Ida B. Wells as Allies against Lynching," *Prospects* 29 (2004).

91. Wells, *Crusade*, 98, 101.
92. Ibid., 103.
93. Ibid.
94. Ibid., 104.
95. Mayo, quoted in Ware, *Beyond the Pale*, 195.
96. See, for example, Seth Koven and Sonya Michel, "Womanly Duties: Maternalist Politics and the Origins of Welfare States in France, Germany, Great Britain, and the United States, 1880–1920," *American Historical Review* 95, no. 4 (October 1990): 1076–1108.
97. Isabelle Mayo, "The Female Accusation" (1894), quoted in Ware, *Beyond the Pale*, 195.
98. Wells, *Crusade*, 105.
99. Ibid., 109, 110.
100. Ibid., 110.
101. Mayo, "The Female Accusation," quoted in Ware, *Beyond the Pale*, 195.

5: Capturing the Attention of the "Civilized World"

1. "Editorial Comment," *The Atlanta Constitution*, June 21, 1893.
2. Sarah L. Silkey, "Redirecting the Tide of White Imperialism: The Impact of Ida B. Wells's Transatlantic Antilynching Campaign on British Conceptions of American Race Relations," in *Women Shaping the South: Creating and Confronting Change*, eds. Angela Boswell and Judith N. McArthur (Columbia: University of Missouri Press, 2006), 11.
3. Ida B. Wells, *Crusade for Justice: The Autobiography of Ida B. Wells*, ed. Alfreda Duster (Chicago: University of Chicago Press, 1991), 113.
4. Ida B. Wells and Frederick Douglass circulated a letter describing and soliciting subscriptions for the pamphlet, which was addressed "To the Friends of Equal Rights." It appeared in a number of black publications including *The Christian Recorder*, April 13, 1893.
5. Wells, *Crusade*, 116.
6. *The Indianapolis Freeman*, August 5, 1893.
7. "No Separate Exhibit Wanted," *Daily Inter Ocean*, November 13, 1890.
8. "For the Colored People," *Daily Inter Ocean*, November 9, 1890; "To Aid the Fair," *Daily Inter Ocean*, July 1, 1892.
9. *The Indianapolis Freeman*, quoted in "Wants to Be Commissioner: Principal Parker Wants to Represent the Colored Race at the World's Fair," *Daily Inter Ocean*, January 28, 1891.
10. *The Indianapolis Freeman*, May 23, 1891.
11. T. J. Boisseau, "White Queens at the Chicago World's Fair, 1893: New Woman-

hood in the Service of Class, Race, and Nation," *Gender and History* 12, no. 1 (April 2000): 36.

12. F. L. Barnett, *The Reason Why the Colored American Is Not in the World's Columbian Exposition* (1893), in *Selected Works of Ida B. Wells-Barnett*, ed. Trudier Harris (New York: Oxford University Press, 1991), 120.

13. Ibid., 122.

14. Ann Massa, "Black Women in the 'White City,'" *Journal of American Studies* 8.3 (December 1974): 333.

15. Robert W. Rydell, *All the World's a Fair: Visions of Empire at American International Expositions, 1876–1916* (Chicago: University of Chicago Press, 1984), 59.

16. Mary Kavanaugh Oldham Eagle quoted in Mary Lockwood, "Mrs. Palmer's Portrait," in Mary Kavanaugh Oldham Eagle, *The Congress of Women* (Chicago: Monarch Book Company, 1894), 817.

17. Boisseau, "White Queens at the Chicago World's Fair," 33–80.

18. Robert W. Rydell, "Contend, Contend!: Editor's Introduction," in *The Reason Why the Colored American Is Not in the World's Columbian Exposition*, Ida B. Wells et al. (Champaign: University of Illinois Press, 1999).

19. Black fairgoer quoted in *The Atchison Blade*, July 23, 1893, in Elliott M. Rudwick and August Meier, "Black Man in the 'White City': Negroes and the Columbian Exposition," *Phylon* 26, no. 4 (1965): 359.

20. Wells quoted in Robert Rydell, "Contend, Contend!," xxvii.

21. *The Indianapolis Freeman*, March 25, 1893.

22. *The Bee* (Washington, D.C.), April 15, 1893.

23. William S. McFeely, *Frederick Douglass* (New York: Norton, 1991), 368.

24. Douglass's previous official address to the World's Columbian Exposition focused on "Hayti and the Haitians." A rousing defense of Haitian independence, it was attended by the twenty-six-year-old W.E.B. Du Bois. Herbert Aptheker, "DuBois on Douglass: 1895," *The Journal of Negro History* 49, no. 4 (October 1986): 264–68.

25. McFeely, *Frederick Douglass*, 370.

26. "To Tole with Watermelons," *The Cleveland Gazette*, July 22, 1893.

27. Fredericka Sprague, quoted in McFeely, *Frederick Douglass*, 370.

28. Rudwick and Meier, "Black Man in the 'White City,'" 359.

29. "Claim Their Rights," *Daily Inter Ocean*, April 14, 1893.

30. *Chicago Daily Tribune*, May 4, 1893; *Chicago Daily Tribune*, September 27, 1893.

31. Christopher Robert Reed, *"All the World Is Here": The Black Presence in the White City* (Bloomington: Indiana University Press, 2002), 148, 155.

32. Rydell, *All the World's a Fair*, 66.

33. *World's Fair Puck* 24 (1893): 279. See also M. Niquette and W. Buxton, "Meet Me at the Fair: Sociability and Reflexivity in Nineteenth-Century World Expositions," *Canadian Journal of Communication* 22, no. 1 (January 1, 1997), www.cjc-online.ca/viewarticle.php?id=400.

34. Jo-Ann Morgan, "Mammy the Huckster: Selling the Old South in the New Century," *American Art* 9, no. 1 (Spring 1995): 88; James C. Davis, "Race and American Narratives of Counter Publicity, 1890–1930," Ph.D. dissertation, Indiana University (2000), 36, 37, 56.

35. "Another Letter from Mr. Douglass," *The Indianapolis Freeman*, April 15, 1893; Rydell, "Contend, Contend!" xxix.

36. I. Garland Penn, *The Afro-American Press and Its Editors* (1891, reprinted New York: Arno Press, 1969).

37. Ida B. Wells, *The Reason Why the Colored American Is Not in the World's Columbian Exposition* in *Selected Works of Ida B. Wells-Barnett*, ed. Trudier Harris (New York: Oxford University Press, 1991), 49–50.

38. Frederick Douglass, *The Reason Why the Colored American Is Not in the World's Columbian Exposition* in *Selected Works of Ida B. Wells-Barnett*, ed. Trudier Harris (New York: Oxford University Press, 1991), 51, 55, 56–57.

39. Wells, *The Reason Why*, 63.

40. Barnett, *The Reason Why*, 134–35, 136.

41. I. Garland Penn, *The Reason Why the Colored American Is Not in the World's Columbian Exposition* in *Selected Works of Ida B. Wells-Barnett*, ed. Trudier Harris (New York: Oxford University Press, 1991), 90–116.

42. Wells, *Crusade*, 117, 118; Dunbar, quoted in Rydell, "Contend, Contend!" xxxii; "Appeal of Douglass," *Chicago Tribune*, August 26, 1893.

43. Douglass, *The Reason Why*, 58; "Appeal of Douglass," *Chicago Tribune*, August 26, 1893.

44. Wells, *Crusade*, 119; Hubert Howe Bancroft, *Book of the Fair* (Chicago: The Bancroft Company, 1893), 972.

45. Louis R. Harlan, "Booker T. Washington in a Biographical Perspective," *The American Historical Review* 75, no. 6 (October 1970): 1583.

46. Booker T. Washington quoted in Rydell, "Contend, Contend!" xxxvi–xxxvii; Wells quoted in "Progress of the Colored Brothers," *Chicago Tribune*, September 3, 1893.

47. Linda O. McMurray, *To Keep the Waters Troubled: The Life of Ida B. Wells* (New York: Oxford University Press, 1998), 206; Wells bemoaned the lack of subscriptions that forced the *Age* to cut back to four pages in Ida B. Wells, "Iola's Southern Field," *The New York Age*, November 19, 1892.

48. Wells, *Crusade*, 238.

49. Alfreda Duster in Dorothy Sterling's "Afterword" to *The Memphis Diary of Ida B. Wells*, ed. Miriam De Costa-Willis (Boston: Beacon, 1997), 193.

50. Stella Reed Garnett, "A Chapter in the Life of Ida B. Wells," unpublished manuscript, April 26, 1951, 1; Ida B. Wells Papers, Box 7, Folder 10, University of Chicago, Special Collections; Alfreda Duster in Dorothy Sterling's "Afterword" to *The Memphis Diary of Ida B. Wells*, 193; "Interview with Alfreda Duster," in *The*

Black Women's Oral History Project ed. Ruth Edmonds Hill (Westport, Conn.: Meckler, 1991), vol. 3, 127. Painting the Sage of Anacostia in the unlikely role of cupid, the *Duluth News Tribune* maintained that Douglass told Wells that "Barnett is a fine Gentleman. He likes you and will make a good husband," and likewise informed Barnett that "Miss Wells was a real nice girl." *Duluth News Tribune*, July 6, 1895.

51. Ida B. Wells, "Two Christmas Days: A Holiday Story," in Mildred I. Thompson, *Ida B. Wells-Barnett: An Exploratory Study of an American Black Woman, 1893–1930* (Brooklyn, N.Y.: Carlson Publishing, 1990), 225–34.

52. "Interview with Alfreda Duster," 128.

53. Wells, *Crusade*, 121.

54. Ida B. Wells, "The Brutal Truth," *Daily Inter Ocean*, July 19, 1893, 17.

55. Ida B. Wells, *The Reason Why* in *Selected Works of Ida B. Wells*, ed. Trudier Harris (New York: Oxford University Press, 1991), 90, 91.

56. Ibid., 83, 85.

57. Ida B. Wells, *A Red Record*, in *Selected Works of Ida B. Wells*, ed. Trudier Harris (New York: Oxford University Press, 1991), 217.

58. Isabelle Mayo to Ida B. Wells, September 12, 1893, Frederick Douglass Papers, Library of Congress.

59. Ibid.

60. Ida B. Wells to Frederick Douglass, March 13, 1894, Frederick Douglass Papers.

61. Wells, *Crusade*, 126.

62. These arrangements are discussed in Sandra Stanley Holton, "Segregation, Racism and White Women Reformers: A Transnational Analysis, 1840–1912," *Women's History Review* 10, no. 1 (2001): 5–25.

63. Wells, *Crusade*, 129.

64. Frederick Douglass to Rev. C. F. Aked, March 27, 1894, Frederick Douglass Papers; Frederick Douglass to Ida B. Wells, March 27, 1894, Frederick Douglass Papers.

65. Ida B. Wells to Frederick Douglass, Manchester, April 6, 1894, Frederick Douglass Papers.

66. Ellen Richardson to Frederick Douglass, Newcastle, England, April 22, 1894, Frederick Douglass Papers.

67. Ellen Richardson to Frederick Douglass, Newcastle, England, May 29, 1894, Frederick Douglass Papers.

68. *The Daily Chronicle* (London), quoted in "Wells's Crusade," *The Sun* (New York), July 26, 1894; Ellen Richardson to Frederick Douglass, Newcastle, England, April 22, 1894, Frederick Douglass Papers.

69. "The Bitter Cry of Black America," *The Westminster Gazette* 10 (May 1894): 1.

70. Ibid., 2.

71. Teresa Zackodnik, "Ida B. Wells and 'American Atrocities' in Britain," *Women's Studies International Forum* 28 (2005): 256–73.
72. Wells, *Crusade*, 149.
73. Wells's *Daily Inter Ocean* articles quote her speeches and are reprinted in *Crusade*. See also Ida B. Wells, "Liverpool's Slave Trade Traditions and Present Practices," *The Independent*, May 17, 1894, 46.
74. Wells, *Crusade*, 135, 141.
75. Ibid., 179.
76. Sarah L. Silkey, "Redirecting the Tide of White Imperialism: The Impact of Ida B. Wells's Transatlantic Antilynching Campaign on British Conceptions of American Race Relations," in *Women Shaping the South: Creating and Confronting Change* eds. Angela Boswell and Judith N. McArthur (Columbia: University of Missouri Press, 2006), 105.
77. Charles F. Aked, "The Race Problem in America," *The Contemporary Review* 65 (June 1894): 827.
78. Silkey, "Redirecting the Tide," 106.
79. Patricia Schechter, *Ida B. Wells-Barnett and American Reform, 1880–1930* (Chapel Hill: University of North Carolina Press, 2001), 101.
80. *Southern Horrors* indicts Alabama bishop Fitzgerald for his statement that those "who condemn lynching show no sympathy for the white woman in the case."
81. Ida B. Wells, "Mr. Moody and Miss Willard," *Fraternity*, May 1894, Temperance and Prohibition Papers microfilm (1977). The careers and racial thought of both Moody and Willard are discussed in Edward J. Blum's illuminating book *Reforging the White Republic: Race, Religion, and American Nationalism* (Baton Rouge: University of Louisiana Press, 2005).
82. Blum, *Reforging the White Republic*, 194.
83. Wells, "Mr. Moody and Miss Willard," 16–17.
84. "The Race Problem: Miss Willard on the Political Puzzle of the South," *The Voice* (New York), October 23, 1890.
85. Excerpt from Frances E. Willard, "President's Annual Address," *National WCTU Annual Meeting Minutes of 1893* (Chicago: Woman's Temperance Publication Association, 1893), 136–38, Temperance and Prohibition Papers microfilm (1977), section 1, reel 4.
86. Lady Henry Somerset, "White and Black in America: An Interview with Miss Willard," *The Westminster Gazette*, May 21, 1894, 3.
87. Ibid.
88. Wells, *Crusade*, 210.
89. "Anti-Lynching Committee," *The Times* (London), August 1, 1894.
90. Wells, *Crusade*, 217, 218.

91. Ida B. Wells to Helen Pitts Douglass, London, April 26, 1894, Frederick Douglass Papers.

6: "Although a Busy Woman, She Has Found the Time to Marry"

1. Ida B. Wells, *Crusade for Justice: The Autobiography of Ida B. Wells*, ed. Alfreda Duster (Chicago: University of Chicago Press, 1991), 250.
2. *Women's Era* 2 (August 1895): 16.
3. *The Indianapolis Freeman*, June 8, 1893.
4. Booker T. Washington quoted in Henry MacFarland, "A Negro with Sense," *The Record* (Philadelphia), April 8, 1894, 12.
5. Ibid.
6. "This Woman's Busy Day," *The Atlanta Constitution*, September 20, 1895.
7. "Interview with Alfreda Duster," in *The Black Women's Oral History Project*, ed. Ruth Edmonds Hill, vol. 3 (Westport, Conn.: Meckler, 1991), 127.
8. Floyd W. Crawford, "Ida B. Wells: Some Reactions to Her Anti-Lynching Campaign in Britain," manuscript of a paper delivered at LaMoyne College, March 2, 1963, Ida B. Wells Papers, Box 9, Folder 2, University of Chicago Library, Special Collections.
9. *The Times* (London), August 1, 1894, 11.
10. *The New York Times*, October 8, 1894, 7.
11. "Southern Governors on British Critics," *The Literary Digest* IX, 2 (New York), September 22, 1894, 231.
12. "A Committee of Impertinence," *The Washington Post*, October 10, 1894; "A Suggestion to the British," *The Atlanta Constitution*, August 7, 1894; "British Anti-Lynchers," *The New York Times*, August 2, 1894.
13. American readers heard that *The Pall Mall Gazette* denounced the committee's work as "Nothing Short of Impertinence," and that *The Yorkshire Gazette* questioned Florence Balgarnie's "tactless screed," but *The Daily Mail's* ongoing support for the venture went unreported. "Nothing Short of Impertinence," *The Washington Post*, October 22, 1894, 4; "Talking Sense at Last," *The Atlanta Constitution*, October 27, 1894, 4.
14. "British Anti-Lynchers," *The New York Times*, August 2, 1894.
15. *The Daily Chronicle* (London), quoted in "Lynching in America," *The Cleveland Gazette*, September 1, 1894.
16. *The New York Times*, July 27, 1894.
17. Ida B. Wells, *A Red Record*, reprinted in *Southern Horrors and Other Writings: The Anti-Lynching Campaign of Ida B. Wells*, ed. Jacqueline Jones Royster (Boston: Bedford Books, 1997), 218.

18. *The Columbus Evening Dispatch*, quoted in "Tennessee Atrocity," *The Cleveland Gazette*, September 8, 1894, 2.

19. Wells's statement of September 2, 1894, is quoted in "The Tennessee Mob," *The Galveston Daily News*, September 3, 1894.

20. "Lynch Law in Bad Odor," *The Washington Post*, September 1, 1894.

21. "Old Unreconstructed *Charleston News and Courier*," *The Cleveland Gazette*, September 15, 1894, 2.

22. Wells, *A Red Record*, 219–20.

23. Ibid., 133.

24. "Lynching Case on Trial," *The Cleveland Gazette*, November 17, 1894.

25. Wells, *A Red Record*, 154.

26. Paula J. Giddings, *Ida: A Sword Among Lions* (New York: HarperCollins, 2008), 316.

27. Wells, *Crusade*, 226, 238.

28. "Ida Wells in California: The Colored Crusader has a Grievance against Methodist Ministers," *The Sun* (Baltimore), March 6, 1894, 3.

29. Higginson, quoted in Patricia Schechter, *Ida B. Wells-Barnett and American Reform, 1880–1930* (Chapel Hill: University of North Carolina Press, 2001), 101.

30. Frances E. Willard, "The Colored People," *National WCTU Annual Meeting Minutes of 1894*, Temperance and Prohibition Papers microfilm (1917), section 7, reel 4.

31. Beryl Satter, *Each Mind a Kingdom: American Women, Sexual Purity and the New Thought Movement* (Berkeley: University of California Press, 2001), 183–88, 216.

32. "Miss Wells Lectures," *The Cleveland Gazette*, November 24, 1894.

33. The WCTU's 1894 resolution as quoted in Wells, *A Red Record*, 146.

34. Ruth Bordin, *Frances Willard: A Biography* (Chapel Hill: University of North Carolina Press, 1986), 223.

35. Carolyn L. Karcher, "The White 'Bystander' and the Black Journalist 'Abroad': Albion W. Tourgée and Ida B. Wells as Allies against Lynching," *Prospects* 29 (2004): 106.

36. Letter from Frederick Douglass et al. in "Lady Henry Somerset's Statement Concerning Accusations of Miss Florence Balgarnie, June, 1895–May, 1896," Temperance and Prohibition Papers microfilm (1977), section 2, reel 32, scrapbook 13, frame 223.

37. Frederick Douglass, "Why Is the Negro Lynched?" *The Lesson of the Hour* (1894), reprinted in *The Life and Writings of Frederick Douglass*, ed. Philip S. Foner, vol. 4, *Reconstruction and After* (New York: International Publishers, 1955).

38. "Through Their Bonnets," *The State* (Columbia, S.C.), June 19, 1895, 1.

39. "British Women's Council," *The New York Times*, June 19, 1895, 5.

40. *The Daily News* (London), June 19, 1895.

41. "The WCTU and the Colour Question," *Anti-Caste*, March 1895, 4, Temperance and Prohibition Papers microfilm (1977), section 3, reel 32, scrapbook 13, frame 215.

42. Vron Ware, *Beyond the Pale: White Women, Racism and History* (London: Verso, 1992), 210.

43. Wells, *A Red Record*, 118.

44. Jacqueline Goldsby, *A Spectacular Secret: Lynching in American Life and Literature* (Chicago: University of Chicago Press, 2006), 82.

45. Wells, *A Red Record*, 80.

46. W.E.B. Du Bois, *The Dusk of Dawn: An Essay Toward an Autobiography of a Race Concept* (New York: Schocken Books, 1969), 11.

47. Wells, *A Red Record*, 154–55.

48. Jacquelyn Dowd Hall, *Revolt against Chivalry: Jesse Daniel Ames and the Women's Campaign against Lynching* (New York: Columbia University Press, 1993), xx–xxi.

49. Wells, *Crusade*, 230.

50. Ibid.

51. Ibid., 238, 255.

52. "Although a Busy Woman, She Has Found the Time to Marry," *Idaho Daily Statesman*, August 8, 1895.

53. *Daily Inter Ocean*, June 28, 1895.

54. Wells, *Crusade*, 240.

55. Ibid., 239.

56. Ibid., 241.

57. Ibid., 255.

58. Ibid.

59. Ibid., 255, 242.

60. "Interview with Alfreda Duster," 132; on Mary Graham Barnett see "Colorful History of Early Chicago," *Chicago Defender*, December 31, 1932.

61. Stella Reed Garnett, "A Chapter in the Life of Ida B. Wells," unpublished manuscript, April 25, 1951, manuscript 5, enclosed in Stella Reed Garnett to Alfreda Duster, April 26, 1951, Ida B. Wells Papers.

62. *The American Lawyer* 5, no. 4 (April 1897): 184.

63. "Interview with Alfreda Duster," 129.

64. Wells, *Crusade*, 164.

65. Ibid., 122.

66. "Interview with Alfreda Duster," 126.

67. *The Indianapolis Freeman*, September 7, 1895.

68. Carolyn A. Waldron, " 'Lynch-law Must Go!': Race, Citizenship, and the Other in an American Coal Mining Town," *The Journal of American Ethnic History* 20, no. 1 (October 2000).

69. "Editorial Comments," *The Atlanta Constitution*, August 20, 1895.

70. Jacks's letter is reprinted in "A Base and Infernal Slander," *The American Citizen* (Kansas City), July 12, 1895.

71. Dorothy Salem, *To Better Our World: Black Women in Organized Reform, 1890–1920* (Brooklyn, N.Y.: Carlson Publishing, 1990), 21.

72. "Colored Women and Miss Willard," *The New York Times*, August 1, 1895.

73. Margaret Murray Washington and Fannie Barrier Williams quoted in Salem, *To Better Our World*, 21.

74. *The Woman's Era* 2 (August 1895): 16.

75. "P.G.," quoted in Richard T. Greener's typescript report of the conference, Rare Book Room, Boston Public Library.

76. *The Woman's Era* 2 (August 1895): 14.

77. Salem, *To Better Our World*, 22.

78. Wells, *Crusade*, 243.

79. Ida B. Wells, *The Memphis Diary of Ida B. Wells*, ed. Miriam DeCosta-Willis (Boston: Beacon, 1995), 150.

80. Wells, *Crusade*, 243.

81. "Interview with Alfreda Duster," 127.

82. Wells, *Crusade*, 251.

83. Ibid., 248–49.

84. Ibid., 251.

85. Ibid., 250.

86. "Interview with Alfreda Duster," 128.

87. Wells, *Crusade*, 249.

88. Ibid., 249–50.

89. Salem, *To Better Our World*, 23.

90. Wells, *Crusade*, 260.

91. Teresa Blue Holden, " 'Earnest Women Can Do Anything': The Public Career of Josephine St. Pierre Ruffin, 1842–1904," Ph.D. dissertation, Saint Louis University (2005), Chapter 5.

92. Wells, *Crusade*, 230.

93. Ibid.

94. "Interview with Alfreda Duster," 127.

7: Challenging Washington, D.C.—and Booker T.

1. Alfreda Duster, interview by Studs Terkel, recorded September 2, 1971, Chicago Historical Society.

2. This phrase comes from Rayford Logan, *The Betrayal of the Negro: From Rutherford Hayes to Woodrow Wilson* (New York: Collier Books, 1965), which first came out under the title *The Negro in American Life and Thought: The Nadir, 1877–1901*.

3. Ibid., 313.

4. Plessy v. Ferguson: *A Brief History with Documents*, ed. Brook Thomas (Boston: Bedford/St. Martin, 1997), 57.

5. "The S.C. Post Offices: No Democrat Need Hope If a Republican Applies," *The State* (Columbia, S.C.), November 4, 1898; "The Murder of Postmaster Baker," *The Cleveland Gazette*, February 26, 1898.

6. "Murder of Postmaster Baker."

7. Loftin survived the assault. But whites in his small Georgia town eventually drove him out of office by delivering their mail to the railway trains that passed through the town rather than patronizing the post office. "Negro Postmaster Retires," *The Dallas Morning News*, February 26, 1898, 2; "Forcing Loftin Out: The Colored Postmaster at Hoganville, Ga., Making but 11 Cents a Day," *The Sun* (Baltimore), February 5, 1898, 6.

8. "Lake City, S.C., Postmaster Baker," reprinted in *The State* (Columbia, S.C.), April 12, 1898.

9. "Ida B. Wells's Petition on Behalf of Frazier Baker's Wife and Children, 1898," *Lynching in America: A History in Documents*, ed. Christopher Waldrep (New York: New York University Press, 2006), 210.

10. *The News and Courier* (Charleston, S.C.), April 21, 1899, quoted in "The Lynching of Postmaster Frazier Baker and His Infant Daughter Julia in Lake City, South Carolina, in 1898 and Its Aftermath," www.usca.edu/aasc/lakecity.htm.

11. Benjamin R. Justesen, "Black Time, White Iceberg: Black Postmasters and the Rise of White Supremacy in North Carolina, 1897–1901," *The North Carolina Historical Review* 82, no. 2 (April 2005): 225.

12. Marvin Fletcher, "The Black Volunteers in the Spanish-American War," *Military Affairs* 38, no. 2 (April 1974): 48.

13. Ida B. Wells, *Crusade for Justice: The Autobiography of Ida B. Wells*, ed. Alfreda Duster (Chicago: University of Chicago Press, 1991), 254.

14. Ibid.

15. Emma Lou Thornbrough, *T. Thomas Fortune: Militant Journalist* (Chicago: University of Chicago Press, 1972).

16. Wells, *Crusade*, 256.

17. Glenda Gilmore, *Gender and Jim Crow* (Chapel Hill: University of North Carolina Press, 1996), 111, 112.

18. Ibid., 112.

19. Ibid., 113.

20. Shawn Leigh Alexander, " 'We Know Our Rights and Have the Courage to Defend Them': The Spirit of Agitation in the Age of Accommodation," Ph.D. dissertation, University of Massachusetts Amherst (2004).

21. Wells-Barnett quoted in Linda O. McMurry, *To Keep the Waters Troubled: The Life of Ida B. Wells* (New York: Oxford University Press, 1998), 253.

22. "Hisses—Groans," *The Cleveland Gazette*, January 7, 1899.

23. David Levering Lewis, *W.E.B. Du Bois: Biography of a Race* (New York: Henry Holt, 1993), 230.

24. Ibid., 226.

25. "B. T. Washington on Lynching," *The New York Times*, April 26, 1899.

26. Ida B. Wells-Barnett, *Lynch Law in Georgia* (Chicago: Chicago Colored Citizens, 1899), 1.

27. Booker T. Washington quoted in Louis R. Harlan, *Booker T. Washington: The Wizard of Tuskegee* (New York: Oxford University Press, 1986), 263.

28. Timothy Thomas Fortune to Booker T. Washington, September 25, 1899, in *The Booker T. Washington Papers* (Urbana: University of Illinois Press, 1976), 5:220.

29. Louis R. Harlan, *Booker T. Washington*, vol. 2, *The Wizard of Tuskegee* (New York: Oxford University Press, 1986).

30. Quoted in McMurray, *To Keep the Waters Troubled*, 259.

31. Booker T. Washington to Emmett Jay Scott, July 21, 1900, *BTW Papers*, 5:589.

32. Emmett Jay Scott to Booker T. Washington, August 13, 1901, *BTW Papers*, 6:186.

33. For biographical details on Robert Charles, see William Ivy Hair, *Carnival of Fury: Robert Charles and the New Orleans Riot of 1900* (Baton Rouge: Louisiana State University Press, 1976).

34. Ida B. Wells-Barnett, *Mob Rule in New Orleans*, reprinted in *Southern Horrors and Other Writings*, ed. Jacqueline Jones Royster (Boston: Bedford Books, 1997), 164–65.

35. "Constitution of the State of Louisiana, Adopted May 12, 1898," in *Documentary History of Reconstruction*, ed. Walter L. Fleming (Cleveland: Arthur H. Clark, 1906), 2:451–53.

36. Hair, *Carnival of Fury*, 146.

37. "Murderer Charles Shot to Death," *The New York Times*, July 28, 1900; "The New Orleans Riot," *Chicago Daily Tribune*, July 29, 1900.

38. Wells-Barnett, *Mob Rule in New Orleans*, 192.

39. Ibid., 169, 193.

40. Ibid., 202.

41. Ibid., 198.

42. Ibid., 164, 166, 202.

43. Quoted in ibid., 202. Alan Lomax, *Mister Jelly Roll* (New York: Duell, Sloan and Pearce, 1950), 57.

44. Wells-Barnett, *Mob Rule in New Orleans*, 202.

45. William Monroe Trotter, *The Boston Guardian*, July 19, 26, 1902; Alexander, " 'We Know Our Rights,' " 277.

46. "For the Negro," *Friends Intelligencer*, January 17, 1903.

47. Ida B. Wells-Barnett to W.E.B. Du Bois, May 30, 1903, *The Correspondence of*

W.E.B. Du Bois: Selections, 1877–1934, ed. Herbert Aptheker (Amherst: University of Massachusetts Press, 1997), 56.

48. Stephen R. Fox, *The Guardian of Boston* (New York: Scribner, 1971), 20.

49. W.E.B. Du Bois, "The Talented Tenth," in *The Negro Problem: A Series of Articles by Representative Negroes of Today*. (New York: J. Pott & Co., 1903), 10.

50. Raymond Wolters, *Du Bois and His Rivals* (Columbia: University of Missouri Press, 2002), 61.

51. Fox, *Guardian of Boston*, 27.

52. Ibid., 32, 39.

53. Ibid., 52, 39.

54. Alexander, " 'We Know Our Rights.' "

55. Thornbrough, *T. Thomas Fortune*, 249, 319.

56. Lewis, *W.E.B. Du Bois*, 302; Fox, *Guardian of Boston*, 62.

57. Wolters, *Du Bois and His Rivals*, 75.

58. Du Bois, "The Parting of the Ways" (1904), cited in Lewis, *W.E.B. Du Bois*, 309.

59. Ida Wells-Barnett, "Booker T. Washington and His Critics" (1904) in Mildred I. Thompson, *Ida B. Wells-Barnett: An Exploratory Study of an American Black Woman, 1893–1930* (Brooklyn, N.Y.: Carlson Publishing, 1990), 256.

60. Ibid.

61. Ibid., 257.

62. Ibid.

63. Ibid., 257, 256, 259.

64. Lewis, *W.E.B. Du Bois*, 306–307.

65. McMurray, *To Keep the Waters Troubled*, 271.

66. "Barnett Appeals for Judge's Seat," *Chicago Daily Tribune*, December 19, 1906; "Canvass of Votes Defeats Barnett," *Chicago Daily Tribune*, November 23, 1906.

67. "Figures Indicate Barnett's Defeat," *Chicago Daily Tribune*, November 21, 1906.

68. "Barnett to Take Bench," *Chicago Daily Tribune*, November 9, 1906.

69. "Tillman Speaks: The Negro Is His Topic," *Chicago Daily Tribune*, November 28, 1906.

70. Wells, *Crusade*, 279.

71. Allen H. Spear, *Black Chicago: The Making of the Negro Ghetto, 1890–1920* (Chicago: University of Chicago Press, 1967), 104.

72. Wells, *Crusade*, 283.

73. Julius Taylor, *The Broad Ax* (Chicago), June 23, 30, July 7, 1906, quoted in McMurray, *To Keep the Waters Troubled*, 275.

74. Wells, *Crusade*, 284–85.

75. Ibid., 286, 285, 287.

76. At least one and possibly both men were innocent of the crimes with which they were charged. Joe James, an Alabama drifter, was convicted and executed for the

miner's murder, but on very dubious evidence. The alleged rapist, a hod carrier named George Richardson, was exonerated two weeks after the riot when Mabel Hallem, the woman whose rape charges sparked the riot, dropped her charges against him. She later admitted that she had never been raped. Roberta Senechal, *The Sociogenesis of a Race Riot: Springfield, Illinois, in 1908* (Urbana: University of Illinois Press, 1990), 19, 167, 158.

77. James L. Crouthamel, "The Springfield Race Riot of 1908," *The Journal of Negro History* 45, no. 3 (July 1960): 170.

78. "Negroes' Hopes in Iron Laws," *Chicago Tribune*, August 16, 1908.

79. William English Walling, "The Race War in the North," *The Independent*, September 3, 1908, 530.

80. "The Call," *The Nation*, February 12, 1909.

81. Ida Wells-Barnett, *Proceedings of the National Negro Conference* (New York: The Conference, 1909), 173.

82. Robert L. Zangrando, *The NAACP Crusade Against Lynching, 1909–1950* (Philadelphia: Temple University Press, 1980).

83. Mary White Ovington, "The National Association of Colored People," *Journal of Negro History* 9, no. 2 (April 1924): 111.

84. Elliott M. Rudwick, "Booker T. Washington's Relations with the National Association for the Advancement of Colored People," *The Journal of Negro Education* 29, no. 2 (spring 1960): 134.

85. Wells, *Crusade*, 323.

86. Mary White Ovington, *Walls Come Tumbling Down* (New York: Schocken Books, 1947), 106; Elliott M. Rudwick, "The National Negro Committee Conference of 1909," *The Phylon Quarterly* 18, no. 4 (Fourth Quarter, 1957): 417.

87. Wells, *Crusade*, 325.

88. Ibid., 327–28; Ovington, *Walls Come Tumbling Down*, 106.

89. McMurray, *To Keep the Waters Troubled*, 281.

90. Lewis, *W.E.B. Du Bois*, 400.

91. Ibid., 399.

92. Ibid., 415, 421.

93. Wells, *Crusade*, 328.

8: Reforming Chicago

1. "Cairo Mob Kills 2," *Chicago Tribune*, November 12, 1909.

2. Ida B. Wells, *Crusade for Justice: The Autobiography of Ida B. Wells*, ed. Alfreda Duster (Chicago: University of Chicago Press, 1991), 311.

3. "Suppression of Mob Violence Bill, May 16, 1905," quoted in Stacy Pratt McDer-

mott, " 'An Outrageous Proceeding': A Northern Lynching and the Enforcement of Anti-Lynching Legislation in Illinois, 1905–1910," *The Journal of Negro History* 84, no. 1 (Winter 1999): 62.

4. Wells, *Crusade*, 311.
5. Ibid., 311–12.
6. Thomas Holt, "The Lonely Warrior: Ida B. Wells-Barnett and the Struggle for Black Leadership," in *Black Leaders of the Twentieth Century*, eds. John Hope Franklin and August Meier (Urbana: University of Illinois Press, 1982), 39–61.
7. Wells, *Crusade*, 312.
8. Ibid., 312, 313.
9. McDermott, " 'An Outrageous Proceeding,' " 65.
10. Wells, *Crusade*, 315, 316.
11. Ibid., 318.
12. "Sheriff Pays for Lynching," *The Atlanta Constitution*, December 7, 1909.
13. McDermott, " 'An Outrageous Proceeding,' " 75.
14. Wells, *Crusade*, 298.
15. Ibid., 299.
16. "Interview with Alfreda Duster," in *The Black Women's Oral History Project*, ed. Ruth Edmonds Hill, vol. 3 (Westport, Conn.: Meckler, 1991), 133.
17. Allan H. Spear, *Black Chicago: The Making of a Negro Ghetto, 1890–1920* (Chicago: University of Chicago Press, 1967), 48.
18. Ibid.
19. "Interview with Alfreda Duster," 137; Wells, *Crusade*, 300.
20. Ibid., 303.
21. Wells-Barnett quoted in Spear, *Black Chicago*, 46–47.
22. Ibid., 301.
23. Ibid., 303.
24. Ibid., 304.
25. Ibid.
26. "Negro Fellowship League's House Warming," *Chicago Defender*, April 10, 1910, 1.
27. Lucius C. Harper, "We Should Pause to Pay Respect to Negro Heroes," *Chicago Defender*, February 9, 1946.
28. "Slayer, in Grip of Law Fights Return to South," *The Washington Post*, October 21, 1910, 11.
29. Or so Wells-Barnett reports, but her memory may not be accurate. Green is quoted in *The Washington Post* as saying, "I tried to kill myself by eating the heads off matches. It did not kill me but only made me sick." Ibid.
30. Ibid.
31. Wells, *Crusade*, 336, 337.

32. Ibid., 304.

33. Ibid., 332.

34. Ibid.

35. Ibid. See also Robin F. Bachin, *Building the South Side: Urban Space and Civic Culture in Chicago, 1890–1919* (Chicago: University of Chicago Press, 2004), 261–62.

36. Wells, *Crusade*, 331.

37. Ibid., 331, 357, 358.

38. Anne Meis Knupfer, *Reform and Resistance: Gender, Delinquency, and America's First Juvenile Court* (New York: Routledge, 2001), 52.

39. Ibid.

40. Wells, *Crusade*, 346.

41. "Illinois Women Feature Parade," *Chicago Tribune*, March 4, 1913.

42. Ibid.

43. "Illinois Women Participants in Suffrage Parade," *Chicago Tribune*, March 4, 1913.

44. Wells, *Crusade*, 352.

45. Ibid., 333.

46. Ibid., 341.

47. "The Ordeal of the Solitary," *Chicago Defender*, June 26, 1915.

48. "Innocent Man Freed from Penitentiary," *Chicago Defender*, May 4, 1918.

49. Wells, *Crusade*, 335.

50. "Appomattox Club Kills 'Jim Crow' Bills in the State of Illinois," *Chicago Tribune*, April 19, 1913.

51. "Ida B. Wells-Barnett Scores Tribune—Disregards Race," *Chicago Defender*, May 9, 1914.

52. "Marshall Field & Co. Discharge Saleswoman Who Insults Afro-American," *Chicago Defender*, June 20, 1914.

53. Robin D. G. Kelley, " 'We Are Not What We Seem': Rethinking Black Working-Class Opposition in the Jim Crow South," *The Journal of American History* 80, no. 1 (January 1993): 75–112.

54. Alfreda Duster in Dorothy Sterling's, "Afterword," in *The Memphis Diary of Ida B. Wells*, ed. Miriam DeCosta-Willis (Boston: Beacon, 1995), 196.

55. Stephen R. Fox, *The Guardian of Boston* (New York: Scribner, 1971), 140.

56. W.E.B. Du Bois, "The Year 1913 in Account with Black Folk," *The Crisis* 7 (January 1914): 133–34.

57. Quoted in Mark Ellis, "W.E.B. Du Bois and the Formation of Black Opinion in World War I: A Commentary on 'The Damnable Dilemma,' " *The Journal of American History* 81, no. 4 (March 1995): 1585.

58. "Help the Soldier Boys to Have a Merry Xmas," *Chicago Defender*, December 15, 1917.

59. Wells, *Crusade*, 390.

60. "Printed Address by Marcus Garvey on the East St. Louis Riots," in *The Marcus Garvey and Universal Negro Improvement Association Papers*, vol. 1, ed. Robert A. Hill (Berkeley: University of California Press, 1983), 213.

61. Ibid., 213, 218.

62. "Lawyer Warns Negroes Here to Arm Selves," *Chicago Tribune*, July 4, 1917.

63. Wells, *Crusade*, 388.

64. Mark Ellis, *Race, War, and Surveillance: African Americans and the United States Government During World War I* (Bloomington: Indiana University Press, 2001), 39.

65. Quoted in William G. Jordan, *Black Newspapers and the War for Democracy, 1914–1920* (Chapel Hill: University of North Carolina Press, 2001), 94.

66. Wells, *Crusade*, 370.

67. Ibid., 372, 373.

68. William M. Tuttle, *Race Riot: Chicago in the Red Summer of 1919* (Urbana: University of Illinois Press, 1996), 21. See also Janet L. Abu-Lughod, *Race, Space, and Riots in Chicago* (New York: Oxford University Press, 2007).

69. Letter to the Editor, *Chicago Tribune*, July 7, 1919.

70. "Meeting of the Baltimore Branch of the Universal Negro Improvement Association and African Communities League," December 18, 1918, in *The Marcus Garvey Papers*, 1:329.

71. "Interview with Alfreda Duster," 153, 154, 171; Wells, *Crusade*, 406; "A Committee of Five," *Chicago Defender*, August 30, 1919, 16; Wells, *Crusade*, 408.

72. Walter White, *A Man Called White: The Autobiography of Walter White* (New York: The Viking Press, 1948), 45–46.

73. Walter White, "The Real Cause of Race Riots," *The Crisis* 19, no. 2 (December 1919): 56.

74. Quoted in Grif Stockley, *Blood in Their Eyes: The Elaine Race Massacres of 1919* (Fayetteville: University of Arkansas Press, 2004), 31; Nan Elizabeth Woodruff, *American Congo: The African American Freedom Struggle in the Delta* (Cambridge, Mass.: Harvard University Press, 2003), 84.

75. White, "The Real Cause of Race Riots," 56.

76. Woodruff, *American Congo*, 87.

77. Ibid., 102.

78. Walter White, "The Real Cause of Race Riots," 56.

79. "Condemned Arkansas Rioters Look to Chicago for Help," *Chicago Defender*, December 13, 1919.

80. White, *A Man Called White*, 51.

81. Wells, *Crusade*, 401.

82. Ibid., 404.

83. Ibid., 403, 404.

9: Eternal Vigilance Is the Price of Liberty

1. Ida B. Wells, *Crusade for Justice: The Autobiography of Ida B. Wells*, ed. Alfreda Duster (Chicago: University of Chicago Press, 1991), 3, 414.
2. Ibid., 415.
3. Ibid.; Wendell Phillips, *Speeches Before the Massachusetts Antislavery Society* (Boston: R.F. Wallcut, 1852), 13.
4. Wells, *Crusade*, 415; see also Alfreda Duster's introduction, xxx.
5. Mary Jane Brown, "Advocates in the Age of Jazz: Women and the Campaign for the Dyer Antilynching Bill," *Peace and Change* 28, no. 3 (July 2003): 380; Robert L. Zangrando, *The NAACP Crusade Against Lynching, 1909–1950* (Philadelphia: Temple University Press, 1980), 18.
6. Jacquelyn Dowd Hall, *Revolt against Chivalry: Jessie Daniel Ames and the Women's Campaign against Lynching* (New York: Columbia University Press, 1993), 197.
7. "Interview with Alfreda Duster," in *The Black Women's Oral History Project*, ed. Ruth Edmonths Hill, vol. 3 (Westport, Conn.: Meckler, 1991), 166.
8. Ibid.
9. Paula J. Giddings, *Ida: A Sword Among Lions* (New York: HarperCollins, 2008), 628.
10. Ida continued to intervene on behalf of prisoners, sometimes making the papers as a result: "Judge Frees Woman Severely Beaten by Jail Matron," *Chicago Defender*, December 12, 1925.
11. Giddings, *Ida*, 630.
12. Ida B. Wells, *The Memphis Diary of Ida B. Wells*, ed. Miriam DeCosta-Willis (Boston: Beacon, 1995), 167.
13. Ibid., 167, 169, 173, 175.
14. Ibid., 173.
15. Darlene Clark Hine, "The NAACP Defeat of Judge Parker to the Supreme Court, 1930," *The Negro History Bulletin* 40, no. 5 (September–October 1977): 754.

Acknowledgments

I am grateful and honored to have been able to write about Ida B. Wells, whose life has been an education to me. That education also came thanks to the librarians and archivists at the University of Chicago Library, the Tennessee State Archives, the Chicago Historical Institute, Harvard University's Widener Library, and the Rutgers University Libraries, who helped me learn about Wells's life. And likewise, this project owes much to the work of a variety of Wells aficionados, who have collected and edited her writings and written about her life. Her daughter Alfreda Duster was her first archivist and biographer, and preserved an invaluable record of her mother's life that has served as one of my major sources. I have also learned much from the work of Wells scholars such as Mildred I. Thompson, Miriam DeCosta-Willis, Linda O. McMurray, Jacqueline Jones Royster, Hazel Carby, Jacqueline Denise Goldsby, Gail Bederman, Patricia A. Schechter, and Paula J. Giddings.

I am also grateful to Tom Slaughter and Lou Masur for encouraging me to write a biography, and indebted to Thomas LeBien for guiding me through the writing of this book with patience, good nature, and a keen editorial eye. Thanks, too, to Liz Maples and the other folks at Hill and Wang who helped move it to print.

ACKNOWLEDGMENTS

I completed this book thanks to sustained encouragement and support from more colleagues, friends, and family members than I can mention here. Jenny Brier, Kat Hindeman, and Kathryn Tanner hosted me in Chicago during portions of my research. And I worked my way through the challenges of this book in conversation with a wide variety of helpful people. Among them were many friends and colleagues in the history department at Rutgers University, most especially Carolyn Brown, Ann Fabian, Nancy Hewitt, Steven Lawson, Julie Livingston, Temma Kaplan, Minkah Makalini, Donna Murch, Bonnie Smith, Keith Wailoo, and Deborah Gray White. Others include Rebecca Welch, Glenn Loury, Kerwin Charles, Farah Jasmin Griffin, Kimberly Phillips, Michael Hanchard, Patricia Sullivan, Eva Thorne, Martha Jones, David Levering Lewis, Barbara Savage, Waldo Martin, Bill Moses, and Alfred Thomas.

I also received particularly helpful commentary from the 1997–98 research group at the Rutgers Center for Race and Ethnicity. Thanks to Keith Wailoo for creating that wonderfully collegial community, which included Nadia Brown, Jeffrey Dowd, Mia Kissil, Dora Vargha, Anantha Sudakar, and Melissa Stein. And double thanks to Melissa Stein for enthusiastic and invaluable research assistance, and to Allison Miller for editorial assistance. I am likewise indebted to Beryl Satter for her careful reading of this book and boundless enthusiasm for its subject.

And finally thanks to my family for love and support, and special thanks to my mother, Juanita Bay, who is always an inspiration to me.

Index

Page numbers in *italics* refer to illustrations.

Abbott, Lyman, 204, 208
Abbott, Robert S., 292, 315
abolitionist movement, 6, 110, 148, 183, 198
accommodationism, 7, 169, 194–97, 233–34, 242
Addams, Jane, 252, 262, 285
African Americans, 13; accumulation of wealth and, 194–95; class prejudices of, 160–61; Columbian Exposition and, 131, 132, 152, 154–57, 162; criminalization of, 98; as critics of Wells, 112–13; disenfranchisement of, 17, 74, 79, 93–94, 96, 108, 119, 186–87, 188, 196, 233; education and, 23–24, 36, 76–78, 195–96, 227–28; emigration from Memphis of, 89, 90–91; lack of history written by, 16–17; Memphis as mecca for, 41; migration movements of, 90–92, 95, 103; "Nadir" of history for, 232–35; political participation of, 24–26, 27, 45;
protest strategies of, 11; Reconstruction and, 15–17, 19–20; self-defense of, 95, 300–301; "talented tenth" of, 253, 258; voting rights of, 33, 44–45, 79, 93, 94, 193, 233–34, 247, 328; World War I and, 297–98, 301–302
African Methodist Episcopal Church, 104–105
Afro-American Council, 231, 234, 238, 239–40, 241–42, 244, 245–46, 250, 255–56, 259–60, 272, 317
Afro-American League, 231, 238
Afro-American Press and Its Editors, The (Penn), 165
Aked, Charles F., 177–78, 183–84
Alexander, Arthur, 275
Alpha Suffrage Club (ASC), 291, 289–90
A.M.E. Church Review, 70, 74, 105
American Atrocities, see Southern Horrors
American Baptist Magazine, 74
American Citizen (Kansas City), 112

American Citizenship Federation, 315
American Colonization Society (ACS), 91–92
Ames, Jesse Daniel, 212, 318
Anderson, W. G., 287
Anthony, Susan B., 156, 163, 204, 212–13, 214, 215–16, *215*, 228, 230–31, 239
Anti-Caste, 134–36, 141–42, 176
antilynching laws, 6, 10, 12, 192, 198, 203–204, 235, 275, 316–17, 318
antimiscegenation laws, 124–25, 130
Appeal-Avalanche, The, 84–85, 99, 113, 192
Argyll, Duke of, 189
Arkansas Gazette, 310
Arkansas Race Riot, The (Wells-Barnett), 313
Armour Institute, 227
Association of Southern Women for the Prevention of Lynching (ASWPL), 212, 318
Atkinson, Miss., 73
Atlanta, Ga., 170, 264
Atlanta Compromise Speech (Washington), 170, 196–97
Atlanta Constitution, 151, 154, 192, 200, 243, 244
Atlanta Journal, 244
Aunt Jemima, 164
Axon, William, 185

Back-to-Africa movements, 91–92
Baker, Frazier B., 236–37, 238
Balgarnie, Florence, 199, 208–209, 221
Baltimore Afro-American, 302
Bancroft, Hubert, 169
Bardwell, Ky., 173, 174, 175, 178
Barnett, Albert, *319*
Barnett, Audrey, *319*

Barnett, Beatrice, *319*
Barnett, Charles Aked, 224–26, *225*, 276, 277, 298, *319*
Barnett, Ferdinand, Jr. (stepson), 298, *319*
Barnett, Ferdinand Lee, 7, 10, 139–40, 152, 165, 167, 170–73, *171*, 190, 198, 225, 228, 234, 245, 250, 260–61, 264, 266, 275, 280, 281–82, 283, 292, 294, 298, 300, *319*, 320, 326–27; as assistant state's attorney, 217, 218; judgeship nomination of, 260, 262; marriage of, 191, 192, 214, 216–21; Wells's wedding to, 214–15; World War I and, 301–302
Barnett, Ferdinand Lee, Sr., 217
Barnett, Florence, *319*
Barnett, Herman, 226, 237, 239, *277*, 298, *319*, 320
Barnett, Hulette (daughter of Albert), *319*
Barnett, Hulette (wife of Albert), *319*
Barnett, Ida (daughter), 226, 234, 246, 277, *319*
Barnett, Martha Brooks, 217–18
Barnett, Mary Graham, 171, 217
Barnwell massacre, 142
Barrett, W. H., 82–83, 84
Beale Street Baptist Church, 41, 76, 79
Bee, The (Washington, D.C.), 70, 158–59
Bentley, Charles E., 260, 270
Bethel A.M.E. Church, 204, 227, 281
Bethune, Mary McLeod, 321
Birmingham Age-Herald, 244
Birth of a Nation, The, 17, 293
black self-help, 195–96
Blaine, James, 198
Blair, Henry W., 204, 212
Blum, Edward, 186
Boisseau, T. J., 156

Bolling, Mr., 19, 20, 22, 25
"Booker T. Washington and His Critics"
    (Wells-Barnett), 257–59
Book of the Fair (Bancroft), 169
Booth, Benjamin F., 43
Boston Guardian, 254–55, 257, 296
Boston Literary and Historical Associa-
    tion, 254–55
Bratton, Ocier, 310
Bratton, Ulysses S., 311
British Anti-Lynching Committee, 6,
    189, 199–200, 203, 209, 220 21
British Good Templar Order, 140–41
British Women's Temperance Associa-
    tion, 140, 149
Broad Ax, 264
Brooks, Grace, 290
Brotherhood of Sleeping Car Porters,
    323 24, 327
Brough, Charles H., 310, 311
Brown, John, 205
Brown, Louis, 60, 61–62, 65, 66
Brown, Mildrey, 126
Brown, William Wells, 135
Brown v. Board of Education, 56, 233
Bruce, Blanche K., 26
Brundage, Edward J., 308
Bundy, Leroy, 301
Bureau of Investigation, 298, 301–302
Burgess, John W., 98
Butler, Stella, 68

Cairo, Ill., 274–75, 279–81, 300
"Call, The" (Walling), 268
Campbell, "Chicken Joe," 292–93
Carnegie, Andrew, 260
"carpetbaggers," 16–17, 27, 97
Cassells, Thomas J., 49, 52–53, 138
Charles, Robert, 247–50
Charleston, S.C., 238

Chase, Calvin, 70
Chesapeake, Ohio, and Southwestern
    Railroad, 45–58, 121
Chestertown, Md., 102
Chestnut Hill, Va., 97
Chicago, Ill., 7, 119, 153, 170, 260, 276,
    278; black middle class of, 170; black
    population of, 276, 278; class divide
    in, 292; corruption in, 324; first
    kindergarten in, 227–28; housing
    shortage in, 306–307; 1919 riot in,
    305–309, *306*; segregation in, 283–84,
    293–95, 296–97; South Side of, 278,
    283, 304, 306–307; State Street of,
    284–85
Chicago Citizens' Committee, 324
Chicago Daily News, 284, 311, 312
Chicago Defender, 285, 292, 301, 311, 312,
    315
Chicago Political Equality League, 252
Chicago Tribune, 211, 237, 252, 266, 290,
    294, 307
Chicago Women's Club, 252, 258
Church, Robert R., 41, 43, 64, 65, 222
City Railway Company, 89–90
Civil Rights Bill of 1875, 56
Civil War, U.S., 15, 17–18, 129
Clark, Helen, 178
Clark, Sarah, 124–25
Clayden, Peter, 183, 210
Cleveland, Grover, 236
Cleveland Gazette, 53, 57, 125, 203, 207,
    302
"Colored People's Day," 158–60, *160*, 161,
    162, 164–65, 168
Colored Women's League of Washing-
    ton, 224
color line, 97, 127, 181, 278; in railroad
    travel, 47–48, 55–56
"Coloured Application to Git out of
    Egypt, A," 92

Columbian Exposition, 131–32, 151–70; African American representation and participation in, 131, 132, 152, 154–57, 162; "Colored People's Day" of, 158–60, *160*, 161, 162, 164–65, 168; Fon people exhibit at, 161–63; International Labor Congress of, 169

Combs, James B., 27

common carriers, 50–52

"Compromise of 1877," 26–27

Comstock Law of 1873, 110

Congregational Union, 284

Conkling, Roscoe, 131

Conservator, 139, 170, 217, 218, 226, 232, 246

Contemporary Review, 183

contraception, 110, 224

convict lease system, 166–67

Conway, Moncure, 205

Cooper, Anna Julia, 48–49, 119–20

Coppin, Fanny Jackson, 105, 141

Coppin, Levi J., 105

corruption, 119, 201, 324

cotton, 201, 309–10

Cotton States and International Exposition, 196

Cowan, William R., 291

Cranford, Alfred, 242

Cranford, Mattie, 242

Crisis, The, 272, 273, 287, 297, 312

Crusade for Justice (Wells-Barnett), 11, 12, 16, 270, 287, 305, 314–15

Cummins, Holmes, 51–52, 53–54

Curtis, Mrs. A. M., 157

Dahomey, 161, 168

Daily Chronicle (London), 180, 183, 184, 185, 201

Daily Inter Ocean, 137, 173, 175, 177, 182–83, 208

Daily News (London), 183, 210

Daily Record, 240

Davis, Frank, 275, 276, 279–80, 316

Democratic Party, 25, 27, 44, 90–91, 92–93, 98, 240

Deneen, Charles, 275, 280–81, 326

De Priest, Oscar, 291, 301, 324

disenfranchisement, 17, 74, 79, 93–94, 96, 108, 119, 186–87, 188, 196, 233

domestic slave trade, 21–22

Douglas, Warren B., 326

Douglass, Ana, 130

Douglass, Frederick, 5–6, 7, 8, 11, 16, 111, 122, 127–32, *128*, 136, 137, 141, 152, 154, 164–65, 167, 172, 177, 178–80, 191, 193, 194, 208–209, 213, 245, 272, 318; Columbian Exposition and, 158–59, 168; death of, 192, 196; on migration, 95; Wells's friendship with, 6, 111, 130–31

Douglass, Helen Pitts, 130, 136, 141, 179, 180, 190, 208–209

Douglass, Joseph, 159

Douglass Civil League, 327

Drake Hotel, 315

Dred Scott decision, 233

Du Bois, W.E.B., 9, 16, 34, 211–12, 231, 242–43, 246, 250–52, *251*, 253, 255, 256–60, *261*, 269–70, 271, 272, 273, 287, 297, 304

Duke, J. C., 103, 104

Dunaway, Louis Sharpe, 310

Duster, Alfreda Barnett, 11, 12, 31, 38, 171, 173, 191, 217, 218, 224, 226, 227, 234, 276, 277, 282, 294–95, 308, *319*, 320

Dyer bill, 316–17, 320–21

East St. Louis, Ill., 298–301, *299*, 308, 326

East St. Louis Massacre, The (Wells-
  Barnett), 301
Echo, The, 183
Economist, The, 184
education, 23–24, 36, 196, 227–28;
  industrial, 195–96, 253, 259
Edwards, Celestine, 176, 177, 178
Elaine massacre, 309–13
election fraud, 4, 25
Equal Suffrage Association, 213
Evans, Matilda, 118
Evening Scimitar, 105
Evening Star, 74
"Exodusters," 90–91

Fellowship Herald, 287
"Female Accusation, The" (Mayo), 148
Ferdinands, George, 144, 146–47, 148,
  149
Fifteenth Amendment, 79, 94
Fisk Herald, 35, 38, 71
Fisk University, 34, 38, 69
Fitts, Annie Wells, 39, 41, 62–63, 64,
  214, 320
Fleming, J. L., 76, 79, 80, 105–106,
  137
Fon people, 161–63
Forbes, George, 254–55, 257
Fortune, T. Thomas, 7, 8, 70, 80, 90, 93,
  106, 107, 108, 110, 111, 113, 114, 141,
  193, 194, 238, 239, 244, 246, 250,
  255, 256
Fourteenth Amendment, 55, 79
Fowler, Ebenezer, 102
Frank Leslie's Popular Monthly, 163
Fraternity, 148, 176, 186
Frederick Douglass Center, 252, 262–63,
  264–65, 270, 305
Freedmen's Bureau, 23, 25
Freed Slave, The (statue), 131

Freeman, The, see *Indianapolis Freeman*
Froman, Alfred, 43, 53, 57, 64

Garnet, Henry Highland, 115
Garnet, Sarah, 115
Garrett, Edward, *see* Mayo, Isabelle Fyvie
Garrison, William Lloyd, 267
Garrison, William Lloyd, Jr., 205, 208
Garvey, Marcus, 299–300, 307
Gate City Press, 70, 94, 104
Georgia, 94, 201, 204
Gill, Nelson, 25
Governor Allen (steamboat), 50
Grace Presbyterian Church, 281–82
Graham, I. J., 60, 65, 66, 67, 69
grandfather clause, 44, 247, 250
Grant, Ulysses S., 17
Gray, Dr., 32, 66, 67
Great Britain, 6, 111; antilynching move-
  ment in, 183–84, 198; reaction to
  Smith lynching in, 134–35; Wells in
  second tour of, 176–90, 192; Wells in
  first tour of, 140–50, 151
Great Migration, 276, 278, 282–83, 306
Green, John P., 242
Green, Nancy, 164
Green, Steve, 286–87
Greer, James M., 52–53
Griffith, D. W., 17, 293
Grimke, Francis, 130
Grimke, Sarah Moore, 130
Grizzard, Eph., 126

Hahn, Steve, 11
Hale, Grace, 134
Hall, Jacquelyn Dowd, 212
Hamilton, Green P., 43
Harlan, John Marshall, 233
Harper, Frances Ellen Watkins, 105, 141

Harper, Lucius C., 285–86
Harper's Weekly, 99
Harris, Armour, 82
Harrison, Benjamin, 134, 155, 156
Hayes, Rutherford B., 27
Hereford, Brooke, 185
Higginson, Thomas Wentworth, 205–206
Hill, James, 26
Hill, Robert, 310
Hine, Darlene Clark, 120
Holiday, Billie, 96
Holly Springs, Miss., 17–18, *18*, 20, 25–26, 28–31
Homestead Act (1862), 91
Hoover, Herbert, 324, 325
Hose, Sam, 242–44, 247, 252
House of Representatives, U.S., Resolution 214 in, 204
Houston, Tex., 302–304
Howard, Kate, 266, 267
Howells, William Dean, 131
Hull House, 252, 262
Hunton, Addie, 320–21
Hurst, Cornelius, 82

Ida B. Wells Club, 214, 219, 227, 323, 324
Ida B. Wells Testimonial Reception Committee, 114, 115, 116–19
Illinois, 10, 265, 275
Illinois Anti-Lynching League, 198
Illinois Equal Suffrage Association, 290
Illinois Federation of Colored Women's Clubs, 325
Illinois Federation of Women's Clubs, 228–29
Illinois National Guard, 300, 301
Illinois Record, 245
Illinois Republican National Committee, 325

Illinois Republican Women's Committee, 214, 225–26
Illinois Women's Republican Club, 327
Imes, B. A., 113
Impey, Catherine, 111, 134–37, *135*, 140–50, 176–77, *178*, 179, 210, 258
Impey, Nellie, *135*
Independent, 267
Indianapolis Freeman, 58, 70, 75–76, *75*, 80, 112, 154, 158, 159, 165, 219
Indianapolis World, 74
industrial education, 195–96, 253, 259
Institute for Colored Youth, 105
integration, 227, 297
International Labor Congress, 169
interracial marriage, 148, 293–94, 296
interracial relationships, 124–26, 127, 130, 148–49, 187, 206

Jacks, J. W., 221–22
Jackson, Daniel M., 324
James, William "Frog," 274–75, 279–80
Jim Crow laws, 4, 6, 7, 51, 56, 94, 96, 98, 108, 122, 124, 129, 130, 152, 194, 197, 211, 234, 294, 296
Johnson, James Weldon, 305, 308, 320–21
Joliet Penitentiary, 282–83, 292–93
Jones, Thomas J., 199–200
Justice Department, U.S., 302, 312

Kansas City, 65, 67, 205
Kansas City Dispatch, 74
Kansas Exodus of 1879, 90, 95
Kimbrough, Victoria, 54
kindergartens, 227–28
kinship networks, 11
Ku Klux Klan, 17, 25–26, 97–98

"ladies' cars," 46–47, 46, 50–52, 54,
  55–56
Lake City, S.C., 236, 238
Lawson, Mrs. Victor, 284
Lawson, Victor, 284, 287
Lesson of the Hour, The: Why Is the Negro
  Lynched? (Douglass), 209
Levin, Louis, 243
Liberia, 91–92
Lincoln, Abraham, 23, 265
literacy tests, 44
Little Rock, Ark., 181
Little Rock Sun, 75
Living Way, 61–62, 70
Lodge bill (1890), 93
Loftin, Isaiah, 237, 238
Logan, Rayford, 232
Loper, Harry T., 266
Londin, Frederick J., 154
Louisiana, 55, 200, 250
Lovejoy, Elijah P., 97
Loyal League, 25
Lynch, Charles, 96–97
"Lynching, Our National Crime" (Wells-
  Barnett), 268
lynchings, 6–7, 11, 12, 85, 94–95, 96,
  108, 110–11, 119, 141–42, 181–82,
  197, 231, 234, 259, 268, 304, 316–17;
  antecedents of, 96–97; of Baker, 236–
  37, 238; Barnwell massacre and, 142;
  British condemnation of, 183–84; of
  C. J. Miller, 173–75, 174; death toll
  from, 3; decline in, 204; Deneen's condemnation of, 280–81; embarrassment about, 202–203; gender politics
  in, 317–18; as hard to punish, 203–
  204; of Henry Smith, 132–33, 136;
  interracial relationships and, 125–26;
  Millington massacre and, 202–203;
  negative press on, 203; postcards of,
  142, 143; Protestants as apologists for,

185–86; public opinion on, 3–4, 6;
  racist ideology of, 96, 98–99; rape
  as justification for, 3, 5, 6–7, 99,
  100–104, 121, 124, 181, 205–206;
  spectacle, 134; as term, 97; white
  justifications for, 5, 6–7, 122–23,
  124; Willard's tolerance of, 187–89; as
  women's issue, 121–22, 127–28; see
  also specific lynchings
"Lynch law," 97
Lynch Law in Georgia (Wells-Barnett),
  244, 248
Lyons, Maritcha, 114–15, 119

MacDonald, A. C., 27
MacDonald Hall, 23
Mammy characters, 164
Manly, Alexander, 240
Marion Headlight, 76
Marshall Field's, 294–95
Martin, R. M., 175
Masons, 31–32
Massachusetts Anti-Lynching League,
  205
Matthews, Victoria Earle, 114, 115, 119,
  223
Mayo, Isabelle Fyvie, 136, 143–50, 152,
  176–77, 178, 179, 206
McClure, James G. K., 284
McCormick, Ruth Hanna, 325
McDowell, Calvin, 83, 84, 85, 86, 90, 99,
  101, 112
McFeely, William, 5–6, 159
McKinley, William, 235–36, 237–38,
  241, 242
McKinney, Susan M., 115
McMurray, Linda O., 68
Memphis, Tenn., 28, 38–39, 40–81, 121,
  203; black elite in, 41, 43, 47, 57, 87,
  112–13; black emigration from, 89,

Memphis, Tenn. (*cont.*)
90–91; black schools in, 76–78; black
vote in, 44; critics of Wells in, 112;
Curve lynching in, 4–5, 82–108, 112–
13, 116–18, 121; Democratic return
to power in, 92; disarming of blacks
in, 85, 87, 95; streetcar boycott in, 90;
white press in, 99–100
Memphis Commercial, 86, 88, 105, 137,
138
Memphis Daily Appeal, 52
Memphis Free Speech and Headlight, 4–5,
45, 76, 78–81, 86, 89–90, 92, 95,
102–108, 116, 124
Memphis Merchants' Exchange, 105
Memphis School Board, 65, 92
Memphis Scimitar, 84, 99, 199, 202
Metropolitan Center, 323
Milholland, John, 271
Miller, C. J., 173–75, *174*
Millington massacre, 202–203
miscegenation, 124–25, 130, 181
Mississippi, 25, 26, 200, 259, 324
Mississippi Constitutional Convention
(1890), 79
Mississippi flood of 1927, 324
Missouri Press Association, 221
Mitchell, John, Jr., 321
Mob Rule in New Orleans (Wells-Barnett),
247–50
mob violence, 4, 10, 87, 96, 98, 103, 108,
122–23, 195, 198, 204, 232, 280, 300,
307, 317
"Model Girl, The" (Wells-Barnett), 72
Montgomery, Ala., 103, 104
Montgomery, Isaiah, 79
Moody, Dwight L., 185, 186
Morris, Charles S., 71
Morton, Jelly Roll, 250
Moskowitz, Henry, 267
Moss, Betty, 83, 117–18, *117*

Moss, Thomas, 83, 84, 85, 86, *86*, 87–88,
90, 99, 101, 107, 112
Moss, Thomas, Jr., 117
Mossell, Gertrude Bustill, 115
"Mr. Moody and Miss Willard" (Wells-
Barnett), 185
Municipal and Presidential Voting Act
(1913), 289
Murray, Abraham Lincoln, 281

Nation, The, 27, 312
National American Woman Suffrage
Association (NAWSA), 290
National Association for the Advance-
ment of Colored People (NAACP), 9,
10, 231, 234–35, 265–73, 275, 278,
281, 287, 292, 293, 295, 296, 297, 301,
304, 308–309, 312–13, 316–21,
327, 328
National Association Notes, 224
National Association of Black Women's
Clubs, 295
National Association of Colored Women
(NACW), 10, 222–24, 228–30, 231,
252, 273, 278, 316–21
National Colored Congress for World
Democracy, 304
National Colored Press Association,
75, 76
National Conference of Colored Women
of America, 222
National Conference of Unitarians,
184–85
National Equal Rights League (NERL),
295–97, 304, 311
National Federation of African
American Women (NFAAW), 222,
223
National League of Colored Women,
222, 223

National Negro Business League, 246, 255–56

National Negro Conference, 268, 269–70

National Notes, 273

National Press Association, 110, 136

National Women's Colored League, 138

Negro Fellowship League (NFL), 276, 281–97, 298, 300, 301, 302, 304–305, 307, 311, 314, 319

Negro Fellowship League Reading Room and Social Center, 284–85, 292

New Deal Paper, 326–27

New Era Club, 119

New Orleans, La., 247–50, 259

New York, N.Y., 108, 114, 115

New York Age, 9, 106, 107–108, 110, 111–12, 113, 114, 127, 170

New York Times, 99, 133, 152, 192, 199, 200, 237

Niagara Movement, 231, 234, 260–61, 261, 268, 272

Nightingale, Taylor, 76, 77, 79

North Carolina, 204, 240–41

Northern, William, 201

"Oberlin girls," 97

Offett, William, 125

"Of Mr. Booker T. Washington and Others" (Du Bois), 252

Olsen, Harry, 289, 291–92

Ovington, Mary White, 267, 269, 270–71, 285

Palmer, Bertha, 156–57

Palmer House, 284

Panic of 1893, 200–201, 247

Paris, Tex., 132–33, 134

Parker, Hale G., 155

Parker, John J., 327–28

"Parting of the Ways, The" (Du Bois), 257

patronage appointments, 236

Patton, Georgia E. L., 140

Payne, Daniel A., 104–105

Pelley, Annie, 274

Pene, Xavier, 161, 162, 163

Penn, Garland, 285

Penn, Irvine Garland, 8, 165, 167

People's Community Church of Christ, 323

People's Grocery, 83–85, 87, 112

Peterson, Jerome B., 107, 108, 113, 114

Philadelphia, Pa., 104–105, 131

Phillips, Wendell, 315

Pierce, James O., 52, 54

Pierce, Leonard, 247

Pinkerton Detective Agency, 133

Plessy v. Ferguson, 55–56, 136, 233

Plummer, Mrs., 264, 265

Police Gazette, 80

poll taxes, 44, 94

Poole, Mr., 68

"Practical Negro Advancement" (Washington), 194

Progressive Farmers and Household Union, 309–13

Protestants, 185–86

Providence, R.I., 114

Public Ledger, 175–76

public protest, 11

Puck, 163

Pulaski, Tenn., 97

Pullman Palace Car Company, 57, 293, 323–24

Quaker Oats, 164

Quin Chapel Committee, 220

"Race Problem in America, The" (Aked), 183–84

race riots, 10, 219–20, 240–41, 265–66, 298–301, 305–309

"Race War in the North, The" (Walling), 267

racial violence, 93–94, 95–96, 97–98, 110, 121, 196

racism, 12; sexualization of, 74

Radical Reconstruction, *see* Reconstruction

Radical Republicans, 56, 204

railroads, 46–57, 121; and black women, 48–49; color line in, 47–48, 55–56; ladies' cars in, 46–47, 46, 50–52, 54, 55–56; Pullman cars in, 57, 293; "smear campaign" against Wells of, 53, 57; smoker cars in, 47, 51–52, 54

Randolph, A. Philip, 323

Ransom, Reverdy, 243, 281

rape, 98–99, 103, 110, 121–22, 129, 205–206, 212, 222, 265–66; of black women by whites, 126–27, 129; false allegations of, 125–26; as justification for lynching, 3, 5, 6–7, 99, 100–104, 121, 124, 181, 205–206; racial politics of, 206

Ray, Mary, 173

Ray, Ruby, 173

"reasonable regulations," 50–52

Reason Why, The (Wells-Barnett), 142

Reason Why the Colored American Is Not in the World's Columbian Exposition, The, 165–67, 170, 172, 173, 175

Reconstruction, 4, 15–17, 19–20, 22–23, 24–25, 44, 50, 56, 74, 90, 94, 96, 233, 258; collapse of, 16, 26–27, 91; myth of, 16–17

redeemers, 27

Red Record, A (Wells-Barnett), 142, 211–12

"Red-shirts," 240–41

Red Summer of 1919, 305–309

Reese, Maggie, 126

reform movements, 110

Republican Party, 25, 26, 27, 92–93, 97, 235, 289, 325; abandonment of black vote by, 93, 233

"Requirements of Southern Journalism" (Wells-Barnett), 104

Revels, Hiram Rhodes, 26

Richardson, Ana, 179–80

Richardson, Ellen, 179–80

Richmond Planet, 321

Roberts, Adelbert H., 325–26, 327

Roosevelt, Theodore, 255

Rosenwald, Julius, 288

Ruffin, Josephine St. Pierre, 115, 119, 138, 221–22, 223, 224, 230

Russell, Charles Edward, 270

Rust College, 23–24, 27, 35, 37–38

Rutt, Chris L., 164

Rydell, Robert W., 158

Sachs, Mr., 288

Saddler, Will, 286

Salzner, Henry, 275

San Francisco, Calif., 205

Sanger, Margaret, 110

"scalawags," 17, 97

Schechter, Patricia, 127

Scott, Emmett, 246

Sears Roebuck, 288

Secret Service, U.S., 303–304

segregation, 4, 50–51, 55–56, 74, 96, 108, 121, 196, 283–84, 293–95, 296–97, 304; of federal offices, 296; by gender, 50–51; *Plessy* case and, 55–56, 233; of schools, 278

segregationists, 158

Selective Service Act (1917), 297

Senate, U.S., 12, 26; Judiciary Committee of, 134
Settle, Josiah, 138
Settles (wealthy Memphis couple), 42
sexism, 7, 12, 118, 191–92
sharecroppers, 309
sharecropping, 20, 41, 169
Shaw University, 23
Sikeston, Mo., 174
Silkey, Sarah L., 141, 184
Singleton, Benjamin "Pap," 91
slavery, 15, 91, 272; domestic slave trade and, 21–22
Slayton, Mr., 204–205
Slayton Lyceum Bureau, 204–205
Smith, Henry, 132–33, 135–36
Smith, J. K., 293
"smoker" cars, 47, 51–52, 54
Social Darwinism, 98–99
"social purity" campaigns, 206
Society for the Recognition of the Universal Brotherhood of Man (SRUBM), 144, 148, 176, 177, 178, 179
Somerset, Lady Henry, 187–89, 208, 209
Souls of Black Folk, The (Du Bois), 251–52, 251, 256, 257
South Carolina, 125, 142, 204, 236
Southern Horrors (Wells-Barnett), 122–29, 123, 177
Spain, 237
Spanish-American War, 237, 238–39, 242
spectacle lynchings, 134
Spectator, The, 184
Sprague, Fredericka, 161
Sprague, Rosa Douglass, 223
Springfield, Ill., 239, 265–66, 275, 282, 300
Spring Valley, Ill., 219–20
Spring Valley Coal Company, 219–20

Squire, Belle, 289, 290
Star, The, 183
steamboat companies, 50
Stewart, William, 83, 84, 85, 86, 90, 99, 101, 112
"Story of 1900, A" (Wells-Barnett), 35–36, 71
"Strange Fruit," 96
Strickland, Elijah, 244
Stricklin, Mr., 101
Strunsky, Anna, 266
Sumner, Charles, 56
Sun (Baltimore), 102
Sun (London), 140, 183
Sun (New York), 186, 201
Supreme Court, U.S., 55–56, 233, 313, 327–28

"talented tenth," 253, 258
Tanner, John R., 245
tarring and feathering, 96
Taylor, C. H., 112
Taylor, Julius, 264
Taylor, Will, 279
Telegraph, The (Macon, Ga.), 192
temperance, 140, 149, 186, 206
Tennessee, 92, 200, 202, 203; "colored car" law of, 51; disenfranchisement in, 94
Tennessee Rifles, 83, 85
Tennessee State Supreme Court, 53–54, 55, 58
Terrell, Mary Church, 120, 222–24, 228–30, 229, 269, 325
Terrell, Robert Herberton, 224
Texas, 94, 200, 204
Third Enforcement Act (1871), 97
Third Ward Women's Political Club, 324
Thompson, William Hale "Big Bill," 291–92, 307

Tilden, Samuel, 26–27
Tillman, Benjamin "Pitchfork," 33, 127,
    240, 262
Times (London), 134
Times-Democrat (New Orleans), 249
Topeka Weekly Call, 138
Tourgée, Albion, 136–37, 138–39, 141,
    142, 145, 172, 173, 208, 258
Tourgée Club, 173
Tremont Temple, 116
Trotter, James, 253
Trotter, William Monroe, 250, 252, 253–
    57, 254, 258, 260, 268, 269, 271, 285,
    295–97, 304
Trout, Grace Wilbur, 290
Truth, Sojourner, 272
Tubman, Harriet, 223, 272
Tunica County, Miss., 102
Turner, Henry MacNeal, 78, 104
Turney, Peter, 202
Tuskegee Institute, 169, 194, 243, 259,
    273
Twenty-fourth Infantry, 302–304
"Two Christmas Days: A Holiday Story"
    (Wells-Barnett), 172

"Understanding Clause," 79
Underwood, Mr., 125
Underwood, Mrs. J. S., 125
unions, 252, 278, 323–24
United States Independent Order of
    Good Templars, 140–41
Universal Negro Improvement Organi-
    zation, 300
Urban League, 304–305, 307

Vance, Myrtle, 133
vigilante justice, 96–97, 198, 204
Villard, Henry, 267

Villard, Oswald Garrison, 267–69, 271,
    272, 296
Visalia, Calif., 41, 62–63
Voice, The (New York), 186–87
Voice from the South, A (Cooper), 120
voting rights, 33, 44–45, 79, 93, 94, 193,
    233–34, 247, 328
Voting Rights Act of 1965, 93

Waddell, Alfred Moore, 241
Walker, Lee, 175–76
Walling, William English, 266–67, 268,
    271, 272
Washington, Booker T., 8, 9, 169–70,
    194–97, 195, 228, 231, 239, 241, 242–
    44, 246, 250, 252–53, 254, 256,
    257–60, 268–69, 271, 273, 288, 297;
    accommodationist platform of, 7, 169,
    196, 198, 233–34; public image of,
    244–45; Trotter's attacks on, 253–57
Washington, D.C., 133–34
Washington, Margaret Murray, 221, 222,
    223, 273
Washington, Portia, 255
Washington Post, 133, 192, 200
Waters, Alexander, 240, 245
Welke, Barbara, 55–56
Wellesley College, 255
Wells, Elisabeth "Lizzie," 15, 16, 17, 18,
    19, 20, 21–22, 23–24, 28–31, 36, 44
Wells, Eugenia, 29, 30, 31, 32, 38–39, 41
Wells, Fannie, 38, 39, 41, 62, 63, 64,
    65, 68
Wells, George, 38
Wells, James (brother), 38
Wells, James "Jim" (father), 15, 16, 17, 18,
    19, 20–21, 23, 24, 25, 28–31, 43, 44
Wells, Lily, 39, 41, 62–63, 64, 65, 67,
    106, 214
Wells, Margaret, 68

Wells, Peggy, 21, 33–34, 68

Wells, Stanley, 29, 30

Wells-Barnett, Ida B., 8, 37, 75, 107, 117, 225, 277, 291, 303, 319, 322; as adult parole officer, 289, 291–92; African American critics of, 112–13; Afro-American Council and, 239–40, 245–46; as agitator, 193–94, 231, 304; ambition of, 44; as antilynching crusader, 3–4, 5–6, 10, 12, 86, 102–103, 108, 109–10, 111, 113–14, 121–23, 132, 173–76, 190, 193–94, 197–214; autobiography of, see Crusade for Justice; and Baker lynching, 237; Bible study classes of, 281; birth of, 3, 17–18; break from Washington of, 242–44, 252, 257–60; California trip of, 62–65; character defamation of, 66–67, 78, 101, 109, 137–38, 221; Charles lynching and, 247–50; childhood of, 15–39; class prejudice of, 160–61; Columbian Exposition and, see Columbian Exposition; continuing activism of, 10–11; criticism of, 192–93; death of, 327; death threats received by, 5, 106–107; and destruction of Free Speech, 104–108; Douglass friendship of, 6, 111, 130–31; early career doubts of, 65, 69–70; education of, 4, 10, 23–24, 27–28, 36–38, 69, 271; Elaine massacre and, 309–13; "Exiled" nom de plume of, 108; financial troubles of, 41–43; Frederick Douglass Center and, 262–65, 270; as head of her family, 31–39; ideas of female leadership of, 121; Illinois-based activism of, 276–313; Impey's invitation to, 137; increasing isolation of, 319–20; interracial cooperation as difficult for, 263–64; leadership credentials of, 9–10, 271–72; as lecturer, 110, 113–14, 115–19, 121–22, 133–34, 218–19; love of books and, 28; Lyric Hall speech of, 116–19; on marriage, 58–59; marriage of, 191, 192, 214, 216–18, 226; in Memphis, 40–81; middle-class aspirations of, 42–43; militant spirit of, 294; Miller lynching investigation of, 173–75; as modern-day Joan of Arc, 192; on motherhood, 226–27; as muckracking journalist, 124; NAACP and, 234–35, 265–73, 316–21; NACW and, 222–24, 228–30, 231, 320, 321; national reputation of, 7, 11–13, 113, 204; Negro Fellowship League and, 281–97; 1919 Chicago riot and, 305–309; parents' deaths and, 28–31; pen name of, 4, 74–75; pistol carried by, 121; political independence of, 93; possible depression of, 68–69; railroad lawsuits of, 45–58, 64, 92, 121; Reconstruction and, 16–17; in run for president of NACW, 321; second British tour of, 176–90, 192; self-defense advocated by, 94–95; sexual improprieties suspected of, 32–33; Smith lynching and, 133–34; as social critic, 13; social life of, 57–78; Spanish-American War and, 239, 242; speech on mob violence of, 241–42; state senate run of, 10, 322–23, 325–27; suffrage work of, 289–91; teaching career of, 32, 34–35, 49, 70–71, 75–76; temper of, 9, 37–38, 264–65; trip to Cairo of, 279–81; in trip to England, 140–50, 151; Victorian sexual ideology of, 66; wedding of, 214–15; white hostility to, 192–93, 198–99; women's support of, 113–22; World War I and, 298–99, 301–302

Wendell Phillips High School, 294

Westminster Gazette, 183, 187, 188
White, George, 238
White, Walter, 308–309, 310, 311–12, 317, 318
"white slavery," 181, 182
white supremacy, 4, 13, 25, 74, 93, 95–96, 98–99, 121, 127, 166, 184, 240–41, 267
Willard, Frances, 185–89, 206–11, *210*, 212, 220–21, 230
Williams, A. M., 280
Williams, Eugene, 308
Williams, Fannie Barrier, 165, 222, 228–30
Williams, S. Laing, 165, 228
Wilmington, N.C., 240–41
Wilson, Woodrow, 296, 304
"Woman in Journalism, How I would Edit" (Wells-Barnett), 76
Woman's Corner columns, 72
Woman's Era, The, 119
"Woman's Mission" (Wells-Barnett), 70, 72
Woman's Political and Social Union, 143
women, 110, 186, 272, 318; ideals of, 72–73; as lecturers, 110; lynching as issue of, 121–22, 124–25, 127–28; political influence of, 231; reform role of, 213; as supportive of Wells, 113–22
women, black, 12, 33, 51, 55–56, 73–74, 186, 193–94, 289–91, 318; class status of, 52; in Columbian Exposition, 156–57; expressions of militancy among, 222; ideals of womanhood and, 118–19; marriage and, 58; media

attacks on, 221–22; public indignities visited upon, 48–49, 120; sexual assaults on, 124, 126–27, 129; volunteerism of, 120
Women's Building Board of Lady Managers, 156–57
Women's Christian Temperance Union (WCTU), 185–86, 187, 188, 206–11, 212
women's clubs, 110, 119–20, 173, 193, 222, 224, 263, 305, 323
Women's Columbian Association (WCA), 156
Women's Columbian Auxiliary Association (WCAA), 156
Women's Era, 221, 224
Women's Loyal Union, 119–20
Women's Second Ward Republican Club, 289
women's suffrage, 110, 186, 206, 230–31, 289–91
Woodall, William, 189
Woodson, Carter G., 285, 286
Woodstock, Tenn., 40, 49–50
Woolley, Celia Parker, 252, 262–63, 264, 265, 270, 305
World Today, 257
World War I, 10, 297–99, 301–302, 304
Wright, Edward H., 286–87, 301, 326
Wright, Silas P., 241

yellow fever, 4, 28–31, 185
YMCA, 284, 287–88, 304